15.

Learning in general, its effects it bestows immortality preserving the fame of those nations where... was cultivated
while others sunk in obliv... ...ther parts
of Literature, is the imm... ...and source
of other Learning, then be... praise the
Deity, By this David appea... ...s Language
and polishes Barbarism... ...me and
brought those days of ignorance wherein were broach'd so
many Heresies, As the source of so many blessings ought not
only to be cultivated, but its professors honour'd and encou-
-raged.

Proposed whether serious matters may be hadled Ludicrously

In ridicule Mr. Mohun affirms it says that if Charles had laugh'd at
the fanaticks rather than seriously oppos'd them, they
cou'd not have gain'd such a Head, instances Hudibras
which did more than all other means to destroy them
ases the Earl of Shaftesbury's Authority concludes with
its being the most effectual method of convincing.
Mr. Dennis denies his assertion of Hudibras says reason
may be a butt for folly, and that nothing can evince
our reason so much, as the Gravity which wisdom
carries with it.
Mr. Pres. determines in favour of a confin'd ridicule.
Mr. Dennis moves that whoever is candidate for the
Censorship may lay in his claim next Friday. agreed

Lustrum. ... that an extraordinary night once a month
be allow'd for the Lustrum and Censor's office.
Mr. Mohun reads the Essay on Criticism Likewise Mr. Hamil.

Mohun Mr. Mohun censur'd. Mr. Dennis accuses Mr. Burke for
neglect. Mr. Hamilton for indecency to the Chair, and
Mr. Mohun for the same. Mr. Mohun accuses Mr. Pres.
for Male-administration. to be tried next Thursday.
House dissolv'd.

Mr. Burke President.
Mr. Mohun   Mr. Hamilton.
Mr. Dennis ...   Mr. Shackleton.

**Thursday May
14. 1747.
Committee**

Mr. Mohun and Mr. Buck... fined for delay. Moved whether
three may proceed to business. agreed and this law

THE HIST AND EDMUND BURKE'S CLUB

The HIST

And Edmund Burke's Club

AN ANTHOLOGY OF THE COLLEGE HISTORICAL
SOCIETY, THE STUDENT DEBATING SOCIETY
OF TRINITY COLLEGE DUBLIN, FROM ITS
ORIGINS IN EDMUND BURKE'S CLUB 1747–1997

DECLAN BUDD & ROSS HINDS

DUBLIN
THE LILLIPUT PRESS

Published by
The Lilliput Press
Arbour Hill, Dublin 7
for
College Historical Society
Trinity College, Dublin 2
Ireland

First published in 1997

ISBN 1 901866 00 9 — Standard Edition
ISBN 1 901866 01 7 — Special Edition

Design by Bill Murphy FCSD
Printed by Criterion Press Ltd, Ireland

To
Ann and Gillie
Gareth, Roland, Julian, Una,
Peter, Aoife and Leila,
who all shared in the making
of this book

CONTENTS

è❧

ILLUSTRATIONS

FOREWORD

The College Historical Society marked its Bicentenary in 1970 in magnificent style with a full week of celebrations in the first week of March. The plan for the celebration year included the production of this Anthology.

Much energy and organisation went into the collection of existing material and in the writing of new. Most of this initial work was done by Declan Budd, Secretary and Convenor of the Bicentenary Sub-Committee, whose idea it was to produce the anthology. He persuaded many Honorary Members to commit their memories to paper. With the help of Ian Ashe, Auditor 1969–70, and Richard Clarke, Record Secretary 1969–70, he collected the other material. It was typed and then annotated ready for the final editing. However, talks between the Officers of the Society and likely publishers never came to fruition. Declan's wife, Ann, some twenty years later prompted her husband and myself to examine again the possibility of publication. After reading the material on one sunny afternoon in June 1993, while sitting in the garden of my house in Brussels, we agreed that it was time to complete the task set in 1970!

The development of modern word-processing systems has made possible the completion on an Apple Macintosh computer of all stages of the work of publication up to final page layout and printing. My sons, Gareth and Julian, both now members of the Society, helped to key in a large part of the text during their vacation. We are very grateful for the work which they did. My youngest son, Peter, shared his journalistic experience with me, editing the final draft of the text to ensure that extracts were accurately copied. I must also record my appreciation of Dr David Mitchell's comments on an earlier draft.

It has been a delight to work with Bill Murphy; he has displayed an easy acceptance of suggestions when they fitted his design and an adamantine rejection when they did not! Tina Murphy has skilfully converted the text into the final layout, and cheerfully made 'last changes' again and again.

No book is without errors. This one has fewer errors now than it had before Avril Forrest took the completed text and applied to it her finely honed proof-reading abilities. She has thereby prevented many embarrassments.

Antony Farrell of The Lilliput Press, himself a past member of the Hist, was immediately enthusiastic when I asked him to publish the book, and has been most helpful. Jeremy Addis of *Books Ireland* was willing to give advice to yet another novice in the ways of book publishing.

The College Historical Society is very grateful to the T.C.D. Association and Trust for its financial support.

Finally I would like to record my thanks to my wife, Gillie, who knows now that the words of dedication to spouses in such a place as this are not formalities. She has provided encouragement and coffee throughout the work, at home and on holiday.

D. Ross Hinds   Brussels
Editor   16 June 1997

PREFACE

THE PRESIDENT OF
THE COLLEGE HISTORICAL SOCIETY
DR CONOR CRUISE O'BRIEN

This valuable history sheds a number of important sidelights on Irish history over more than two hundred years. The Hist, like Trinity itself, has often stood, during this period, in a difficult and fraught relation with the rest of Ireland. But there is something in such a relationship that can stretch the mind and stimulate the talents. And in no case is this more evident than in that of Edmund Burke, Trinity's most illustrious son, founder of 'the Club' and ancestor of the College Historical Society.

Conor Cruise O'Brien
30 September 1996

ACKNOWLEDGMENTS

We would like to acknowledge the following sources of material:

The National Gallery of Ireland, Dublin, for reproductions of portraits; Grace Duncan, Dublin for photographs of the 1970 Bicentenary Celebrations taken by her late husband George Duncan; Noel Dagg for his uncle's extensive papers on the Hist; Trinity College Dublin for reproductions of paintings and drawings; Victoria Glendinning for an extract from *A Fretful Midge* by Terence de Vere White; the *Irish University Quarterly* for extracts on the Hist; *Blackwood's Magazine* for an article on the Hist; *T.C.D., A College Miscellany* for poems and other writings; Claire McCutcheon for the photograph of the Inaugural Meeting of 10 November 1937; the Governors of Portora Royal School for reproduction of the painting of Rev. Henry Francis Lyte; and the *Irish Times* which published Dr Owen Sheehy Skeffington's contribution in 1970, and supplied the photograph of the Corresponding Societies Debate of 5 March 1952.

INTRODUCTION

Certain features of the Hist must strike the reader of this anthology. First, the Society has enjoyed an amazing continuity over two hundred years. The laws, in essence, remain unchanged. The office of Auditor, a title once peculiar to the Hist, is the same.

Secondly, the Hist has maintained a forum of free speech. The Society has trained Hyde and Carson, Tone and Ashbourne, Emmet and Glenavy. The views of all creeds and colours, radicals and reactionaries have been given a fair hearing, and understanding has bred toleration. Year by year, new members join the Hist, idealists, and cynics of every discipline, and there they thrash out the problems of the world.

A student society should be radical and humane in advance of the thinking of each era. The motions for debate are evidence of the Society's avant-garde spirit. The Society was the platform for rebel thinkers — Tone, Emmet, Davis and Dillon; for savants like Kells Ingram, Rowan Hamilton and Joly; for authors Lecky, Stoker and Le Fanu; for poets such as Moore and Wolfe and for politicians like Henry Grattan, Isaac Butt and Edward Carson. Oscar Wilde and Samuel Beckett were ordinary members. Such a standard, carried aloft for over two hundred years, is a stark challenge to the present generation.

This anthology has been compiled by members of the Society. It embraces aspects of the Society's history, for which we are indebted to the late T. S. C. Dagg. His nephew C. N. Dagg has given to the Society all the research material used in the preparation of the Dagg *College Historical Society, A History*. We are grateful to our Honorary Members who contributed to this anthology and permitted us to use extracts from their works. We are indebted to the Governors and Guardians of the National Gallery of Ireland for their permission to reproduce photographs of portraits in their possession.

Declan Budd
Secretary and Convenor,
Bicentenary Sub-Committee

T. S. C. Dagg, Auditor 1906–07, author of College Historical Society, A History

THE HISTORY OF THE SOCIETY TO 1920

The only complete history of the College Historical Society is College Historical Society, A History *(Kerryman, 440pp) by T. S. C. Dagg. It was published privately in 1969, after the death of the author, but in a run of only twenty-five copies, none of which was available for sale. The section of the anthology which follows has been condensed from Dagg's work. Part of the Introduction to that book, by T. S. C. Dagg's nephew C. N. Dagg, is reprinted below.*

INTRODUCTION

THE FIRST SUGGESTION THAT A History of the College Historical Society should be written is found in the Committee minutes of 1905, but until now no such history has appeared. T. S. C. Dagg, who is the author of the following history from the foundation of the Society in 1770 to the year 1920, was Auditor of the 'Hist' in the year 1906.

During the time he held office he determined that he would compile a history of the Society and he spent much of his spare time over many years collecting information from every source available. Most of the information in the Journals and minutes has never before been published and should prove of interest to all lovers of Irish history and especially to the members of the College Historical Society.

The first draft of his book ran to some fifteen hundred pages and he was reluctantly persuaded to condense it. When he died in his ninetieth year, in December 1964, the book was roughly in the form now presented in this limited edition, except that over forty full page illustrations[1] have had to be omitted.

---

[1] Many of these are included in this volume.

BURKE'S CLUB

In Dublin University there is a tradition, which has been handed down from generation to generation, that the College Historical Society, 'the greatest of all the schools of the orators', sprang from two associations of a similar character that existed in Dublin in the middle of the eighteenth century — Burke's 'Club' and the 'Historical Club' — of which a brief account is given in this chapter.

The 'Club' founded by Edmund Burke and a few of his fellow students is the earliest debating society composed of students of the University of which any definite record remains. The minute book of this club, a treasured possession of the College Historical Society, relates that the first meeting took place on Tuesday, 21 April 1747, in a house in George's Lane, now South Great George's Street, the members present being Edmund Burke, Matthew Mohun, William Dennis, and Andrew Buck. Mohun was elected the first President, and Dennis the first Secretary.

The minute book of the Club, most of which is in Burke's handwriting, consists of one hundred and ten closely written pages, and contains an account of the proceedings of thirty-five meetings. Burke, who sat six times as President and twice as Censor, was the moving spirit and was never once absent from the meetings. The minutes vary in length and importance, some being merely concise notes of the evenings proceedings, while others record carefully the speeches of the members.

The flavour of events can be gleaned in the following extract of a letter by Dennis:

Dublin, May 28 1747

Dear Richard,

I have prosecuted Mohun (while a private member) with the utmost vigour, and when Censor expelled him, and now for my good services I am threatened with expulsion by Burke, who is a terrible fellow, and is very active (at getting me punished) in the Club, though I have hitherto shown myself a good member. I'm now accused of a design of destroying the Club when, alas! no, no one has a greater desire to preserve it: nay, so strong is it, that though I find in myself a strong desire to keep the Chair when I get it,

Edmund Burke, portrait in the possession of Dr Brendan O'Brien, Dublin, by courtesy of Dr O'Brien

yet my regard for four or five members quells it. The approbation I met with in the character of Cato (Censor) has made me so much more a stickler for liberty, that not bearing any encroachment on it in our assembly, I am deemed a criminal; and what's worse, my accuser a violent one, and my judge the person whom I've injured; you see the justice.

The letter continues:

Friday morning, May 29 1747

Burke is now writing the proceedings of the assembly, and just saying he'll pass over part of the Debates because he is tired, you see he is semper idem, as lazy as you imagine, though I must do him the justice to say he designed writing last night; what prevented it heretofore was our expectation of your first challenge and likewise Ned thought it preposterous to be threshing his brains for you when he is writing for the public; pray laugh heartily now lest you should split when you see the subject he chose and the manner he has treated it, but I will not anticipate your pleasure by acquainting you any more. I wonder Ned did not acquaint you with several important affairs which have happened in town, but I'll supply his place.

Here follows an account, part mock heroic, part serious, of the Black Dog Prison riots of 21 May 1747.

To rescue one of their number who had been arrested by a Catchpole in Fleet Street and was being carried off to this torture den, the students of Trinity College sallied out on the evening of Thursday 21 May 1747. They caught up the bailiff, rushed him into the College, and soused him in the trough under the pump. Then, headed by one of their number known as 'Gallows' Walsh, the scholars resolved to storm the Black Dog itself, effect a general gaol delivery and release all the prisoners. They carried the bailiff half drowned and stark naked with them from the College gates along Dame Street, up Cork Hill and through High Street, and accompanied by an ever gathering mob they made a determined attempt to break open the Marshalsea, and only failed to batter in the gate from want of artillery. Roe, the constable of the adjoining Castle of Newgate gaol, who was well supplied with cannon, fired upon the assailants.

Dennis mentions in his letter that two of the mob were killed and several others wounded — but apparently these were townspeople who joined in the attempt to storm the gaol and were not students. He continues:

Excuse the shortness of this, but I shall be more prolix in my next, till when believe me your sincere and humble servant,

William Dennis
or Cato the unfortunate!

Henry Grattan by Martin Archer Shee 1769–1850, courtesy of the National Gallery of Ireland

The Hon. David Plunket (Lord Rathmore) states that Burke's Club and several successive debating societies, of which Grattan, Avonmore and Hussey Burgh were members, though entirely composed of students of the University, had held their meetings outside its walls.

How long the 'old' Historical Club, which was in existence in 1744 or the Historical Club, founded in 1753, continued to function we have no definite knowledge. Francis Hardy in his speech at the opening of the Fourth session of the Historical Society in 1772 congratulated that Society on the position it had attained as compared with many institutions of a

John Fitzgibbon, Earl of Clare

similar character, but of limited duration, which had at different periods been founded in the University; and Christopher Temple Emmet began his speech at the close of the tenth session with the following words: 'Ten sessions this Society has seen, since from the embers of another Institution it shone a fairer Phoenix in a purer Flame: the hands that struck the sparks of first existence long feared that their blaze, like the shortlived meteor would glitter for a moment to decay for ever, but oppposition taught that blaze to struggle into brightness.' The other institution to which Emmet referred, and which had apparently ceased to exist shortly after the foundation of the Historical Society, was presumably the Historical Club founded in 1753. In a footnote to his auditorial address (7 November 1844) Charles Hemphill, afterwards Baron Hemphill, referring to this Club, states: 'I have heard, however, that Mr Yelverton (afterwards Lord Avonmore, Chief Baron of the Exchequer) Mr Scott (afterwards Earl of Clonmel) and the Rev. Patrick Hare (the Auditor's grandfather) were chiefly instrumental in its establishment.' Brougham says that Grattan and Flood were also members of it. Mrs Ella B. Day in her book *Mr Justice Day of Kerry* wrote that Day became a member of the Historical Club, and that his contemporaries were Henry Grattan, John Foster (the last Speaker of the Irish House of Commons), and John Fitzgibbon (afterwards Earl of Clare).

The Fellows' Common Room, Trinity College

The last quarter of the eighteenth century was the golden age of Irish eloquence, and amongst the great orators of this period the names of Burke and of Grattan, Flood, Yelverton, Burgh and other members of the Historical Club hold an honoured place.

Of Burke's oratory in his College days we have preserved for us the views of the members of the Club, when on one occasion they voted him thanks for the matter of his oration but not for his delivery of it.

Of his oratory in later years Grattan has left us the following impressions:

I have heard Burke. He is ingenious, oratorical, undaunted. . . . Burke is unquestionably the first orator of the Commons of England. Boundless in knowledge, instantaneous in his apprehensions — abundant in his language, he speaks with profound attention, and acknowledged superiority, notwithstanding the want of energy, the want of grace, and the want of elegance in his manner.

As an orator he has been surpassed by some, as a practical politician he has been surpassed by many . . . but no other politician or writer has thrown the light of so penetrating a genius on the nature and working of the British Constitution, has impressed his principle so deeply on both of the great parties in the State, and has left behind him a richer treasure of political wisdom applicable to all countries and to all times.

When Burke died on 9 July 1797, Canning wrote to Lord Malmesbury:

There is but one event, but that is an event for the world, Burke is dead . . . he had among all his great qualities, that for which the world did not give him sufficient credit, of creating in those about him very strong attachments and affection, as well as the unbounded admiration, which I every day am more and more convinced was his due . . . he is the man that will mark his age, marked as it is itself by events, to all time.

Henry Grattan, who was in College from 1763 to 1767, entered the Irish Parliament in 1775, and his speeches there and in the British House of Commons rank amongst the masterpieces of parliamentary oratory.

The late T. M. Kettle says: 'The proud, full sail of the Grattan utterance is as noble and individual in its way as that of Shakespeare himself. There is as rich political wisdom in him as in Burke.' (Introduction to *Irish Orators and Oratory*)

Barry Yelverton entered College in June 1753, aged seventeen, and obtained a scholarship in 1755. Sir Jonah Barrington says:

It would be difficult to do justice to the lofty and overwhelming elocution of this distinguished man, during the early period of his political exertions. To the profound, logical, and conclusive reasoning of Flood, the brilliant, stimulating, epigrammatic antithesis of Grattan — the sweetened, captivating, convincing rhetoric of Burgh or the wild, fascinating imagery and varied pathos of the extraordinary Curran, he was respectively inferior; but in powerful, nervous language, he excelled them all. A vigorous, commanding, undaunted eloquence burst in rolling torrents from his lips, not a word was lost. Though fiery, yet weighty and distinct, the authoritative rapidity of his language, relieved by the beauty of his luxuriant fancy, subdued the Auditor without the power of resistance, and left him in doubt, whether it was to argument or to eloquence that he surrendered his conviction.

Walter Hussey entered in October 1758, and graduated in 1762. In after life he assumed the surname of Burgh. The following graphical sketch of him has been given to us by Grattan:

He was a man singularly gifted, with great talent, great variety, wit, oratory, and logic; he, too, had weaknesses, but he had the pride of genius also, and strove to raise his country along with himself, and never sought to build his elevation on the degradation of Ireland. — I moved an amendment for a free export, he moved a better amendment, and he lost his place.

HISTORICAL SOCIETY

THE HISTORICAL SOCIETY met for the first time on Wednesday, 21 March 1770 when the following thirteen students 'who first united into a body and obtained the use of the Common room from the Provost and Senior Fellow' were present:

Michael Truel (who took the Chair as Senior Member); William Day,

Scholar, afterwards F.T.C.D.; Richard Cary, Scholar; Charles Dennis; Henry Duquery, Scholar, afterwards M.P. Sergeant-at-Law; James Whitelaw, Scholar, author of *History of Dublin*; John Barton, Scholar; John Harvey, Scholar; Thomas Johnson, Scholar; Henry Doyel afterwards Filazer of Exchequer, Chairman of Quarter Sessions; Ponsonby Gouldsbury, Scholar; Robert Robinson, Scholar; Michael Cahill, Scholar. Chapter IV of the Laws prescribed the duties and powers of the Auditor:

The Office of the Auditor shall be to inspect and supervise the laws, journals, and accounts, and to act as Comptroller of the several officers of the Society.

The office of Auditor originated as far as is known in the Historical Society. It has always been regarded as one of much distinction both inside and outside the University, and election to this office is, perhaps, the highest honour that can be conferred upon a student by his fellow students. The title has been adopted by several other debating societies in College and elsewhere.

Chapter XI (the last chapter) dealt with the admission of members. No person below the standing of Senior Sophister was admitted, except Fellow Commoners, who when they had arrived at the standing of Junior Sophister had the privilege of being proposed as candidates. Graduates whose names were off the College books but who were under the degree of Senior Bachelor were also eligible for membership. The election was by ballot, an adverse vote of one seventh of the members present being sufficient to reject a candidate. The subscription at entrance was a guinea, and elected candidates were required to subscribe their names to the following certificate:

I promise and vow, upon my honour and reputation, to conform myself to all the laws of this Society, so long as I shall continue a member thereof, under the penalties in them enacted. And if (by any motive whatsoever induced) I should hereafter withdraw from it, I never will (as I value the above-mentioned pledges) make an ungenerous use of any knowledge of the Society's proceedings, acquired by me whilst I am a member of it. I also promise, that I will never divulge any proceedings of the Society which in my judgement may tend to the prejudice of this Society, or of any individual thereof.

The signatures of 997 members are appended to this certificate in the book containing the first code of laws.

The proceedings opened each night at six o'clock, in the Common room, with an examination in the portion of History appointed at a preceding meeting. On the conclusion of the History examination the members adjourned to an inner room for tea and coffee. A Chapter of laws and the abstract of the proceedings at the previous meeting were then read. The question for debate was next declared from the Chair, discussed and voted upon. Essays and poems were received, read from the Chair, and ordered to lie on the table for the perusal of the members till the following meeting. Motions were submitted, candidates for admission were proposed; new members were balloted for; the portion of History for debate was appointed for the next meeting; and the Society then adjourned.

The second session, which opened on 24 October 1770 was one of considerable activity and progress. Early in the session steps were taken by the Society to secure the comfort of the members. The Society's room was matted, the seats were covered with green baize, and a canopy was provided for the Chair. A steward was elected monthly to 'provide all things necessary for the accommodation and refreshment of the Society'. A porter was also employed to attend on the Society.

The lighting of the Common room in which the debates were held appears to have been a matter of some expense, as Duquery and Whitelaw were ordered to wait on the Bursar 'in order to enquire whether the College will take upon it the expense of the branch which was a gift from it to the Society'.

The monthly subscription was raised to three shillings 'English', and the 'admission fine' to one guinea.

That the Society was not altogether free from molestation would appear from an entry in 26 December 1770: 'that an advertisement offering a reward of five guineas for the discovery of the persons concerned in breaking and abusing the tables and benches belonging to this Society be drawn up and posted in several of the most public places within the College'.

During the session, committees were appointed to collect and codify the Laws, to methodise and register the abstracts and essays, and to supervise and correct the Journals and records, and to have them transcribed into a book provided for that purpose.

The Society did not confine itself entirely to the pursuits of History, Composition, and Oratory. A Committee of ten members was appointed 'to collect subscriptions for the relief of the poor at this period of distress and misery', and at the meeting following their appointment they placed a sum of £6 at the disposal of the Society. The number of charitable collectors was subsequently increased so as to include the whole Society, and the charity, which was at first confined to those connected with the College, was extended to the outside poor, including the prisoners in the City Marshalsea, and the Four Court Marshalsea.

A special book was kept in which the sums contributed were recorded. The following are typical of the grants made by the Society, lists of which appear frequently in the Journals:

To ye Widow English — 5s 5d
To Michael Dunne — 2s 8 ¹/₂d
To George Webb — 1s 0d per week in bread
To the Rev Mr Moxam — £1 2s 9d
To the prisoners in the Four Court Marshalsea — 11s 4 ¹/₂d
To the City Marshalsea — 11s 4 ¹/₂d

A Committee of three members was appointed 'to enquire into the state of the Four Court Marshalsea,' and, later 'to distribute the five guineas amongst the poor prisoners'.

William Preston, Chairman at the closing meeting of the third session, devoted a large part of his speech to the advantages to be derived from taking part in the debates, even by those members who did not intend to follow a profession in which public speaking was required. 'They will', he said, 'be freed from that faulty diffidence, that painful embarrassment, and bashful timidity, that too often attend sensibility, and throw a shade on genius; that keep modest merit in obscurity, and make the wise man appear in the company of fools as the fool ought to appear in the company of wise men.'

The third session (1771–72) appears to have been one of steady progress for the Society, which was now firmly established. Nine candidates for membership were proposed at the opening meeting, but of these five were rejected. Among those rejected was John Philpot Curran, and the Society thus deprived itself of a share in the honour of training this renowned orator.

The following interesting account of the Historical Society at this time is given by Lord Rathmore:

In 1782 when Plunket was admitted into the Society . . . the patriotic party in Ireland, with whom nearly all the youth of the University sympathised had achieved their short lived triumph. From their places in the House of Commons, the members of the Historical Society listened night after night to the eloquence and shared the enthusiasm with which Henry Grattan and his associates stirred the Irish people to assert their independent nationality. They saw an army of nearly 90,000 volunteers assemble and line the streets of Dublin, through which the patriot members walked to their regenerated assembly; and whilst every Irishman of ardent imagination regarded these events as the beginning of a meridian age of independence and posterity, none foresaw the future of humiliation and disaster which closed the history of the last century in Ireland.

ORATORS

At that moment of intense political and social excitement, the Historical Society must have presented splendid lures to such an ambition as was young William Plunket's, and afforded him at the same time an opportunity peculiarly suited for the development of his special powers. He entered into the competition of the Society with all the energy of his character, and although the greater number of his associates were his seniors, he seems almost at once to have taken a leading part amongst them, and soon to have become the master spirit of their debates. During his career in this Society, Plunket formed around him a company of friends and admirers, amongst whom were afterwards found some of the most remarkable Irishmen of their day.

Charles Kendal Bushe, of whom the greatest modern authority on the subject said that 'his merits as a speaker were of the highest description' and that 'his power of narrative has not perhaps been equalled'.

Magee, afterwards Archbishop of Dublin, and author of the comprehensive and eloquent argument on the Atonement, still a text book in

Peter Burrowes

the Irish Divinity School. Peter Burrowes, an honest but eccentric genius, possessed too of such rare powers of real pathos and of honest denunciation, that in these respects his reported speeches are second only to those of Curran. George Miller, afterwards University Professor of History, and author of the masterly work, *History Philosophically Considered*. Sir Laurence Parsons, the liberal and popular Irish patrician, who so brilliantly opposed the Union; Theobald Wolfe Tone, and Thomas Addis Emmet.

Another friend was Whitley Stokes, who obtained a lay fellowship; he

The House of Commons, College Green, Dublin

Irish Volunteers in College Green

also took a degree in medicine, and may be considered as the founder of clinical instruction in Ireland. In public life he endeavoured to develop the natural resources of the country, and in private life he was deeply loved by all who knew him. In his diary Tone wrote of him: 'In the full sense of the term, I look upon Whitley Stokes as the very best man I have ever met.'

15

William Conyngham Plunket

Of William Conyngham Plunket's oratory Lecky has written:

Even as an orator — though his place is in the foremost rank — his popularity was somewhat limited by the extreme severity of a taste which rarely stooped to ornament, or indulged in anything that was merely rhetorical or declamatory. But in the power of rapid, lucid, and most cogent extemporaneous argument; in the grave, dignified, reasoned, and persuasive eloquence, which is most fitted to charm and subjugate an educated audience, he has very seldom had an equal, scarcely ever a superior . . . In the Imperial Parliament he was at once recognised as one of the very greatest of orators and debaters. . .

Rev. Paul Limerick, Secretary College Historical Society 1775–76, Chaplain of the Presidency of Fort William, Bengal. Appointed Bishop of Calcutta, but the ship in which he was coming to England for consecration was lost at sea in 1810. Minitature portrait in the possession of the Society.

Edward Mayne in his speech at the opening meeting of the ninth session (1777–78) exhorted the members to attend the weekly meetings regularly:

to shift from the company of ladies, from the pleasure of seeing and being seen, from the delights of the bottle, or from other even rational amusements, for the variety of an assembly of men, for the conversations of persons of sense, for the sweets of friendship, for the improvement of the manners, for instruction and experience in the most noble of Sciences, and in the scarcest of excellent Arts.

The demands for Free Trade and for Parliamentary Independence, the example of America, the eloquence of Grattan and others in the Irish House of Commons and rise of the Volunteers inspired many students to become members of a Society where they were afforded opportunities of debating the burning topics of the day. The number of students in the University had also increased considerably, and the admission of Junior Sophisters into the Society at the beginning of the twelfth session led to a large influx of new members.

Christopher Temple Emmet

The first Irish debate was held on 6 January 1779, when the question 'Whether an Union with Great Britain would be of advantage to Ireland' was decided in the negative by eight votes to six, Christopher Temple Emmet being teller for the noes, and John Steward for the ayes. Another debate which reflected the spirit of the times in Ireland, 'Whether Universal toleration should be encouraged by a wise legislature,' was carried in the affirmative by seventeen votes to four. Up to this time the debates had been mostly on questions of ancient history or on general subjects of a non-political character, but during the next four years the most burning political questions relating to Ireland, or to Great Britain and America as affecting Ireland, were discussed by the Society.

The following is an account[2] of the attendance of the students in the Irish House of Commons:

The student's passport was his gown. He rapped at the wicket, and the porter looked through a grating; the applicant held up his gown, and the door was opened, admitted him, and again closed . . . when I first entered College I was very fond of using this privilege. It was a proud thing for a 'Gib' to present himself to a crowd around the door, hear many a cry, 'make way for the gentleman of the College,' pass the avenue made for him, find the door expand to the 'open sesame' of his gown, and himself admitted alone to the great council of the nation, while the suppliant crowd were excluded.

After the fire (27th February, 1792), the business of the house was adjourned to the speaker's chamber, and the students of Trinity College were particularly favoured. At the end of the apartment, behind the speaker's chair, there was a deep and convenient gallery, which was exclusively devoted to gownsmen. They were instantly admitted here on presenting themselves, and listened to the debate at their ease, while the public in general now found it difficult to obtain passes, and when they got permission, were confined to a narrow strip of gallery, from some parts of which they could neither see nor hear.

This proud distinction the gownsmen, however, soon forfeited. Lord Fitzwilliam had been sent over as a popular viceroy, and, on his sudden recall, a strong feeling of disappointment prevailed. On a night when the subject was brought before the house, our gallery was full, and I remember well the irrepressible excitement that seemed to actuate us all. At length it broke out. Grattan rose to deprecate the measure as one calculated to cause great disturbance in Ireland, by what was considered the perfidy of the government, first exciting the high hopes of the people by promised measures of liberal policy, and then dashing them, by the sudden removal of the man who had been sent over expressly to accomplish them. At the conclusion of Grattan's inflammatory speech, the enthusiasm in the gallery was no longer capable of restraint. We rose as one man, shouting

---

[2] *Ireland Sixty Years Ago* by the Right Hon. John Edward Walsh, 2nd edn Dublin 1849, p. 175 *et seq.*

and cheering with the boisterous tumult of a popular meeting. When this subsided, Foster's peculiar voice was heard through his nose, ordering the students' gallery to be cleared, and a sergeant-at-arms, with a posse of messengers, entered among us. We were pushed out in a heap without the slightest ceremony, and were never again suffered to enter as privileged persons.

From the year 1779 onwards, many of the debates partook of the spirit of political excitement prevailing at the time, and from the divisions it was not difficult to see on which side were the feelings of the majority of members of the Society. During the session 1779–80 the following questions were debated:

'Whether America was justifiable in her secession from Great Britain,' decided in the affirmative nem. con.

'Whether any member of a community can be justifiable in proposing a condition without which he will not serve his country,' decided in the affirmative.

'Whether Ireland could possibly subsist independent of any other Nation,' decided in the negative.

An important innovation, the appointment of a paid secretary, was made in this session. This officer was required to attend in the Society's room on Wednesday evening from the hour of six o'clock to half past eleven o'clock, and he was also required to attend on the Auditor every Wednesday at ten o'clock. William Bruce was appointed to this office, and attended for the first time on 22 March 1780, from which night onwards his signature is appended to the records of the proceedings. It was apparently customary for the Secretary to sleep in the Society's rooms on the nights of meeting, as on the first night of his attendance a resolution was passed 'that the Secretary be allowed to put up a bed in the tea-room'.

Laurence Parsons, who had been Auditor for the last period of the session 1779–80, was elected Auditor again in the session 1782–83. At this time he represented the University in the Irish House of Commons, and was one of its most brilliant and attractive personalities. His election to Parliament while occupying the Auditorial chair is unique in the Society's annals. Parsons afterwards became second Earl of Rosse.

19

SPECULATIVE SOCIETY

On 21 May 1783 the first steps were taken to establish a connection between the Historical Society and the Speculative Society of Edinburgh. A committee of three members, Gabriel Stokes, Chairman, William Baker (Auditor), and Thomas Addis Emmet, was appointed to consider the conditions under which members of the Speculative Society of Edinburgh might become members *pro tempore* of the Historical Society, and on 11 June resolutions, which may be briefly summarised as follows, were adopted.

That the establishment of a connection between the two Societies would tend to the advantage of both: that members of the Speculative Society be admitted members of the Historical Society having made and subscribed the usual declaration; that they be entitled to compete for the awards in History, Oratory and Composition and be allowed to speak, vote and ballot on all public business; that they shall have full use of the Library; and that they shall be excused from serving in any office, and from all fees, subscriptions and punishments.

Thomas Addis Emmet and Stephen Dickson, who were at this time medical students at Edinburgh University, and members of the Speculative Society, were mainly instrumental in bringing about the connection between the two Societies. In the years 1783, 1784 and 1785 Emmet was one of the five Presidents elected by the Speculative Society in each session, and Dickson was one of the Presidents elected in the years 1783 and 1784. On the death of his elder brother, Christopher Temple Emmet, in 1789, Emmet resolved, on the advice of Sir James Mackintosh, with whom he had formed a fast friendship, to quit physic for law, and he proceeded to the Irish Bar, whereupon he became a non-resident member of the Speculative Society.

Emmet's[3] connection with the Speculative Society terminated on 20 November 1798 when the following record appears in the minutes of that Society:

---

[3] Thomas Addis Emmet later went to the U.S.A. and was one of three people who looked after Thomas Paine, author of *The Rights of Man*, in his old age, when all others had abandoned him. He was an executor of the will of Paine, when he died in 1809 in Greenwich, New York. cf. *Paine* by David Freeman Hawke, W. W. Norton, New York and London 1974.

Thomas Addis Emmet, 1765–1827

The Secretary (Mr Waugh) moved, and was seconded by Mr Henry Brougham, that as Thomas Addis Emmet had acknowledged himself a member of the Executive Directory of the Irish Union and had confessed himself privy to carrying on a treasonable correspondence with France, his name should be erased from the List of the Speculative Society. A ballot was

21

taken on this motion, after it had lain on the table for three weeks, and it was carried unanimously.

In the Journals for 26 February 1783 we find the following entries:

The Bursar's Compliments to the Historical Society. The Board requests the favour of the use of the Historical room for a few days, as His Excellency the Lord Lieutenant is to breakfast in the College on Monday next, the 3rd of March.

The Historical Society present their compliments to Dr Ussher. They have much pleasure in complying with the request of the Board, and have unanimously agreed to accommodate them with the use of their room for a few days.

The following note is appended by the Secretary to the record of the proceedings for 26 February:

The Historical room being very much deranged in consequence of His Excellency the Lord Lieutenant breakfasting therein on Monday 3rd March, the Society were necessitated to postpone meeting therein until Wednesday 12th March, 1783.

On 19 November 1783 four compositions were read, for one of which 'A Defence of the Age', Plunket was awarded a medal; and a 'Particular Medal' was awarded to Standish O'Grady for an elegy on Dr William Cleghorn, which concluded with the following lines:

Say — how he liv'd a succour to th'oppress'd,
Great without Pride; and Lib'ral without shew,
In Friendship faithful, gen'rous to a Foe,
Admir'd, not envied, Vanity he scorn'd;
And dying bless'd that Land — which living he adorn'd.

A composition entitled 'The Incognitos, a Northern Tale,' signed 'Borealis,' met with a different fate, as the usual motion of thanks to the author was negatived nem. con. and the following resolution was passed by thirty-seven votes to twelve:

*That a poem signed 'Borealis', containing very unjust and scandalous abuse of
the Volunteers of Ireland and also the most unjust calumny of several
respectable private characters, be burned by the hands of the porter, in
presence of the Society.*

The record proceeds 'And the porter being called in the said poem was
burned accordingly.'

WOLFE TONE

O<small>N</small> 19 N<small>OVEMBER</small> 1783
Theobald Wolfe Tone was proposed for membership by George Miller,
seconded by William Conyngham Plunket, and elected, and on 3 December
he attended his first meeting.

Tone took an active part in the proceedings of the Society, where he
made many friends and was held in high esteem by his fellow members. In
that part of his autobiography referring to his College career, he writes:

*As it was, however, I obtained a scholarship, three premiums, and three
medals from the Historical Society, a most admirable institution, of which I
had the honour to be Auditor, and also to close the session with a speech from
the Chair, the highest compliment which that Society is used to bestow. I
looked back on my College days with regret, and I preserve, and ever shall, a
most sincere affection for the University of Dublin.*

On the first night of the sixteenth session, 26 October 1784, Charles
Kendal Bushe was elected a member.

On 15 December 1784 Tone was teller for the Ayes and Bushe was teller
for the Noes, in the debate 'Whether we are more indebted for the
constitutional liberty of Great Britain to bad than good Princes?' On
5 January 1785 Bushe was awarded a medal for Oratory with the
exceptionally large number of 287 returns; Richard Graves, afterwards
F.T.C.D., and Dean of Ardagh, receiving the second medal with 181
returns. On the same night Bushe was also awarded a special medal offered
for the best elegy on Francis Blake Woodward, a former member of the
Society. A couple of nights later the following motion was passed by 34
votes to 25: 'That the extraordinary thanks of the Society be given to Mr

Theobald Wolfe Tone Auditor 1785–86, artist unknown,
courtesy of the National Gallery of Ireland

Bushe for his very proper, steady, and polite conduct in the Chair on
the last night of meeting, when spirited exertions were necessary.' On
23 March he again acted as one of the tellers in a debate on the question of
the King's prerogative, and on the opening night of the next session he was
chosen to deliver the speech from the Chair.

The friendship between Bushe and Plunket which began in the
Historical Society lasted until it was terminated by death. During their
career at the Bar they became 'famous forensic gladiators,' and after long
years of professional competition they found themselves ranged together as
Solicitor General and Attorney General. Finally Plunket became Lord
Chancellor and Bushe Lord Chief Justice of Ireland.

Charles Kendal Bushe

Tone's first appearance in the debates was on 9 June 1784 when he was one of the pleaders on the question: 'Is an absentee tax admissible in a Free State?' which was carried in the affirmative nem. con. On 30 June 1784 when Richard Jephson and William Stawell were awarded medals for their distinguished merit in debate, Tone was declared to be entitled to the remarkable thanks. At the beginning of the next session, 1784–85, Tone was absent for some time, but on 5 January 1785 when he and three other members were proposed as Presidents for the four ensuing nights, he was 'elected unanimously' and the others were 'elected'. A few nights later he was one of the four members nominated for the office of Auditor, but he was not elected on that occasion.

On the following night, however, it was proposed by Graves seconded by Goold, and carried in the affirmative nem. con. 'that an extra medal be presented to Mr Tone for his exertions in Oratory during the last period'.

On 2 November 1785 George Miller obtained leave to resign the office of Auditor and nominated Gabriel Stokes, Abraham Stewart, Wolfe Tone and Charles Kendal Bushe as candidates from whom to choose his successor. On the following night Tone was elected Auditor.

On 4 January 1786 Tone was awarded a medal for Oratory, with 103 returns, being second to Richard Jebb, who gained the first medal with 139 returns, and on the following night he was awarded a medal for History. During the last month of his Auditorship, Tone was absent, and an entry on 8 February relates that 'Mr Magee, Vice-Auditor on behalf of Mr Tone, resigned the office of Auditor.'

At a meeting on 3 May when a composition entitled 'John and Mary', signed 'Swift secundus' was submitted, a motion was passed that 'it be burned at the hand of Mr Bilson, ye porter.' The record proceeds: 'Mr Bilson was accordingly called in and burned the said composition.'

The following entry appears in the Journals of 1 November 1786:

The Society being informed that Mr Tone had been robbed of three medals presented to him by this Society, a motion was made by Mr Plunket and seconded by Mr Magee, that the Society do come to the following resolution:

'Resolved that the Treasurer be ordered to furnish Mr Tone with three medals in place of those of which he has been robbed, as well to testify our respect for so valuable a member, as because we would wish to perpetuate those proofs of our discernment. Carried in the affirmative nem. con.'

On 15 April 1789 Tone proposed a motion that an extra silver medal be awarded to the author of the best poetical composition 'on the late happy recovery of his present Majesty'. The motion was seconded by Bushe, and a few nights later three compositions were submitted, for one of which a medal was awarded to Wheaton Bradish.

One of the members, Ezekiel Sharkey, having printed, in a volume with other poems, a poetical composition for which he had obtained a medal from the Society, a motion that he had acted illegally and that such a proceeding ought not to be a precedent was discussed on several nights, and was finally 'not put'. A motion was thereupon proposed by Tone, seconded by Thomas Nunn, and passed, that no person who had obtained a medal for composition should publish it as having received a medal without obtaining leave from the Society.

Tone was chosen to close the twentieth session with a speech from the Chair, and in it he gives a deplorable picture of the Society at the time. His opening sentence reads: 'At the close of a troublesome and tempestuous session, which has been marked by a variety of important incidents, I have the high honour to meet you in the situation to which your goodness has raised me.' His duties as Chairman, he stated, would be 'to censure indecency and impropriety without consideration whom he might offend, and boldly tell you of your faults, though at the certain forfeiture of your favour'.

After references to the proud position held by the Society in the past, and to the many members 'now high in the estimate of their country,' he proceeds:

But why do I recur to glories that are past: Let me not consider what the Historical Society has been, let me, painful as it is, lay before you what you are.

In the long detail of your follies and your faults, there is one which pre-eminently cries aloud for the most unqualified and decided condemnation. I mean the vindictive spirit of sanguinary personal resentment, which has through this whole session disgraced your proceedings, and would, if prosecuted with the same acrimony in which it commenced, have degraded you into a mob of gladiators. Other of your misdeeds affect the form but this strikes at the life of the institution.

What! Shall the Historical Society be no more mentioned but as a theatre of War and of Tumult? Shall the civil Magistrate rest from our broils, or must an eternal succession of bail-bonds and recognizances perpetuate our disgrace?

Shall the laws of the country be insulted, the discipline of the University condemned, and disorder, and misrule, and anarchy be let loose upon us at the will of any hot-headed or giddy young man, who may choose these walls as the scene of his riotous valour, and turn the seat of science into a field of blood? Not for such heroes was this Society instituted; not such were the views of our wise and able founders; not such was the practice of this assembly while the Historical Society deserved that name, while we moved obedient in our proper orb round the centre of our institution, not as we have of late appeared breaking our order, and shooting wildly across the system, glaring and fiery and portentous!

He denounces strongly the recurrence of duelling:

It has been my fortune to be unwilling witness to many quarrels in this Society, very few of which came to a termination in the field, and in none did any serious mischief occur, except to the reputation of this institution. I did with great satisfaction congratulate myself that the demon of duelling was laid, though not in a red sea and, as I hoped, would walk within these hallowed walls no more. . . .

Unwillingly I am compelled thus to observe on the dangerous spirit of contention which has through this session haunted your debates, it is now my duty to see whether you have carried the same active, ardent spirit into the necessary and essential parts of your business, into History, Composition and Oratory. What is the result of the enquiry? In all these obsolete pursuits your faculties have been chilled and torpid, but when the hot fit returned, your desperate and paralytic exertion of strength was exhausted either in a silly and contemptible impeachment, or a more baneful and destructive personal quarrel. But let me come to particulars. What has been your attendance on History? A wretched evasion of the spirit of your laws by a thin attendance of members not half prepared, endeavouring to distribute the poor modicum of information, which one or two had collected, among the needy remainder, and so impose on the Chairman and save sixpence! What have been your debates? Night after night have they been begun and concluded by the two pleaders, not infrequently by one single pleader, and if they extended beyond these narrow limits, instead of clear and spirited investigation of the question, running out into commonplace harangues or more ruinous contention and invective.

On the subject for Compositions, silence is mercy — this is not your era for Compositions!

His concluding words are not, however, without encouragement and hope:

Dark and gloomy as are our prospects, I do not yet despair of the republic. Let us but set ourselves seriously to the work of reformation — in pointing out what I have thought wrong in our past proceedings, I have in effect laid down the rules which I would have you pursue. Fly like the pestilence the spirit of private quarrel — if any troublesome and petulant member breaks the good order of the Society with his personal resentment, instantly remove the evil thing from amongst you, and dismiss him to his proper station, the Bear Garden. Let not the sacred fire of your resentment be dragged forth on every trivial occasion, nor the censure of this Society be a weapon in the hand of every peevish individual who may raise himself into imaginary consequence on the stilts of an impeachment. Be assiduous in History. Be bold yet temperate in debate — be candid and cautious on the merits of Compositions — think of your past glories, the infamy of desertion, the greatness of the reward, the easiness of acquisition. This do and ye shall live! Omit it and you are nothing!

A letter which appeared in Walker's *Hibernian Magazine* for December 1793, purporting to be from a visitor to Dublin, presumably from across the Channel, gives an amusing account of a tour through the College, with sarcastic criticisms of its general condition, but concluding with the following:

Up a pretty flight of stairs on our left as we came out of the Dining Hall I was highly pleased with a noble room elegantly fitted up in the most modern style, with a taste and expense I had not observed since I entered the College walls till then; this I find is a room ceded about 23 years ago by the Board to a Society of young gentlemen who since that time to the present day have had the exclusive care of it, and who are well known through the three kingdoms by the name of the Historical Society.

An unusual entry appears in the Journals of 20 November 1793, when it is recorded that on the proposal of the Treasurer, Samuel Kyle, the Society unanimously agreed that 100 flannel waistcoats be granted by the Historical Society, for the use of the British Army in Flanders, and a Committee was appointed to receive subscriptions for purchasing the waistcoats.

EXPULSION 1794

On 2 April 1794 an incident occurred which led within a very short time to the expulsion of the Society from the College.

It appears that William Connor, an old member of the Society, who, owing to a serious breach of College discipline committed some years before, had been forbidden by the Board to appear in College, attended the meeting on this night. The Rev. George Miller, F.T.C.D., then Junior Dean, upon observing that Connor was present, requested the Auditor, Lewis Kerr, to inform him that if he did not immediately quit the Society he would move for his expulsion. The Auditor declined to deliver this message, whereupon the Chairman, Henry Adair, was appealed to, but he also declined. The message was then conveyed to Connor by the Secretary and he immediately withdrew. There followed an exchange of resolutions between the Board and the Society, resulting in the Society meeting outside the College.

Edward Lawson occupied the chair at the opening meeting of the twenty-sixth session, which was held in the Exhibition Room, William Street, on 22 October 1794 and at which eighty members were present. In his speech he bitterly denounced the Board's decrees expelling them from the College, and he expressed the view that reconciliation was utterly impracticable.

. . . Far from expecting an amnesty at present, you must regard this very moment as the opening of a new campaign. . . . Already is your inheritance offered to younger brethren, and colonists and culprits of all sorts and sizes are invited to people your forsaken habitation. . . .

At the meeting on Wednesday, 31 December 1794 the Auditor submitted the following report:

An Account of the transactions between the Historical Society and Senior Fellows of Trinity College, Dublin.

The Historical Society of the University of Dublin, finding with extreme concern that every submission on their part, has only appeared to enflame that hostility with which the heads of the college have pursued them for eight months past, esteem it a duty which they owe to themselves and the public, to vindicate their own conduct from industrious misrepresentation; to explain the utility of their institution and to shew by a full and plain statement of facts, in what manner the CHARTERED GUARDIANS OF NATIONAL EDUCATION have, in this instance, executed the important trust reposed in them.

In 1770, several students, observing the insufficiency of the academical course as a qualification for active life, obtained a grant of apartments in college, for the purpose of devoting one evening in every week to the cultivation of those useful branches of the Belles Lettres which were totally neglected in the under-graduate course. COMPOSITION in prose and verse was periodically encouraged; and an extensive examination in HISTORY (chiefly that of Great Britain) was regularly succeeded on each meeting by a DEBATE on a moral or historical question; in which EVERY ALLUSION TO CONTEMPORARY PERSONS OR EVENTS WAS STRICTLY AND UNIFORMLY PROHIBITED. Eminence in each of these branches was rewarded with prize medals, and other suitable distinctions, and a library of the most useful publications was gradually formed, to accommodate members with the loan of such books as their various studies might require.

To preserve the respectability of the institution, no persons were eligible but students of advanced standing, proposed by two members and balloted for (after due notice) one black bean in seven excluding. But all Fellows of the College were admitted of course as honorary members, and invariably treated with every mark of respectful attention.

Governed by these principles, and animated by a motive more powerful than any system of mercenary reward, or slavish compulsion, the general ambition of conciliating the esteem and applause of friends and fellow students, the

THE HIST AND EDMUND BURKE'S CLUB

Historical Society prospered twenty-four years, in the bosom of the parent University, contemplating with conscious pride a perpetual succession of their members rising to conspicuous eminence in Life, but particularly in the learned professions. Yet so far were their pursuits from obstructing the attainment of abstract science, that all the present Junior Fellows (one or two excepted) were active members of the Society previous to their education and pledged by the most solemn promises to support and protect it.

But the late Provost (a strenuous patron of the institution) being abroad in his last illness, this harmony was at length interrupted by the Rev. Geo. Miller, F.T.C.D., who on the second of April, 1794, desired the chief officers, the Auditor and then the Chairman of the Society to order Mr C——, a member then present, to leave the room, or he would move for his immediate expulsion; and upon their declining to deliver this message; he communicated it by the Secretary; in consequence of which Mr C—— withdrew. Soon after, a member whose name happened not to be on the college books (unacquainted with a circumstance, which indeed was known to very few, that Mr C—— had been privately forbidden by the Board, some years before, to appear in College) moved for the appointment of a committee to enquire into the cause of his abrupt departure. In the debate which arose on this motion nothing in the slightest degree disrespectful was said of any of the Fellows; and the Society adjourned without a decision.

The account then sets out *seriatim* the proceedings which followed and the communications which passed between the Board and the Society, and includes a description of the Board's examination of the Auditor, Lewis Kerr, on 20 December which ended in his receiving a public admonition in the College Hall.

The account concludes as follows:

Of the justice and wisdom of the Board, and their zeal to promote the literary improvement of the rising generation, some estimate may be formed from the above unadorned narrative. It remains for them to shew why they have inexorably interdicted the meetings of a society so constituted and conducted; endeavoured to prepossess the heads of the bar and the church against those members of each profession who attended it, with the sole view of qualifying

themselves for their respective duties in life; and inflicted so severe an academic
censure on a gentleman whose only crime was signing an earnest and humble
supplication for the re-establishment of an institution no less ornamental to the
University than important to the nation.

Signed by order of the Society,
Robert Burrowes, Sec.

Resolutions proposed by the Auditor, seconded by J. R. Galbraith, that the
said report be now received, and be laid before the public by the
Extraordinary Committee, were agreed to, one voice dissenting.

Resolutions were also passed conveying the warmest thanks of the
Society to the Auditor for his temperate, manly, and firm conduct when
called before the Board, and offering to support him if he should deem an
appeal to the Visitors expedient.

At the meeting of 1 April 1795 the Auditor read the following letter:

To the Historical Society of Dublin.

Gentlemen,

The Speculative Society of Edinburgh conceive themselves highly indebted to
you for your friendly communication of the 21st January, 1795, which they
have ordered to be inserted on their records. They do not fail to meet with
equal warmth the obliging expressions of esteem and regard which that letter
contains, nor to take the deepest concern in whatever regards the interests of
an Institution, their amicable connections with which they so highly value. As
this connection is founded on the basis of their common literary pursuits, the
Speculative Society conceives that it subsists independent of the private
regulations by which each Institution is governed, and ought not, therefore, to
be affected by such changes in those regulations as either may find it
convenient or proper to adopt. As, therefore, the Speculative Society do not
conceive that the original compact of 1783 is in any degree affected by the
circumstances announced by the Historical Society, they beg leave to assure
that they consider it as subsisting in its original force, and will be happy to
receive with all usual privileges such members of the Historical Society,
bringing with them proper certificates, as may favour them in their
attendance during their residence in the City of Edinburgh. In obedience to

an unanimous resolution of the Society, dated the 17th current, we have the honour to subscribe ourselves, Gentlemen, your most humble Servants,

F. Jeffrey, President,
Walter Scott, Secretary

Francis Jeffrey (Lord Jeffrey) was President of the Speculative Society in 1794–98; Lord Advocate 1830; M.P. for Edinburgh 1833; Lord of Session 1834; and Editor of the *Edinburgh Review*.

Walter Scott, afterwards Sir Walter Scott, was Secretary and Librarian of the Speculative Society 1791–95.

INTERN 1795

THE 26TH SESSION OF THE COLLEGE Historical Society which now held its meetings in the Exhibition Room, William Street, had not been long in progress before some of the members, no doubt realizing the difficulties of the Society's existence outside the walls of the College in opposition to the governing body decided to accept the conditions upon which the Board were willing to re-grant the use of the rooms formerly occupied. The Extern Society had removed their furniture, books etc. when they left College on 31 December 1794 and the Society's room was refurnished by the Board. Thomas Langlois Lefroy was unanimously elected Auditor for the re-constituted Society within College.

Thomas Langlois Lefroy, Auditor 1794–95

The customs of the Old Society were followed, and similar laws were enacted. Members were fined 'for standing at the fire', 'for appearing without academic dress', 'for not answering History' — the fine for the last mentioned offence being still the substantial sum of 11 shillings 4 and a half pence — half an Irish guinea.

The opening meeting of the second session of the re-constituted Society was held on 20 October 1795. Forty-three members, including nine Fellows of the College, were present. Thomas Langlois Lefroy delivered the opening address in which he advocated the study of a general outline of Modern History in preference to the particular periods of History studied by the Society. In acknowledging the 'general support and parental kindness' of the rulers of the University he remarks that if the Society should fall it would be from its want of zeal and energy.

Never was there a folly more glaring, more mischievous, than separating the interests of this Society from the interests of the University, and representing them as distinct and even contrasted. . . . But I trust even this short experience has convinced us that to be relieved for the present and secured for ever from an indiscriminate throng of Externs was no less serviceable to this institution than absolutely requisite for the good of the University. . . .

He also refers to the advantage of meeting within the University 'instead of by stealth in a suspected haunt.'

An entry on 4 January 1797, which may be regarded as a sign of the times, is a notice by the Librarian that on the next night of meeting he would move 'that no member shall appear in this Society in full military dress'.

George Moore, in his speech at the close of the session, announced 'You stand now unrivalled. Your former competitors rejected the protection of the University, you received it. They have sunk into non-existence — you have swelled into importance.'

The members of the Society in common with the general body of the students were much perturbed by the political ferment prevailing at this time. The United Irishmen were seeking to establish a Republican Government and to this end had invited the assistance of France. The patriotic feelings aroused by the threat of an invasion led to the establishment of Volunteer Defence Forces throughout the country, and a College Corps was formed, and divided into four companies, commanded by the four law Fellows. This corps had its guard-room in the rooms of the Historical Society and took part in all the military movements around Dublin.

MOORE & EMMET

EARLY IN THE SESSION TWO students entered the Society who were destined to rise to fame, although by different paths. These were Thomas Moore, elected on 22 November 1797, and Robert Emmet, elected a couple of nights later, on 6 December. United by a similarity of views and kindred genius, an intimacy of the closest kind sprang up between them. Not long after their entry into the Society we find them both taking an active part in the proceedings. On 10 January 1798 Moore made his first appearance in debate, supporting the negative on the question: 'Is the study of the Sciences of more advantage than the study of *Belles-Lettres*'; and on the same night Emmet was appointed Chairman of the Committee elected to bring in questions for debate. A month later, on 7 February Emmet and Moore both spoke in support of the question: 'Is unlimited freedom of discussion the best means of stopping the progress of erroneous opinion?' which was carried by 27 votes to 20, Emmet being the teller for the Ayes.

The students of the University could not long remain unaffected by the party spirit which was prevalent throughout the country. The great majority were no doubt loyal to the existing constitution but many of them, as has so often been the case in Trinity College, ranged themselves on the popular side. In his *Life of Lord Edward Fitzgerald*, Moore, in his Journals, gives a vivid account of Emmet's career in the Society:

. . . *not only had I myself from early childhood taken a passionate interest in that struggle which, however darkly it ended, began under the bright auspices of a Grattan, but among these young men whom, after my entrance into College, I looked up to with most admiration and regard, the same enthusiasm of national feeling prevailed. Some of them, too, at this time of terror and torture I am now speaking of, were found to have implicated themselves far more deeply in the popular league against power than I should ever have suspected.*

A youth destined to act a melancholy but forever-memorable part in the

Robert Emmet, original pencil sketch (1802) in the National Library of Ireland, by courtesy of the Director

troubled scenes that were fast approaching had now begun to attract, in no ordinary degree, the attention both of his fellow students and the College authorities in general. This youth was Robert Emmet, whose brilliant success in his College studies, and more particularly in the scientific portion of them, had crowned his career, as far as he had gone, with all the honours of the course; while his powers of oratory displayed at a debating society, of which, about this time (1796–97) I became a member, were beginning to excite universal attention, as well from the eloquence as the political boldness of his displays. He was, I rather think by two classes, my senior, though it might have been only by one. But there was, at all events, such an interval between our standing as at that time of life, makes a material difference; and when I became a member of the debating society, I found him in full fame, not only for his scientific attainments, but also for the blamelessness of his life and the grave suavity of his manners.

Of the popular side in the Society, the chief champion and ornament was Robert Emmet; and though every care was taken to exclude from among the subjects of debate all questions likely to trench upon the politics of the day, it was always easy enough by a side wind of digression or allusion, to bring Ireland and the prospects then opening upon her within the scope of the orator's view. So exciting and powerful in this respect were the speeches of Emmet, and so little were the most distinguished speakers among our opponents able to cope with his eloquence, that the Board at length actually thought it right to send among us a man of advanced standing in the University, and belonging to a former race of good speakers in the Society, in order that he might answer the speeches of Emmet, and endeavour to obviate what they considered the mischievous impressions produced by them. The name of this mature champion of the higher powers was, if I remember right, Gerahty; and it was in replying to a speech of his one night that Emmet, to the no small mortification and surprise of us who glorified in him as our leader, became embarrassed in the middle of his speech, and (to use the parliamentary phrase) broke down. Whether from a momentary confusion in the thread of his argument, or possible diffidence in encountering an adversary so much his senior (for Emmet was as modest as he was high-minded and brave) he began, in the full career of his eloquence, to hesitate and repeat his words, and then, after an effort or two to recover himself, sat down.

The manner and appearance of Emmet in the Society are thus described by Moore:

Were I to number, in deed, the men, among all I have ever known, who appeared to me to combine, in the greatest degree, pure moral worth with intellectual power, I should among the highest of the few, place Robert Emmet. Wholly free from the follies and frailties of youth — though how capable he was of the most devoted passion events afterwards proved — the pursuit of science, in which he eminently distinguished himself, seemed, at this time, the only object that at all divided his thoughts with that enthusiasm for Irish freedom which, in him, was an hereditary as well as national feeling, — himself being the second martyr his father had given to the cause.

Simple in all his habits, and with a repose of look and manner indicating but little movement within, it was only when the spring was touched that set his feelings and — through them — his intellect in motion, that he at all rose above the level of ordinary men. On no occasion was this more peculiarly striking than in those displays of oratory with which, both in the Debating and Historical Society, he so often enchained the attention and sympathy of his young audience. No two individuals, indeed, could be much more unlike to each other than was the same youth to himself, before rising to speak and after; the brow that had appeared inanimate and almost drooping at once elevating itself in all the consciousness of power, and whole countenance and figure of the speaker assuming a change as of one suddenly inspired.

Before the close of the session in which the two friends joined the Society, events happened which led to the expulsion from the College of Emmet and eighteen other students. Two scholars, Power and Ardagh, who had absented themselves from the presentation by the College of a loyal address to the highly unpopular Viceroy, Lord Camden, previous to his departure from Ireland, were publicly expelled. This led to a General Visitation by Lord Clare, Vice-Chancellor of the University, which took place in 1798. The Visitation disclosed the existence in the College of four Committees of the United Irishmen, and also of some Orange Societies. Nineteen students were expelled, eight of whom were members of the Historical Society, *viz.* Robert Emmet, Peter McLoughlin, Thomas Corbet, William Corbet, Arthur Newport, John Browne, Michael Farrell and Martin John Ferrall.

Moore became a successful competitor for honours in Composition and in his *Journals* he gives the following account of the circumstances under which he obtained the Society's medal:

A struggle in which I myself was, about this time, engaged with the dominant party in the Society may be worth dwelling on for a few moments.

Thomas Moore, portrait by Martin Archer Shee 1769–1850, courtesy of the National Gallery of Ireland

— the circumstances attending it being, in no small degree, perhaps characteristic as well of the good as the bad qualities of my own character at that time of life. Besides the medals given by the Society to the best answers in history, there was also another for the best compositions sent in at stated periods, either in prose or verse. These productions were all to be delivered in anonymously, and on the night when they were to be read aloud for the judgement of the Society, a reader for each was appointed by rotation from

among the members. Taking it into my head to become a candidate for this medal, I wrote a burlesque sort of poem, called an 'Ode upon Nothing, with Notes by Trismegistus Rustifustius, etc., etc.,' My attempts at humourous writing had not been many, and the fun scattered throughout this poem was in some parts not of the most chastened description. On the night whenever it was to be read, whether by mere accident, or from a suspicion that the poem was by me, I was voted by the Society to be the reader of it; and as I performed my task con amore, though tremblingly nervous during the whole operation, — and in some degree acted as well as read the composition, its success was altogether complete, applause and laughter greeted me throughout, and the medal was voted to the author of the composition triumphantly. I then acknowledged myself in due form, and the poem was transcribed into the book of the Society appointed to receive all such prize productions.

A number of the members objected to the indelicate nature of some of the passages in the composition, and proposed that they should be removed. This led to much discussion, and in the end Moore, as he tells us, 'took an opportunity of quietly removing the composition from the books'.

An echo of Emmet's insurrection appears in the Journals for 16 November 1803 when a medal, open to all members of the University, was offered for the best elegy on the death of Lord Kilwarden.

A new gown was required at this time for the use of the Chairman, and the Committee appointed to purchase it reported somewhat tersely: 'The gown which the Chairman now occupies has been chosen by us, and it cost £14.12.6d.'

Considerable disorder prevailed at some of the meetings of the tenth session, and on one night — 8 February 1804 — a record of the proceedings consists purely of fines.

MERGER 1807

ON 25 JANUARY 1807 A MOTION proposed by the Auditor (J. H. North), seconded by Hugh George Macklin, was passed, conveying the thanks of the Society to John Kinchella 'for his attention to the Society and active diligence in procuring for them the transfer of the books and Journals, etc., of the Extern Historical Society'. On the following night the Auditor through the Chair informed the Society that the Committee appointed to communicate with the Extern

Society had received the Journals, essay-books, etc. On the next night the Committee of the Extern Society arrived during the debate, and a motion by the Auditor, seconded by John Jebb, that they should be permitted to hear the remainder of the debate and be received immediately after the decision on the question, was agreed to unanimously. The Committee of the Extern Society attended accordingly and after the division on the debate presented an address, in which they stated:

'To you who are associated as we once were, for the advancement of liberal knowledge, we are glad to afford an increase of suitable materials (and we should add) new incentives to your laudable career, while we thus incorporate and identify with yours the memorials of our progress in the same pursuit.'
The address was signed by J. Kinchella, Chairman; William Henry Ellis; Robert Blakeney; Hutton King; James Clancy, and J. Hamilton, Secretary.

The report on the conduct of the Auditor, J. H. North, mentions that 'his disinterested zeal and unwearied exertions in recovering for us the library of the Extern Society, and improving the happy opportunity of re-union with them, appears in an especial manner to merit the gratitude of the Society'.

During the session 1809–10 a debate on the subject 'Should universal toleration be a part of the British Constitution?' led to the Auditor being summoned before the Provost, and being questioned 'as to certain inflammatory expressions said to have been used'. The Auditor reported to the Society that 'after an exhaustive enquiry he had denied the charge as absolutely unfounded'.

A committee was appointed on 5 February 1812 to present an address to General Sir William Parker Carroll, who had served with great distinction as a field officer in the Spanish Forces, and had taken part in the battle of Albuera. The address and the General's reply were couched in flattering terms:

The Historical Society conceive it due to the character of their Institution to express the high sense which they entertain of the exalted heroism, directed by the most splendid military capacity, which has been evinced in the person of one of their earliest and most distinguished members. . . . it was reserved for you, Sir, (we feel it with pleasure, we acknowledge it with gratitude), to make this Institution subservient to the noblest of purposes — the defence of our country and the liberties of mankind. Accept, Sir, in the name of the Society by which we are deputed, the warmest congratulations of the youthful heart.

General Carroll in his reply recalls his days in the Society:

How often, in the active scenes in which it has been my lot to be engaged on the theatre of the world, has memory transported me to the spot whence this memorial of your kindness is dated. How often have I turned to the scenes of my early and happy youth there passed to the companions who then shared with me in its pursuits and pleasures, and who, like me, in journeying forward have delighted to linger over scenes of intellectual pleasure and moral improvement, the traces of which are indelible on every heart.

Another distinguished officer whom the Society could claim as a former member was General Ross of Bladensburgh, who was mortally wounded whilst leading the British troops against Baltimore.

At the meeting of 22 December 1812 a communication received from the Provost, Dr Thomas Elrington, was read by the Auditor, Richard Hastings Graves, objecting to some of the subjects chosen for debate.

The subjects to which the Provost referred were: 'Does a standing army contribute to the liberty of the subject', 'Should the elective franchise be unlimited', and 'Should capital punishments be entirely abolished'. These had been discussed in one form or other, session after session without the slightest objection by the Board.

Some nights later the Provost addressed the following jejune remarks to the Society reproving them for debating the well-worn subjects 'Was Brutus justifiable in putting Julius Cæsar to death?', 'Was the execution of Charles I justifiable?' and 'Should the liberty of the Press be restricted?':

Provost Thomas Elrington, portrait in the Portfolio of Trinity College pub. W. H. Benyon, Cheltenham.

Provost's House.

27th January 1813

The Provost regrets to find himself again obliged to notice the questions debated by the Historical Society. To admit a defence to be made for assassination must be injurious to morality. To discuss the right of a subject to put a monarch to death who by the Constitution was exempted from personal responsibility, unquestionably tends to weaken those principles of loyalty which at a time like the present should be cultivated with peculiar care. It is no longer safe to sport with questions, such as these, which but a few years ago might without much hazard have been made the subject of discussion. The example of Brutus can no longer be considered as harmless, for we have seen its effects, in stimulating, in a Christian country, to the murder of a lawful king: the splendour of a voluntary devotement has thrown a false lustre round the assassin Marat, and increased the temptation to the crime by diminishing its deformities: whilst even in England the malignant sophistry which argued in support of the murder, as but private justice, has not terminated in theory, and the wretch who hesitated not to put these pernicious principles in practice, has not wanted those who were ready to lament and defend him.

Nor has the crime of Cromwell been less fertile in the production of evil, as France can terribly witness, nor is the contagion less dangerous to these kingdoms, nor less to be guarded against by a Society whose principles it would be the fondest wish of the Friends of Democracy to corrupt. The circumstances of the times render it also improper to debate upon the propriety of removing those restraints which make the author responsible for the evil which his writings tend to produce, as the subject almost unavoidably connects itself with the political controversies of the present day.

On 3 March 1813 another communication was received from the Provost:

The Provost has hitherto indulged the hope that his advice will be sufficient to regulate the conduct of the Historical Society but finding that immediately after his disapprobation of a question relative to the law of libels the same question has been debated with but a slight variation in its form, and finding that another question touching upon a prerogative of the Crown uninterruptedly exercised has also been made the subject of debate, he thinks it necessary to inform the Historical Society that he will, should the statutory regulations prescribed by the Board be again transgressed, feel it his duty to have recourse to such measures as shall be effectually corrective.

Macneile Dixon has described Elrington as 'a man who made up in piety what he lacked in distinction of mind and character, and presided with rigour and inefficiency over the College until 1820'. One of his pupils,

Valentine Lawless, elected a member of the Society in June 1790, afterwards Lord Cloncurry, in his *Personal Recollections* referred to him as:

A learned man, but stupid and blockish, and thoroughly imbued with the narrowest views of his class and profession. It was he who accomplished the suppression of the Historical Society, then obnoxious to all who dreaded progression, as a nursery of genius and patriotism, and as opening a common field whereon the rising generation of Irishmen were learning mutual respect for each other. . . .

From the next report on the state of the Society, read on 9 January 1813, the conditions appear to have become worse, and this was attributed to the exclusion, under the new regulations, of the experienced senior members: 'Disorder and irregularity have appeared on many occasions, particularly on extra nights. Your Chair, repeatedly insulted by threats of impeachment, has failed to command that respect, which from the character of the Society, and of the members who filled it, it was entitled to. This conduct if persevered in must lead to your destruction.'

The election for the position of Auditor of the twentieth session was held on 10 November 1813. The election was very closely contested, and appears to have given rise to a lot of unpleasantness. The result of the ballot was that Carrol Watson was elected Auditor with 61 votes, as against 58 votes cast for Richard Stack. When the Auditor entered upon his office he was interrupted in the discharge of his duties by a discussion which arose relative to the ballot. On the following morning, 11 November, four members of the Society, Lendrick, Robinson, Hamilton (three ex-Auditors) and Smith, supporters of Stack, waited upon the Provost to obtain his views on the qualifications of certain members to vote at the election. Later in the day the Provost set out his views in a paper which he gave to them:

11th November, Gentlemen; It appears to me of some importance that my opinion of the questions asked me this morning relative to the Historical Society be distinctly understood. My opinion is that when the name of a student is struck out of the College books he instantly ceases to be a member of the Historical Society, and should his name be replaced on the books of the College he must be proposed to the Society and balloted for as a new member.

My opinion on the other question proposed is that when any person claims to be a member of the Historical Society he is bound to prove his right not only by referring to his election into it, but by showing that his name is on the College books; and that if he should allege that it has been omitted, or taken off by mistake, he is bound to prove the allegation, and to procure it to be replaced, before he can be admitted to act as a member, but that for the single night, on which he has made the claim, he may be allowed to remain in the rooms, but not to speak or vote.

I am, gentlemen, your most obedient Servant,
Thomas Elrington.

When the Society re-assembled at six o'clock on the following Wednesday, 17 November, the officers proceeded to elect James Lendrick as pro-Auditor, a motion by the Librarian, Alexander Millar, seconded by William Boyd, that a pro-Auditor was unnecessary, being defeated by 36 votes to 35. A motion was then brought forward by Lendrick, seconded by the Auditor (Watson) that the regular business of the Society be suspended to consider a motion respecting the election of the present Auditor. This was carried, and a further motion to proceed to a new ballot for Auditor was proposed. An amendment to this was proposed and passed — that the names of Messrs Hill, Horner and Hancock be erased from the ballot of last night. In the new election which then took place each candidate secured an equal number of votes, and the Chairman gave his casting vote in favour of Stack.

Before the next night of meeting Watson went to the Provost, and obtained the following further explanation on the question which had been submitted to him:

Understanding that doubts have arisen as to the meaning of the opinion I gave relative to the rights of persons whose names are replaced on the College books to be considered as thereby restored to their place in the Historical Society I think it necessary to state that it was intended not as a new modification of any existing right, but as a declaration that no such right existed — that the person replaced on the College books should be balloted for before he can be considered as a member of the Society. It is in the power of the Society to extract from such members new admission fees, but to do so would obviously be most unreasonable.

24th November

(Sgd.) Thomas Elrington

Whether or not use was made of the Provost's communications to secure the disqualification of the three members mentioned, he expressed his strong dissatisfaction at the manner in which his paper was referred to in the Journals of 17 November:

The Provost is much dissatisfied with the manner in which the paper given by him to Messrs. Lendrick, Robinson, Smith and Hamilton is mentioned in the Journals of the Historical Society. The paper contained a determination of an abstract question, not, as the entry implies, a decision of the case of Messrs. Hancock and Horner, of which the Provost knew nothing. It now seems necessary that the paper itself, and also the further explanation of it given on the 24th inst. to Mr Watson, should be entered on the Journals of the Historical Society.

1st December, 1813

At the next meeting on 8 December a motion was passed that the ex-secretary, Richard Bevan, should be examined by questions put from the Chair relative to the manner in which the Journals of 17 November had been drawn up. This examination was continued at the meetings on 15 and 22 December, and at the latter a motion was proposed by Lendrick, seconded by the Auditor (Stack): 'that it is the opinion of the Society that the Journals of 17 November are falsified, and through the interference of Mr Watson.' An amendment proposed by Watson that he be allowed to bring forward a witness for the examination of every member who pleased, and that questions be put to the witness through the Chair, was passed. John Boswell, an ex-Treasurer, was then called upon as the first witness, and his examination extended over the following three nights.

At the meeting on the third night, 12 January 1814, Charles Wolfe was in the Chair, and during the examination of Boswell a question put to him by Watson led to a heated dispute between Watson and another member,

Dickson. This dispute was reported to the Board, who instituted an exhaustive inquiry into it. Details of this inquiry are recorded in one of Dr Elrington's note books. The inquiry was held on Saturday, 15 January, and the following Monday and Tuesday, and Elrington's notes extended to thirteen pages. Sixteen members of the Society, including three Fellows of the College, Sadleir, Singer and Hincks, who were present at the meeting on 12 January, were interrogated.

A quarrel arose when Watson put his question to Boswell, Dickson implying that the answer had been put into Boswell's mouth. Watson accused Dickson of lying and Dickson called Watson a rascal. Later in the evening Dickson apologised to the Society, but said it was not to be understood as an apology to Watson who had given him the lie. When the Society broke up at midnight, Dickson went to Watson, apparently with the intention of settling the dispute, but further altercations arose. Singer, one of the Fellows present, came to Dickson and told him that if the matter were not settled he must bring it before the Board, and asked Dr Sadleir to tell Watson the same. Next morning Singer proposed that if Watson apologised for the lie, Dickson should apologise for the rascal. Difficulties, however arose as to which of them would apologise first, and the Board becoming aware of the quarrel decided to hold the inquiry. Under the date 18 January 1814 Elrington made the following note of the board's decision:

Provost reads principle part of evidence.

Dr. Dav.	*Mr Watson off (Books). Mr D. privately admonished.*
Dr. Pr.	*Rusticate both six months and privately admonish.*
Dr. Ph.	*Both names off; rule against replacing Watson.*
Dr. St.	*do.*
Dr. Gr.	*do.*
Vice P.	*do.*
	NAMES TAKEN OFF.

Beneath this is the following entry in secret script : 'Jan. 19, 1814 — Sent for Mr Hincks and said to him that I thought it would be better if he did not go to the Historical Society for a considerable time.'

The outcome of the proceedings was that a committee of five members was appointed at the meeting of the Society on 19 January 1814 to correct the Journals of 17 November.

Amongst the members who obtained medals for poetical compositions during the session 1813–14 and the previous session were Charles Wolfe, author of *Lines on the Burial of Sir John Moore*, and other poems, and John Martin Anster, the translator of Goethe's 'Faust'. Wolfe's name appears frequently as a reader of compositions, and as a member of committees to select subjects for debates, etc. On 8 June 1814 when the Auditor, William Brooke, moved that the voluntary apology offered to the Society by John O'Brien for his conduct to the Chairman on last night of meeting be considered a perfectly satisfactory one, we find Wolfe moving a somewhat sweeping amendment which was carried by 43 votes to 14 — 'that the Auditor's motion be considered useless'.

The following entries regarding this matter appear in Elrington's notebook:

4th June, 1814. Jun. Dean was in bed when the disturbance happened in the H. S. — heard it at 6 next morning. Mr O'Brien called to him, stated that he wished to offer an atonement to Sir Stack. Afterwards Mr O'Brien told Sir Stack that he was sensible of impropriety of his conduct — left it to the Society.

P. Calls in J. Dean to state his ideas as to whether the business should be entered into by the Board. J. Dean states that he thought reviving the discussion might lead to bad consequences — might revive the quarrel now made up.

P. puts the question: shall the Board proceed in Mr O'Brien's case? Agreed to bring it forward. Dr. Lloyd rather against it — Dr. Stokes against it — Dr. Barrett absent.

6th June, 1814. Mr John O'Brien throws himself on the mercy of the Board — he had struck Sir Stack in the Hist. Society — he had immediately made an apology in the strongest manner — he had conceived that he received the lye.

Agreed not to punish him.

7th June, 1814. The Provost stated a question as to whether the Board should make any regulation as to the Historical Society.

Rev. Charles Wolfe

Rev. Samuel O'Sullivan, who was elected a member on 8 December 1813, gives the following description of the proceedings at the meetings of the Society at this period:

After the History examination the members adjourned for tea and coffee to a withdrawing room. . . . As the hour of debate drew nigh, you saw the groups thronging out into the Society's room, and broken up into small distinct

50

parties. Here you might discern amidst their friends and admirers, rival candidates for the oratory prizes, and veteran speakers arranging with their partisans the order of their proceedings. . . . The Chair is now taken, two pleaders on each side open the debate; then the voluntary speakers. The debate being over the doors are closed, and private business is transacted, and the most interesting part of the proceedings commences. You see young men ardent in their mutual opposition, and inflamed by the excitement of debate, and yet observing the most unbroken respect for established forms, and the most entire submission to the President's authority.

EXPULSION 1815

THE TWENTY-FIRST SESSION (1814–15) opened in the most promising fashion, and without any sign of the disaster that was soon to overtake the Society. Wolfe, who had been chosen to open the meeting, and who was unable to attend sent an apology which was considered satisfactory. An extra night was therefore appointed for hearing his speech, which he delivered on Saturday, 12 November and for which he was awarded a gold medal. Amongst the members elected at the beginning of the session was Henry Francis Lyte, author of the famous hymn 'Abide with me'.

At the meeting of 1 February 1815 the Auditor read the following letter from the Register:

To L. Foote, Esq., Auditor of the Historical Society:

Sir,

I am directed as Register to communicate to you that the Board, having heard with great concern that altercations destructive to College discipline have taken place in the Historical Society; and feeling it necessary to consider what measures they may be compelled to adopt respecting the Society itself, direct the names of James Howlin and of John Walker be struck off the list of members; and that the Society do not in any respect discuss the circumstances of their quarrel.

I am, Sir, Your very humble servant,
Robt. Phipps, Register.
Trinity College, Dublin, 31st January, 1815

Rev. Henry Francis Lyte, painting at Portora Royal School, Enniskillen, by courtesy of the Governors

No information is forthcoming of the nature of the quarrel between Howlin and Walker or of the 'unusual degree of tumult and confusion' which it caused.

The Register's letter of 31 January was followed almost immediately by another communication, which the Auditor himself placed before the Society at the next meeting, 6 February 1815.

A motion was then proposed by the Auditor requesting a committee to wait on the Provost and Board to ascertain the 'private business' they were to transact.

The entries in Elrington's note-book on 11, 14 and 15 February make interesting reading:

11th February, 1815.

Register read memorial from Hist. Society. To be considered on Tuesday next.

14th February, 1815.

Dr, Nash would take five names off Hist. Society.

Dr, Dav(enport) would make no reply, but do nothing against them.

Dr, Prior. Do., but would get someone to intimate disapprobation.

Dr. Stokes. Send for Auditor and tell him verbally what is meant by Private Business.

Dr. Hodg(kinson). Order before Board and reprimand.

V. P. agrees with Dr. Nash. Agreed by a majority to reprimand the five signers, using the words 'for sending a memorial to the Board so unprecedently disrespectful'. Explain 'Private Business' to mean All questions relating to individuals in the Society.

15th February, 1815.

All present except Dr. Davenport.

Sirs Hamilton, Foote, Wolfe, Brooke, Ius., and Graves (Herc.) attended.[4]

Provost:— I do not recollect any duty to which I have felt such reluctance as that which I am now called upon to perform. When I remember the characters you have supported in College, reflect upon the friends who are interested in your conduct or call to remembrance the Dead, I feel aggrieved indeed to be obliged to say that I am desired by the Board to reprimand you

---

[4] The 'Sir' prefixed to the surname designates the Bachelor, and corresponds to the 'Ds.' (Dominus) in the Calendar. It was in use generally until the latter end of the eighteenth century.

*and each of you having sent a Memorial couched in Terms so unprecedently
disrespectful to the Board —*

*I feel yet more grieved to say that I consider the punishment as light when
compared with the offence.*

*By private business is meant All things relating to the conduct of Individuals
in the Historical Society.*

The arguments which had been set forth so eloquently in the Committee's
address certainly deserved more consideration and a fuller answer than were
given to them by the Board, and at the meeting of 15 February 1815 the
Society apparently came to the conclusion, whether rightly or wrongly, that
the Board had resolved to terminate its existence. The remaining
proceedings on this night are briefly told.

The question of debate was then read and discussed, and a question was
selected for that night three weeks. A resolution was then moved by
Hamilton, and seconded by Foote, to suspend the regular business for the
purpose of taking into account the present state of the Society. This was
carried unanimously in the affirmative, whereupon the following
resolution was proposed by Hamilton, seconded by Foote:

*That a committee of seven be appointed for the purpose of resigning for the
present into the custody of the Provost and Board the rooms hitherto
appropriated to the use of the Historical Society, the late regulations of the
Board being in the opinion of the Society inconsistent with the successful
prosecution of the objects for which it was instituted, and that this committee
be empowered and directed to take such steps as to them may appear most
effectual for the securing the property of the Society, until a favourable
opportunity occurs for the revival of an institution the utility of which the
experience of twenty years has most satisfactorily evinced.*

The Chairman then nominated Foote (Senior) Chairman of the Committee
of seven, the other members being Hamilton, Brooke, Wolfe, George
Abraham Grierson, O'Sullivan and George Robinson. The Chairman
appointed eleven o'clock on Thursday for the meeting of this Committee.

The Society then adjourned *sine die*.

The Journals of this last night are signed: 'Lundy Foote, Secretary'.

This is the last entry in the Society's Journals, but the following further information is given in Elrington's note-book:

April 29th, 1815.

Application from B. W. Hamilton, C. Wolfe, M. O' Sullivan and Geo. Robinson, four of the committee of the Hist. Socty. for their books etc.

Agreed to let them make Inventory and take everything except their books. Register to ascertain whether there is any Law as to the books.

Dec. 10th. 1815.

An application having been made by some of the Students for the re-institution of the Historical Society, it was refused; the Registrar is to notify this to the persons applying.

In *College Reflections*, the Rev. Samuel O'Sullivan gives a long account of the proceedings on the last night, and the speeches on the motion for adjournment. He tells how one member, who was in the habit of ridiculing the proceedings of the Society, rose from the back benches and speaking in a tone of mock-heroic proposed an amendment that the Society, for the purposes of perishing phœnix-like, should collect all the benches, desks and books into a large funeral pile, in the centre of which the members should stand assembled, the Chairman's robe being reserved to serve as a pall for the collected ashes. When all was prepared one member (himself) should fling a lighted torch into the pile, returning the next day to collect and pay appropriate honours to the ashes. John Sydney Taylor closed the debate with a speech in favour of the motion of adjournment, which concludes as follows: 'having existed to this hour in the fullness of reputation and utility, you will leave behind you a spirit to animate the exertions of worthy successors, and a pure and perfect model according to which they may fashion the structure of a future Society.'

O'Sullivan describes how he arrived after the meeting was over, and on entering through the open door he found the room silent and deserted, the lights still blazing, and everything in the most perfect order, except that some person had cast the President's robe as a pall over the forsaken chair of state, and that the busts of great men which ornamented the various niches had their faces towards the wall.

In 1831 the following resolution was carried unanimously:

That as the members of the 'Oxford Union Society' are Honorary members of this Society, the members of the 'Cambridge Union Society' are likewise hereby admitted Honorary members of the Dublin Historical and Literary Society. . . . That the Secretary be directed to write to the Secretary of the Cambridge Union informing him of the same.

During the session 1831–32 the question 'Is the Constitution of Great Britain more favourable to the liberty of the subject than that of America?' was decided in the negative. Isaac Butt who spoke on the affirmative was adjudged the best of the eight speakers who took part in the debate, and William Torrens McCullagh, who spoke on the negative, the second best.

ISAAC BUTT

AT THE OPENING MEETING OF the session 1832–33, held on 1 November 1832, McCullagh was elected President, Butt, Secretary, and John Finlayson, Treasurer. At the expiration of a month Butt resigned the office of Secretary, and before the close of the session McCullagh resigned his office as president, and Butt was elected to succeed him, the other candidates being Joseph Pollock and Cæsar Otway.

Early in the session the questions of the reading room and the petition to the Board of Trinity College for re-admission were again brought forward. On 15 November 1832 Butt gave notice that he would move for a petition to the Board of Trinity College, and on the following night a similar notice was given by Pollock, but there is no further reference to this subject.

On 13 December 1832 the following motion was carried: 'That this Society be in future called the "College Historical Society".'

Butt took a prominent part in the debates. On the nights on which he spoke he was usually adjudged the 'best speaker', and at the end of the session he was awarded a medal for Oratory. Amongst the subjects debated were: 'Is the Impression of seamen justifiable?' — decided in the negative by the chairman's casting vote; 'Is the constitution of Great Britain more favourable to the subject than that of America?' and 'Was the separation of the United States of America from England beneficial to the latter?' —

Isaac Butt Auditor 1834–35 portrait by John Butler Yeats, 1839–1922, courtesy of the National Gallery of Ireland

both decided in the affirmative. The question 'Ought duelling be restricted by legislative enactment?' — decided in the affirmative by a majority of one, after seven members had spoken on the affirmative and six on the negative, Thomas MacNevin and Butt being amongst the latter, and Butt being voted the best speaker. 'Whether Emigration so far as it can be put into operation is a remedy for Irish distress' which was decided in the negative, which side was supported by Butt who was adjudged the best speaker of the night. 'Should unanimity in juries be required?' — was decided in the affirmative, Butt, who spoke on that side being again voted the best speaker.

At the close of the session 1832–33 Butt, who was President, delivered an address on the subject of 'Oratory'. In the last few pages of the Address he gives some interesting information about the Society:

Gentlemen of the Old Historical Society we are now the legitimate successors. Our title has been acknowledged by the kindred institutions in the Universities of the sister kingdom. The resolutions of the Oxford and Cambridge Societies, by which all members of our Society are declared honorary members of these bodies, may surely be fairly interpreted as a recognition of our claim; I would that it were equally acknowledged at home. Gentlemen, there is a subject upon which I know that a difference of opinion exists, and therefore it was not my intention to advert to it at all; but as in the course of your debates this evening, allusions have been made to the relation in which we stand to the heads of our own University, perhaps I may be excused if I say a few words in reference to this — I confess myself anxious for the introduction of this Society within the precincts of this College; that we should meet in that very room whose walls once echoed to the eloquence of a Curran and a Bushe. There are those among you who think that this object could never be attained without forfeiting that freedom of independence which ever should be the first — the proudest characteristic of a Society such as ours. I think differently; and I am not ashamed to say that I have made personal exertions to carry my object into effect; but while there still exists a difference of opinion among you, I would not put forward my private sentiments from this place, were it not that those exertions have but convinced me of their hopelessness, and I feel that the question can never be submitted to your consideration. The hope that I long had fondly cherished — that, as far as academic matters is concerned, was nearest to my heart, is gone, and the anticipations, which were the objects of it, are now classed in my mind with those ideal dreams, in which, with respect to everything that concerns us, we all sometimes indulge. But while a formal recognition of our title to the honours of our great ancestors is wanting, let us prove the verity of our descent by the splendour of our achievements. I feel — I know I am persuaded, that from this Society great things will be produced; we will draw around us the youthful talent of our country, and train them in that power which may enable them to benefit her. The glory of the days gone shall return with more than pristine splendour. We shall yet send forth a Grattan to represent her in the senate — a Curran to shed the blaze of eloquence upon her bar — a Kirwan to redeem her pulpit taste. And I will not — I cannot believe that better days are not in store for my unhappy, but still loved, my native land. This may not be the place to give utterance to my feelings, but I cannot help it. I see good for Ireland. An orator shall yet rise whose voice shall teach her people wisdom, and whose efforts shall procure for him the epithet of the father of his country. It may be but the dream of an enthusiastic heart; but I do believe that the time will come, when faction shall flee away and dissension shall be forgotten; when Ireland's orators and Ireland's statesmen shall only seek their country's good; when law shall be respected and yet liberty maintained; when 'in all her borders shall be neither wasting nor violence, and no complaining in her Streets'. And when I contemplate this Society collecting and training those youthful and ardent spirits, whose practised powers may yet achieve this good; when I think that through the instrumentality of this Society, my country may be blessed, my soul rises with the grandeur of the vision; and if my labours in your service were toilsome and severe, instead of pleasant and delightful, still, Gentlemen, I would gladly undergo them all, and think myself more than repaid by the privilege of indulging for one moment as I do now, in this grand place — this noble — this ennobling contemplation.

Isaac Butt was elected Auditor for the session 1834–35. He resigned, however, after a couple of months, and was succeeded by Moses Wilson Gray, who, towards the close of the session, was in turn succeeded by William Ribton. Amongst other members who held prominent positions in the Society during this and the three succeeding sessions we find William Archer Butler, afterwards Professor of Moral Philosophy; John Thomas Ball, afterwards M.P., Lord Chancellor, Vice-Chancellor of the University; Thomas MacNevin, author of the *Life of Sheil*, etc.; R. Graves MacDonnell, KNT., C.B., K.C.M.G., Governor of Hong Kong; Geo. Bomfort Wheeler, editor of *Hecuba of Euripedes, Virgil*, etc.; Richard Armstrong, Q.C., Sergeant-at-law, M.P.; John Edward Walsh, Q.C., M.P., Master of the Rolls; Joseph Sheridan Le Fanu, novelist and poet; James Anthony Lawson, M.P., Justice of the Common Pleas and Queen's Bench;

Thomas Davis, poet and patriot; William Keogh, M.P., Justice of the Common Pleas. The last five were on the Committee together.

LE FANU

THE FOLLOWING EXTRACTS FROM letters written to his father and mother by Joseph Sheridan Le Fanu, poet and novelist, while he was a member of the Society, give some insight to its workings:

6th January, Wednesday, 1836

. . . as to my oration at the Historical Society it went off far better than I could have hoped. I acquired the character of being possessed of the most imperturbable Brass — a reputation which I much coveted. . . .

1st March, 1837

On the 19th of this month the College Historical Society will give a great dinner at Morrison's rooms — I have been placed on the Committee, and to all who have that honour a ticket will cost 16/-. Where is that to come from? I have not a rap.

I cannot leave town until July as my office in the Society will not expire until then.

Saturday, 1st July, 1837

I have been awarded one of the two Historical Society medals. I shall not receive it however until the beginning of next Session. The grand dinner of the Society has been blown up by the conduct of the radicals and in its stead we have gotten up a conservative dinner with Butt in the Chair (I am just beginning to become acquainted with him, by the way, and like him greatly) and in the way of lions we are to have Carleton and Mortimer O'Sullivan, and to give us gravity and respectability Samuel O'Sullivan, Mr Litton the barrister and Professor Longfield. The tickets are 15 shillings each and one shilling to the servant.

Joseph Sheridan Le Fanu, Auditor 1838–39

15th April, 1838

*. . . I have now got my Hist. Soc. Medal and also the last No. of the
University Mag., which I can send down together in one parcel when you
please — or if you please. They are endeavouring to revive an Historical
Society within the walls of College and under a most despotic system. I hope
it may not succeed. . . .*

April, 1839

My dear Mother,

. . . I am still President of the Historical Society having been pressed in a very complimentary manner to retain the office upon my own terms, these being the exemption from the liability to being called upon to deliver an address etc. Wallis has been speaking and was in the greatest raptures with my national ballad and the minute I had done reading it he exclaimed 'Shake hands!' and after a pause 'Le Fanu! say what you like you must have some of the real right feeling in you or you could never have written that.'

Your most affectionate son,
Joseph T. S. Le Fanu

The next volume of records we have is entitled 'Minutes of the Proceedings of the Historical Society', and begins:

Many gentlemen being desirous of forming an Historical Society for the promotion of Eloquence and Composition, twenty persons were elected, ten Conservatives and ten Liberals, to form the nucleus of such a Society. These being specially summoned met at Mr Kearney's rooms, 27 College, on Thursday, 14th day of March, 1839.

From the other resolutions passed at this meeting on 14 March we learn that the Society was to be called 'The Historical Society' and that graduates and undergraduates of the Universities of the United Kingdom: members of the Society of Queen's Inns; members of the Queen's College of Physicians, and of the Royal College of Surgeons, Dublin, were to be eligible for membership.

At a meeting held on the following Tuesday twenty-four candidates for membership were proposed and amongst those elected we find the names of John Dillon, under-graduate, 28 College, and William Magee, under-graduate, 27 College. Of the twenty-one candidates elected, six had been members of the former Society.

THOMAS DAVIS

At the meeting on 26 March Joseph Sheridan Le Fanu was elected President; Charles Palmer Archer, Vice-President, and Thomas Osborne Davis, Auditor. A committee of seven was also elected. The Secretary and Treasurer were not elected by the Society, but were nominated by the Auditor, who announced his appointment of Francis Kearney as Secretary, and of Thomas Wallis as Treasurer.

The first debate on 26 March 1839 was on the question 'Ought vote by ballot be introduced at elections?' The pleaders on the affirmative were Kearney and Lawson, and on the negative Murray and Wallis, and the debate was adjourned until the next night. On the next night Mullins and Davis spoke on the affirmative, and the motion was carried by a majority of one, eight members including Davis and Dillon voting on the affirmative, and seven on the negative.

Some of the members of the Society were apparently not satisfied with the accommodation in Leitrim House, as on 9 April the Auditor was directed 'to inquire into the possibility of obtaining a room at the Metropolitan Conservative Society, Dawson Street, and to report on the same to the Society'.

As he would be unable to deliver an address at the close of the session, the President, Le Fanu, on 16 April announced his intention of resigning, but on the proposal of Davis seconded by Wallis, the Society decided that no address should be delivered, and that instead members should be elected on the next night to read papers on the last night of meeting, and that no papers should be read at the intervening meetings. Upon this Le Fanu consented to remain President. A few nights later Davis brought forward another motion that two persons should be chosen to read papers on the last night of meeting of the session.

Among the members who took part in the debates during the session were Ball, Davis, Dillon, Wallis, Lawson and Magee.

On the last night of the session, 25 June 1839, there was no debate, and Davis read his paper on 'The Constitutions of England and America'. An unanimous vote of thanks was given to him 'for his eloquent and audible address'. At this meeting the following officers for the ensuing session were elected:

President   —   Thomas Davis.
Vice-President   —   Harcourt Mooney.
Auditor   —   Charles Palmer Archer.

The opening meeting of the session, 1839–40, was held in the Commercial Buildings on Tuesday, 5 November 1839. At this meeting Davis read a paper 'On some parts of the constitution of the United States' and a vote of thanks to him, moved by Lawson seconded by Le Fanu, was passed unanimously. Other places of meeting during the session were Radley's Hotel, Dame Street, and the Northumberland Rooms.

A committee to revive the laws, consisting of Synan, Carley Davis, Wallis and Bagot, was elected on the last night of the session.

On 19 June 1840 the following entry appears:

A letter from Cambridge was read announcing to the members of the Historical Society that they had been elected honorary members of the Cambridge Union.

On the following night a reciprocal motion proposed by Carley seconded by Davis was passed unanimously 'That the members of the Cambridge Union be elected honorary members of the Historical Society.'

The following entries appear in the minutes for the last night of the session, 26 June 1840:

Mr Macnamara then left the Chair, which was taken by Mr Davis who read an address to the Society on 'The utility of Debating Societies in remedying the defects of an University education', — on the conclusion of which Mr Dillon took the Chair, when it was moved by Mr Wallis seconded by Mr C. Bagot that the marked thanks of the Society be given to Mr Davis for his able address. Passed unanimously.

Moved by Mr Wallis seconded by Mr Cangley, that Mr Davis be requested to furnish the Society with a copy of his address, in order that it may be printed. Passed unanimously.

In this address Davis denounced the system then pursued in the University, as not being adapted to the tastes and capacities of the students, and he

Thomas Osborne Davis, President of the Extern Society 1839–40, by Sir William Burton 1816–1900, courtesy of the National Gallery of Ireland

advocated the Lyceum system of ancient Greece. He also revealed himself as an enthusiastic reformer and as an ardent patriot. Gavan Duffy says that from the time Davis delivered this address he stepped into the lead among his contemporaries, 'not seeking it, for there was no man more modest, but naturally, as of right, because other men would have him for their leader'.

At the opening meeting of the session 1840–41 Davis delivered another address: 'Developing some interesting passages of Irish history, principally relating to the sixteenth century', for which he was awarded the marked thanks of the Society.

At the meeting on 18 December 1840 Davis brought forward a lengthy proposal for re-modelling the Society, beginning with the following:

That a committee be appointed consisting of the President, Auditor, Messrs. Wallis and Davis, to consider and report to the Society on the following plans for extending this Society and increasing its utility.

First, that the Society shall permanently rent or purchase a room or rooms, the rent at present not to exceed £50 per annum.

The Society shall be called the Dublin 'Lyceum'. Its general business shall be managed by a committee consisting of a President, Vice-President, Treasurer, two Secretaries, who shall be elected for three years, and of the Presidents and Secretaries of the sections, who shall be elected on the first meeting in January to serve for one year.

On 29 January 1841 Davis was excused from reading his paper, and Moore read a paper on 'The Jamaica Emigration Scheme, showing it to be an attempt to entrap Irishmen into slavery and destruction.'

The entry in the minute Book on 12 February 1841, is headed 'The Dublin Institute', and underneath 'Historical Society'. After the date appears the statement: 'Society met at its rooms[5] in Marlboro' St.' Davis's scheme, or some modification of it, had apparently been adopted under the name of 'The Dublin Institute'. Two further reports of the Committee of five were brought forward by him on this night. The Society approved of

---

[5] In 1840 No. 2 Marlborough Street was occupied by the Dublin Savings Bank, popularly known as the Penny Bank. In that year the Bank moved to larger premises in Lower Abbey Street, and in the following year, 1841, the upper part of No. 2 was rented by the Historical Society. It was a three-storey building, and there was a large hall on the second floor which seated about a hundred people. From June 1843, when the Historical Society terminated its tenancy, it was occupied by a variety of tenants. From 1872 to 1903 it was used as the City Morgue. During 1904 and 1905 it was rebuilt, and in 1906 it became the famous Abbey Theatre. See article entitled 'The Abbey Theatre' by Mr P. J. Stephenson on page 24 of the *Dublin Historical Record*, Vol. XIII, and note on p. 26, Vol. XV of the *Record*.

the conduct of the Committee 'in transferring the meetings from the Commercial Buildings to No. 2 Marlboro' St.,' and also of the terms which they had arranged for taking the upper part of that house.

YOUNG IRELAND

Early in 1841 several members of the Society joined O'Connell's Repeal Association, and, later, helped largely to form the Young Ireland party. In 1833 O'Connell[6] had started a movement for the repeal of the Union, but had suspended activities during the five years that Thomas Drummond was Under Secretary for Ireland. In April 1840, he revived the movement, and founded the 'Loyal National Repeal Association of Ireland', with its headquarters in the Corn Exchange, Burgh Quay. Gavan Duffy tells us that it met with little success and would probably have perished were it not that early in 1841 'half a dozen young men, mostly barristers or law students, and half of them Protestants, silently joined the Association'. The most notable of these were Thomas Davis and John Blake Dillon, and amongst other members of the Historical Society who joined were Thomas MacNevin, James O'Hea, John O'Hagan, Michael Doheny, John Edward Pigot, Daniel Cangley and Thomas Wallis.

In 1842 *The Nation* newspaper, which became the mouthpiece of Young Ireland, was founded by Duffy, Davis and Dillon, and made its first appearance on 15 October 1842. The title was suggested by Davis, who became the principal contributor and in the three years until his death on 16 September 1845, a stream of patriotic prose and verse flowed from his pen. Duffy, who was the first editor, states: 'But Davis was our true leader. Not only had nature endowed him more liberally, but he loved labour better, and his mind had traversed regions of thought and wrested with problems still unfamiliar to his confederates.' An English journalist jeeringly alluded to the youthful contributors to *The Nation* as '*Young Ireland*', and the nick-name, invented as a reproach, was adopted as a distinction.

---

[6] Daniel O'Connell had himself attended Hist debates in 1796–97 when waiting to be called to the Bar. In *Daniel O'Connell, His Early Life and Times* by Arthur Houston p. 156 O'Connell is quoted as saying, 'I spoke twice against the partition of Greece into small portions.'

Differences which arose between O'Connell and the Young Irelanders over the British Government's proposal to establish non-sectarian colleges, styled by O'Connell 'godless colleges', and other questions of policy, led to an unhappy and ever-widening rift. O'Connell had proclaimed that no political amelioration was worth one drop of blood, while the Young Irelanders held that in certain circumstances force might become justifiable. The death of Davis in September, 1845, deprived the Young Irelanders of their chief counsellor and leader. At the meeting on Monday, 8 November 1841, Dillon, the ex-President, delivered his address on 'Patriotism'. On the termination of the address, the Auditor (Hancock) moved, and the Secretary (Cogan) seconded, 'That the warm thanks of the Society are due and hereby given to Mr Dillon for his very able address, and for his dignified conduct while President of this Society.' — passed nem. con.

On 16 January 1843, Davis was elected an honorary member. His last appearance as a speaker in the debates was in April 1841, when he spoke in favour of a tax on absentees.

INTERN 1843

AT THE FIRST MEETING OF THE session 1843–44, which was held in new rooms which had been secured in Great Brunswick Street, William Hancock gave notice of the following motion: 'That in case it should appear that the Board of Trinity College are determined to prevent students from continuing members of this Society I will propose that an offer be made to the Board to unite the Historical Society with the Society within the College by the Board upon the condition that all the present members of the Historical Society be admitted as members of the Intern Society.' On the same night J. E. Pigot gave notice of the two following motions: 'To bring under the notice of the Society the proceedings of the Committee, and of Mr Hancock, with respect to their proceedings relative to any correspondence with the Board of Trinity College.' After the discussion of the last motion, to move 'That Mr Hancock's conduct was unauthorised by the Society, and therefore an improper assumption of a power of interference which is contrary to the obvious interests of the Society and the credit of its members.' A notice of a further motion was given by John Kells Ingram as follows: 'On the next

John Kells Ingram from Supplement to T.C.D.
8 May 1907

William Connor Magee

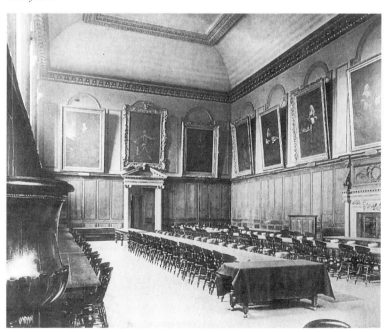

The Dining Hall, Trinity College

night I shall move that the conduct of Mr Hancock in the late communications with Dr Sadlier was highly praiseworthy, and entitles him to the thanks of the Society.'

The meeting on 4 November 1844, at which no members were elected, was the last meeting of the Extern Society.

J. C. MacDonnell, in his *Life of Archbishop Magee*, tells of the important part played by Magee in bringing about the re-establishment of the Society within the University:

. . . Afterwards, in more peaceful times, the students sought to make amends for their loss by forming a society outside the walls of the College and the jurisdiction of the University. For in Dublin, unlike Oxford and Cambridge, the University has no power outside the College precincts, and provided the students are guilty of no misdemeanour and return to their College at proper hours, they cannot be interfered. Various attempts were made to restore the College Historical Society to its old status as a recognised University institution, meeting within the walls of Trinity College, but the authorities were afraid, and thought it better that it should debate in places where they were not responsible for its proceedings.

W. C. Magee was one of the few who commenced a fresh agitation when Dr. Sadleir was Provost of Trinity. He was decidedly favourable to the restoration of the College Historical Society, as was also Dr. MacDonnell who succeeded him as Provost. Some of the other members of the Hebdomadal Board were more timid or cautious, and were not easily converted to the movement. In this agitation Magee was associated with H. E. Chatterton, now Vice-Chancellor of Ireland, Henry Jellett, now Dean of St. Patrick's and myself.

. . . He had already distinguished himself in the exiled Society, outside the walls of Trinity College, Dublin, as a ready speaker.

It was the business of the Auditor to deliver an address at the opening of the Session. It was resolved among the few promoters of the change, who were only numerous enough to form a committee, to make Magee Auditor, and to trust him to forward their cause by his opening address. . . .

Strange to say the return of the Society was not popular among many of the students. They were unwilling to give up the freedom from collegiate control which they had enjoyed outside the walls. Magee's task, then, was a difficult and delicate one as he had to please and thank the Heads of the College who had shown their readiness to welcome back their prodigal children, but who showed their caution by tying them down with very rigid rules, and at the same time to conciliate the more restive spirits who chafed under the idea of any restraints.

The meeting was crowded. Provost Sadleir himself took the Chair, Magee's address was completely successful, and at least silenced, if it did not at once convince, all the gainsayers. It was the first of a long series of oratorical triumphs. From that day the success of the Society was complete. The College soon after gave the Society a separate building, with a library and committee-rooms, for its own use. Members flocked in and it became the famous institution it still is — the training ground not only of the judges and bishops, but of many useful men in less exalted spheres.

The address occupied more than an hour in delivery. But though it has not the epigrammatic terseness which characterises the styles of his prepared addresses in later life, it held his audience enchained in rapt attention, and sealed the success of the Historical Society. . . .

The first meeting of the Society was held on 13 May 1843, 'by order of the Provost' when nine of the original members were present, and also the Rev. Chas. Graves, F.T.C.D., who was at that time Junior Dean. A number of laws were read to the Society by J. C. MacDonnell, on whose motion, seconded by Magee, they were adopted as the laws of the Society. The following officers and Committee were then elected:

Auditor	—	W. C. Magee.
Treasurer	—	H. Jellett.
Secretary	—	J. C. MacDonnell.
		H. E. Chatterton,
		Edward Sullivan,
		J. L. Robinson,
		W. A. Battersby,
		T. Twigg.

On 4 March 1846 a letter was read from the Secretary of the Oxford

Rotten Row and the Rubrics in Library Square, Trinity College before the building of the Graduates' Memorial Building. The dormer window at the end of Rotten Row at the extreme left of the picture is the window of the bed-room in which John Kells Ingram composed one night 'The Memory of the Dead', *which contains the lines* 'Who fears to speak of '98?'

Union Society thanking the Historical Society for the marks of goodwill they had shown in forwarding a copy of their regulations, etc., and transmitting in return a copy of their own principal documents. The letter had the following postscript:

P.S.:–

The Secretary would call the attention of the C.H.S. to Rule XXXVIII of the Oxford Union Society, where they will see, what probably they were aware of before, that all members of the Historical Society, Dublin are members of the Oxford Union Society.

Some nights later, with the approval of the Board, a motion was adopted making the members of the Oxford and Cambridge Union Societies honorary members of the College Historical Society.

In his address, at the opening of the session 1849–50, the Auditor, Edward Light Griffin, remarked:

It cannot have escaped the notice of anyone who is at all familiar with the working of this Society that the study of Oratory has acquired amongst us a vast preponderance over those of History and Poetry. I cannot resist the conviction that it may be partly traceable to some peculiarity in the temper and circumstances of the Irish people which predisposes them in favour of oratorical display.

Thirty-nine new members were elected during the session 1852–53. Alexander Edward Miller, Treasurer, 1851–52, was elected a life-member subject to the approval of the Board.

The finances of the Society at this period were not flourishing and in reply to an application for assistance made to the Board on 2 February the Auditor read the following letter from the Provost:

'I have much pleasure in informing you that the Board have voted a sum of £20 towards clearing off the debts of the Historical Society

I have also the pleasure of enclosing my own mite of £2.'

The following letter, written by a student, G. B. Morgan, who was present, contains a reference to the opening meeting of the session 1853–54, held on Wednesday, 9 November and to its somewhat abrupt adjournment:

37 Trinity College,
10th Nov. 1853

My dear mother,

. . . The Historical Society met last night in the Dining Hall. Henry gave me a ticket. Mr Richey delivered an eloquent address previous to receiving his medal, for the last year, which was well merited. Napier, the member, followed, and his speech was succeeded by a capital one from John Kells Ingram, F.T.C.D., and Professor of Oratory to the University, in which he bestows the highest encomiums on Mr Richey; who was his pupil and had taken very high honours in the University. It was Ingram who wrote the

celebrated song: 'who fears to speak of ninety eight'. He was enthusiastically cheered by the under-graduates on the commencement and end of his speech; and also on leaving the room. The Provost, as chairman, acted very badly, leaving the room very prematurely, and, thus, putting a stop to the proceedings before the time. We, thus, lost a speech from Butt, who was there. The under-graduates kept up shouts of 'Butt!', 'Butt!', while the Provost was leaving, to annoy him. Indeed the Provost behaved very shabbily.

The closing debate of the session 1856–57 took place in the Dining Hall on Wednesday, 10 June 1857, at eight o'clock (College Time), the President in the Chair. We are told that there was a very numerous attendance of students and visitors, including a large number of ladies. The motion discussed was 'That the Reform Bill of Lord Grey was not formed in accordance with the wants of the country'. Somerset B. Burtchaell and Isaac Butt spoke on the affirmative and the motion was carried in the affirmative. The President then delivered an address to the Society, in which he stated:

I was looking over some old papers a few days ago and came across and opened, — I confess, not without some emotion, — the closing address I myself delivered in 1828. It was not delivered within the walls of the University; we were then exiled, we were obliged to take shelter outside in the city. The address was composed within the walls, and when I thought of all the interval since that period, now nearly thirty years ago, . . . I own I could not look back upon it without deep and thrilling emotion.

In his address at the opening of the session 1857–58 the Auditor, William Bradford, alludes to the lack of interest taken in the Society by the Fellows of the College:

You will agree with me that the spirit of a meeting depends, in some measure, on the Chairman, yet somehow those who have devoted their lives to the purposes of education come seldom amongst us, or consent to preside. . .

(The Board ruled that a Fellow or Professor must preside.)

We had thought, gentlemen, that we would have been favoured tonight with the presence of Ladies. . . . But we are doomed to disappointment, and once again has the order gone forth that 'Nought of Beauty shall enter here.' I dismiss this subject as unpleasant.

Amongst the members elected at the beginning of the session were W. E. H. Lecky and J. P. Mahaffy.

Edward Gibson, afterwards Lord Ashbourne, was elected Auditor for the session 1858–59. Among his contemporaries were David Robert Plunket, afterwards Lord Rathmore, and William Edward Hartpole Lecky. Gibson, Plunket, and Lecky all represented the University in the British House of Commons in later years. Many years afterwards, in 1891, these three gold medallists in Oratory were brought together once more at the annual T.C.D. Dinner which was given in the Middle Temple Hall, London. Gibson, then Lord Ashbourne, presided, and Lecky proposed the Houses of Parliament, to which the Archbishop of Dublin and Plunket (who was then M.P. for Dublin University, and First Commissioner of Works)

Officers and Medallists 1858–61: Isaac Bond, David R Plunket (ex-Auditor), Henry Stewart Freeman Wills (ex-Auditor), Edward Gibson (ex-Auditor), Conway Cartwright, W. E. H. Lecky

Edward Gibson, Lord Ashbourne Auditor 1858–59

responded. The meeting revived many old memories. Next day Plunket wrote to Lecky:

I will not resist to write to you one little line to tell you how thoroughly I enjoyed your most charming speech yesterday evening — so eloquent, so graceful, and in such perfect taste. It was to me like a very pleasant whiff of

*fresh air from the far-off hills of our old friendship — a friendship which I
am glad to know holds fast and firmly.*

The names of Anthony Traill, afterwards Provost, and Gerald Fitzgibbon,
afterwards Lord Justice of Appeal, appear amongst those of the new
members elected on the second night of the session.

 The debates were well supported, as many as eleven or twelve speakers
taking part on occasions. Lecky, Plunket, and Gibson spoke often.

DAVID R. PLUNKET

AT THE OPENING MEETING OF
the session 1859–60, held on 9 November 1859, the Auditor, David R.
Plunket, delivered a brilliant address on the subject of public speaking at
the present day:

*. . . There is, indeed, but one responsibility, I know of, that you incur on
entering our guild, it is to be patriotic Irishmen. This Society is now in its
ninetieth year. Called into being at first at the moment when the spirit of an
awakening freedom and a new-born nationality began to breathe upon this
land, it has watched that freedom's progress, — tenderly nursed that
nationality. For ninety years it has sent forth the best and greatest Irishmen.
— Gentlemen as I speak these words, great memories come thick upon me.
This Society had existed for scarcely twelve short years when Ireland was
roused from the ages of torpor and slavery, and a people of serfs became in one
day a nation of free men; and if you ask me how this was accomplished, I
answer — pre-eminently by the Eloquence sent forth by this Society; and if I
am to say what guarded that freedom and that independence well and long,
and when that freedom fell and that independence was extinguished in the
ignominy and despair of the nation, — what it was mitigated the disaster
and half effaced the shame, — I must answer again — it was the Eloquence
sent forth by this Society. And, as the mind passes on over years and years of
our country's oppression, and suffering, and sin, what was it that still guarded
her interests, and pleaded her cause? I must answer still — it was the
Eloquence sent forth by this Society. And when the Emancipation had at last
been carried, and that great justice had been done, what was it that, through
times of plague, of rebellion, of famine, ever held forth hope and comfort, and*

what at last has helped to win for Ireland peace, prosperity, and plenty? I answer still, — it was the Eloquence sent forth by this Society. Finally if I am asked what it is that this day reflects the ancient fame of Ireland in the British Senate, brings back the bygone glory of her Bar, and makes the old Halls ring again, I answer — it is the Eloquence sent forth by this Society. And we, young men, — what have we to do with this? It is a grand position that we stand in. Behind us stretches away the history of our country, over ages of sorrow and oppression; it brightens as it approaches the present; and the future is full of hope and promise. In the day of Ireland's sore distress the men sent forth from this Society did not fail their country; shall it be said that in the hour of her prosperity we were found wanting?

Gentlemen, these are the great thoughts by which I would seek to rouse my fellow-members to renewed exertions; these are the inducements that I would hold out to those who have not joined us to do so now. I have no others to offer; I desire to offer no others; for if you are not roused by ambition, — if you care not for friendship or good fellowship, — if you are cold to patriotism, I have no wish that you should become one of us.

In a letter written by Lecky a few days later he refers to Plunket's address:

We had the Historical opening night last Wednesday, and one of the grandest addresses I have ever heard from Plunket. He delivered it instead of reading it, and his delivery is I think better than that of any speaker I know; I should be inclined to put him pretty much at the head of the living speakers in Ireland. Dudley another of our Historical men, has got Mr. Maturin's curacy: I heard him preach last Sunday. A son of Fitzgibbon, the lawyer, is, I believe, to be the star this year. Napier has given a gold medal for composition which has been gained by Gibson, whose essay he praised to the skies. Gibson is publishing it with his name and moderator distinctions. I am, as usual, going on with Divinity, writing, reading, and studying oratory.
. . .

During the session we find Lecky, Plunket, Gibson and Fitzgibbon, still taking a prominent part in the debates. The number of speakers, however, was not so great as in the previous session. Pitt's policy was again debated,

Lecky opening on the affirmative that it was partial and unjust, and Fitzgibbon and Mahaffy supporting the negative. The motion was again carried in the affirmative.

W. E. H. LECKY

The following extracts from the *Memoir of Lecky* by his wife, contain some allusions to his oratorical gifts:

He had had from boyhood a passion for oratory, and found full scope for it in the Historical Society, which he joined two years after he had entered College, and where, in 1859 — in his second session — he won the Gold Medal which was awarded annually. 'On one evening of that session', writes Judge Snagge, 'he rose to his feet in the debate and, to the amazement of us all, poured forth a stream of mellifluous and finished eloquence that carried all before it. It was meteoric. It was not a speech, it was a recited essay, but it raised the standard of debating rhetoric enormously.'

In paying tribute to Lecky's memory at the first meeting of the Society after his death the President (Lord Ashbourne) gave his own recollections. He said he heard him make his first speech in that Society, over forty years ago, in the year 1858, and he remembered the surprise with which they all saw him rise and come forward.

'He spoke very much as he spoke all through life, with an extraordinary wealth of language, with the most marvellous affluence of illustration, with the most singular gift he (the President) ever knew of giving the most appropriate designations to every person and subject, no matter how numerous, that he desired to describe.'

Lord Ashbourne believed that the great success that Lecky achieved among his contemporaries by being awarded the Gold Medal for oratory had a considerable effect on his character and his future. It no doubt stimulated him and gave to his shy nature the self-confidence which he needed.

A 'College Friend', writing in the *National Review*, March 1904, says:

W. E. H. Lecky

His speeches were always carefully prepared during long walks on the West Pier at Kingstown, though they were not committed to memory. A few notes on a slip of paper about two inches long and about one wide, crumpled up in the waistcoat pocket, were all he carried to remind him of the points in the subject. The language was always admirable, rising at times to a high pitch of eloquence, perhaps occasionally a little too ornate, but producing a distinct thrill through the audience. It was said sometimes that the matter was more emotional than argumentative, but those who had to reply found the task by no means an easy one. . . .

He frequently practised extempore speaking to himself in his own rooms, and no honour he received was so highly prized as the Gold Medal of the Historical Society.

In a letter to Knightly Chetwood, Lecky wrote:

Yesterday we had a closing night at the Historical, which was a rather formidable thing for me, as I had to open and reply. The subject was Journalism — that its growth is beneficial to Society. We had, I believe, about three or four hundred people there, Napier, of course, in the chair. I found that I was not the least nervous and liked it all very well. The subject, however, not being in my line, I did not make one of my best speeches. Also, not having the fear of conservatism and the clergy before my eyes, I had the audacity to review (in its relation to political and sectarian public opinion) the struggle for nationality in Ireland, and to launch a diatribe at the political clergy. . .

This evening the Committee have made up the Oratory marks, and I have got the Gold Medal, which is, I confess, very gratifying to me. . . My marking, they seem to think, is the highest which has been in the Society for some years. It is a fraction above what Plunket got last year, but perhaps they have got into a way of marking higher than they did then. Gibson tells me that one of the speeches I withdrew was marked very high, so perhaps it would have been better if I had kept that in and had withdrawn my speech of last night.

EDINBURGH 'SPEC'

THE RECORD OF PROCEEDINGS OF the session 1863–64 has some interesting correspondence about the relations of the Society with the Speculative Society, Edinburgh:

To the Secretary of the Speculative Society, Edinburgh.

Sir,

I have given to the Historical Society of Trinity College an account of the reception which I received as their President at the Centenary Banquet of the Speculative Society in Edinburgh, on the 14th of October last. It has been very gratifying to the Historical Society to learn that the friendly relations and reciprocity of privilege which had been established between the two Societies, in the last century, have been revived under such happy auspices and in so genial a spirit.

I forward a transcript of resolutions and correspondence recorded in the books which contain the authentic minutes of our proceedings, from which it appears that when in the year of 1794, the Historical Society was exiled from Trinity College, its manly independence and its fidelity to the principles on which it was founded cemented the union with the Speculative Society which had taken place in the year 1783. It is with no common satisfaction that we find that the cordiality with which the two societies then fraternised has been renewed at a time when the Historical Society, by the wise liberality of the heads of the University has the status and secured the freedom in which it now stands, an established and honoured institution within the walls of Trinity College.

I have but to express a heartfelt desire that the union of the two Societies, so highly begun and so highly auspiciously revived, may be as cordial as their devotion to literature and as lasting as their love of truth.

I have the honour to be,

Your very faithful,

Joseph Napier,
President of the Hist. Soc.

On 2 December the Secretary read the following letter, dated 25 November 1863, from the Secretary of the Speculative Society:

Sir Joseph Napier

I have had the honour of laying your letter of the 12th. inst. before the Speculative Society, and I now beg to enclose the formal minute in which they express the gratification with which they record it. I beg also to thank you on their behalf for the extracts from the records of the Historical Society which you kindly transmit, and I enclose the counterpart from our own minutes containing the resolutions passed here on the occasion of the union of the two Societies.

Edmund Burke, statue at the West Front, Trinity College

May I beg that you will take an opportunity of conveying to the Historical Society the assurance of the continued sympathy with their pursuits, and interest in their prosperity, felt by the members of the Speculative Society.

The movement for the erection of statues to the memory of Edmund Burke and Oliver Goldsmith, which resulted in Foley's two masterpieces that stand at either side of the entrance gate to the College, was at this time on foot, and in February 1864 the general Committee was authorized to solicit subscriptions towards the erection of the contemplated statue to Burke.

Fifty-five subscriptions of 10s. each were received, and a sum of £2.10.0d was added out of the funds of the Society, making up a total of £30, which was forwarded to the Burke Committee.

On 9 December 1863 a motion was brought forward to limit the 'primary speakers' to twenty-five minutes each, and the subsequent speakers to ten minutes each, and the opener in his reply to fifteen minutes. On the next night , however, the Society affirmed 'that the law limiting the speakers to thirty minutes is a good one and ought to be enforced'. Reference to this motion is made by Maurice C. Hime, afterwards Headmaster of Foyle College:

I remembered when I joined the Society in 1861 or 2, there were three or four born orators in it, but few, if any, of the ordinary members had at that period ever obtained any College honours. I was idiotic enough to think that they must be rather stupid asses — not that they were. Many of them distinguished themselves much afterwards in life. I presently proposed a motion that the speeches should each be limited to twenty minutes. George Chadwick, afterwards Bishop of Derry, Shore, who afterwards distinguished himself as a preacher and literary man in London, and a number of other long-winded friends were furious with me; and they managed to induce a number of the Society's heroes to come and oppose my motion. Gerald Fitzgibbon, just then called to the Bar, afterwards Lord Justice, David Plunket, afterwards M.P., (Lord Rathmore) and I think Edward Gibson, afterwards Lord Chancellor (Lord Ashbourne), and others. R. O'B. Lane (Schol.) afterwards K.C., and a Police Magistrate of London, seconded my motion. Lane promised to write it out, and stick it up on the gate. I had not myself seen it there. Chadwick however had, and he brought much laughter to the members present and tears of vexation almost to my eyes, when he said: 'Ore rotundo,' among numerous other cutting remarks, 'Mr Hime has derided some of us men as incapable of speaking because we do not get scholarships or honours, but I will let him know that an orator is born not made, and that a man may win College honours and yet not know how to spell. When Mr Hime affixed his motion to the gate that our speeches should be limited to twenty minutes, I think Mr Chairman, and Gentlemen, he might have limited his own spelling and spelt "limited" with but one "t".' In point of fact it was Lane, one of the cleverest men in our class — 1859–62

— who, as I have said, was guilty of the blunder, but, of course, beyond looking daggers at him, I was helpless. We were, of course, beaten hollow when we came to the voting, all the most distinguished members orating against us and voting accordingly.

David R. Plunket, Lord Rathmore, Auditor 1859–60

In the notices of the meetings the time was always given as 'College Time'. Thus the notice announcing the opening meeting for 11 November 1868, stated that 'The Chair will be taken at eight o'clock (College Time) by the Right Hon. The President'. 'Doors open at half-past seven o'clock (College Time).' The clock in the pediment of the dining hall kept the College time, 'giving fifteen minutes of grace to all students who resided outside the walls'. College time was abolished in the nineteenth century, since when all the clocks inside the College record the same time as those outside.

From the revival of the Intern Society in 1843 until the session 1864–65, the Auditor's addresses, with one or two exceptions, were on the subjects of Oratory, of History, or the Claims or Objects of the Society. The Auditor for the session 1865–66, Richard O'Shaughnessy, departed from the usual custom, and delivered an address on 'Sociology', and from this time onwards the subjects chosen covered a wide field.

INAUGURAL CONTROVERSY A{.T THE OPENING}

meeting of the session on Wednesday, 14 November 1866 the Auditor, Richard O'B. Lane, delivered a brilliant inaugural address on 'Science in Politics'. In his address the Auditor foreshadowed President Wilson's famous League of Nations and suggested a 'Confederacy of the West', as a means of avoiding anarchy and confusion. Reviewing the position of the European powers he stated that England 'must modify her maritime supremacy, her commercial rapacity, and her imperial arrogance. By the cession of Gibraltar she must evince the genuineness of her sympathy with European national rights'. He also censured her severely regarding her relations with Ireland.

The usual motion 'That the thanks of the Society be given to the Auditor for his address', was, in accordance with the programme of the evening, to have been proposed by Lord Chief Justice Whiteside and seconded by Mr Justice Keogh, but neither came forward when the time to propose the motion arrived, as they evidently disapproved strongly of the views expressed by the Auditor. The situation was, however, saved by Professor Webb, F.T.C.D., rising and proposing the motion. The Chairman then asked: 'Does anyone second the resolution?' but no one rising to do so, the motion was allowed to drop, although as one report stated, 'there were many gentlemen on the platform who thoroughly approved of it, and it was most cordially received in the body of the hall'.

The Lord Chief Justice then rose and instead of the second motion usually proposed, 'That the Auditor's address be printed at the expense of the Society', he submitted the following: 'That this meeting regards with satisfaction the statements of the Auditor with regard to the progress of the Society during the past session'. This motion was seconded by the Rt Hon. Mr Justice Keogh in a speech filled with historical and classical allusions, in which he took strong exception to the detracting spirit in which the Auditor had spoken of England, and to the proposal that Gibraltar be ceded to Spain.

The late James T. Andrews, in a letter, gives a brief account of the disturbance created by Lane's address:

. . . Richard Lane's address as Auditor caused one of the greatest scenes of disorder at any of the meetings. He chose as his subject 'The Hegemony of the Nations of the West', quoting in it Tennyson's lines:

'When the war drums throb no longer, and the battle flags are furled,
In the parliament of man the Federation of the world.'

Amongst other courses to be pursued by England to forward this desirable result he advocated the giving up of Gibraltar to Spain. This and other parts of his address elicited shouts of disapproval, and there was a considerable display of objection to all his proposals. Lane was anticipating the present craze for the League of Nations. Professor Webb alone moved that the thanks of the Society be given to the Auditor for his address, but as no one seconded it was not put. The usual motion that the Auditor's address be printed at the expense of the Society was not proposed by any speaker. A motion as to the satisfactory progress of the Society was carried, on which Mr Justice Keogh delivered a very impassioned imperialistic speech, in which he stated the duty of England was summed up in the old adage, 'Parcere subjectis et debellare superbos'. I was on the Committee at the time, and at a meeting of it we were considering what was to be done as to printing the address, when the Rev. G. A. Chadwick, afterwards Bishop of Derry, came in as an honorary member, and said if we printed the address at the expense of the Society the College

Historical Society would be ruined. However, as we did not want the expense to fall on the Auditor, the address having already been printed and Judge Keogh like the other speakers having got a copy before the meeting, we passed the following resolution: 'That without expressing approval of the various topics alluded to in the Auditor's address we desire to thank the Auditor for the eloquence and research therein, and resolve that it be printed at the expense of the Society.' And nothing detrimental to the Society occurred in consequence.

The opening meeting of the session 1868–69 was fixed to take place on the usual day, the second Wednesday in November, and notices were published in the press announcing the names of the speakers, tickets were issued, and all arrangements made, when at two o'clock p.m., only six hours before the hour at which the meeting was to begin, the following order was issued by the Board:

The opening meeting of the College Historical Society advertised to be held this evening has been postponed by order of the Board.

Th. T. Gray,
Junior Dean.
T.C.D., 11th November, 1869

A special meeting of the Society was held immediately, and a memorial was presented to the Board complaining that their decision had placed the Society in a position of great embarrassment, and that the suspension of their proceedings might have a most detrimental effect on the Society. The memorial concluded with the following paragraph: 'And we further most respectfully draw the attention of the Board to the indefinite nature of their order, and request to be informed at their earliest convenience how long the prohibition is intended to operate.'

It should be mentioned that Sir Dominic Corrigan, M.D., and Sir D. R. Plunket, both of whom had been invited to speak at the opening meeting, were opposing candidates in a parliamentary election which was due to take place shortly after the date fixed for the meeting. Early on Wednesday, 11 November a letter was received from Dr Corrigan expressing his inability to attend the meeting and this additional information was given to the Junior Dean and included in the memorial.

At the meeting on 18 November a reply was received from the Registrar, John Toleken, stating:

. . . there is no objection to the appointment of any day for holding the inaugural meeting of the Society provided that such day be after the conclusion of the Irish Parliamentary elections. I may add that the postponement of the meeting was regarded imperative by the information which was laid before the Board that great disorder was likely to occur if the meeting should take place.

The postponed opening meeting took place on Wednesday, 2 December 1868. The following is an extract of an account of the meeting which appeared in the London *Times* of 4 December:

On the platform were the two most prominent combatants in the late electoral duel — Sir D. Corrigan and the Hon. David Plunket — and around them were the Ministers of various religious denominations and other gentlemen representing every shade of political sentiment. The Society is popular with all classes on account of its national traditions, of the distinguished names inscribed upon its roll, and the generous spirit which it infuses into the educated youth of the country. Additional interest was excited on this occasion by the fact that Mr. O'Hea, the Auditor, by whom the inaugural address was to be delivered, is a Roman Catholic gentleman. It is a remarkable circumstance that some of the ablest essays heard in the Society of late years have been composed by students of the same creed. No more satisfactory evidence need be offered of the willingness of the Roman Catholic youth to avail themselves of the educational facilities afforded in the University, with its increased liberality, and to enter into friendly competition with their Protestant fellow-citizens for the honours which are awarded to the highest merit. They have proved themselves able successfully to encounter the most accomplished of their rivals in a fair and open field. The prizes which they have honourably won have been awarded with generous alacrity, and their fellow students have witnessed their triumphs, not merely without jealousy, but with sincere pleasure. Last evening presented no exception to the rules. Mr O'Hea's address, which was marked with great ability, elicited a hearty tribute of praise from the assembly. Its subject was the influence of

University life upon national life. The spirit in which he treated it, and the feeling entertained towards the institution and his colleagues, may be inferred from the following passage, which was received with acclamation:

'As the University generates an atmosphere of intellectual thought, so does this Society create one of political opinion. In its debates many a young member has heard, perhaps for the first time, the expression of sentiments directly opposite to his own, and when the first feeling of astonishment wore away he began to understand that it is possible for honest minds to differ on the same subject, and at that moment his political education has begun. . . Is it not our bane in this country that we are so often banded into hostile camps, and seldom meet on neutral ground — that our opinions are formed for us, and are associated with old rancours, and old grievances, the old crimes — that we are made to fight under banners which were hostile once, but which need not be so longer, and to shout angry war cries which in out hearts we loathe. . . And is it not good for this country that there should be in her University a school, though it be only for the purpose of debate, in which every fact in Irish History is referred to, and every point in Irish Politics is canvassed, and yet no angry word is spoken, no sentiment of bigotry is uttered, no party cry is raised, no tie of friendship is broken?'

The name of Alfred Perceval Graves appears occasionally among the list of speakers in debates, and the following, written by him to T. S .C. Dagg on 25 August 1923, contains some interesting reminiscences:

. . . But I do remember the excitement caused when Sir William Rowan Hamilton rose to speak, and the curious feelings which his oration, for it was more than a speech, aroused in us. It was delivered ore rotundo as if from the floor of the old Parliament House eighty years before, with studied gestures and in long flowing periods. He wore his graduate's gown, forty years old no doubt at the time, and was happily reminiscent of his early and later College days, though perhaps a trifle egotistical about them. Small wonder, for he reached the highest classical as well as mathematical honours in his class — after declining to take a Virgil from his entrance examiner on the score of knowing it by heart, as he proved to the incredulous don who started passage after passage from the twelve books only to hear them correctly repeated and rendered into perfect English by the young prodigy.

Lecky also I listened to, and years after, hearing him speak at a presentation to Earl Roberts after the Boer War, enjoyed anew the peculiar rise and fall of his voice in his Gibbon-like sentences.

The address delivered by Abraham Stoker, Auditor, at the opening of the session 1872–73 was on the subject of 'The Necessity for Political Honesty'.

Cecil Robert Roche, the Auditor elected for the session 1873–74, chose 'Federalism' as the subject for his inaugural address.

The night fixed for the opening meeting was Wednesday, 12 November and at the Committee meeting on Friday, 7 November the Auditor submitted a letter from the President informing him that the Board 'contemplated directing the Society to hold its opening meeting with closed doors'. He was directed by the Committee to send a letter to the President setting forth the claims of the Society to hold a meeting without any unusual restrictions.

On the following day a letter was received from the Board stating:

. . . at this time, and under the present circumstances, the public discussion of the subject of Federalism, however discreetly treated in the Auditor's address, would be prejudicial to the character of the College and injurious to its peace. They have therefore come to the conclusion that they cannot give their consent to the use of the College Hall for the discussion of the subject of Federalism on Wednesday next.

The Committee decided to submit this letter to a conference of the members and a conference at which sixty-eight members were present was held in the new buildings on Saturday, 8 November.

The Chair was taken by R. O'B. Furlong, ex-Treasurer, and after motions to apply for the use of the hall for the opening meeting, excluding members of the public, and to hold the meeting outside College, had been rejected, O'Hea, ex-Auditor, proposed and Stoker, ex-Auditor, seconded, the following series of resolutions:

1. *That the Board's order be published in the newspapers, and notice be given that the Auditor's address will not be delivered on next Wednesday as announced.*

Edward Carson, a cartoon of the Member for the University

2. *That a sub-committee be appointed to prepare and present a respectful remonstrance with the Board of the subject of their order; to ask respectfully the reasons for their exceptional action with a view to removing the misapprehension under which they labour, and report to the Society on the result of their action.*

3. *That this meeting adjourn to next Wednesday in the Society's rooms at 8 o'c.*

These resolutions were carried.

A special general meeting of the Society was held in the new buildings on Monday, 17 November, at 4 p.m. when the sub-committee reported that before they had time to draw up the memorial to the Board they received a letter from the Auditor in which he stated that he had not the slightest doubt that the Board would not depart from their decision, and that rather than plunge the Society into a contest with the Board which might 'end disastrously to either our liberty or our prosperity', he withdrew his address. He added that if he were allowed to deliver an inaugural address on some other subject it might be conveniently delivered at the first meeting of the Society in the new year. A motion was then proposed that the Auditor should read a new address on Wednesday, 14 January and when several members and the Auditor had addressed the meeting the motion was put to the vote and lost by eighteen votes to thirteen; whereupon the Auditor handed in his resignation. The Society then passed a motion: 'That the Auditor's resignation be not accepted,' but he wrote stating that on mature consideration it would be impossible for him to continue to occupy the post of Auditor 'after the great encroachment made on the just rights and privileges belonging to that office by the vote of Monday week'.

Amongst the members who joined the Society at the beginning of the session 1873–74 were some who afterwards distinguished themselves in widely different walks of life. Amongst these were William Ridgeway (Sch.), Arthur Warren Samuels (Sch.), Oscar Wilde (Sch.), Edward H. Carson, and Arthur Patton.

The following is the official account of the opening meeting of the session 1874–75, held on 11 November, as it appears in the minutes:

The minutes having been read and confirmed the Auditor, Mr Charles L. Matheson, B.A., delivered the inaugural address.

It was then proposed by the Honble. David Plunket, Q.C., M.P., and seconded by the Rev. Canon Reichel, D.D., and resolved:

'That the thanks of the Society be given to the Auditor for his address.'

Owing to a disturbance in the hall further proceedings were suspended, and the President declared the meeting adjourned to Wednesday 18th November, 1874.

We must seek elsewhere for a picture of the scene that was witnessed in the hall. The following graphic description appeared in the *Freeman's Journal* on the next day:

Last night the most extraordinary scene which was ever enacted within academic walls took place in the Dining Hall of Trinity College. The night was fixed for the inaugural address of the Auditor of the Historical Society, an office this year filled by Mr Charles Louis Matheson. During the week College circles had been greatly excited by the coming meeting. The cause of the excitement had sole reference to the election for the University which will take place on Dr. Ball's elevation to the bench. We need scarcely say that the only 'live' candidates for the seat about to be vacated are Mr Gibson, Q.C., of the Irish and Mr Miller Q.C., of the English Bar.

There can be no doubt whatever that in the under-graduate world Mr Miller's candidature is eminently unpopular. His candidature has not been managed with good taste or good sense, and he is the supposed political nominee of the most successful and most unpopular Irishman of the time — Lord Cairns. The managers of the inaugural meeting had committed the error of inviting Mr Miller and two of his prominent committee men to speak, while no such invitation was extended to Mr Gibson. Hinc illae Lachrymæ. Hence the rumours of war with which Old Trinity resounded all during the week; hence the unparalleled row of last night. The meeting took place as we have said in the Dining Hall, a fine apartment in the heart of the College buildings, and reached by several stone steps. To the man who arrived at the College about twenty minutes to eight, an extraordinary scene presented itself. The door at the top of the Dining Hall steps was half-open, and on the steps was a surging, swaying densely packed crowd of human beings trying to fight their way up and in through the door. Into this crowd the new arrival had to force himself, and then after some minutes of desperate crushing he was fairly taken off his feet, and swept through the open door. Inside this door was a hall, and to pass into the Dining Room it was necessary to fight one's way through another door, where the crush was almost as bad as outside. Broken hats, coats torn up the back, collars rent away, were common results of the double scrimmage, while the well-meant efforts of the stewards only made confusion more confounded. At eight o'clock the hall was filled to overflowing with a vast throng, in which the learned professions were very largely represented. Everywhere the undergraduate element was conspicuous, collarless, stick-bearing, uproarious, and 'spilling for a fight'. At eight o'clock precisely the Right Hon. Sir Joseph Napier, the President of the Society, accompanied by the Auditor and the platform guests, entered the hall in long and dignified procession. Their appearance was the signal for the outbreak of the wild scene of tumult, uproar, and riot, which raged for two long hours. Mr Gibson and Mr Miller were both in the procession, and the roof rung with cheers for Gibson and groans for Miller. Whistles and bugles added to the din, while on all sides were heard the sharp crack of the explosive fire-works known as Ashantee bombs. When Sir Joseph and those accompanying him had taken their seats on the platform, Sir Joseph rose and attempted to address the meeting. The din continued unabated, and not a syllable of the right hon. baronet's remarks could be heard a few yards from the platform. Sir Joseph, who appeared much distressed and annoyed by his reception, resumed his seat, and the Auditor then came forward to read his address. After he had read a few sentences the din died away, and Mr Matheson was very well heard during the greater portion of a conspicuously able and interesting address. Towards the close, however, the trifling incident of a young lad fainting again evoked the spirit of uproar and disturbance, and the latter portion of the Auditor's address was lost. . . . The Rev. Canon Reichel then came forward to second the resolution proposed by Mr Plunket. The Rev. Canon, as a 'Millerite', was received with a deafening yell, before which, after a little dumb show, he retired. Mr Miller, Q.C., then advanced to the front of the platform to move the second resolution. His appearance brought to a climax the tumult. The Ashantee were flung by the handfuls. The key-buglers and the penny bombs whistlers outdid their previous efforts. The undergraduates yelled, screamed, roared, brayed. The seats were broken in the body of the hall. The wooden panelling was thumped with the fragments of the seats. . . . For nearly an hour Mr Miller stood his ground, and all this time the riot grew worse and worse. Sir Joseph Napier made several efforts to secure a hearing but not a syllable could be heard above the din. No written description can give any adequate idea of the tumult, the appalling noise, the braying trumpets, the shrieking whistles, the showers of exploding fire-works, the bewildered pigeons flying hither and thither, the missiles from outside, the free fights, the infernal tumult which reigned all round. At one time the surging crowd swept up to the very edge of the platform. The stewards checked their further advance, a violent altercation appeared to take place, and it seemed as if the platform was about to be stormed. The only idea of the wild confusion can be given by saying that the scene represented a dozen election nominations condensed into one. At last Sir Joseph Napier rose and left the hall, the stewards surrounding him and fighting their way down through the crowd. Some minutes of tumult ensued, and the platform guests began to leave. Such were the aspects of the scene that it was thought advisable to surround Mr Miller with a bodyguard, consisting of Dr Traill and other muscular Christians. Dr Traill is a great favourite with the undergraduates and way was made for him, though the other members of the bodyguard were hustled rudely. All then left the room, the wearers of the high hats narrowly escaping without being 'bonneted'.

The following describes the meeting in a letter which T. S. C. Dagg received from the late Rev. Canon T. B. Wilson, Hon. Member, who was then Correspondence Secretary:

The meeting began in the usual way by the reading of minutes, and the names of candidates for membership. This formality was carried through in dumb show, and the President called upon the Auditor to read his address.

Then, though Mr Matheson was personally most popular, the storm burst with redoubled fury, and not a syllable could be heard. The Hall resounded with shouts and cheers, and crackers and small rockets were let off on all sides. In the midst of the pandemonium two carrier pigeons were released, and dashed

Provost Anthony Traill, from Supplement to T.C.D. *14 May 1904*

to and fro, one of them at last taking refuge in the arms of Mr Justice Keogh!

In vain the President appealed for order, and the Auditor asked for fair play, but nothing availed, and he had to give up the attempt to make himself heard. As a last resort, and in the hope of stilling the storm, the President called on Mr David Plunket to speak. At first this most popular speaker was listened to, and there seemed good prospect of peace until, in an unfortunate moment, the speaker ventured on a quotation apropos of what was in all minds

> *The sunset of life brings me mystical lore*
> *And coming events cast their shadow before.*

This was the end. The turmoil grew worse, and finally the President rose and adjourned the meeting, and thus ended what was probably the stormiest meeting in the annals of the College Historical Society.

During the session 1875–76 the debate on the motion 'That Capital Punishment ought to be abolished' was opened by Edward Carson on the affirmative, which side was also supported by J. H. M. Campbell: ten speakers also took part in the discussion, and the motion was decided in the negative by a majority of six votes. The motion 'That the system of Land Tenure in Ireland needs reformation' was supported by six speakers, including R. S. D. Campbell (Auditor) and J. H. M. Campbell, and opposed by five speakers, amongst whom were Edward Carson and Arthur W. Samuels.

At the meeting on 22 March 1876 a dispute on a point of order arose between the Auditor and James Shannon, a prominent member of the Society who occupied the Chair, which resulted in the suspension of Shannon, and the appointment of a special committee to consider the relative duties of the Auditor and Chairman. After an animated discussion extending over several meetings the special Committee expressed the opinion that Rules 20 and 21 of Chap. XII, Sect. 2, show conclusively that a Chairman has no power to judge points of order, and that the Auditor is the person in whom alone that power is vested.

Campbell at first chose the subject of 'Land Tenure in Ireland' for his inaugural address, but when at the beginning of October he sent a copy of the address to the President, he received a reply stating: 'the general topic of Land Tenure in Ireland is too inflammable and explosive for the occasion in College, however carefully considered and discussed, to be trusted for safe handling; and I am confident the Board would interpose, if necessary, to veto the selection'.

When asking the Board for the use of the Dining Hall for the opening

James H. M. Campbell, Q.C., M.P., Lord Chancellor, First Lord Glenavy, Chancellor of Dublin University, Chairman, Seanad Éireann, painting by Leo Whelan in the Regent House, Trinity College, by courtesy of the Provost and Board

meeting, the application was also made for consent to modify the rule regarding the wearing of evening dress, so as to allow graduates or undergraduates to attend in academical costume should they so prefer. In conveying their consent the Board stated that 'if the evening dress be not worn under academicals care should be taken that students admitted to the meeting should appear in proper and becoming dress, and not in the careless costume which has sometimes been admitted on former occasions'.

The subjects debated were similar to those discussed in the previous sessions. We find Carson speaking in favour of the Abolition of the Social and Political Disabilities of Women; an Hereditary Legislative Chamber, and Pitt's Irish Policy; and against Municipal Corporations being replaced by Paid Commissioners; the approval of Cromwell's Character; the Maintenance of the Connection between Church and State in England, and Lecky's Views on Federalism.

On 21 March 1877 a motion was proposed by E. J. Lefroy, seconded by Henry Harden, and carried, 'that members be allowed to wear their caps during the debate, save the speakers for the time being'.

On 27 March 1878 Arthur W. Samuels, and Edward Carson, were proposed for a vacant seat on the general Committee, and on the following night Samuels was elected.

At the opening night of the 109th session, 1878–79, the Auditor, John Ross, alluded to the death of Mr Justice Keogh. 'We have lost a staunch friend', he said, 'by the death of one of our Vice-Presidents, Mr Justice Keogh. It was as a member of this Society that his eloquence first attracted attention; and throughout all his eventful career he ever displayed a deep interest in the School where his great faculties were trained.'

Disturbances occurred at the opening meeting, as a result of which the Board decided to refuse permission to hold next year's opening meeting in the Dining Hall. They relented, however, on receiving satisfactory assurances from the Committee.

At the end of January 1879 Edward Gibson was elected a Vice-President of the Society, and a few nights later the following letter from him was read:

I feel very much gratified indeed by the honour conferred on me by the College Historical Society in electing me Vice-President.

I shall always feel the deepest and most sincere interest in the welfare and advance of the Society, and gladly welcome any new link which binds me more closely to it.

I am anxious to elicit a good essay from the members of the Society on 'Primary Education' with a contrast of the German, English, and Irish systems, and shall give a prize of £10:10:0 to the writer of the best. Would you kindly see that this is known amongst those members likely to compete.

The essays to be sent in before 20th October, and their merits to be decided on by myself, either alone or with the assistance of some other gentlemen whom I may select.

The prize was won by John Cooke.

APPROVAL FOR DEBATES

DURING THE SESSION 1882–83 difficulties arose again with the Board regarding the subjects for debate. On 22 November a list of forty-two subjects was submitted, of which the Board approved, with the following exceptions:

Nos.	6	concg.	Municipal Corporations.
	7	"	Grand Jury System.
	11	"	County Boards.
	14	"	Pitt's Irish Policy.
	19	"	Federalism.
	23	"	Daniel O'Connell.
	24	"	Political Agitation.
	29	"	The Young Ireland Party.
	31	"	Parliamentary Procedure.

A letter was sent to the Board pointing out that nearly all these subjects had on many previous occasions been debated by the Society with the sanction of the Board, and expressing the hope that the Board would reconsider their decision.

On 17 January the Committee selected for debate on 7 February, the motion 'That Grattan's denunciation of the Union has been justified by the results', which appeared as No. 19 in the list of subjects entered in the Committee minutes of 22 November. The debate was duly held on 7 February, P. J. Smith, Nationalist M.P., in the Chair, and after nine speakers had participated in the debate it was adjourned. At the conclusion of the debate, the Chairman made a strong Home Rule Speech, which was fully reported in the daily press. On the following night the debate was continued, and the motion was carried in the affirmative by a majority of six votes. Some days later the Registrar wrote inquiring what subject had been debated on the fourteenth, and on being informed, he wrote inquiring whether the Society had obtained permission from the Board to debate this subject and, if so, when.

The pro-Correspondence Secretary, H. D. Conner, furnished the information asked for, and on 1 March he received the following letter from the Registrar: 'I beg to inform you that I have before me the list of subjects furnished on 23rd November, 1882. The subject in question is not in that list. Probably the Board will expect the answers of the Historical Society on Saturday next, the 3rd inst.'

To this letter Conner replied stating that the subject in question was among those in the list which the Committee had directed their Secretary to submit to the Board on 22 November 1882.

The committee assume that the Correspondence Secretary did not submit the subject as directed, but if by inadvertence it is left out the committee had no opportunity of finding out that such was the case, as the Board did not return the list which was submitted to them. It appears by the minute book of the Committee that the subject was submitted on the date mentioned, and as the then Correspondence Secretary has ceased to be so and is now out of town, the committee has no way of investigating the matter further.

On the following day the Registrar wrote to Conner: 'I have read to the Board at their meeting today your letter of the 1st and 2nd March '83. The Board instruct me to say that they observe no apology has been made for the flagrant violation of the Rules of the Historical Society. The Board direct that the meetings of the Society be suspended during the present month (March).'

On 7 February 1883 the Rt Hon. Edward Gibson, Q.C., M.P., Vice-President, was elected President. Gibson occupied the Chair for the first time as President at the opening meeting of the 114th session (1883–84). At a Committee meeting a few nights before the opening meeting a resolution was passed that all students should be required to wear caps and gowns, and 'that no sticks be admitted'.

In the debate on the subject 'That the Church of England ought to be disestablished', held during the session 1885–86, H. S. Lunn and Douglas Hyde were amongst the six speakers on the affirmative, and C. Litton Falkiner and G. F. Brunskill amongst the six speakers on the negative.

Douglas Hyde, President 1931–50, President of Ireland, from the painting in the Conversation Room of the Society

Twenty-seven speakers participated in the debate on the motion 'That the Political Institutions of 1782 deserve approval', which extended over three nights. Amongst the speakers on the affirmative were W. M. Crook, Douglas Hyde and D. M. Wilson, and amongst those on the negative were H. B. Kennedy and William Moore. The motion was decided in the negative.

When notifying the subject for the President's composition medal at the end of the session Lord Ashbourne wrote as follows:

. . . There is a point in the existing laws which I think not unworthy of the attention of the general committee. At present it is the Auditor, or pro-Auditor, who is the judge of order, and not the chairman of the meeting. This, altho' absolutely opposed to the precedents of all public assemblies, may often be convenient when the Chairman has no experience, and is perfectly ignorant of the Society, and its ways. But when the President or Vice-Presidents are in the Chair, it is almost absurd for a member of the Society to be able to appeal from the ruling of the Chair to the Auditor. I would be glad if the committee and the Society considered if they could not render the rule a little flexible. This would be done by introducing words which would make the Auditor, whenever the President or Vice-Presidents were in the Chair, available to give any advice in reference to the laws that might be asked for by the Chairman.

The Correspondence Secretary was directed to write to Lord Ashbourne approving of the sentiments of his letter, but the Committee do not appear to have acted on his suggestion, and wisely retained without any modification one of the peculiar and distinctive features of the Society.

After the History examination in June 1886 the following letter was received from the examiners:

In presenting to the committee the results of the examinations for the History medals, we desire to state that the answering of each candidate was of a very superior standard; and that so far as we could draw any distinction between the answering of the two candidates, Mr Waugh appeared to each of us to have a slightly more accurate knowledge of the subject, but that any advantage he possessed in this respect was counterbalanced by the superior style of Mr Hyde's answering.

Each of the candidates was awarded a gold medal.

LAWS & CANVASSING

A BREACH OF THE LAWS against canvassing, which occurred in the contest between H. S. Lunn and T. B. Moffat for the office of Auditor for the session 1886–87, gave rise to a lot of unpleasantness. A letter received by T. S. C. Dagg from the late Rev. Canon Lyster refers to this incident:

In 1886 there was a very bitter contest for the Auditorship between
T. B. Moffat and H. S. Lunn, now Sir Henry Lunn, which aroused more
heated feelings than I have ever known on such a matter. Lunn was a rather
aggressive Englishman, and was unpopular with a section of the members. At
that time a White Cross Association for the promotion of social purity had
just been formed in College, and Lunn was a member of the committee.
Scandalous lies were told about Lunn in connection with this in order to
influence the electors. Moffat himself had nothing to say to this, — he would
have been utterly incapable of anything dishonourable. In the end Moffat was
elected by a considerable majority. The feeling against Lunn went so far that,
during his absence from College, his rooms in No. 26 were forcibly entered,
and the furniture broken up.

Lunn relates these occurrences at some length:

The story of the Home Rule movement had led me away from my life in
College. At the end of my second year I was elected Treasurer of the
Theological Society, and had secured the oratory medal and the President's
prize essay for the year; I was elected Secretary of the Historical Society, and
President of the University Temperance Society. At that moment it seemed
that the blue ribbon of University life — the Chairmanship or as it was
called 'the Auditorship' of the Historical Society, which corresponds to the
'Unions' of Oxford and Cambridge — was within my reach, but I was to
have a proof of the truth that Thomas à Kempis puts thus: 'They say that to-
day take thy part, to-morrow may be against thee, and often do they turn
round like the wind'. It was a lesson for life.

What happened was truly Irish. The well-known son of a very well-known
father went to the rooms of the Historical Society one day and said 'I'm going
to sit here day after day and tell lies about Lunn till he is beaten for the
Auditorship.' He then started a number of legends which had no foundation
whatever in fact, mainly bearing on my relation to the Purity Society, with
which I had nothing whatever to do, except having given the inaugural
address. He depicted me in graphic terms taking a dark lantern to
Mecklenburg Street, a notorious street in Dublin, and turning it on the faces
of men who were going to certain houses. The story flew round the University

that I had been the means of the dismissal from the Bank of Ireland of two highly respectable clerks whom I had met in this street. A letter from the Secretary of the Bank of Ireland, stating that no clerks had been dismissed, did not kill the rumour. As the year went on the excess of popularity which had led to my being elected to the posts named above was steadily vanishing. I was pelted with eggs. My rooms were screwed up one Saturday night, and I was due to preach on the Sunday. I descended by a ladder and took my service, putting the ladder in W. M. Crook's rooms for the day, and returned to my bed at night. The next day the carpenter came and extracted screws about eight inches long with the heads knocked off.

Finally while I was away on the Home Rule campaign, the loyalist student 'moonlighters', as they proudly called themselves, broke into my rooms, passed a unanimous resolution consigning me and Parnell to the Abyss, destroyed my furniture, broke my pictures up, cut my bedding to pieces, and poured oil from my lamp on it. They stopped when they realized that if they lit it they might burn half Trinity down. . . .

It will be judged from these incidents that my candidature for the Chair of the Historical Society . . . was not successful, and I was defeated by a considerable majority by a man whom I had beaten by a large majority the year before for the Secretaryship.

The President's gold medal for composition presented at the beginning of the session 1887–88, was won by Douglas Hyde, and the silver medal by William Moore.

In the Committee minutes of 13 February 1889 we find the following letter from the President referring again to the rights of the Chairman:

I shall be very glad to take the chair at the Historical Society on the 13th, unless something unforeseen prevents me. I do not know whether any change has recently been made, but amongst the rules some time ago was one reserving all points of order for the Auditor or pro-Auditor. If this rule is still in existence it would be well to have it re-considered. It is open to obvious objection. It is opposed to the general practice of Parliament and Societies. Whoever is in the chair should have the power and the discretion to control and guide the meeting, and he could, whenever he thought desirable, speak to the Auditor. In my own case the rule is simply absurd. I am the President of the Society and Lord Chancellor of Ireland, with abundant experience of both Houses of Parliament, being also an ex-Auditor, and yet a pro-Auditor could over my head (and it might be against my clear opinion) declare what was order. I pointed out these clear considerations on a former occasion, but, I suppose owing to a change of officers, nothing may have been done.

The Committee after some discussion directed the Correspondence Secretary 'to inform his Lordship that they regretted the anomaly existing at present, but that, inasmuch as the Society refused to sanction any alteration in the rule referred to when the subject was discussed two years ago, they were powerless in the matter'.

In his inaugural address entitled 'Oratory in the University and in Public Life', at the opening meeting on 9 November 1892, the Auditor, F. Leopold Leet, claimed further recognition from the governing body of the College of the functions discharged by the Society:

So far back as the year 1858, you, my Lord President, then Auditor, endeavoured to obtain for the Society's medals and prizes a more immediate University prestige, and suggested the advantage of associating the Professorship of Oratory with the functions of the Society. At that time the Professorship was held by Dr. Ingram, who was also a Vice-President of the Society, and it seemed not unlikely that the suggestion would be taken up. Perhaps it was, and then put on the shelf for further consideration. But whatever may have been its fate, it is a matter for regret that the specific business of the Society does not receive the same official sanction which is accorded to the various desiderata of the College curriculum.

The inaugural address of the Auditor, F. N. Greer, at the opening meeting of the 124th session on 8 November 1893, referred to the unique position of the Society:

. . . kindred associations in other Universities are located in palatial buildings; they are equipped with every luxury and comfort that can be devised; but we have no barbaric opulence, no splendour of external decoration on which to

*pride ourselves: our sole boast is in our vigorous existence for 123 years
through good report and ill, in the names of our founders and those who have
since cast a lustre on our Society, our University, and our country. . . .*

The question 'That the establishment of a Dublin University Union is
desirable' was debated in January and was decided in the affirmative by a
majority of one vote.

On 7 February 1894 the Correspondence Secretary was instructed to
write to Lord Ashbourne asking him to take the chair at an extraordinary
meeting to be held to consider how the interests of the Society would be
affected by the proposed Union Building, and on the following night he was
directed to write to the Graduates' Memorial Committee inquiring what
steps they had taken in regard to the proposed building to preserve the
separate individuality of the College Historical Society.

An extraordinary general meeting of the Society was held in the front hall
on Wednesday afternoon, 4 April 1894, Lord Ashbourne, the President of
the Society in the chair, when the following resolutions were passed
unanimously:

*Moved by Lord Justice Fitzgibbon, seconded by Professor Cherry: 'That in
any scheme for the establishment of a Dublin University Union the
Independent and separate existence of the College Historical Society, and its
traditions, should be preserved.'*

It was also moved by Mr Justice Madden, seconded by J. H. Campbell, and
supported by the Auditor: 'That the Society desires an opportunity of
considering any scheme for the formation of an Union before it receives the
final sanction of the University Authorities.'

On 4 December 1895 the following resolution was passed: 'That the
sub-Committee appointed to watch over the interests of the Society in the
matter of the Graduates' Memorial scheme be, and is hereby, thanked for
their services, and be hereby dissolved.'

The Auditor for the session 1896–97, Beauclerk Upington, hailed from
South Africa, and the destiny of that country was the subject of his address.
Lecky was one of the speakers at the meeting, and gave his impressions of
President Kruger:

They (the Transvaal Boers) have at their head a man who, with greatly superior abilities, represents very faithfully their character, ideals, and wishes. I can speak of him with some personal knowledge. He has been more than once in my house, and I have come in contact with several men who have known him well. In many respects he resembles strikingly the stern Puritan warrior of the Commonwealth — a strong stubborn man, with indomitable courage and resolution, with very little tinge of cultivation, but, with a rare natural shrewdness in judging men and events, he impresses all who come in contact with him with the extraordinary force of his nature. He is the father of no less than seventeen children. He belongs to a sect called the Doppers, which is derived from the Dutch word for an extinguisher, because they are desirous of extinguishing all novelties since the Synod of Dort. Ardently religious, he is said to believe as strongly as Wesley in a direct personal inspiration guiding him in his acts. He is a great hunter of the most savage wild beasts. One finger is wanting on one of his hands; it was broken in a hunting expedition, and it is a characteristic trait that he then and there amputated it himself. In a semi-regal position, and with even more than regal power, he lives the life of a peasant; and though, I believe, a just, wise, and strong man, he has all his countrymen's dread of an immigration of an alien element, and all their dislike and suspicion of an industrial and mining community.

The Rev. T. A. Finlay, F.R.U.I., occupied the chair when the motion 'That a Catholic University should be established in Ireland' was debated and was carried in the affirmative. Standish O'Grady presided at the debate on the motion 'That Dickens is the greatest novelist of the century', which was decided in the negative. Timothy Harrington, M.P., occupied the chair when the motion 'That the career and conduct of Daniel O'Connell are worthy of our admiration' was discussed, and was decided in the affirmative.

In February 1897 prizes of £10.10s.0d and £5.5s.0d were offered by Edward Carson, M.P., for the best essay and second-best essay on Queen Victoria's reign. Two essays were received and forwarded to Carson, and the prizes were awarded to J. de B. Saunderson and E. H. Kenny.

BURKE CENTENARY

On 9 November 1897, the day before the date fixed for the opening meeting, a letter was received from the President stating that as this was the centenary year of the death of Edmund Burke, the Auditor's address must therefore be on that subject. The Auditor thereupon obtained from the College Library biographies and numerous other books relating to Burke, and working all through the night, assisted by the Record Secretary (R. R. Smylie) searching the volumes for information as required, he completed his address in time for the meeting.

The Burke Memorial Banquet was held in the Dining Hall of the College on 7 December 1897. Some interesting details about the banquet is given in the *Memoir of Lecky* already referred to:

The year of 1897 was the centenary of the death of Burke. Lecky's study of Burke was fresh in the memory of those who had read his 'History of the Eighteenth Century', and when Dublin University resolved to commemorate the centenary of one of its greatest alumni, the Provost asked Lecky to propose the memory of Burke on the occasion, and he could not refuse. On 7th December a State Banquet was given in the dining hall of Trinity College, at which the Provost, Dr. Salmon, presided and the Lord Lieutenant was present. Burke's fine portrait had been transferred from the examination hall, and placed wreathed in palms, before the guests. There was a magnificent display of flowers and Old College silver on the table, and the Doctors in their red gowns gave much colour to the scene. But the chief interest was the speaking, which was, as usual on such occasions in Ireland, of a very high order.

The following is an extract from Lecky's speech on that occasion:

But Burke certainly owed much to us. In that charming picture of Irish eighteenth century life, the Leadbeater Papers, you will find many letters to the son of his old school-master, written from this place describing his life here. We claim him as the founder of our Historical Society, and it was certainly here that he first practised the art of debating, of which he became so great a master.

On the visit of Queen Victoria to Ireland in 1900 an illuminated address was presented to Her Majesty by the voluntary societies and clubs of

Trinity College. The first signatory to the address was that of the Auditor, E. V. Longworth.

The address of John Edward Walsh, Auditor, at the opening meeting of the session 1900–01 was entitled 'Trinity College in the Nineteenth Century', and in the preamble he makes the following reference to the new Graduates' Memorial Building:

We await with some anxiety the announcement of the regulations which are to control this 'Union'. . . . The importance of the Society to the University was well pointed out by Professor Mahaffy, when proposing 'Long Life and prosperity to the College Historical Society' at the banquet given in this Hall, in 1897, to the memory of our great founder, Edmund Burke. 'At no time,' said the learned Professor, 'was it more important to have in this University a Society which keeps alive the sacred flame, which strives to save Ireland from the disgrace of losing one of her brightest qualities which holds aloft the beacon of eloquence and the surge of over-instructed and stammering mediocrity.

Lecky was one of the speakers, and the *Memoir* by his wife contains a brief reference to the meeting and his speech:

Lecky had promised to attend the opening meeting of the Historical Society, and when that body met on 7th November, he found himself once more with two old friends and fellow gold-medallists — the Lord Chancellor, Lord Ashbourne, and Lord Justice Fitzgibbon. The subject for discussion was Trinity College in the nineteenth century. Lecky said in the course of his speech that there was no institution which was so closely connected with all that was best and most illustrious in Irish intellectual life.

The address delivered by the Auditor, James Andrews, at the opening meeting of the session 1902–03, was on 'Imperial Federation', and the speakers were James H. M. Campbell, ex-Auditor, Vice-President, at that time Solicitor-General for Ireland; Winston Churchill, M.P., the Rev. T. A. Finlay, and the Rt Hon. Lord Justice Fitzgibbon. His Royal Highness the Duke of Connaught also addressed the meeting.

Left: Rt Hon. Gerald Fitzgibbon Lord Justice of Appeal from the painting in the University Club by courtesy of the Committee

Above: Provost John Pentland Mahaffy

It is one of the privileges attaching to my office to congratulate past members of the Society upon the distinctions which they have recently won. The Right Hon. W. E. H. Lecky has been enrolled as one of the original members of the Order of Merit; Sir Robert Anderson has been created a Knight Commander of the Bath; the Hon. Sir Frederick M. Darley has been elected a Knight Grand Cross of the Order of St. Michael and St. George; and Mr Justice Ross has been appointed a member of His Majesty's Privy Council in Ireland.

On 26 November 1902, on the proposal of the Auditor, seconded by the Treasurer, the Record Secretary was directed to write to the Oxford and Cambridge Unions inviting them to a joint debate to be held in Dublin in 1903.

On 18 February 1903 a letter was received from Mr H. Asquith stating that the representatives of the Oxford Union Society would be F. W. Curran (Lincoln), ex-Librarian, and H. Thorpe (Wadham), Junior Treasurer. The debate was held in March, and the following letters from the Provost and Dr Mahaffy, referring to the visitors, appear in the Committee minutes:

Provost's House,
Trinity College.
4th March, 1903

Dear Mr Fitz-Gerald,
I forgot to say anything to you about Dr. Mahaffy's willingness to give
bedrooms to your other two guests. If it can be availed of I think it would be
the pleasantest way. Dr. M. had a nasty fall which has given him a shake,
but I should hope he would be well enough to talk to you to-morrow. The
only difficulty he made was that which I felt myself, namely about keeping
my servant up to a very late hour. The difficulty would be all the more
because if they were leaving by the early mail boat the servants would have to
be up early to let them away. I dare say he and I could give our guests a latch
key for each couple; and I hope you would not carry Irish hospitality to
excessive lengths. I don't think that men who do not take their meals at a
hotel are very welcome there, and we could give them here everything but
bedrooms.

Very sincerely yours,
Geo. Salmon

1, T.C.D.

Dear Sir,

I have offered to the Provost to give two of your English visitors beds in my
house here in College. They will have breakfast with the P., and I suppose
lunch in the Common Room. But if they arrive at 9 p.m. to-morrow evening
and want supper I can't manage it as my house in town is wrecked and some
of us sick. So some of you must look to that. No doubt the P. would give all
four supper, I can supply them with a latch key, provided some of you will
escort them to my rooms, and see that they enter quietly and soberly.

I am so sorry I am so laid up that I cannot help personally.

Yours sincerely,
J. P. Mahaffy

The joint debate took place on Friday, 6 March at 8.30 p.m., the subject chosen being 'That this House disapproves of the principle of Party Government'.

W. E. H. Lecky died on 22 October 1903 and a resolution of regret and sympathy was sent to Mrs Lecky. The following is an extract from an 'In Memoriam' notice in *T.C.D.*, 9 November 1903:

Entering College in the late fifties, Lecky made the Historical Society his sole intellectual exercising ground, and soon made his mark as a fluent debater. In 1895 he was elected member for the University in Parliament, where 'his transparent honesty and his manifest indifference to all posts and emoluments made him trusted even by politicians'.

Subjects discussed during the session 1904–05 included 'That Misgovernment justifies rebellion', decided in the affirmative; 'That the growth of State interference with private rights is to be deplored', decided in the affirmative; 'That the principles of the '48 Movement in Ireland are no longer applicable to Irish politics', decided in the negative; 'That the recall of Lord Fitzwilliam in 1795 was justifiable', decided in the negative; 'That the abolition of the Vice-royalty in Ireland is desirable', decided in the affirmative.

OXFORD

IN DECEMBER THE COMMITTEE agreed to accept the invitation of the Oxford Union Society to an inter-debate to be held at Oxford in the following February. The report of the debate, extending over almost two columns, which appeared in the *Oxford Review* of 18 February 1905 makes interesting reading. H. L. Murphy, who was the opening speaker on the negative, spoke for about twenty minutes:

. . . apart from the pleasure he and his companions had in being present at the debate of that Society, they had a special pleasure in being able to discuss a political question, because during the last hundred years political speeches had been completely debarred in the Dublin Society.

The assertion that the conduct of the Irish Parliamentary Party was not conducive to the best interests of Ireland seemed to him to be a strong and sweeping statement, and one which must go far to shake one's ideas with regard to popular institutions and representative government.

. . . It was said by a member of Mr Isaac Butt's party that it was the duty of Irishmen to be gentlemen first and patriots afterwards. Personally, his firm conviction was that in the case of Ireland it was the duty of a man to think first of his own country and afterwards of his own self-respect and dignity — (applause). Those who opposed the motion could not rely on facts for doing so. In the last twenty years what had the Irish Party done? When Parnell first started the idea of an Independent Party the Irish peasant was little better than a serf, now he was, at any rate, a free man. Ireland was then honeycombed with secret societies, and crime was rampant throughout the land; now they had hope and trust in the future.

Land reform had been secured for the people, and whatever the mover of the motion said, it must be remembered that the tenant farmer represented the wealth and the dominant class of the country. The crowning piece of all, the gaining of Ireland's political independence, they trusted the Irish Party to obtain. It should be stated that during its career the Irish Nationalist Party had trusted to the fairness and justice of England, and to the great forces of Liberalism which were working in this country. The demand of the Irish people was one which, when obtained, would result in Ireland taking her place amongst the great nations of the world.

Another report which appeared in the *Oxford Magazine* of 22 February was prefaced by the following paragraph:

The debate last Thursday was by far the most interesting of the Term. For the first time, we believe, in the history of the Union, it was visited by delegates from the Historical Society, Trinity College, Dublin, an institution which dates back to 1770, more than half a century before the foundation of the Oxford Union. The delegates displayed that eloquence which we associate with Irish speakers, and those members who were present were rewarded by an admirable debate.

*Officers and Committee 1905–6, back left to right: M. H. Meeredy, M. C. Green Librarian,
J. H. G. Brookes, R. J. Maunsell, H. S. B. Taylor Correspondence Secretary, H. L. Cowdy
ex-Auditor; seated middle left to right: T. S. C. Dagg Treasurer, H. L. Murphy Auditor,
J. G. Dougherty; seated front: D. L. C. Dunlop, R. J. H. Shaw*

The memorial to Lecky took the form of a statue, the work of John
Goscombe, R.A., which was unveiled in 1906 by Lecky's old friend and
predecessor as Member for the University, David Plunket, Lord Rathmore.
In his peroration Lord Rathmore said:

> . . . *Yonder stand the statues of Oliver Goldsmith and Edmund Burke, the
> warders of our gate, and close at hand, in the thronging thoroughfare, the
> effigy of Henry Grattan, illumined through the genius of Foley with all the
> fire of patriotism. It is well that here within these academic courts should rest
> the monument of another, not less illustrious in his time than they were in
> theirs, the patient, the indefatigable student, the philosopher, the orator, the
> historian, who re-wrote the annals and vindicated the character of his
> countrymen, that future generations of students within these walls, looking
> upon this memorial, should be stirred to follow his example and gather hope
> and courage from his career to win success and renown for themselves, to
> render faithful service to their country, as he did, and add fresh honours to
> the name and fame of old Trinity.*

The Auditor, T. S. C. Dagg, announced in his inaugural address in 1906
that the dispute between the College Societies and the Board regarding the
occupation of the Graduates Memorial Building had been settled:

It is with profound satisfaction that I am able to state that a solution of the difficulties in regard to the Graduates' Memorial Buildings has now been agreed to by the Governing Body of the College, on the lines originally recommended by our Society and the University Philosophical Society. However much we may regret that this arrangement was not adopted in the first instance — a course of action which would have saved considerable and, as it now appears, unnecessary expenses to the two Societies — we are confident that it is the one which will work for the benefit not only of the College Historical Society, but of the whole body of Students in the University.

UNIVERSITY & STATE

THE AUDITOR'S ADDRESS WAS on the subject 'The University and the State', and the passage referring to the Royal Commission was as follows:

It is not surprising to us in Trinity College that amongst the multitude of statements placed before the present Royal Commission only one contains any suggestion as to the representation of the students on the Governing Body; but what does appear to call for some comment is that the invitations for evidence on behalf of the Commission, which have been so liberally distributed amongst all other classes throughout the country, failed to reach any students representative organization within the walls of this College. The question under consideration is one which would seem to concern ultimately the welfare of Irish University students, and, despite the fact that these may not be in a position to regard College life through the lengthy telescope of half a century, their opinion on the subject might perhaps be of some value. We are not without experience ourselves of the injurious effects which have resulted from ignoring students' opinion on matters which entirely concern them; and the Irish Undergraduate may regard the provisions about to be made for his supposed welfare with somewhat the same feelings of mingled hope and apprehension as those with which the patient watches the drug which the apothecary is compounding for him, ignorant of its contents, but in a slightly better position in that he at least has been asked for symptoms of his ailment.

The Auditor was directed to write to J. H. M. Campbell, M.P. (member for Dublin University) requesting him to ask in Parliament why the

College Historical Society had not been invited to give evidence before the Commission.

On 1 May 1907 the following motion, proposed by the Auditor, seconded by the Treasurer, was passed in silence:

That the members of the College Historical Society have heard with deep regret of the death of John Kells Ingram, LL.D., D.Litt., ex-Vice Provost of Trinity College, Dublin, and a Vice-President of this Society since 1856, and they desire to express their sympathy with his relatives in their bereavement; and further that the Society do now adjourn as a mark of respect to his memory.

A letter was received from Dr Ingram's son, W. Alex. Ingram, in which he stated: 'It is a source of sincere gratification to all of us to know that we have in our great loss the sympathy of a Society in which my father was so much interested during so many years.'

On 6 February 1907 the Committee decided to hold a debate on 27 February on the subject of 'The present University proposals' and the Record Secretary was instructed to communicate with the Board with a view to obtaining their sanction.

About a month later the following letter was received from R. H. Gwynn, F.T.C.D.:

> *Dublin University Defence Committee,*
> *40, Trinity College,*
> *Dublin*
> *8/3/07*

> *Dear Sir,*
> *I am instructed by the Provost, at the request of the Organising Committee, (1) to say that if the C.H.S. desire to hold a meeting in order to pass resolutions (with set speakers not in the ordinary method of debate) in defence of the University in the present crisis, they should write to himself (if possible stating details, such as the resolutions and speakers proposed — this may however be done subsequently) personally and obtain from him the sanction required; and that he himself would regard such a meeting with approval*

whether held by the C.H.S. separately or (as he suggests in order to get a mass meeting of students) in conjunction with the Philosophical and other College Societies, and that he would grant the use of the Examination Hall or Dining Hall.

(2) To request the co-operation of the C.H.S. in the Graduates' meeting for the 22nd (a) in obtaining speakers, should it prove necessary to provide a second platform for an 'over-flow' meeting in the Dining Hall or G.M.B., (b) in providing and organizing stewards.

The Defence Committee trust that you will bring these requests before your Society's committee at the earliest opportunity, and hope that they may count on your support in the effort to enable the University by the end of term to have uttered a clear and unmistakable protest by the voices of all its members, so that the Bill which is expected before next term has far advanced may find us united and ready.

Yours faithfully,
R. M.. Gwynn,
Sec. Org. Committee

On 9 December 1908 Sir Maurice O'Rorke, M.A., LL.D., was elected a Vice-President of the Society, and on 12 May the following letter from him was received:

University College,
Auckland, N.Z.
25th March, 1909.
W. L. Murphy, Esq.,
Rec. Sec., Coll. Hist. Soc.

Dear Sir,
I was very much surprised but gratified by your note of 18th December ulto., announcing my election as a Vice-President of your famous Society. I call it famous as I have always understood it was founded by the great Edmund Burke. I have no idea to whom I owe thanks for the honour conferred on me.

I have only paid one visit to my beloved native land since I left it for Australia in 1852 immediately on taking my B.A. degree. My M.A. I did not obtain till 1896 when the University also honoured me with an LL.D., I fear I shall never again see my Alma Mater, but I would take a run home if I were to see the Members of Parliament for Ireland entering their old chamber and bowing in reverence to the paintings of Grattan, Curran, and Plunket, the champions of their race in its dying struggle for the protection and preservation of the Irish Race. You may imagine how shocked I was on my visit to my native land in 1896 to find that the population of that unfortunate country had fallen from some nine millions in '52 to four and a half millions in 1896.

Such is the result of what the dominant partner of poor Erin calls paternal government!

I trust the Almighty will some day redress the wrongs of my unfortunate country.

Yours faithfully,
G. Maurice O'Rorke

On 1 December 1909 the following note of motion was handed in: 'That the sum of £5 be granted by this Society towards the cost of the National Monument which is to be erected in Dublin to the memory of Theobald Wolfe Tone (ex-Auditor) on the understanding that the Society's contribution is expended solely on the proposed monument.' Proposed by T. S. C. Dagg (ex-Auditor), and seconded by A. P. I. Samuels (Treasurer). On the following night when the motion came up for discussion, J. G. Dougherty (ex-Auditor) called attention to a report in the press that the Treasurer of the Memorial Fund had absconded with the subscriptions that had been received, and the motion was in consequence withdrawn.

At the meeting on 12 November 1912 the following notice of motion was handed in: 'That this Society disapproves of any legislation which would tend to separate Trinity College from the rest of Ireland, believing such legislation opposed to the best interests of their University and this Society.' Proposed by E. M. Stephens, seconded by C. S. Power. At the meeting on 20 November the pro-Auditor (Arthur C. Davies) declared the motion to be out of order, whereupon D. Coffey proposed that the House do now adjourn to consider the conduct of the pro-Auditor in refusing to accept the motion. The motion for adjournment was carried on a division, and the House adjourned accordingly. On the following night, on the suspension of Standing Orders, the following motion proposed by T. S. C. Dagg, ex-Auditor, seconded by J. H. Monroe, ex-Auditor, was carried unanimously: 'That the recent publication of the proceedings at the private business of the Society in the daily press is unprecedented, and is to be condemned, and that any member communicating to the Press, directly or indirectly, is guilty of a gross breach of confidence, and of conduct dishonourable to the traditions of the Society, and which renders him liable to expulsion.' During the discussion of the motion the House was informed that a representative of the newspaper in which the report had appeared was outside the Hall, and had asked whether he might be furnished with a report of the proceedings. Another member immediately proposed a motion to adjourn the House in order that the members might put the intruder under the pump, but after some discussion wiser counsels prevailed, the motion was rejected, and the newspaper representative departed in blissful ignorance of the fate which had threatened him.

During the session 1913–14 the following motion proposed by B. St J. Galvin, seconded by Kevin E. O'Duffy, was rejected by twenty-nine votes to thirteen:

'That the Correspondence Secretary be instructed to write to the various Parliamentary leaders to secure that the College Historical Society shall be granted the privilege of a special gallery in the Irish House of Commons in the event of the Government of Ireland Bill being made law.'

On 3 June 1914 Charles L. Matheson, K.C., First Sergeant-at-Law, and Douglas Hyde, LL.D., President of the Gaelic League, were elected Vice-Presidents.

WAR & 'REBELLION'

THE EUROPEAN WAR BROKE OUT in August 1914, and at a Committee meeting held on 10 September the following resolutions were passed:

'That the inaugural meeting be postponed indefinitely.'

'That the Librarian be empowered to make arrangements concerning the use of the rooms by the gentlemen now in military training in the College Park, at a small subscription.'

C. S. Mullan was appointed pro-Correspondence Secretary during the absence of B. St J. Galvin, and J. H. Magowan was appointed pro-Librarian during the absence of Kevin E. O'Duffy, and before the end of the year many further changes became necessary.

On Easter Monday, 24 April 1916, at noon, the Sinn Fein Rebellion burst forth in Dublin.

One of the cadets of the Officers' Training Corps who took part in the defence was T. C. K. Moore, who was Record Secretary of the Historical Society at the time. In the following term he was Editor of *T.C.D.*, and in his first editorial he made reference to the Rebellion:

Front Square, Trinity College, during the Easter Rising in 1916 from Supplement to T.C.D. 19 June 1916

Trinity has never passed a more anxious moment than on that fateful first night of the rebellion, when the houses held by the enemy loomed ominously over the low building, where a handful of students watched and waited for an attack; while the tramp of rebel feet and the sound of rebel challenges came clearly through the darkness; while the outposts of the enemy rattled the gates of the College. They were not attacked: perhaps it was the vigilance of the defenders, perhaps the Sinn Fein leaders were ignorant of the small numbers of the garrison. Yet we cannot help cherishing the hope that our College was defended by something even more powerful than rifles and bayonets, and that the honoured fame of our University made the rebels loath to attack it. The love of Trinity and the pride in it are the heritage of all Irishmen, and whatever be the form of our government, whatever the party in power, we believe that they will regard our College as one of Ireland's greatest possessions.

On 20 July 1916 the Board made a grant of £25 to the funds of the Society, and in the following December they awarded £5 as compensation for chairs removed during the military occupation.

The Peace Inaugural Meeting of the Society for the 149th session was held in the Dining Hall on Wednesday, 29 January 1919. In his address the Auditor, T. C. Kingsmill Moore, stated that as no Opening Meeting had been held since November 1913, it devolved on him to present a report of the affairs of the Society extending over some five years.

The subject of the Auditor's address was 'Socialism and the War', and the speakers were His Grace the Lord Primate, Professor W. Alison Phillips, Mr W. B. Yeats and Mr Thomas Johnson. A supper was held after the meeting to which the Provost, the President of the Society (the Rt Hon. Sir John Ross, Bart.), the four speakers and the officers of the Society were invited.

The Committee, at their meeting on 7 May decided that all customary medals be awarded this year.

Statements submitted by the Treasurer showed that the Society was in a sound financial condition.

The following letter from the Provost was read at the Committee on 23 April:

Could you give any facilities to American students to read in your rooms till your members come back, and you can elect them if you choose. They are strange here and wandering about — Come and see me.

V. Sincerely,
J. P. Mahaffy

An invitation was sent immediately to the officers and men of the American Army residing in College offering them the use of the Society's rooms so long as they remained in College. The invitation stated: 'It may perhaps be founded by Edmund Burke, the great champion of the rights of the American Colonies during their struggle with the Mother Country.'

At the meeting of the Committee on 3 December 1919 the following letter from the Honorary Secretary of T.C.D. was read:

3rd December, 1919

Sir,
At a shareholders' meeting of T.C.D. it having been brought up that the question of precedence of the College Historical Society was not carried out, the following motion was passed unanimously:-

Yours faithfully,
William Starkie, Hon. Sec.

That the shareholders of the T.C.D. Publishing Company do regret that the customary order of precedence due to the College Historical Society has been lately neglected owing to mistakes of printers, and do hereby authorise and confirm the usage both in the Society reports and in the lists of fixtures, of the order of precedence in the introduction to the College Calendar.

THE
SOCIETY'S RECORDS

The Society has always retained records of its proceedings. A selection from the archives is given in this section.

BURKE'S MINUTE BOOK 1747

A full transcript of the minute book is given by A. P. Samuels: The Early Life, Writings and Correspondence of the Right Hon. Edmund Burke.

When the Society adjourned in 1815 and left College, it took with it the journals and other records, including the minute book of Burke's Club. Walter Berwick, who was Treasurer of the Society when it was revived outside College in 1820, had the book in his library, and said that he had picked it up on the quays for a few pence. It remained in Berwick's library until 1868, when he was killed in a railway accident, and it was probably dispersed with his other books. In 1877 it was discovered by Walter Fitzwillam Starkie, Secretary, in a second-hand bookshop, and was restored by him to the library of the Society, where it remained until the 1960s, when it disappeared for a number of years. It is now in the College Library for safekeeping.

April the 21st 1747

Being assembled in George's Lane, the Club proceeded to the chusing a President by lot, which was done, the seniority being determined as follows

Mr Mohun, President
Mr Dennis, Secretary
Mr Burke
Mr Buck

A fundamental law for the club propos'd, but not determin'd.

Voted, whether each member shall produce a system of Laws for the approbation of the Assembly which was agreed on accordingly.

Accusation for Lampoon

Mr Buck accus'd for Lampooning Mr Kinselah by Mr Burke, answer'd by Mr Buck who pleas, that the Assembly had no right to trie him. Mr Burke replies. Mr Buck rejoins, with this plea, that as the crime was committed out of the Assembly, it did not properly come under their cognizance therefore, they had no right either to accuse or condemn him. The President determines in his favour. Mr Burke declares against his determination, and maintains that the crime was committed in the assembly. Mr Buck replies and Mr Dennis backs him with this plea, that it was no crime that Mr Burke accus'd him off, that it was not committed in the assembly, and lastly that He approved of the lampoon, and by accusing Mr Buck, was liable to accusation for ill nature. Mr Burke answers, but is interrupted by Mr President who dissannuls the accusation.

Accusation of scurrility

Mr Buck accuses Burke of scurrility, is answered by him. The Assembly dismiss'd till Friday the 24th of April at which time Mr Dennis is appointed to speak an 'oration on Ld Lovat', and Mr Burke to deliver an essay on society.

PETITION TO THE BOARD OF TRINITY COLLEGE DUBLIN 1825

In September 1902 the late Dr H. C. Bailey, then Registrar, kindly allowed T. S. C. Dagg to make a copy of the Petition presented to the Board in 1825. It reads:

To

The Reverend and Learned

The Provost and Senior Fellows

of

Trinity College Dublin

We, the Undersigned Graduates and Undergraduates, deeply sensitive of the anxiety, ever evinced by your reverend and learned Board for the advancement of the Students in the different branches of useful knowledge, and humbly hoping that our present unrivalled state of discipline may be received as an evidence of our dispositions, and as a pledge that we shall in all cases, continue to render a strict obedience to any regulations that your Reverend and Learned Board may judge it expedient to prescribe — humbly solicit the permission of your Reverend and Learned Board to form within the College under such rules and regulations as your Reverend and Learned Board may impose, An Historical Society, for the purpose of improving our knowledge of Modern History and acquiring that facility in Composition and Speaking which the nature of our future Professions imperatively requires.

The following text appears on the folder containing the petition

Notice:

Such gentlemen as are desirous of signing the Petition to the Board for leave to form an Historical Society in College are requested to call at the Room No. 13, 3rd left, where the petition is now lying for signature from ten o'clock a.m. till eleven, and from four o'clock till five and after Night Roll —

Gentlemen are particularly requested not to tear down this notice
— March 31st, 1825.

This petition was granted to the College Historical Society on condition that it was publicly displayed and kept in good repair.[7]

Of the 227 signatories 1 was a Fellow, 7 afterwards became Fellows, and 75 were Graduates, of whom 62 were Scholars at the time of the Petition. Among the signatories were John Gregg (afterwards Bishop of Cork), Joseph Napier (afterwards Lord Chancellor), Charles Lever (Novelist), and Gerald Fitzgibbon (afterwards Master in Chancery).

The decision of the Board is recorded in the following minute:

'April 9th, 1825. An application (by Memorial) to the Board by a great number of students having this day been presented, the Board directed the Regr. to communicate that the Board do not consider it expedient to accede to their request to have a debating Historical Society formed by the students.'

In a footnote at the end of his Address Napier mentions that fifteen out of the seventeen Junior Fellows then in College offered any assistance in their powers to forward the prayer of the Petition.

MEMORIAL TO THE BOARD 1902

TO
THE BOARD OF TRINITY COLLEGE, DUBLIN.

A MEMORIAL
FROM
The President, Vice-Presidents, Members, and Past Members of
The College Historical Society.

Supported by others interested in the welfare of the Society.

---

[7]   There is a discrepancy between the note on the folder and the Board's minute; one says the petition was accepted, the other says it was rejected.

At an extraordinary general Meeting of the College Historical Society held on Wednesday afternoon, the 4th of April, 1894, the Right Hon. the Lord Chancellor, President, in the Chair, the following resolutions were adopted:—

It was proposed by Lord Justice Fitzgibbon, and seconded by Professor Cherry, Q.C.:

'That, in the scheme for the establishment of a Dublin University Union, the independent and separate existence of the College Historical Society and its traditions should be preserved.'

It was proposed by Mr Justice Madden, seconded by J. H. M. Campbell, Q.C., and supported by the Auditor:
'That the Society desires an opportunity for considering any scheme for the formation and management of such an institution before it receives the final sanction of the University authority.'

The distinctive features which characterise the Society as an 'independent and separate' body are briefly as follows:-

In the first place it is a Debating Society:

As such the 'Historical' still maintains its pre-eminent position. The appendices to the Auditor's addresses, setting forth the subjects debated, the number of members who have taken part in the discussions, the names of the distinguished Chairmen who have presided at the weekly meetings, and who have frequently expressed their appreciation of the high standard of speaking, bear ample testimony to this.

In addition to a gold and a silver medal and certificates of proficiency in oratory, the Society annually awards a gold and a silver medal in Composition. The Oratory medal was instituted in the year 1781, the History medal in the year 1777, and the Composition medal, which is now presented by the President, in the year 1770.

The average attendance of members on each night of meeting during the past three sessions has been: session 1899–1900, 33; session 1900–01, 34; and session 1901–02, 48.

In the second place it is a Social Institution:

As such the Society discharges a very important function. It is, in fact, a Club managed by Students for Students, and, like every Club, enjoys the right of electing its members.

For many years following its foundation in 1770 the Society enjoyed the use of the room now known as the Fellows' Common Room for the purposes of a Club; and through a long series of years has, through the generosity of the Provost and Board, occupied the suite of rooms, the use of which it now enjoys, consisting of a reading-room, library and writing-room, smoking-room, committee-room, and lavatory. These rooms afforded its Members many of the conveniences and advantages of a Club, while their position, comfort, and privacy rendered them most suitable for this purpose.

The Society's property includes a library of 1700 volumes, the complete Record of its proceedings from 1770, the original minute-book of the Historical Club, in the handwriting of Edmund Burke, founded in the year 1747; also a variety of manuscripts, paintings, photographs of groups of Officers from 1864, and upwards of fifty portraits or engravings of distinguished old Members.

The Ordinary Members of the Society at the present time number 220, each of whom pays an annual subscription of £1.1s. There are 147 old Members of the Society who have, from time to time, been elected Honorary Members, with the sanction of the Board. They enjoy all the privileges of Ordinary members, excepting the right to share in the government of, and to hold office in, the Society, and are deeply interested in the welfare of the Society, which forms for them a strong link with their old University.

On many occasions the Historical Society has been treated as representing the general body of the Students. At the time of the Tercentenary celebrations in 1892 the Auditors and Secretaries were entrusted by the Board with the duty of forming a committee to organize the celebrations on the Students' part, when, it is believed, this duty was performed with general satisfaction.

The Historical Society has long been regarded as the representative Undergraduate Society of the University by similar Undergraduate Institutions in the sister Universities. By mutual courtesy the Members of the College Historical Society have been considered Honorary Members of the

Speculative Society of Edinburgh since 1783, and of the Union Societies of Oxford, Cambridge, and Durham since the restoration of the Society in 1843; while from 1789 up to that date the rights of membership of the College Historical Society were extended to Graduates of Oxford and Cambridge.

The Graduates' Memorial Buildings have now been completed for upwards of five months. Shortly after the inaugural ceremony, a Report containing suggestions upon possible schemes of management was submitted, on behalf of the Society, to the Board; but, up to the present time, the Society has not been afforded 'an opportunity for considering any scheme for the formation and management of the Institution'.

Experience has shown that the social functions of the Society are a necessary supplement to its position as a Debating Society. As a voluntary Institution the majority of its members are first attracted to the Society by the advantages it offers as a Club. When once elected, many members gradually come to realize the far greater advantages it holds out in the direction of self-culture as a Debating Society. If the Society's permanent existence as such is to be assured, it is absolutely essential that it should be enabled to continue to discharge its social functions as a Club, as it has from the time of its foundation in 1770, and to offer privileges over and above mere membership of a Debating Society.

Your Petitioners therefore pray that in the event of any change in its circumstances in the near future the Society may be placed in a position to maintain its distinctive features as a Debating Society and as a Club, which are mutually essential to its 'independent and separate existence', and thus to continue to enjoy the prestige which it has derived from association with this great and ancient University.

Signed (up to the present date),

Ashbourne, President, C.H.S.

Hedges Eyre Chatterton, Vice-President.

C. Palles, Vice-President.

Gerald Fitzgibbon, Vice-President.

J. G. Gibson, Vice-President.

Edward Carson, Vice-President.

W. E. H. Lecky, Vice-President.

Frederick R. Falkiner, Vice-President.

Geo. A. Derry and Raphoe, Vice-President.

James H. Campbell, Solicitor-General, Ex-Auditor, Vice-President.

Robert Walsh, D.D., Ex-Auditor, Vice-President.

John Ross, Judge of the High Court, Ex-Auditor, Vice-President.

Samuel Walker, Lord Justice of Appeal, Vice-President.

Seymour Bushe, K.C., Vice-President.

The following have already authorised their names to be added:

His Grace the Lord Primate.

His Grace the Archbishop of Dublin.

The Right Hon. Lord Justice Holmes.

The Right Hon. Mr Justice Andrews, LL.D.

The Right Hon. Mr Justice Kenny.

The Hon. Mr Justice Wright.

Arthur Warren Samuels, K.C., LL.D., Hon. Mem.

Miles Kehoe, K.C., Hon. Mem.

J. F. Vesey-Fitzgerald, Hon. Mem.

C. L. Matheson, K.C., Ex-Auditor, Hon. Mem.

R. M. Hennessy, K.C., Hon. Mem.

Charles A. O'Connor, K.C., Ex-Auditor, Hon. Mem.

Alex. F. Blood, K.C., Hon. Mem.

John F. Cooke, K.C., Hon. Mem.

Richard R. Cherry, K.C., LL.D., Ex-Auditor, Hon. Mem.

H. D. Conner, K.C., Hon. Mem.

John Wakely, K.C., Hon. Mem.

William Moore, K.C., M.P., Hon. Mem.

D. F. Browne, K.C.

T. C. Herbert Wilson, K.C., Hon. Mem.

Gerald Fitzgibbon, Jun., Hon. Mem.

Frank N. Greer, Ex-Auditor, Hon. Mem.

November, 1902

OPENING MEETING 1920

Extract from the Minute Book of the College Historical Society

Account of events previous to Opening Meeting (1920)

In order to explain the absence of Mr (late Colonel) Cecil L'Estrange Malone from the Opening Meeting of this Society, the following facts may be recorded.

The suspicions of the Officials of the Society were aroused by various rumours and reports as to whether the Government intended to prevent Mr Malone from addressing the meeting, owing to a speech he was alleged to have made at the Albert Hall, London, on Sunday 7th November 1920, and owing to the present disturbed state of the country. The Provost sent for the Auditor, and he telephoned Dublin Castle to find out if they intended to prohibit Mr Malone from speaking on that evening. The reply was in the negative.

At 7:30 on the day of the Meeting the Auditor, arriving early, met Mr Malone, and they proceeded to the Common Room where the Auditor explained to Mr Malone that the College Historical Society wished to treat the subject of 'Bolshevism' in an academic and not a political manner. Mr Malone said that he understood that.

Just then the Provost arrived and sent the Librarian for the Auditor, the former remaining with Mr Malone in the Common Room. At this time one guest arrived and was introduced to Mr Malone.

About five or six minutes after, a Staff-Major in company with a plain clothes man went into the Common Room, and approaching Mr Malone said 'Mr Malone?' 'I am he,' replied that gentleman. 'You are under arrest, Sir, in connection with a speech you recently made in London,' said the Staff Major, and at the same time the plain clothes man put his hand on Mr Malone's arm, and the Officer sat down at the desk in the corner of the Common Room, and proceeded to write on some papers he had.

The Auditor then came up the stairs and went over to the newly made prisoner and said, 'Of course, Mr Malone, you may be quite sure we did not know anything about this, and I am sure you will not suppose we were leading you into any kind of trap.' Mr Malone took the whole occurrence very well, and said, 'Oh yes, I know that.'

The officer and party of four plain clothes men departed with their prisoner.

Some further remarks have been supplied by Fintan O'Connor, Secretary 1921–22 as follows:

The arrest was of Col. Cecil L'Estrange Malone M.P. (Westminster, of course); It was on the occasion of Barry St.J. Galvin's Auditorship Opening Meeting.

Malone had made a speech a few days earlier in London when he said he hoped the day would soon arrive when all the Cabinet Ministers would be hanging from the lamp posts and the gutters of Downing Street 'would be running with their blood'!

He was a charming fellow and stayed in hiding one night in my rooms on the ground floor of no. 28 in the G.M.B. Cathal O'Shannon (Senior) was one of the few with me in the upstairs Fellows' Room of the Dining Hall when the Provost arrived with Staff Officers from the Castle to arrest him.

DOUGLAS HYDE BECOMES PRESIDENT

A letter to the Society from Douglas Hyde President of Ireland and President of the Society 1931 to 1950.

A Chara,

Excuse the pencil but I cannot leave my bed yet. I was very sorry not to see you when you called the other day about the presidency of the C.H.S.

It is a pity you cannot induce Lord Carson to take it. He would suit admirably. If you cannot get anyone better, and the Society think that I would make a good president, I need not say I would esteem the honour highly, and will do my part to make as good a one as I can, though I know I will be a very poor successor of statesmen and men of affairs like Ashbourne, Ross and Lord Glenavy.

My address after the next fortnight will be: *Ratra House*
    Frenchpark,
    Co. Roscommon

Inaugural Meeting 10 November 1937. From left to right front row: R. Brereton Barry S.C.,
Douglas Hyde President, W. Ivan McCutcheon Auditor; back row: Canon Stuart Harry,
Jim Larkin, Frank McDermott. Photo loaned by Claire McCutcheon, Ivan's daughter and
Senior Member of Committee 1972–73

I am working on the O'Mahony pedigree for one of the clan in London, but I
think he confounds Ó Mathamhna of Munster and Mac Mathghamhna of
Oriel!

Thank you for your subscription to Béaloideas.

Mise le meas mór
An Craoibhín
(Douglas Hyde)

THE LAWS

Since the Laws for Burke's Club were drawn up, the Society has had a meticulous concern for the meaning and application of its Laws. While the issues are internal, the principles learnt are of wide application and have formed the basis for many other sets of rules when Hist members moved to apply their experience in wider spheres.

Many Sub-Committees have laboured to make fine distinctions in the interpretation of the Laws. Two were selected for inclusion here to give a flavour of the genre. The first attempts to define academic nudity, while the second investigates the power of the Auditor to impose fines.

ACADEMIC NUDITY

Gentlemen,

We, your sub-committee appointed to inquire into academic nudity, beg to report as follows.

Being deeply sensible of the gravity of the trust committed to us and its importance in as much as has devolved upon us the duty of deciding the exact custom and tradition of the Society and, in addition, we had the benefit of the vast and well-nigh mythical learning of Mr J. S. Alcorn, whose acquaintance with the subject of nudity is almost unparalleled and whose punctilious respect for decorum has established him as par excellence the academic Mrs Grundy.

Law 4 of the fundamental rules prescribes that annual members shall wear academic dress at meetings of the Society. By the statutes of the University and College, academic dress is defined as a proper gown and cap and hood according to the degree. The meaning, then of the words 'academic dress' is clear and indubitable, but the problem arises, what constitutes academic nudity. Recourse to dictionaries is of little avail. Nudity, it was suggested, may be defined as the entire absence of costume and hence, *a fortiori*, academic nudity is the entire absence of academic costume. That this explanation is unsatisfactory may be demonstrated by a simple example.

A plain, billy-cock hat is without a doubt an article of dress, but, if any man were to appear clad in a billy-cock hat and nought else besides, the law would certainly step in and such a person would be considered to be in a state of nudity for all practical purposes. The problem can best be solved if we consider as relevant the injunction 'Let all things be done decently and in order', an injunction whose high apostolic authority is augmented by its adoption in the advertisements of Queen Elizabeth, 'our Foundress', and its incorporation thereby in English Law. The word 'nudity' had for most people in its subjective intension, if we may use a technical term of the schools, the thought of unseemliness, indecency, and disorder. And hence we may conclude that academic nudity is such absence of academic costume as a reasonable man would consider indecorous or unseemly. And therefore it is requisite, in our opinion as reasonable men, that as a bare minimum every annual member being either bachelor, or scholar of the house, should wear a full, seemly gown, and every annual member being a pensioner or sizar, should wear the customary, lesser gown, commonly called the jib's gown.

Tradition and the plain meaning of the law demand that the gown should be worn visibly and above all other garments. Indeed, that academic dress should be worn visibly beneath other dress by way of lingerie or underwear, is a subversion of the purpose for which such costume was ordained, to wit, the identification of the wearer as a member of the University.

Furthermore, the gown must be a gown. A collection of black rags held together by pins, or a concentration of dark coloured ribbons assembled by cords is not a gown, and any member who attempts to appear in such a costume merits rebuke and punishment.

It is difficult and, indeed, almost impossible to prescribe within exact limits the exact length and breadth that a gown should possess. But we recommend the Auditor should permit no annual member to be present at the meetings of the Society whose gown does not cover at least three-fourths of the total area of his back and does not reach to within at least a hand's breadth from his knee.

Before concluding this report, we desire to express our sorrow that one ancient custom of the Society has been allowed to fall into desuetude. Formerly, all members came to the meetings attired in the square cap that the collegiate statutes prescribe; and during the meeting, they had their caps in close proximity to their persons. This is no longer done. We suggest that the officers, at least, revive this venerable and worthy custom.

We desire to add also that we did not think it necessary to inquire if there were any auditorial rulings *in hac re*. Had there been any such, our learned Auditor would have been *ex officio* acquainted with them and this sub-committee would never have been appointed. Brevity, gentlemen, is the soul of wit, as has been laid down by Shakespeare W. in Hamlet's case, and so we will end by briefly summarising our findings, recommendations, and suggestions:–

(1) That a gown is the very minimum of academic dress.

(2) That the gown must be worn visibly above all other clothing.

(3) That the gown must be of the usual pattern, proper, decent, and seemly, and must cover at least three-fourths of the area of the back and reach to at least within a hand's breadth of the knee.

(4) That it is desirable that officers should bring with them to meetings their caps.

Such, gentlemen, is the conclusion and result of our labours which we commit to you in sure and certain hope that they will not have been in vain, but will bring forth fruit abundantly, some thirty-fold, some forty-fold, and some an hundred-fold.

> (Signed)
> H. E. Woulfe Flanagan.
> R. P. McDermott.
> M. T. Porteus
> [8]Dated this   day of 19

---

[8] The manuscript has no more precise date than this, but R. P. McDermott won a Gold Medal for Oratory in the session 1932–33.

LAWS & PROCEDURES DEALING WITH FINES

Report of the Sub-Committee appointed to enquire into and report on the subject of the Society's laws and procedure in dealing with fines.

Mr Chairman, Mr Auditor, and Gentlemen of the College Historical Society, your sub-committee has held four meetings and interrogated one witness, Mr J. E. Lynch; we have also examined the records of the Society and the Auditors' Ruling book. We have come to the following conclusions:

In the first place, there undoubtedly exists an anomaly between the laws of the Society about fining on the one hand and on the other the custom followed by many Auditors: the only body that is given by the laws unlimited powers of fining is the General Committee, by Law 6 of part 1 of Chapter XI of the Laws. The Auditor is nowhere given unlimited power to fine: in six places in the laws he is given power to fine a fixed sum on a specific occasion; these places are: Law 17 of Chapter V, Law 6 of Chapter IX, Law 7 of Chapter X, Law 4 of Part II of Chapter XII, and Part VI of Law 3 of Chapter XIV. By one law he is given a more extended power of fining, but this too is restricted; we refer to Law 22 of Chapter XII (Part II). It is worth while quoting from this Law: 'If any member on being called to order by the Auditor shall not submit he shall be fined by the Auditor in a sum not exceeding two shillings and sixpence. If having been fined two shillings and sixpence he shall still persist he shall then be fined five shillings.'

This, sir, is an exhaustive account of all the laws which deal with the Auditor's power to fine. It is obvious at once that the extent to which the Auditor exercises his powers of fining at present is quite contrary to the laws; apart from the six statutory instances the Auditor may by the laws only fine for a breach of order: yet in the last session alone the Auditor has fined for such offences as ignorance of the laws, an incorrect count on the part of the balloting officers, and wasting the time of the House, all of which fines are plainly outside the powers of fining given him by the laws. Moreover, for many offences he fined without previously calling the offender to order, a procedure which is as clearly contrary to the laws.

We must also call your attention to one ruling of an ex-Auditor which is undoubtedly in our opinion inconsistent with the laws; this ruling was given by Mr E. O'Mahony, ex-Auditor, on 11 March 1931, and runs as follows: 'An Auditor is entitled to fine a member of the Society for any act done on the Society's premises.'

This ruling, sir, appears to us to be totally at variance with Law 22 of Chapter XII (Part II). Nor are we alone in this opinion: it is necessary to quote from the minutes of the meeting at which this ruling was given:

'Under the heading of general business the Auditor announced that he proposed to inflict a fine of five shillings on Mr G. for rowdyism in the Society's rooms, and one of two and six on Mr A. for aiding and abetting him. Mr Auchmuty and Mr Sweetman on a point of order asked the Auditor to refer them to a law authorising the Auditor to impose fines for offences committed outside the debating hall. Messrs Diarmuid Murtagh M.A., LL.B., and D. P. Owens questioned the legality of the Auditor's action. . . . The Auditor stated that he believed a ruling had been given on the matter by previous Auditors, but as no such ruling could be found in the ruling book, he was prepared to give a ruling of his own if members asked him to. Accordingly, at the request of Messrs Murtagh and Gore-Grimes, the Auditor ruled: "An Auditor is entitled to fine a member of the Society for any act done on the Society's premises." Mr Murtagh proposed and the ex-Auditor Mr C. B. McKenna, Sch. (mod. B.A., M.Sc., LL.B.), seconded a privileged motion of adjournment: "That the House do adjourn to consider the Auditor's conduct." The motion was put to the House and carried by 16 votes to 12.'

This ruling, therefore, which we consider contrary to the laws, was an interpretation of no specific law, but was given on the strength of a ruling which was found to be non-existent; moreover, the House to which it was given was so dissatisfied with it that it adjourned its meeting. There can be little doubt that it would have been deleted but for the congestion of private business at the time on account of the attempt to impeach the Auditor. This ruling is the only pretext which an Auditor can give for extending his powers beyond those given him in the laws, and if this ruling were taken in its full significance, it would actually be legal for the Auditor to fine any member of the Society for an act committed five years ago (as, for example, upsetting a coffee cup) by someone who was not a member of the Society, as long as the act was committed on the Society's premises!

We ought, however, at this point explain the view of Mr J. E. Lynch. He would reconcile this ruling with Law 22 of Chapter XII by claiming that the ruling was not an interpretation of Law 22 but of Law 19 of Chapter XII (Part II), which states: 'The Auditor shall in all cases be sole interpreter of the Laws and judge of order for the night.'

By virtue of this law, according to Mr Lynch's view, the Auditor may extend his power of fining as far as he likes. Thus Mr O'Mahony's ruling is consistent and Law 22 is not relevant. This view does not commend itself to us, since we consider that Law 19 only gives the Auditor power to interpret the laws; and the only interpretation which can be put upon Law 19 by the Auditor is that he can interpret the laws, and so on ad infinitum. On the other hand he cannot interpret either Law 19 or Law 22 as giving him unlimited powers of fining; or if he does, it is no more consistent than if he interpreted these laws as giving him permission to drive a steamroller through the Society's premises.

There are two more questions which arise about the laws governing fines; the first is: Can the Auditor fine himself? In our opinion, according to the laws and rulings of the Society, he cannot. To do so, he would first have to call himself to order; if he then decided that he did not submit to himself he would have to fine himself a sum not exceeding two shillings and sixpence; if after this he found himself persisting in contravening order he could fine himself five shillings: only by this absurd method of self-examination could he fine himself. The second question is: Can the Auditor warn or fine the Chairman? There are no laws or rulings directly governing this point, but the peculiar position of the Chairman is clearly incompatible with either his being called to order or fined.

Such, sir, are the anomalies and inconsistencies which we find to exist between the laws, and the customs and rulings of the Society. We therefore, as in duty bound, make the following recommendations in order to remove this unsatisfactory state of affairs:

1. That the ruling given by Mr O'Mahony on 11 March 1931: 'That an Auditor is entitled to fine a member of the Society for an offence done on the Society's premises' be deleted by motion.

2. That after Law 23 of Chapter XII (Part II) the following laws be inserted:

   Law 24. The Auditor shall have power to fine any member of the Society for any act committed by that member in the debating hall during public or private business which shall be judged by the Auditor to be contrary to the laws, rulings, or procedure of the Society, or to be an act of obstruction or discourtesy or for any act wherever committed which in his opinion tends to cause a disturbance in the proceedings.

The Auditor shall have no further power of fining except where such a fine is specifically set out in the laws.

Law 25. The Auditor shall have power to fine himself in all cases where he has such power to fine any other member.

3. That the Auditor do make a ruling which shall forbid any Auditor to warn or fine the chairman.

This, sir, seems to us to solve the various questions which are raised about the laws dealing with fines. Our references also direct us to enquire into the procedure of the Society in dealing with fines. In this matter there are no such large questions raised as in the other, and we consider that the procedure is quite clear. On the occasion of this sub-committee's appointment the then Auditor confessed his inability to decide whether the discussion of a fine which continued till 5 a.m. should be ipso facto finished or merely adjourned.

After considering Law 15 of Chapter XII (Part I), we are convinced that when discussion of a fine is curtailed by law, that discussion is adjourned till the next occasion on which fines are considered in private business.

It is unlikely, sir, that anyone will deny that the laws of the Society dealing with fines are at the moment in a very unsatisfactory state and in need of amendment. Our recommendations are in our opinion neither drastic nor inadequate; they neither increase nor diminish by very much the powers of fining either which the Auditor possesses by law, or which he at present arrogates to himself. But they define and clarify the extent of these powers, and make the laws consistent with the rulings and customs of the Society. We do not think that they present any loophole by which they can be evaded, and they seem to solve the various questions which are at the moment undecided. It is therefore with confidence that we commend them to the consideration of the Society and sign ourselves

A. T. Hanson.
G. C. Overend.
W. W. L. Rooke

1938

MOTIONS DEBATED
1770–1970

A selection of the motions for debate by the Society is given below.

1770	4 April	Whether that Egyptian Law which ordained the perpetuation of professions from father to son was a beneficial institution.
		Which of the three forms of government, viz., Monarchy, Aristocracy or Democracy, is to be preferred.
1771	7 May	Whether a Member of Parliament ought to pursue his own sentiments or those of his constituents in Parliament.
	12 May	Whether Universal toleration should be encouraged by a wise legislature.
		Is it possible that Great Britain will regain her former greatness?
		That America would not flourish more as a Monarchy than as a Republic.

1779	6 January	Whether an Union with Great Britain would be of advantage to Ireland.
1780	19 January	Whether Ireland could possibly subsist independent of any other nation.
		Whether the power which the king possesses of bestowing pensions is dangerous to the constitution.
	21 March	Whether a certain qualification of estate ought to be deemed requisite for election into the Irish Parliament.
	5 April	Whether Mr Burke's plan if adopted in the entire would be advantageous to the Constitution.
		Whether a Law making the duration of Parliaments annual would be of service to Great Britain.
		Whether the aggregate body of the citizens should be allowed the discussion of political questions.
1781		Is it consistent with political freedom to force men to military service?
	5 December	Whether a standing army is dangerous to a free state.
		Is it consistent with their character, and would it be useful to the public, that clergymen should introduce subjects of political disquisition to the public?

Whether he may be supposed to possess greater public virtue who never joined a corrupt administration than he who, having done so, voluntarily resigns the most lucrative employment to return to the service of the public.

Is a passion for military glory consistent with the principles of real virtue?

Has a state a right to prevent its subjects emigrating?

Is it likely that the Independence of America will be injurious to England?

1783		Is an Infant State likely to derive more benefit from a Monarchical than a Republican form of Government?
		Is a strict adherence to Party under the British Constitution consistent with real Patriotism?
		Is more danger to be apprehended from increase of the Aristocratic than of the Democratical influence in our Government?
1786		Are popular discontents a benefit to Liberty?
1789		Are popular commotions of advantage to a Nation?
1851	15 January	Is a Member of Parliament bound in all cases to vote in accordance with the expressed opinion of the majority of his constituents? Negative unanimously.
1852	8 December	Does America possess the qualities requisite to become a supreme power? Affirmative.
1862	12 March	That the abolition of the Viceroyalty would be a wise measure. Affirmative.

1863	28 February	That Great Britain should have interfered to prevent the construction of the Suez Canal. Negative.
	23 December	That the complaints of the Colonies against the transportation system are unjustifiable.
1864	13 January	That the emigration from Ireland affords serious grounds for apprehension for the future prosperity of the country. Negative.
	16 March	That a general congress would be advantageous to Europe.
	29 March	That the policy of England should be directed towards the early independence of her colonies.
	20 April	That the movement in favour of the business education of women deserves our approbation.
	4 May	That unanimity in the verdict of juries should not be required.
	18 May	That municipal corporations should be superseded by paid commissioners.
1865	29 March	That the introduction of voting by ballot at parliamentary elections is desirable.
1866	7 February	That capital punishment should be abolished.
	13 June	That the law relating to the tenure of land in Ireland requires alteration.
1867	March	That agitation has done more detriment than service to the best interests of Ireland.
	24 April	That the system of government by party has not been beneficial to the public welfare.
1868	8 January	That the representation of minorities is a sound principle, and admits of being practically worked.

	8 April	That women ought to be admitted to the learned professions.
	9 December	That even though vested interests should be preserved, it would be iniquitous and unjust for the state to appropriate the property of bodies corporate as that of private individuals.
1869	31 March	That in the present condition of society early marriages are undesirable.
	15 December	That the state support should be given to secular education only.
1870	16 March	That the present demands for university reform are unreasonable.
	11 May	That the present system of Competitive Examinations has been carried to excess.
	1 June	That the Sensational Tendencies of the present age exhibit marked symptoms of degeneracy.
1871	4 January	That morality decreases with the increase of civilization.
	26 April	That a Court for Divorce and Matrimonial Causes should be established in this country.
	3 May	That a Tax should be imposed on the Landed Property of Absentee Landlords.
1874	21 January	That the principle of Trade Unionism is sound.
1876	23 February	That the Social and Political Disabilities of Women ought to be removed. Affirmative.
	17 May	That Political agitation has done more harm than good to Ireland. Negative.
	6 June	That the system of land tenure in Ireland needs reformation. Affirmative.

1877	17 January	That a hereditary chamber, endowed with legislative powers, is essential to the welfare of the nation. Affirmative.
	9 May	That the connection between Church and State in England should be maintained. Negative.
1878	1 May	That the character and career of Daniel O'Connell are worthy of our approval. Affirmative.
1881	2 February	That the political sentiments of the Young Ireland party deserve our approval.
1882	10 May	[Society adjourned in consequence of the assassination of Cavendish and Burke.]
	14 June	That the objections to the construction of the Channel Tunnel are well founded.
1883	14 February	That Grattan's denunciation of the Union has been justified by the results. Affirmative.
1884	19 March	That Darwin's theory of evolution is sound. Negative.
	23 April	That the career of Thomas Davis deserves our admiration. Affirmative.
	22 March	'That the character and policy of Queen Elizabeth deserve our approval' — amendment moved 'That, while approving of the career of Queen Elizabeth, we disapprove of her gross extravagance in hosiery'. Lost, original motion carried.
	30 April	That the efforts to revive the Irish language should be encouraged. Negative.
	7 May	That Trade Unions are calculated to promote the best interests of the working classes. Negative.

1885	17 March	That a system of proportional representation is desirable. Affirmative.
	9 December	That the Church of England ought to be disestablished. Negative.
1886	10 March	That Nationalisation of the land is desirable. Negative.
1889	11 December	That the Franchise should be extended to women. Negative.
1892	4 May	That the institution by the State of Pensions for the aged is desirable. Affirmative. That the exodus of Irish boys to English Schools deserves our disapproval. Affirmative.
1895	18 December	That International Sporting Contests are conducive to friendly relations between States.
1896	16 December	That the present system of advertising is deleterious to the public state. Affirmative.
1897	27 January	That the extension of the franchise to women is desirable. Affirmative.
1898	9 May	That members of Parliament should be paid. Negative.
1898	11 May	That the intervention of America on the Cuban Question is unjustifiable. Affirmative.
	7 December	That the present condition of Secondary Education in Ireland is unsatisfactory. Affirmative.
1899	31 May	That any attempt to further the Irish Literary Movement will result in provincialism. Negative. Mr W. B. Yeats in the Chair.
	7 June	That the movement to establish Sunday Journalism is to be condemned. Negative.

1901	4 December	That it is incumbent on the State to undertake the Housing of the Poor. Negative.
1902	5 February	That Irish Railways should be owned by the State. Affirmative.
1903	4 March	That women should be admitted to all the privileges of this University. Affirmative.
	15 November	That the American Government should take measures by which the lives and liberties of the Black Population would be secured.
1905	7 June	That the Gaelic League is deserving of the support of every Irishman. Affirmative.
1906	16 May	That the education provided in public elementary schools should be fully secular. Affirmative.
	30 May	That the Gaelic League is deserving of general support. Affirmative.
	18 December	That this Society deplores the increase in the power and influences of Trade Unions. Negative.
1908	12 February	That the emancipation of the coloured races is a danger to 'civilization'. Affirmative.
	26 February	That Ireland must be governed according to nationalistic ideals. Negative.
	11 March	That Democracy is the ideal form of Government. Negative.
	27 May	That this Society would deplore any interference with the liberty of the Press. Affirmative.
	17 June	That this Society deplores the technical tendency of modern education. Affirmative.

1909	17 February	That the fewest possible restrictions should be placed on the choice of subjects in a University Career.
	24 February	That this Society deplores the rapidly increasing power of the Cabinet.
	21 April	That this House approves of the appointment of natives to the governing body of India.
	9 June	That the present growth of Athleticism is to be deplored.
1910	9 February	That in the opinion of this Society the present fiscal system has proved disastrous to Ireland.
	18 May	That Modern Society is rotten at the core.
	8 June	That this Society deplores the growth of Sunday Pastimes.
1910	15 June	That material prosperity is conducive to the production of good literature.
	30 November	That this Society approves of the application of the principle of Federalisation to the United Kingdom.
1911	25 January	That this Society approves of the action of the United Irishmen in 1798.
	1 February	That this Society approves of the principle of the referendum.
	8 February	That in the opinion of this Society the Divorce Laws should be reformed.
	15 March	That this Society views with concern the spread of Western Civilization among Eastern Nations.
	22 March	That undue freedom is accorded to the British Press.

	24 May	That this Society deplores the growth of the Military Spirit in Universities.
	22 November	That an Academic Education is essential for the conduct of Public Affairs.
1911	13 December	That this Society disapproves of European Aggression in Africa.
1913	26 February	That the value of Polar Exploration does not compensate for the incidental sacrifice of human life.
	14 May	That the attempt to revive the Irish Language and Literature meets with the approval of the Society. Affirmative.
	3 December	That this Society is of the opinion that the law may on occasion be justifiably disregarded. Affirmative.
1914	4 February	That this Society deplores the growth of Cosmopolitanism to the prejudice of Nationality. Negative.
	11 March	That this House views with approval the modern feminist movement. Affirmative.
	6 May	That this House approves of Socialism. Negative.
	20 May	That this House approves of compulsory military service. Affirmative.
	10 June	That this House approves of Vivisection. Affirmative.
	18 November	That this House is of the opinion that a lasting international peace can only be secured by the growth of Democracy. Negative.

1914	25 November	That this House disapproves of the sale of alcohol after eight o'clock. Negative.
1915	10 February	That this House approves of Conscription. Negative.
	3 March	That this House disapproves of Socialism. Negative.
	5 May	That this House is in favour of the Feminist Movement. Negative.
	9 June	That this House is in favour of Trade Unionism. Affirmative
	1 December	That this House condemns the attitude of the U.S.A. in this war. Affirmative.
1917	14 February	That this House is of the opinion that an Universal Peace can be secured by a League of Nations to enforce it. Negative.
	27 February	That this House considers that in time of war the civil authorities should subordinate to the military. Negative.
1919	28 May	That a Minimum Wage Scale is practicable and desirable. Affirmative.
1920	11 February	That Pitt's Irish Policy is worthy of approval.[9] Negative.
	25 February	That it is desirable that War criminals should be brought to trial. Negative.
1921	2 February	That this Society welcomes the Restoration of the King of Greece. No Vote.

[9] Note by T. S. C. Dagg: Since the board banned debate on current politics, this motion was a cloak for criticism of the effects of the Act of Union. The vote was, as always, anti-Union.

	23 February	That it is the duty of every citizen to assist in the working of the new Home Rule Act. Affirmative.
1922	15 March	That two Legislative Chambers are essential to Good Government. Affirmative.
	31 May	That Military Interference in politics is to be deplored. Affirmative.
1923	21 February	That this Society desires the immediate political reunion of Ireland. Affirmative.
1924	6 February	That the admission of women to Universities has been justified. Negative.
	13 February	That a return to despotism is necessary for the rejuvenation of Europe. Affirmative.
	14 May	That Ulster has been betrayed. Negative.
	11 June	That Animal Life should not be sacrificed to Sport. Negative.
	18 June	That Nationalism rather than Internationalism is the hope of the future. Negative.
1927	25 May	That this House disapproves of the participation of women under 25 in jurisdiction. Affirmative.
1928	8 February	That there is no future for Socialism. Affirmative.
	16 October	That patriotism is the last refuge of a scoundrel. Negative.
1931	18 February	That women should be admitted to membership of the College Historical Society. Affirmative.
	25 November	That the Unity of Ireland is an impossible ideal. Negative.

1932	9 March	That divorce should be permitted in Ireland. Affirmative.
	18 May	That this House has confidence in the present Government of the Irish Free State. Negative.
1941	19 February	That this House disapproves of Sweepstakes. Affirmative.
	21 May	That this House considers that Irishmen should not fight in foreign forces. Affirmative.
1943	12 May	That women should be allowed on the floor of the College Historical Society. Negative.
1944	26 January	That this House approves of State Monopolies. Negative.
	6 December	That there is no solution for Partition. Negative.
1946	13 March	That this House approves of General Franco. Negative.
1947	12 March	That this House would Welcome the Provision of Facilities for Divorce in Ireland. Affirmative.
1948	25 February	That this House approves of Birth-Control. Negative.
	10 November	That Éire should revert to full membership of the British Commonwealth. Affirmative.
1950	29 November	That this House would arm now to take the North. Negative.
	22 February	That Communism is a bad means to a good end. Affirmative.
1952	14 May	That this House deplores Racial Segregation. Affirmative.
1952	26 November	That there is no such thing as a National Culture. Negative.

1957	8 May	That Ireland should rejoin the Commonwealth. Affirmative.
		That this House approves of Emigration. Negative.
1958	10 December	That this House favours amalgamation with the National University of Ireland. Negative.
1959	18 November	That White Africa is doomed. Affirmative.
1961	1 March	That this House condemns Apartheid. Affirmative.
	29 November	That this House condemns the practice of Birth Control. Negative.
1963	23 January	That this House would enter the Common Market unwillingly. Negative.
	27 February	That Abortion should be made legal. Affirmative.
	13 November	That Socialism is a refusal to face the facts. Negative.
1964	5 February	That every effort should be used to revive the Irish Language. Negative.
	28 April	That the U.S. get out of Vietnam. Affirmative.
1965	19 January	That the State should not legislate for Private Morality. Affirmative.
1966	27 April	That the Vatican Council was a Flash in the Pan. Negative.
	9 November	That this House looks forward to a United Europe. Affirmative.
1967	18 January	That this House would support Euthanasia. Negative.

1968	7 February	That Merger means Murder [on the proposal by the Minister for Education to merge T.C.D. and U.C.D.]. Affirmative.
1969	22 January	That this House would march on Stormont. Affirmative.
	26 November	That Armed Aggression is a justifiable instrument in Foreign Policy. Negative.
1970	18 February	That Trade Unions are the Guardians of Progress. Negative.

WRITINGS
ON THE SOCIETY

A FAMOUS STUDENTS' CLUB (1747)

The first speeches of Edmund Burke

In celebrating recently the centenary of Edmund Burke, a reference was made to an interesting record of his early efforts as a speaker, which exists in the 'Proceedings of the Club' a small society founded by him on the 21 April 1747 while in his third year as a student in Trinity College, Dublin. Very little is known of these unpublished minutes, but scant attention has been paid to them by the compilers of the *Works, Correspondence and Life of Burke*. The earliest mention of them is, we think, in Todd's *Life of Milton*; and James Prior, in his *Life of Burke* (1826), quotes a passage from Todd which he had extracted from these minutes. Sir Joseph Napier speaks of them in a published lecture delivered in Dublin in 1862, and the Rev. Dr Robert Walsh quotes from them in his address to the Trinity College Historical Society in 1864, who say the book was lent to them by Judge Berwick. The book disappeared subsequently to this; but it was ultimately picked up in a local bookstall some years ago by a Trinity College student, who presented it to the Historical Society. In 1882 a paper called 'Hibernia' was published in Dublin, its chief contributors being young university men: it had a purely local and mere fugitive existence; but in its pages, however, the first and hitherto only attempt was made to deal with the 'Proceedings of the Club'.

To Burke's Club the Historical Society above mentioned, which is the oldest debating society in the United Kingdom, traces its descent. In its arena most of the great Irish orators for the past hundred years have learned the art of debate, and laid there the foundation of their future fame.

The 'Proceedings [or minutes] of the Club' is a small quarto volume, and contains 111 pages of closely written matter, a portion of which is in Burke's handwriting, when he in turn filled the position of Secretary to the club. Burke, as is well known, was educated in the little Quaker town of Ballitore, in Co. Kildare, by Abraham Shackleton, a Quaker who came from Yorkshire, and founded a school here in 1726. Burke entered Trinity College in April 1744, and the following[10] is inserted on the fly-leaf of the minutes: 'Edmond Bourke, pens. filius Iohannis Generosi, Annum 16 agens, natus Dublinii, educatus sub ferulâ mag. Shackleton. Dr Pellisier.' This was written (17 December 1813) and signed by Dr Barrett, the celebrated 'Jacky' of whose eccentricity many stories still survive.

Of the college life of Burke not much is known, and what has been gathered is chiefly derived from his correspondence with Richard Shackleton, the son of his master, with whom he maintained a lifelong friendship.

In a letter written to his friend in November 1744 he says: 'The Society, if you remember, we had thoughts of erecting, goes on slowly. . . . Members for our purpose are very scarce; and though we had the number, we shall always think it imperfect while it wants you.' Some little gathering of his friends was formed, for he speaks of it again in these terms: 'Dear Dick, your neglecting to answer our last letter has very much surprised the whole club.' Of its exact nature we are left in doubt; but that Burke was a youth of great warmth of feeling is matter beyond dispute from these letters, and that he cultivated and maintained strong friendships which lasted through all the struggles and storms of life, there is ample evidence.

The club at once set to work on the formation of a code of laws: they are

---

[10] The first page of the minutes are reproduced in this Anthology.

a model of their kind, and a remarkable example of youthful legislation. The first is typical of the formality of the time: 'Decency and good manners, virtue and religion, must guide their whole behaviour, and no word, gesture, or action contrary thereto pass uncensured.' The club was to meet on Tuesdays and Fridays, and sit from five to nine o'clock. On the first evening an oration was to be made on a given subject by an appointed speaker, and a paper read, 'the author passing his word and honour that he wrote it originally for that time and purpose'. On Friday evening a speech was to be delivered out of some book, 'with proper emphasis and action', and a paper on some moral subject, the remainder of the time to be taken up in reading or debating as the president appointed. This office was held for a week: the president opened the club 'with an harangue'; he had to sum up the arguments in debate, decide the point at issue, and give his reasons for his judgments. It met regularly twice or thrice weekly until 10 July and Burke sat six times as president and twice as censor; of the thirty-five meetings recorded he was never once absent.

Mohun was the first president and Dennis the first secretary, and on assembling the personal element at once entered into the proceedings with Burke accusing Buck of 'lampooning Mr Kinsella'[11]. The president supported Buck's plea that they had no right to condemn for anything done out of the assembly, and that Burke was liable to an accusation of 'ill-nature': he decided against the charge, and also against one of Buck's accusing Burke of 'scurrility,' and summarily dismissed the meeting, appointing Dennis 'to speak an oration on Lord Lovat', and Burke 'to deliver an essay on Society', on the next night of meeting.

The minutes vary in length and importance: some are merely concise notes of the evening's proceedings, while others are fairly exhaustive, the speech having been carefully written out and entered.

On the subject of Irish manufactures there was evidently some free speaking on the old and oft-renewed complaint as to the injury inflicted by English legislation on Irish industries. Buck declared it 'his opinion that such subjects are not fit matter of debate in this assembly', and moved that a law be made to restrain them in the choice of their subjects, 'for that all such which in the discussion of the question will make us show any dislike

---

[11]   The Minutes of Burke's Club spell the name "Kinselah".

to his Majesty or his Ministry is improper; that questions relating to the Government of our country are ticklish points not fit to be handled'. Later on he succeeded in carrying a law to this effect notwithstanding the opposition of Burke, who contended that such restraint would 'take away their spirit' and 'destroy their oratory'.

The measures adopted by this youthful band of statesmen and legislators were of an exceptionally heroic nature, and the attitude taken toward public offenders forms a striking illustration of Burke's own position later as the great censor of his age; and it is easily seen where he acquired his earliest lessons in the conduct of affairs. We find Mohun soon brought to trial, and in his absence the 'assembly thinks he should not be defended by an advocate'. The president postpones the trial; but the club passes a law to the effect that 'the absence of an accused member implies his guilt, and that sentence be passed on him unless the president interpose' and that 'a Lustrum be held once a month'. The members proposed themselves for this office, urging their own claims.

On May the 12th, Burke, who had already acted as secretary, appears as president and delivered 'an harangue' from the chair to the effect that 'he represented the dignity of the assembly, and would act with the utmost rigour, and would, was there no law, do it through his benevolence and regard to the Society, and that he would act absolute and free within the laws'. A curious subject is proposed for discussion — 'Whether an absolute pride or servile complaisance in a president be most commendable.' Burke recapitulated the arguments advanced, and 'determined pride to be the least faulty of the extremes, but recommended the medium'.

Two trials soon come off, and the 'crimes' committed were 'indecency and contempt of the president', who, Hamilton had said, was 'damned absolute', which was very probably the case, if we are to judge by his opening 'harangue'. Mohun not only assented to this, but was guilty of 'constant insolences, contempt, and absence from the assembly, with disregard to the repeated fines and censures'.

On the 26th May Burke was ordered to make a declamation in praise of painting, and the minutes record as follows:

'There are three arts, called generally by way of eminence polite — poetry, painting and musick. That painting is in many things not inferior to poetry, and doubtless superior to musick, that it gives us all the beauties of nature with the additional pleasure that the mind takes in comparing them and finding their resemblance with the original. That it greatly tends to the furtherance and improvement of virtue by putting before our eyes the most lively examples of the reward of it, or the punishment of the contrary. Like St Paul preaching at Athens (a piece of Raphael), it convinces some, astonishes and pleases all. Portraiture particularly useful by showing our ancestors who have done well: we may be incited by their example, for which end the Romans kept the statues of their ancestors in their houses.'

We have interesting evidence from these minutes, as well as from Burke's and Dennis's letters, of the part the students played in Dublin street riots of the time. In a letter of Burke to Shackleton in 1746, he gives a graphic account of the Sheridan and Kelly theatre riots. On 29 May Dennis is ordered 'to make an oration to dissuade the scholars from engaging in the riots'. A joint letter of the friends to Shackleton was written that evening, in which light is thrown on the internal workings of the club. This letter was first published in the *Dublin National Magazine* (1830), and in it Dennis says, in connection with an attempt to rescue a student from arrest: 'The mob attempting to force the "Black Dog" (Newgate Prison), the gaoler fired, killed two, and wounded others. Five scholars were expelled for the riot, and five more admonished.' Among the latter was Oliver Goldsmith.

An amusing contrast in the choice of subjects is shown in the order of the president Ardesoif, that as he had not his speech on drunkenness well by heart, on the next night 'he produce one on love'. The subject of absenteeism on that occasion engaged their attention, and Burke introduced a bill 'to tax the absentees ten per cent of their estates.' He urged 'that 'tis the only means of preserving some part of the little money in the kingdom, which, appropriated to the Dublin Society, might prove a great advantage to it'.

Subjects of a religious kind were occasionally introduced to the club, and on this evening Burke was ordered 'to make an extempore commonplace on the Sermon of our Saviour on the Mount'. There was a strong current

of religious feeling in Burke's nature, which shows itself in his correspondence with Shackleton. The minutes record that he took:

*'Occasion to observe how much the Christian morality exceeds the best
heathen by refining our passions, and not only our actions, but their spring,
the heart. Our divine Physician heals the corrupted source; the others are but
surgeons tampering with the outward sores, and very defective in that. . . .
The heathens, even the wisest and best, were employed a long time in
searching what was good — or virtue — and that the most learned were
much puzzled in their inquiry, and the ignorant could know nothing at all.
But the gospel by substituting faith, which the most ignorant can have, gives
us the precept, and leaves us immediately to the practice. That the morality
inculcated in this excellent sermon conduced so admirably to the improvement
of society, that had its rules been observed, we should have a heaven upon
earth. But since men are so wicked that this cannot be, those who do may be
sure of finding it in a better place.'*

On May the 30th, Burke 'moved that he may accuse Mr Dennis', and we
have an example of his early efforts in the art of impeachment. He spoke
as follows:

*'That he is sorry to be so frequent in accusations, as it may seem cruel in him,
particularly since he is now obliged to accuse a member who had filled with
applause the greatest posts in the Society, and till very lately behaved himself
perfectly well; but since all things are of late turned upside-down amongst us,
and that the best members are become the worst, his love to the Society
overbears all other considerations and obliges him to show — First, that Mr
Dennis had transgressed the laws in accusing its president while in office, and
that not with a calm accusation, which would have lessened his crime, but
with the utmost insolence, and refusing to be silent at his order, continuing
his insults to the chair and the private members by exclaiming for his liberty.
Secondly, that, continuing his ill-behaviour, to insult the Society he used
obscene words without provocation, and forced, for this same end,
unbecoming insolent laughs. Thirdly, to complete all his crimes, he declared
he disregarded the censure, and by that means he endeavoured to have the
punishments of the assembly set at nought. That what aggravated the*

accused's crime was the repetition and long continuance of it, and unless such offences be punished, it must bring inevitable ruin on the Society. He desires the president not to be moved with a crafty insinuation the accused might use, "that the offended person was his judge", but considering himself intrusted with the care of the Society, he should, disregarding evil tongues, give a sentence on Mr Dennis, which he demands from him as a debt he owed to the Society, and for the omission of which he would be accountable another day.'

Dennis made an equally able defence, denied the insolence, but admitted 'that he might be a little warm', and that his crimes 'had no foundation but in the malice of the accuser'. Burke replied and prayed for judgment, and the president, after recapitulation, gave the sentence of 'admonition'. Nobody seems to have been a bit the worse for these apparently serious impeachments, fines, and censures. Burke and Dennis were the best of College friends, and occupied the same rooms.

The above is an extract from Blackwood's Magazine, *February 1898.*

THE HISTORICAL SOCIETY OF TRINITY COLLEGE, DUBLIN — FIRST ERA
From: The Irish Quarterly Review, *June 1854 no. XIV p. 305–28.*

How long this early Historical Society[12] lasted cannot now be ascertained, but it is probable that on Burke's leaving College (where he took his A.B. degree in 1751) the Society declined. Certain it is, that, in 1753, another Society was formed, a volume of whose Journals was in the possession of The Historical Society, when it was dissolved in 1815; but unfortunately it has been lost, as has also been the first volume of the proceedings of the Society of 1770, in the interval that elapsed between the dissolution and the establishment of the present Society. This Society of 1753 appears at first to have been established merely for the cultivation of historical

---

[12]   The reference is to Burke's Club.

knowledge, but after it had been formed for somewhat more than a year, a monthly debate was added to the original plan. Among the members of this Society were Yelverton, afterwards Lord Avonmore, and Scott, afterwards Earl of Clonmel.

Yelverton might well be the founder of a Debating Society; his eloquence was magnificent. One speech, delivered in 1782, in favour of the Roman Catholic Claims, is thus characterized by Grattan, when speaking of the Penal Code: 'It', the Penal Code, 'was detailed by the late Lord Avonmore — I heard him — his speech was the whole of the subject, and a concatinated and inspired argument, not to be resisted: it was the march of an elephant, it was a wave of the Atlantic, a column of water 3000 miles deep. He began with the Catholic at his birth, he followed him to his grave; he showed that, in every period, he was harassed by the law — the law stood at his cradle, it stood at his bridal bed, and it stood at his coffin.' The following extract, from the proceedings of the Society, at the meeting, June 11, 1757, seems to refer to the Club formed by Burke, some ten or twelve years before, and it renders it probable that the latter continued its meetings up to this time, at least. 'A Committee sat to take into consideration a scheme for incorporating with the old Historical Club. Resolved, that it is impossible for the Club, under their present circumstances, to incorporate with the above Club. Stopford, Chairman.'

The volume of Journals from which this is taken, brings down the proceedings of the Club to Saturday, October 29th, 1757, on which day the Club adjourned to November 1st, of the same year. How much longer this Club continued to meet we have no means of ascertaining, or whether The Historical Society of 1770 owed its origin in any way to it. The fact of this volume of its proceedings, with one or two from the library of these older Societies being in the library of the Society of 1770, would seem to point out that it did.

We can use the guidance of the Journals of the Society from the year 1773; it had then attained to a very successful position, the average attendance of members at that time amounting to upwards of eighty.

Mr Ball thus opens his speech, from the chair, at the end of the summer session of 1774:

'*Self applause should never be otherwise than cautiously, never otherwise than deservedly bestowed. It is an unfading wreath, the present of God himself, whose flowers the heart of man cannot ravish, and the breath of malice cannot blast. Let us not profane the holy gift! 'Tis profaned when offered by the hand of self-love! 'Tis profaned when offered at the shrine of vanity!*'

Having thus prepared his hearers, the account, which follows, of the Society's debates is certainly not very flattering.

'*One gentleman*', he says, '*arises and opens the debate by modestly informing the society that he 'has nothing to say, for that indeed he has not studied the question,' and sits down. Another arises to oppose the last and to that purpose, with equal modesty, assures us that 'the arguments of his learned and respectable friend, who opened the debate, carry with them such weight and authority, 'twould be presumption in him to attempt an answer, and — besides — indeed — being prevented — by necessary avocations — he has not studied the question either,' and he sits down. The President, after some minutes spent in the most awkward silence imaginable, is forced to arise and put the question to the vote. And that question, which was proposed for the improvement of our language, the exertion of our genius, the exercise of our reason, and the discovery of truth, that question which perhaps involves in it some of the most interesting points in philosophy, or deepest principles of Government, is left to be determined by the blind, fortuitous, and tumultuous aye or no of a majority, who scarce know their own mind, and who are not ashamed in pronouncing this aye or no, to express, in the most public and dogmatical manner, an opinion, which, from their silence a little before, they might be fairly presumed to be absolutely incapable of supporting by a single argument.*'

One evening during the long vacation [of 1793], when most of the members of the College had dispersed, [Mr Miller, then Junior Dean,] perceived an hackney coach drive into the square, and three young men, whom he recognised, alighting from it, accompanied by, *horribile dictu!* two females. This was too much for the good Dean, and he at once laid the affair before the Board. The authorities being naturally much displeased, issued an order excluding the delinquents from the precincts of the College.

On the re-assembling of the students for the winter, and the resumption of the meetings of The Historical Society, the Dean, as an ex-officio member, happening to attend, perceived one of those who had been excluded in the room, whereupon he requested the Auditor to have the offending party removed; he then appealed to the Chairman, but neither of them was willing to exert their influence or authority: applying then, personally, to the gentleman himself, he retired rather than involve the Society in a dispute with the authorities of the University, and thus it was thought the affair would have ended. But the dispute was not allowed to rest there: the Society, imagining its independence invaded, appointed a Committee to investigate the affair. Mr Miller, hereupon, conceiving this as tantamount to an inquiry into his conduct as Dean, and thus overthrowing all discipline and rule, laid the affair before the Board; and that body, not sorry for an excuse to bring the Society, hitherto more independent than they thought agreeable, under more direct control, published a code of rules which among other commands, forbade any one to continue a member of the Society whose name was no longer on the College books, and ordered that the name of the proposer of the inquiry into the Dean's conduct should be erased from the list of the Society.

To this message a Committee of the Society returned an answer explaining their conduct with regard to the inquiry; alleging that the Board was mistaken in its object, which was merely to discover the reason of a member being forced to retire from their meetings, and hoping that the Board would not insist on the name of the proposer being erased from the books; the Committee also pointed out the ruinous effects of the order for the exclusion of the extern members, as destructive to the prosperity of the Society, and hoped that the Board would reconsider the question.

Upon receipt of this answer the Board declared that they were more than ever convinced of the impropriety of the extern members being still allowed to attend the meetings of the Society, and ended by resuming possession of the rooms where the Society had been accustomed to assemble; offering, however, the use of them to any of the students who might choose to meet subject to such restrictions as the Board should think proper to prescribe.

The Society, upon this, adjourned to the Assembly Rooms in William Street. In this room an address was drawn up and sent to the Provost, in which, after detailing the particulars of the dispute from the first, they thus conclude:

'Thus exiled from the University, the Historical Society cannot prevail upon themselves to bid a melancholy farewell to a place, where their institution has flourished four and twenty years, without offering the humble tribute of their gratitude for the kind protection with which you have so long honoured them. Anxious for the continuance of your good opinion, they wish to impress upon your recollection, that they have always observed the highest respect for the heads of the College; that the concessions which they have offered proceed as far as is consistent with the spirit of gentlemen, and the honor of a Society which aspired to your protection, and that they have never abused that freedom in their general constitution which is, perhaps, as necessary to the utility and character of such an institution, as it is incompatible with the control attempted to be exercised by the Board. To your judgment the Historical Society submit how far a separation from the College may effect the cause of polite literature, the existence of their Institution, and the interests of the University committed to your charge.'

The Society does not appear to have received any answer to this address, which we may account for by the illness of the Provost[13], who died early in the following September. In him the Society lost one of her warmest supporters, who might have prevented the secession from College had he been at his place at the Board.

The members of the Society then resident in London called a meeting at the Crown and Rolls, Chancery Lane, and drew up an address, thanking the Society for the manly stand that had been made, and offering their assistance in any way that might be deemed useful during the struggle.

The College Board did not stand tamely by while the Society thus proceeding independent of their support, as we may gather from the following resolutions:

---

[13]   John Hely Hutchinson.

'Resolved, that the late public admonition of Lewis Kerr, Esq. our worthy Auditor, by the Board, for discharging a trust reposed in him by the Society, appearing to us a continuance of the unmerited persecution exercised by the Heads of the College against this Society; we are determined to support him if he should deem an appeal to the visitors an expedient measure, and that we do hereby empower him to draw upon our Treasurer from time to time for which sums as may be requisite for that purpose. Resolved, that the warmest thanks of this Society be presented to Lewis Kerr, Esq., our worthy Auditor, for his temperate, manly, and firm conduct when called before the Board for presenting the address of this Society to that Body.'

While the dispute thus went on it was not confined to decrees on one side, or resolutions on the other; the Press was called in to the aid of the belligerent parties, and squibs of every kind appeared; now it was a farce, now a burlesque poem or a satirical song; at one time the language used was Greek or Latin, at another the vernacular tongue was laid under contribution. From among these various efforts of wit, and satire we select one, quoted by Madden in his *Life of Emmet*, in which grave humor (sic!) and bitter irony are conspicuous:

'At a full meeting of the Vintners, Publicans, and Courtezans, in the City of Dublin, held the 1st of May, 1794, Mrs Margaret Leeson[14] *in the chair. Resolved, 1st. That the thanks of this meeting be presented to the Vice Provost and Senior Fellows of Trinity College, Dublin, for their public spirited suppression of the Historical Society.*

2ndly. That the said Society has considerably injured our respective trades, by employing the Gentlemen of the University (formerly their best customers) one whole evening in the week in literary pursuits, and wasting many other evenings in preparation for it.

3rdly. That the kind interference of the College must cause the custom of the College to return gradually to us, and the time of the young gentlemen to be more profitably employed, than in the pursuits of the said Institution.

---

[14]   Mrs. Leeson was a brothel-keeper in Dublin in the late eighteenth century. See *The Memoirs of Mrs Leeson [Madam]*, Edited by Mary Lyons, The Lilliput Press 1995.

That the Provost and Senior Fellows be made free of our Society, and that the freedom of the same be presented to them in a quicksilver box.

Mrs Leeson having left the chair, and Mrs Simpson being called thereto, Resolved — That the thanks of this meeting be given to Mrs Leeson for her very proper conduct in the chair. Signed by order,

Catherine Grant, Secretary.'

But we will not dwell any longer on this dispute. It is painful to find a body of men, distinguished by learning and talents, engaging in this petty and unnatural warfare with those who were placed under their control for guidance and instruction.

Bushe was chosen to deliver the customary speech on the first meeting of the Society after their separation from the University. For this speech, we refer our readers to Mr Phillips' *Specimens of Irish Eloquence*: for purity of style and vigor of thought, it may be set beside any afterwards delivered by its distinguished author.

The Society continued to meet for a considerable time after this separation; but, as the members dropped off, and as the Society established in the University as its successor increased in fame, the original Society declined gradually, until, in 1806, a meeting was called, at which it was resolved to hand over the Journals and other property to the Intern Society, whose career it will be our object to follow.

THE HISTORICAL SOCIETY OF TRINITY COLLEGE, DUBLIN. — SECOND ERA.
From The Irish Quarterly Review *September 1854 No. XV p.502–27.*

In November 1797 Moore entered the Society, having previously been a member of a junior debating society, that served in some measure, as a training school for the more advanced Association. In a few days after, another name was added to the Society, destined to win for itself a painful notoriety in the troublous times that followed, we mean Robert Emmet.

United by a similarity of views, and a kindred genius, of the same standing in College and in the Society, an intimacy of the closest kind sprang up between the poet and Emmet.

How different the fate that awaited each! The one the favoured associate of the rich and noble, yet not the less beloved by the lowliest peasant of his native land, has but the other day sank calmly to rest, the wreath of fame resting upon his brow, the regrets of all classes and parties following him to the grave. The other —

> '*Oh! Breathe not his name, let it sleep in the shade,*
> *Where cold and unhonour'd his relics are laid:*
> *Sad, silent and dark, be the tears that we shed,*
> *As the night dew that falls on the grass o'er his head.*'

The halo of such names as Burke, and Grattan, Plunket and Bushe, failed to preserve the Society from the repeated assaults of that body which might have been expected to have been its warmest supporters, and the members of the Board unhappily succeeded in bringing to a successful issue their determined hostility to a Society to which every one of them once owed allegiance, from which they had each received the encouragement and support so necessary to the first efforts of the orator or the writer!

It has been asked, can a Society exist in a University whilst freedom of discussion is its object, and the result a certain independence of action and thought. The fate that twice overtook the Historical Society is pointed out as a proof in the negative.

But we do not think that those who are themselves the guides of youth in the pursuit of knowledge, the appointed guardians of learning, must necessarily be opposed to such an Institution. Rather let us suppose that such hostility resulted from misrepresentation, that such constant interference with the affairs of the Society resulted from an overweening care for its welfare. Anything, rather than imagine that, for a paltry breach of etiquette, or a private and insignificant dispute between its members, the Society should incur the hostility of the authorities of the University, and that its destruction could alone atone for the offence. We sincerely hope that the Society which at present occupies the position twice vacated by its predecessors, may never incur a like hostility from its natural guardians; that it never may be again in the power of the enemies of the University to point to the acts of her Governors as partaking, not of the liberality and enlightenment of the nineteenth century, but of the obstructive folly of the Middle Ages.

Before concluding, however, there is one assertion which his Grace [the present Archbishop of Dublin] had made, and to which we must refer. He declares that a system which he advocates 'tends to form accurate reasoners, able statesmen, sound divines, good lawyers: the other showy demagogues, popular preachers to ignorant fanatics, and pleaders qualified for appealing to the passions of illiterate jurymen'. Now, without going beyond the limits of the Historical Society, will his Grace call such men as his distinguished predecessor, Archbishop Magee — Dean Graves — or the many other divines whose names have been mentioned in the preceding pages, mere popular preachers to ignorant fanatics? Will he persist in terming Curran, Plunket, or Bushe, as but pleaders qualified for appealing to the passions of illiterate jurymen? It was by painful practice in a Debating Society, after having been laughed down for his action and mode of delivery, that Curran at last educated himself so as to become one of Ireland's greatest orators. It was while addressing the Historical Society that Bushe earned from Grattan the praise —'that he spoke with the lips of an angel'. With such names as these on our side, to which we may add those of Burke, and Yelverton, and Grattan, and Moore, and Croker, and Sheil, with a host of others, a few only of whose names we have recorded — with such names, we repeat, on our side, we appeal from the dictum of his Grace, and with all deference for his high authority and great talents we ask, has the only result of the Historical Society been to produce showy declaimers, agitating demagogues, popular preachers to ignorant fanatics, and pleaders qualified for appealing to the passions of illiterate jurymen?

T.C.D., A COLLEGE MISCELLANY

The Opening Meeting

Thank you for your card, Mr Honorary Secretary,
But I fear I must regretfully decline.
Thank the Auditor and the Council
For the invitation pretty,
Thank the Treasurer and Chairman,
Thank the Library Committee,
Give the essayist my greeting
For I shan't be at the meeting,
I propose to spend the evening at a tavern in the city.
And so, Mr Secretary,
No, Mr Secretary,
I fear I must regretfully decline.

Thank you for your card, Mr Honorary Secretary,
But I fear I must regretfully decline.
I don't want to hear the paper
On 'Democracy and Duty,'
Or the vote of thanks to follow
By the Minister for Beauty
Or Professor Jabez Bower
Ramble on for half an hour,
Or the Paraguayan Consul, or the Dean of Rumti-Footi.
Which is why, Mr Secretary, I, Mr Secretary,
Fear I must regretfully decline.

Thank you for your card, Mr Honorary Secretary,
But I fear I must regretfully decline.
You are really most obliging
To invite me to your meeting,
And to come at 7:30
For preliminary eating,
But you'll start your blasted session
Without me in the procession
Or wearing out my trousers on your adamantine seating.
Very well, Mr Secretary,
Hell! Mr Secretary,
I fear I must regretfully decline.

W. A. G. (R. B. D. French)
31 October 1935

An Appeal For National Unity
(An address to the Historical Society)

'Tis with pleasure I confess that I rise now to address
This gathering of aliens and traitors,
And if what I say to you is unpleasant it is true;
Those who praise you are at best prevaricators.
West Britons though you be,
Listen carefully to me
Since you'll hear the things you should have heard before.
As a nation's voice I speak
(And you are few and weak)
And that nation's voice is now an angry roar.

The people pure and plain have begun their glorious reign,
Ponder deeply upon this piece of information,
And it's aliens like you that these pure and plain ones view
With peculiar pain and irate indignation.
My twenty-six fair counties —
Home of liberty and bounties —
Your ill-doings can no longer tolerate.
Did you vote Fianna Fáil ?
Are you any use at all
To my Christianised Republican — Free State?

Grattan, Berkeley, Swift and Co. let me tell you will not go
Down with us who guide the destinies of Ireland.
Your professors I complain go a-roving over Spain
Writing literature repugnant to the Sireland.
'Tis a crime far worse than arson
To have bred the Baron Carson,
In fact you'd best be quietly interred
In conclusion may I add
That the paper we have had
Was easily the best I've ever heard.

Colyn (R. P. McDermott)
15 November 1934

౭☙

Extract from an Editorial, Thursday, 14 May 1931

In the Historical is the very antithesis of this (The Philosophical Society). Its members tread daily over volcanic fires of politics, anarchy and schism. Intrigue susurrates in the air: laws are made to be broken: officers are elected to be dismissed: periodicals magically vanish or are secreted in coal boxes: meetings are thronged with noisy partisans. We disagree with the Jeremiahs who bewail the decadence of its manners and the degeneration of its oratory. The debates are as good as ever — but intolerably unpunctual: timed for eight o'clock they rarely begin for another half-hour, a small but irritating fault. However, the Hist. certainly cannot be called moribund; it is dangerously alive. With skilful guidance it should prosper from this unrest: but it will need brave and shrewd governors.

Society Snips
We have pleasure in printing below some papers for the forthcoming Entrance Examinations, to be held by the various College Societies. If you are interested, write out your answers on a clean sheet of paper, and sign with two specimens of your usual signature in block capitals. If you send them to the Senior Lecturer you will hear from him in due course.

Historical Entrance
[A correct answer to the first question qualifies the candidate for immediate election to the chair of that officer who has been the latest to resign.]

1. What had Edmund Burke to do with the Society?

2. Repeat the rules of the Society.

3. Give five reliable means of bringing about (a) the election, (b) the resignation, of any officer.

4. When is the Silence Room? Why isn't it?

5. A, having procured the election of B to the office of Treasurer, finds that he owes the Society, in the person of B, twenty-five shillings. He knows something about B's private history. How can he avoid paying the twenty-five shillings?

6. What is wrong with (a) the cigarette machine, (b) the treasurer?

7. Repeat the formula for referring to the Philosophical Society.

Philosophical Entrance

1. What do you know about the College Historical Society? (Any answer whatsoever to this question disqualifies the candidate.)

2. Give ten different ways of saying 'This, Mr President and Gentlemen, is the best paper I have ever heard.'

3. Give the position of the Encyclopaedia Britannica in the Library.

4. Give one hundred reasons by which to persuade any newcomer to College not to join the Historical Society.

5. Who were: Alan Cobham, Rev. Hartford, Kant, Mr Jessop's cousin?

6. Can you write a paper for tonight's meeting?

7. Assert, prove, reassert and disprove your total ignorance of everything.

Lament of An Auditor

Oh, who'll be persuaded to speak?
I've had nothing but "noes" for a week;
Bernard Shaw was offensive,
Shirley Temple's expensive;
And the platform's beginning to creak.

Mussolini has cabled "Decline!"
Windsor pleads an engagement to dine;
My platform grows littler
With the failure of Hitler:
And I fear I shall have to resign.

The professor of Greek in Rangoon
Has promised to 'phone me at noon.
The recorder of Dingle's
Afflicted with shingles,
So I think we'll postpone it till June.

Pseudo (A. T. Hanson.)
4 November 1937

As Some Day it may Happen
(With apologies to Gilbert and Sullivan)
Sung by: The Lord High Executioner,
(With apologies to Ko-Ko). With chorus of Satellites.

As some day it may happen that our numbers overflow,
I've got a little list — I've got a little list
Of Society offenders who might well be down below,
And who never would be missed from the portals of the Hist.!

All those who on a point of order raise a point of fact —
"Circumlocutionaries" who refuse to be exact —
And the idiots who criticise the subject every night
Who tell us what it should be, why the wording isn't right;
And those who split my lordly ears by thumping with their fist —
They'd none of them be missed from the portals of the Hist.!

Chorus:
He's got 'em on the list — he's got 'em on the list;
And they'll none of them be missed from the portals of the Hist.!

There's your high and mighty officer who doesn't know the rules,
And your anti-monarchist — I've got them on the list!
All honorary members who behave like silly fools,
They never would be missed from the portals of the Hist.!
All jiblets, ignorami — I despise 'em everyone —
And those who, as I look around, are clearly 'out for fun';
And the man who thinks he's clever when he hops on the unwary,
Incapable, unfortunate Pro-Record Secretary.
But it really doesn't matter whom you put upon the list,
For they'd none of 'em be missed from the portals of the Hist.!

Chorus:
You may put 'em on the list — you may put 'em on the list;
And they'll none of them be missed from the portals of the Hist.!

G. S.

MY TIME IN THE HIST

In these pieces Honorary Members recall their time in the Hist. The period covered stretches from 1878 to 1970. Each item was written at the request of the Bicentenary Committee, with the exception of two which are excerpts from books already published.

SIR JOHN ROSS – AUDITOR 1878–79, PRESIDENT 1913–25, GOLD MEDALLIST

In the following year (1878) I was elected Auditor of the College Historical Society, after a keen contest with Mr Samuels now the Right Hon. Mr Justice Samuels, and delivered the auditorial address on 'Imperialism in the Nineteenth Century'. The Lord Chief Justice of the Common Pleas, afterwards Lord Morris presided. The speakers were the Hon. David Plunket, afterwards Lord Rathmore, Mr Butt, Q.C., the Solicitor-General, afterwards Lord Justice Fitzgibbon, and Professor Dowden of Shakespearian fame.

The meeting would have been a great success, but the boisterous spirits of the students exhibited themselves to an extravagant extent. The speakers were much perturbed by the explosion of squibs and other fireworks at short intervals. Finally the Auditor was chaired down the hall, round the square, and at last deposited, in a state of exhaustion at his rooms. My sufferings, on reading my presidential address, were such as to deter me from ever looking into the auditorial address, which I am sure would horrify me quite as much. I am glad to say that these opening meetings are no longer attended with the uproar and disorder which used to take place.

On the death of Lord Ashbourne in 1913, I was elected President of the College Historical Society, and retain the honour to the present time. The opening meetings are usually addressed by eminent public men. Lord Randolph Churchill made his first notable speech on the Historical platform, and other speakers have been Lord Parmoor, Sir John Simon, and Mr J. R. M. Butler, M.P.. Among those who were my contemporaries in the Historical Society were several who afterwards attained to high distinction, such as J. H. M. Campbell, afterwards Lord Glenavy, now the President of the Senate in the Irish Free State; Charles O'Connor, now Master of the Rolls in Ireland; Richard Cherry, afterwards Lord Chief Justice of Ireland (all of them auditors); Mr Justice Samuels, who, taking up the unfinished work of his gallant son, Arthur Samuels, killed in the War, has published *The Young Burke*, in which appears a most interesting account of the origin of the Historical Society. Edward Carson, now Lord Carson, was very able in debate, and his speeches were remarkable for their sincerity. While in College, his mind never rose to the great intellectual height he was to reach in after years. We used to say of him at the Bar that he improved every year, and probably the highest type of mind is one that is always growing. The one thing about him that impressed us all was his transparent integrity and courage.

An eminent man, connected with Trinity College, once complained in my presence that, while representing Dublin University, Carson had agreed to the partition of Ireland. I said that if I ceased to believe in Carson, whom I had known from my youth, I must cease to believe in men; that I was convinced that neither power, nor money, nor any other inducement would make him swerve from what he thought just and right.

Dr Kells Ingram, F.T.C.D., in his young and ardent days, had written the famous lyric, beloved of all Irish Nationalists:

'Who fears to speak of Ninety-eight?'

In his later years he was of the opinion that most of the Irish grievances had been removed, and that any that remained would disappear without the necessity for violent agitation.

The above is an extract from The Years of my Pilgrimage *by Sir John Ross, London, 1924.*

T. C. KINGSMILL MOORE – AUDITOR 1915–19, GOLD MEDALLIST

On August 1st, 1914 the College Historical Society was flourishing. The annual election for officers and committees had taken place and the new Auditor was occupying his mind with the preparation of his inaugural address and the selection of speakers. Three days later came the war: and with the war a steadily worsening of conditions in the Society. As usual, the members represented all grades of current political opinion, but the extreme nationalists were few, the great majority being either Unionist or Redmondite nationalists, and both of these classes regarded service in the armed forces as a manifest and compulsive duty. An estimate, made shortly after the war was ended and necessarily incomplete, reckoned that '253 of our present members (about 75 per cent of the average yearly membership) served in His Majesty's Forces. The inclusion of past members brings the total to approximately 700. With every fit member serving in the forces, the number available for carrying on the Society was at one time reduced to a fifth of its normal total'.

Almost at once, the Society was denuded of officers. Before the vacation was over, Auditor, Correspondence Secretary and Librarian were in uniform, shortly after Christmas the Treasurer was also commissioned. The opening meeting was perforce abandoned, leave of absence given to the serving officers and pro-officers appointed. In February 1915 the Treasurer, Correspondence Secretary and Librarian sent in their resignations and an election was held to fill their places. Leave of absence to the Auditor was continued throughout the session, the work being done by a pro-Auditor.

Throughout the 1914–15 session, the Society functioned along normal lines. Twelve debates were held, and though the attendance diminished, there was always an adequate number of speakers. Medals were awarded for Oratory and Composition. It was the policy of the authorities to encourage students in medicine and engineering who were in their final year to complete their courses before joining up and those who had been successful in the Indian Civil examinations remained to do their course in Indian Law and oriental languages. As the demand for men in the services was not yet critical, the physical standards for enlistment were high, and many who were subsequently to serve were initially rejected. Thus, there remained for a time in the Society a nucleus of knowledge and experience.

Elections for the 1915–16 session were held in June and it still was possible to fill all the officer-posts with senior men, three at least being filled by persons already rejected for the army on grounds of health. It was clear, however, that a crisis was at hand. To hold an opening meeting was impossible. Attendance at debates was getting dangerously small. There seemed to be no reservoir of experience from which to draw officers for ensuing sessions. Almost at once, the new Treasurer was leaving to take up a commission. Above all, it was necessary to take measures to preserve the unwritten conventions and practices of the Society. A committee was set up to consider and report what alterations were necessary on the existing rules and they drew up a set of temporary regulations which were adopted in November. To preserve continuity the existing officers and Committee were to hold office until the June after the first opening meeting. Any vacancy was to be filled by election by a committee composed of the officers and members of the general and library Committees. Meetings were to be confined to one a term and a debate at such meetings was optional. After the adoption of these rules, the Society for two and a half years did little more than keep alive. After the vacancy caused by the resignation of the Treasurer had been filled, the officers remained almost unchanged.

Two officers who had previously been rejected as unfit for service were given commissions, but after an accident one was wounded and returned to take up office. Meetings for private business were held as often as was necessary and there was an occasional debate, but the Society was clearly languishing. The Auditor was living in the country and was not always available. This caused discontent and there was a motion to remove him, which failed, but discontent continued and on February 5th, 1915 the Committee passed a motion that it was desirable to have a re-election of all officers. Accordingly, the officers handed in their resignations and, on February 11th a new election was held. The Record Secretary was elected Auditor, and the other offices were filled by new names. As the temporary regulations had not proved satisfactory, a committee was appointed to frame new temporary laws which were adopted in May. These laws provided, among other matters, that there should be new elections to offices and Committee seats each session, but that each officer should be eligible for the office which he then held, or for a lower office (thus preserving continuity of tradition while allowing replacement of any officer who had not been satisfactory). As a further measure to maintain tradition, members who had attained M.A. standing were allowed to remain on as ordinary members for a limited period. No opening meeting was to be held until the beginning of the session after peace was declared.

With the election of the new officers and committees, fresh life was injected into the Society. Debates were held more regularly and in June, pursuant to the temporary laws, there was an election. In the session 1918–19 trust in the existing officers was shown by the re-election of all to their former positions.

On November 11th came the Armistice, and the next day the President of the Society, Sir John Ross, then Lord Chancellor, sent for the Auditor to urge on him the necessity of holding a Peace Inaugural Opening Meeting at the traditional time in November, and the temporary laws forbade such a meeting till after peace had been declared, but the Society was determined to hold such a meeting on the first Wednesday in Hilary Term, 1919, and set about repealing the obstructive law, a procedure which required a two-thirds majority in favour at two successive meetings. To this, there was unexpected opposition. Since November, the Society had resumed almost full working, and a number of Honorary members turned up to oppose holding an opening meeting at such an unprecedented time. The debate was heated, and the Auditor rose to reply with such vigour as to overturn the auditorial chair, breaking its back; but the motion was carried by more than the necessary majority. When the day for the meeting came, the country was in the grip of the lethal influenza of 1919, and the Auditor delivered his address with a temperature of 102 degrees. In spite of the influenza, the meeting was crowded and successful. From then on, normal working prevailed, and membership grew rapidly as men returned from the colours. At the last meeting of the session, a motion was passed repealing all the temporary laws.

Our troubles were over. The policy of holding a limited number of debates, of retaining meetings for private business at more frequent intervals to ensure all the routine working of the Society, and the provisions whereby officers could remain in office for extended periods, had preserved all the traditions intact. The Auditor at the Peace Inaugural had held office continuously from February 17th 1915 to June 1919, save for an absence of eight months in the Royal Flying Corps, and was able to pass on his experience to his successor. The finances were in a satisfactory condition. The storm had been weathered.

GARDNER BUDD – SECRETARY 1925–26, VICE-PRESIDENT 1960–76

The early twenties was a flourishing time for the Hist. Although the membership was much smaller than now, the Society had then a wealth of first class speakers and the standard of debate was high. Rows and ructions were infrequent but that is not to say that there was any lack of student fire and courage. Revolutionary ideas were freely advocated and were not any the less effective in the absence of demonstrations to support them. The traditions of a liberal forum and hearing what the other man had to say were vigorously upheld by all from the Auditor down to the youngest novice.

The Society was very fortunate in its auditors during this period. Such men as Ralph Brereton Barry, W. D. L. Greer and Mark Wilson would have added lustre to any University Society. All of them were gifted speakers. Ralph Brereton Barry was outstanding in both serious debate and after-dinner speaking, a rare combination. Many members rose to high rank in later life. Of the above mentioned Ralph became a distinguished member of the Senior Bar, W. D. L. Greer became Bishop of Manchester and Mark Wilson was Chief Justice of the West African Court of Appeal.

The year one remembers best is naturally that in which one was most concerned with the Society's affairs and that was for me the 1925–26 session when I was Record Secretary. It was W. D. L. Greer's year as Auditor. The Treasurer was F. H. Boland, now Dr Boland, Chancellor of the University and President of the Society. His work and career in the United Nations is well known to all of us and made him a figure of international repute. His interest in the Society is as keen now as it was then, and all its members owe a debt of gratitude to him for his advice and guidance in all the Society's problems referred to him.

The event of most public interest at that time was the proposed visit of Lord Birkenhead to speak at the Inaugural Meeting of the year. He was a famous figure in those days, having had a lightning career in Parliament, and at the Bar and becoming Lord Chancellor of England. Justly renowned as a brilliant orator, he was original in style and had a penchant for interspersing his speeches with brilliant shafts of wit. Irishmen particularly remember his association with Lord Carson and later his part in the negotiations culminating in the Treaty of which he was a signatory.

The Society considered that it had brought off a great coup in securing him for its platform. There was a tremendous rush for tickets and high excitement about his visit. Then, about forty-eight hours before the time of his projected arrival, the blow fell. The Auditor received a telegram from Lord Birkenhead regretting his inability to speak at the opening meeting owing to public engagements. There was consternation. The reasons given did not sound very convincing to the Committee. It was decided to consult the President of the Society (Lord Glenavy) with a view to seeing what could be done, but he did not seem to favour any positive action which disappointed us. We came away from his house somewhat mystified. When we got back to the College it was decided to call an immediate meeting of the Committee to discuss the situation.

The ensuing meeting lasted into small hours of the following morning when a decision was reached to send over an emissary from the Committee whose instructions were to find out exactly what the position was, and to endeavour to persuade Lord Birkenhead to keep his engagement if at all possible. The two senior officers could not be spared so close to the meeting, and consequently the lot fell on the Record Secretary. I was to go over by the mail boat to London that very morning, which I did.

Before leaving, and on the way, a little planning had to be done. Lord Birkenhead was then Secretary of State for India and probably not addicted to receiving every strolling student who knocked at his door. I had however, a good friend in the shape of Ivison McAdam (now Sir Ivison), then the holder of high office in the English National Union of Students. He kindly agreed to gain entrée for me and to vouch for my credentials. Having arrived in London I dined with him and we set off together to Grosvenor Crescent where Lord Birkenhead then lived.

As a young student on a mission such as this I was in a state of some trepidation but we were received with great kindness and immediately put at ease by our host. I started explaining the nature of my mission and had not got very far when Lord Birkenhead, to my considerable surprise said that he had been looking forward very much to coming over to us but he was in a difficult position owing to communications and advice which he had received. He then gave me some documents to read. Despite what they contained he was ready and willing to go. He said that he had no personal fears but wished to avoid a demonstration of any sort because of his public position. We discussed ways and means of avoiding trouble, many of which had already been considered before I left. He then expressed his confidence in the Society to take all steps called for in the circumstances and proceeded to make various arrangements by telephone. I gathered that it was to be given out that it was believed he had left for Scotland.

Business over, we attempted to take our grateful leave but Lord Birkenhead would not hear of any immediate departure. He seemed to have a very good knowledge of Ireland generally, and the College and

Society in particular. He asked numerous questions and on discovering that I hoped to go to the Bar reminisced about his own career in an entrancing fashion. We were only allowed to go at a late hour and with the arrangement that he would expect to see me at Euston. I went to my room in some elation of spirits and proceeded to ring up the Auditor and glee-fully tell him the good news which was received with joy by him and those with him at the other end. I then fell asleep, but fate struck again.

In the small hours the 'phone awoke me. Billy Greer at the other end told me that I would have to take it from him that Lord Birkenhead should not travel and that I was to put him off immediately. I had no option but to endeavour to do so but it was to prove to be not at all simple.

First of all a 'phone call to his house went through but the butler said he regretted that his lordship had left for Scotland and of course he could not deliver a message in the circumstances: nor would he budge from that attitude. What to do then and yet observe a proper degree of discretion? The India Office seemed a possible source of communication but whatever high official was on night duty reacted with astonishment and some asperity to an unknown individual, describing himself as an Irish student, ringing up at that hour of the night with what , I suppose, sounded an odd sort of explanation. I could only think of politely suggesting that the responsibility was now over to him, which was not too well received. Later, however, he rang back in a more kindly frame of mind to say he would see what could be done. Meantime I had rung up Ivison McAdam and enlisted his aid. He was most sympathetic and said he would go round to Grosvenor Crescent and see what he could do. It was then time to go off to Euston to take the last stand there.

Arriving at Euston I had no difficulty in finding a senior official, I think it was the Station Master himself, on the platform, I assumed for the purpose of seeing Lord Birkenhead off. He was uncommunicative and re-ferred me to some other gentlemen on the platform. Apparently official personages, they were also uncommunicative but asked some searching questions as to my identity and credentials. On paper, at any rate, these were nil. Then at last Ivison McAdam, having seen Lord Birkenhead and put him off, arrived and all was cleared up. I thanked him very heartily and jumped into the train, starting a rather doleful return to Dublin and the Inaugural Meeting without any glittering prize. It went off well just the same, though I was somewhat fearful of my meeting with our President, who I gathered was not very pleased with me. He said nothing but had a distinct twinkle in his eye when he greeted me that evening.

W. B. STANFORD – VICE-PRESIDENT 1951–84

Two incidents stand out vividly among my memories as an undergraduate member of the Hist (1928–32). The first was the impeachment of Eoin O'Mahony as Auditor in 1930 for (to quote the indictment of 19 November 1930) 'his conduct in relation to the Opening Meeting'. The complaints of those moving the impeachment (who included a subsequent Minister of State and a Regius Professor of Laws) mainly centred on O'Mahony's substitution of the toast of 'Ireland' for the traditional 'the King' at the auditorial supper (where the toasting and counter-toasting led to some comical confusion). But other matters were also raised, including the fact that the Auditor had arranged for the menu of the supper to be printed by the University Press in elegant green Irish type — an unforgivable offence, apparently, in the eyes of some members. The first motion against the Auditor was debated from 12 noon to 7.52 p.m. on Wednesday, 12 November 1930 — a continuous performance which attracted many casual visitors until it merged into an ordinary meeting of the Society. This impeachment, and three subsequent attempts, failed, and O'Mahony continued to preside over one of the liveliest sessions in the Society's recent history.

The second incident happened at an ordinary debate in May 1931. Jim Larkin took the chair for a debate on the motion 'That in the State the individual should conform to the wishes of the Majority' (which was lost). It was a rather dull evening until Larkin began to give the chairman's summing up. He held many of us spellbound — he was the only truly spellbinding orator I have ever heard directly — with his account of the sufferings and degradations of Dublin's poor. When he left the debating hall many of us crowded eagerly round him, as if he were the Pied Piper of Hamelin, begging him to lead us anywhere, to tell us anything we could do, then and there, to remedy this monstrous injustice, as he had presented it. (One must remember that most students in those days were far less interested in social reform than the majority of students now: they were better academics and worse citizens on the whole.) I can still see and hear his reaction and response — huge, powerfully built old man that he was. He pushed his way on through us to the door of the G.M.B.: 'Ah, I'm a bit tired tonight, boys. Come and see me about it another day.' I don't think any of us did. But we had experienced for a few minutes the kind of oratorical power that in other circumstances has altered the course of history.

GARRET GILL – SECRETARY 1930–31, GOLD MEDALLIST

In my time in the Hist most debating societies we met had their distinctive styles. Oxford Union speakers had to be witty and frivolous; redbrick colleges tended to be heavily serious. In the Hist you followed your natural bent. There were echoes of Oscar Wilde in the speeches of Donough Bryan (Auditor 1928–29) and Terence de Vere White (Auditor 1932–33). No one who heard it will have forgotten the booming out reverberating reciting of Belloc's poem 'Balliol men' by Pope O'Mahony (Auditor 1930–31), though its relevance to the subject for debate must have been obscure. For a comprehensive and persuasive opening speech you could rely on Desmond Owens (Treasurer 1932–33) but for sharp shooting and entertaining attacks on previous speakers you looked to Owen Sheehy

Skeffington (Librarian 1930–31). Then there was the wild figure with tattered gown, crooked tie and draggled hair, who made his maiden speech in May 1934, with words and ideas tumbling over each other in their profusion — but Mr McDowell would have been *sui generis* in any Society.

In the Autumn of 1932, in company with J. J. Auchmuty (Auditor 1931–32), I represented the Hist in the USA, meeting about thirty American Colleges in debate. There, they debated to win. Some colleges had a debates coach, a Professor of Forsenics and a department of speech; important debates were rehearsed for weeks beforehand. In New Orleans our opponents each had a long narrow box before them — their card index file on the subject for debate. Insofar as debating has any practical effect they may have been right, but I think we, members of the Hist, had better fun and better learned to tolerate and enjoy a diversity of minds and opinions including such speeches as that of 'Mr J. G. McClintock (a maiden) who under cover of making a speech, read a short paper to the house upon his success as a breeder of dogs' (See T.C.D. for 3 March 1932).

EOIN O'MAHONY – AUDITOR 1930–31, GOLD MEDALLIST

In the late Summer of 1925 the Auditor was preparing his platform for his Opening Meeting and he thought that he would like to have F. E. Smith, Earl of Birkenhead as one of his principal speakers.[15] Knowing the close association during the Ulster Volunteer period of 1912–1914, he approached the President of the Historical Society, Lord Glenavy (The Chairman of the Senate at that time) to ask his help. The President was not enthusiastic but

---

[15] Editor's note: This account does not tally in all its details with that of Gardner Budd.

promised to write to the noble lord. A few days later, he told the Auditor that F. E. Smith had written to say 'no'. He was afraid of being assassinated in Ireland, according to the President.

The Auditor, an Ulsterman, went straight to the Irish Prime Minister and said that he thought it a terrible slur on Ireland's good name when, within four years of the signing of the Treaty of 1921, one of the chief English signatories was afraid to set foot on our shores. Mr Cosgrave agreed with him and, while he denied that there was any danger, he promised Birkenhead a military and police guard for the whole of his short stay in Ireland. The Auditor then went to London to reassure the Galloper and F. E. said that, for himself he had no fears, but he produced a letter from the Society's president warning him not to come. The proposed visit was whispered all over Dublin and Roger Casement's loveable but difficult brother, Tom, sent Birkenhead a telegram worded as follows: 'You murdered my brother. If you set foot inside Trinity College, I'll shoot you.'

On his return from London, the Auditor was met at Dun Laoghaire by his Officers and two taxis conveyed them all to Lord Glenavy's mansion. The President received them in bed and wine was served. After a decent pause the Auditor conveyed that he had persuaded Lord Birkenhead to come, that he had been willing to come all the time and that it was merely an excessive zeal on the President's part for F. E.'s safety which had caused him to hesitate. The President, Lord Glenavy, showed signs of intense rage, dashed his glass to the ground and threatened to resign the Presidency of the Society. The Auditor then told the President what he, and the men of Ulster, thought of him and Lord Birkenhead was dropped from the panel of speakers.

It was up to the President to repair the damage he had caused and he suggested that he should persuade his life long friend and political opponent, T. M. Healy, the Governor General, to take the Galloper's place. Never in the history of the Society was there such a brilliant Opening Meeting. It was of course Tim's meeting. He dominated the proceedings from the beginning to the end and every page of the *Irish Times* was filled with photographs of the gathering. The supporting speakers — The Bishop of Cashel Dr Miller, the Labour Leader, R. J. P. Mortished and Senator General Sir William Hickie paled into insignificance beside him.

At the supper afterwards, Tim excelled himself in his wickedest, most puckish and impish mood and became blazingly indiscreet for the King's representative. He purported to reveal the names of those who shot Private Aspinall, an English soldier from Spike Island or Haulbowline some nine months previously. His two uniformed and immaculately dressed A.D.C.s immediately jumped him to attention, seized him by the shoulders and the legs and conveyed him out of the Supper Room and down the Dining Hall steps to the waiting Viceregal Rolls Royce. Meanwhile, Tom Casement had concealed himself in the Dining Hall with a flask of whiskey and a loaded revolver thinking that Birkenhead would be smuggled into the meeting at the last moment. Disappointed of his prey, he made for the United Arts Club and poured petrol down the side of the house to which he set fire. He anticipated the work of Dublin's developers by forty-five years. It's an ill wind.

During the outstanding Auditorship of Donough Bryan of 1928–29, the College and the Society both took part in celebrating the bicentenary of the births of Edmund Burke and Oliver Goldsmith. Stephen Gwynn gave the address on Goldsmith and Birkenhead was invited to give the Oration on Burke — a performance unworthy of both. He was taking no chances on this occasion. In avoiding Tom Casement he took the wrong Boat Train and woke up in Belfast. The address was stolen completely from John Morley's essay on Burke which he appeared to have picked up on the train or on the boat. Appropriately, there was a patronising reference to Burke's debts. Mr Cosgrave, Taoiseach, was the principal guest at the Provost's luncheon party. Next day, Birkenhead spend the morning golfing at Malahide and was due to inaugurate the Burke Bicentenary Fund for the Society in the Graduates Memorial Building at 3 p.m. with the President of the Society in the chair. It was fortunate that he was an hour late because it enabled the packed audience to hear the President at his very best. He recalled the Society in the 1870s when the Lord Chancellor President Sir Joseph Napier had vetoed his Inaugural on Land Purchase as being too revolutionary. After Christmas, he delivered the same Opening Address when the new President Chancellor Sir Edward Sullivan Lord Chancellor censured him for his lack of courage! Claiming to have been a pioneer on Land Purchase from his undergraduate days, the President said that he had turned his Inaugural Address into an article for John Morley's *Fortnightly Review*! To his annoyance, he got no acknowledgment from Morley and to add insult to injury, Morley absorbed the article and published it as his own!

The Bicentenary Debate on Literary Censorship was memorable with Cecil Harmsworth in the Chair and Michael Stewart, now British Foreign Secretary (Oxford Union) leading for the affirmative against Censorship which lost by 241 to 91 votes.

My best friend in the Hist was Diarmuid Murtagh of Athlone, founder of the Military History Society of Ireland, beside whom I sat in school refectory. There was no better speaker, no shrewder judge of debating and of Oratory. He knew all the orators by heart from Grattan's day until our own time. He told me that the most brilliant and convincing speech he ever heard was that delivered on the result of the German Presidential Election in April 1925 when Hindenburg won. The speaker was Frederick Boland, now Chancellor of Dublin University and President of the Hist. But Murtagh had erred in his dates. On that night, no speech was made by Fred Boland. His speech was almost certainly delivered on the following 25th November with the College Chaplain, Canon Forrester, in the chair. The motion for debate was 'That Germany's Participation in the War was justified'. It was of course defeated but the whole house admired the argument and the speaker's courage in facing an extremely hostile audience.

OWEN SHEEHY SKEFFINGTON – LIBRARIAN 1930–31, GOLD MEDALLIST

My memories of the Hist go back to the autumn of 1927 when I first entered Trinity College. When my name went up on the 'Intending Members' list one member proposed in the Suggestion Book that I be not admitted, because if the Hist were to admit such 'Sinn Féiners' it would find itself 'admitting de Valera next.' As a not-very-well-informed Junior Freshman, I did not know whether this was to be taken seriously or not; some of my slightly less junior contemporaries did take it seriously and warned me about 'talking politics'. This advice I did not take, and when I got to know the Hist I realized that any fears of serious prejudice on such a basis were quite groundless there, and that this particular 'suggestion' was a joke.

The Auditor in my first year was Brendan Lloyd, mild but effective, though something overshadowed by the sheer ebullience of two of his officers, C. J. Pelly and the late Oliver McCutcheon (who *ought* to have been Auditor the following year). Debates were impressive. The then existing Neophyte Debating Society — which admitted students up to Junior Sophister standing only — ensured that the more rumbustious heckling and the less co-ordinated types of oratory were mainly confined to it, where you had to be *good*, or at any rate be telling a good story, to be allowed to finish a sentence. Two results of this were that in the Hist it was rare for a Junior Freshman to do more than listen, and the speeches there tended to be more crisp, co-ordinated, and mature and less subject to irrelevant or brainless heckling than has sometimes been the case since the demise of the Neophyte in the 1940s.

Attendances ranged around the 30 or 40 mark, except when there was a row on in Private Business; there were usually five debates in the Michaelmas term, seven in each of the other two, and no 'Hon. Members Debate,' so that ordinary members had more chances than now to participate. It is true that, as still happens, quite a few members never attended debates. The Conversation Room was heated by an open fire at each end, and by, at one end, the heated discussions of Private Business intrigues, tribulations, and simulated indignations, and at the other, by Rugger or Cricket Club tactics and politics. Each group knew the other to be quite mad. I belonged to both, having both types of lunacy in the family.

In the 1927–28 session there were still rumblings of the Hist politics of a few years previously — centred around a mysterious former Auditor called 'Hoppy' whom I never knew. As a consequence, there was a successful campaign (no canvassing, of course, good heavens no!) against McCutcheon for Auditor and in favour of the brilliant but much senior Donough Bryan, who, after a spell with the Oxford Group, was some years later to meet a tragic death.

Private Business in the Hist was very strictly conducted, and few points conceded without prolonged procedural argument. The midnight closure rule was always observed. One object of the opposition was, consequently, to talk out the 'making absolute' of fines, some of which mounted by the session's end to astronomic figures, such as 7s. 9d. or even 15s. 11d. I remember towards the end of the 1929–30 session that the Committee decided to hold a twelve-hour Private Business meeting, in order to spike the guns of the opposition, who had usually found it all too easy to talk out Private Business between the end of the debate (usually 10.30 p.m.) and midnight. The occasion was an epic one. Every trick was tried by the opposition, most effectively led by the late Gerard Sweetman — so grimly killed this year — and Marshall Dudley. Privileged motions were used to their maximum capacity; as I remember it, for instance, a motion to give leave of absence to the librarian (R. P. P. Wallace) was spoken to for over three hours, despite the fact that Wallace made it perfectly clear at the outset that he did not want and would not take leave of absence. It was urged that he *looked* as if he wanted it, that he worked too hard for the Society, that a rest would do him good, etc., etc.

Numbers thinned out during the lunch hour, but the opposition kept all their supporters there until there were very few others left. They then withdrew in a body, leaving one of their number to point out that there was no quorum (eleven members) and to call for an immediate adjournment. The chairman saved the day by peering doubtfully round at the five or six people still present and saying that, in order to make quite sure that there was not a quorum present, he would ask the record secretary to read out the names of all the members of the Society and ask those who were present to signify this fact. It took about fifteen minutes; and the house was full to capacity (and the buffet empty) by the time the full list had been read. Bueno McKenna was the Auditor that year, and an exceedingly good one, both as a crisp and cogent speaker and as an efficient administrator and committee man.

The Auditor in the following year, 1930–31, was in many ways a very different character. He certainly was not an efficient committee man, though of engagingly original, generous, and mercurial temperament. He was one of the best undergraduate speakers I have heard in the Hist. He had won the oratory gold medal the previous year, and he was at his very best at this time, when he was in his middle twenties, some four years older than his fellow members, having spent some time in the U.C.C. Medical

School before coming to T.C.D. He was, of course, Eoin O'Mahony — the 'Pope' — whose untimely death has recently saddened us all.

A really full account of 'the O'Mahony row' would take more space than I have at my disposal. Suffice it to say that he had decided not to toast the King at the Auditorial Supper after the opening meeting (November 1930), and that a majority vote on the Committee had confirmed the fact that such a matter lay within the auditorial prerogative. On the night of the meeting, after an 'address' brilliantly delivered — and the word seems unusually appropriate — from the backs of a few envelopes, and on the topic of 'Canada in Travail', the 'Pope' took me aside — I was his librarian — and said: 'I want your advice before we go in to this supper: these fellows are going to get the chairman (Professor Alison Phillips) to toast the King; what am I to do?'

In the light of the Committee decision and his own earlier stated intention, I said: 'My advice is for you to get in first!' The 'Pope' did not look too happy at this advice, I thought, but I only later found out why. Some of his opponents had just asked him, in fact, if they might ask Phillips to give the toast, and the 'Pope' had said: 'I wash my hands of the whole matter; you can do what you like.' This he had not told me: and so he looked unhappy; and in fact he had decided to let the whole matter go as his opponents wished it.

However, as he went in to the supper, he heard one of them say: 'Thank God we have taught him to behave like a Trinity man and a gentleman.' This was just too much for the 'Pope', and when the moment came, he sprang to his feet and shouted: 'Gentlemen, I give you the toast of Ireland!' Farce followed. All rose to the toast. Some could be heard saying: 'Ireland — and the King. I mean, the King and Ireland.' We sat down amidst some confusion and hilarity, to which the foolish chairman added by jumping up and proposing the royal toast, which was drunk by some and not by others. O'Mahony's opponents then left in high dudgeon, and so did the chairman; it was thought at first that the latter — an Englishman — was deeply offended, but he later explained that he had some trouble with his bladder.

The session that followed was filled with the efforts of O'Mahony's opponents to impeach him, and of his friends to prevent (a) them from doing so, and (b) him from quixotically resigning. New members flooded in on both sides, and those of us who were on the Auditor's side decided to obstruct Private Business week by week, and prevent the impeachment motion from coming up until at least the majority of the new members had got tired of attending. The session was a memorable one; many new orators were heard. I remember humorous and persuasive Joe Shields (till recently Irish Ambassador at the Vatican — it just shows how careful you have to be!). I recall, too, a more astringent orator, who was brought to the fore by this row, a classical scholar, a fighting Kerryman, and a spellbinder, Gold Medallist in Oratory 1933–34, Noel Hartnett, of course.

The end of the affair was farce like the beginning — though it is true that a serious motion to drop the royal toast and 'all other political toasts' was passed and ratified that year. By March, however, it was impossible to stall the anti-O'Mahony motion any longer; a twelve hour private business meeting was held again. The impeachment motion was reached and passed, though not before an amendment of mine had been added: to insert in it, after the Auditor's name, the words 'and all his officers and Committee'. And so we all stood impeached, both his supporters on the Committee and his opponents. At the next meeting we each in turn solemnly submitted our resignation to the Society, starting off with the Auditor; and each in turn was solemnly refused. Good fun while it lasted; and not bad political training. Hist issues are not always important, but learning to wield the instrument of speech and use fairly the structures of democratic procedure can be of vital importance.

I have said enough; but I cannot stop; a not uncommon Hist defect. I think of a magnificent Jim Larkin speech at an ordinary meeting in 1931 which made us all feel that if he had asked us there and then to storm the Dáil, we would at once have done so. I think again of Harold Laski's brilliant performance at Jimmy Wellwood's opening meeting in 1934. Speaking after Mr de Valera who had been just two years in office, and was speaking at a Hist opening meeting for the first time, Laski — the best speaker I have ever heard — began his speech thus:– 'There is one thing at least that Mr de Valera will have to admit, and that is that we English are always ready to forgive.' This received a great cheer from about half the audience, and in particular from those who did not favour Mr de Valera. Laski's sentence, however, despite the audience's impression, was not yet finished. He went on: '. . . those whom we have most grievously wronged'.

There was a moment of stunned silence, and then a wild cheer from the other half of the audience: a splendid initial stirring up of listeners! It was Laski, also, some years later, speaking to the Hist on Edmund Burke (of all people!) who heard a vote of thanks proposed and seconded to him in rather unfriendly terms by a former Free State Minister and a visiting Professor. The first had said that he knew Laski to be a 'Muscovite' (which he was not), and that, of course the Muscovites had done a service to the world 'by making murder respectable': they called it 'liquidation'.

The Professor was less offensive, but he did make a rather weak joke about Laski's name, and also said that while he himself was only an academic, and a bit out of touch with the big world, he did gather that Laski had 'something to do with politics'. Laski made a brief reply: he said that he was 'particularly impressed' by the Irish politician's remarks about murder and liquidation, because he, Laski, was merely a university teacher, whereas Mr X (let us call him) 'as a former member of the Cosgrave Government, had had, of course, practical experience'. Turning then to the Professor, he observed that 'to the Ivory Tower inhabited by Professor Y, apparently no light penetrated'. However, he would urge him, he said, to take advantage of the fact that he was for once out in the open, to look about him a bit 'before lapsing back into that state of resentful coma, which the universities call Research'.

A double oratorical knock-out, and much appreciated by the Hist audience. Later that evening at a dinner to Laski, he paid tribute to Churchill, with whom he had recently been unsuccessfully tangling in the courts, and to Mr de Valera, about whom he said that he was one of the few politicians 'willing to listen to advice'. And he added: 'He never takes it, of course; but still he does listen.' And he praised Irish hospitality, expressing his joy at getting for the first time since the war two eggs at breakfast. When a later speaker referred to the fact that we had at least given Laski two eggs, the voice of O'Mahony interjected: 'And two targets!'

These last memories are of a mere twenty-three years ago, not forty. I had better stop. The Hist has been — is — good fun. It provides a wonderful (*stet*, as Myles na Gopaleen would say) stamping ground and 'workshop' for those who value wit coupled with rational debate, who favour persuasion rather than the bludgeon, who are prepared to give a fair hearing as well as demand one. And, as for procedural devices . . . Well, there are very few that have not at some time in the past two hundred years been given a trial run in the College Historical Society. Moreover, there, at any rate, the rule of law is paramount; and the final arbiter is the House itself — if the House so wills. If democracy has any meaning, it is upon such concepts that it stands.

ॐ

TERENCE DE VERE WHITE – AUDITOR 1932–33, GOLD MEDALLIST

My first speech was the worst I have ever heard. I heard it quite distinctly because my voice seemed to leave me and speak from a distant point in the ceiling. When it stopped suddenly, I had two impulses equally strong — to burst into tears and to run away. I resisted both and waited with a strange feeling of disembowelment for the voice in the ceiling to start again. After what seemed like a fortnight, it uttered a few, hasty, valedictory remarks, one more sententious than the other, and then came back to me. I returned quickly to my seat and left the hall as soon as decency allowed. After that I kept out of Trinity until I felt that the report of my shame might have died. No one, of course, cared a damn.

By degrees I got up courage to speak again and attained some degree of success by adopting an epigrammatic and would-be sophisticated style which was not common in Trinity, if sadly familiar elsewhere. It was effective for a while; but when my audience became accustomed to the trick, they ceased to be impressed by it.

Taken in by my manner, the Society selected me and Donough Bryan, who died not long afterwards, to represent it in an inter-university debate in Galway. Donough was twenty-seven and I was sixteen. Our rivals were serious-minded men. Dudley Edwards, now professor of Modern History in University College, Dublin, and Carrol O'Daly, now a High Court

Judge, represented University College. Dudley Edwards was very much in earnest and Carrol O'Daly very much in Irish, so that when my time came to speak, I felt that a degree of flippancy was almost a duty. Donough Bryan had spoken before me in his pleasant, thoughtful way but without sufficient bite to dispel the inspissated gloom which threatened to smother us.

I provoked a certain amount of laughter and was delighted with myself. Donough Bryan took me to task afterwards. There was a danger in this, he said. A diet of champagne would pall at last. Use it for light relief, not as the substance of speeches. I wish I had taken his advice.

The College Historical Society, originating in an earlier Society, founded by Edmund Burke, belongs to the history of Ireland. Here Wolfe Tone and Robert Emmet began their public careers: here Thomas Davis first preached the doctrine of nationality: here Isaac Butt and Edward Carson first found a platform.

If in the main it took its tone from the University, there were times when the Society proved too revolutionary and explosive to be allowed to function within the College walls. And, for some years, it suffered banishment. It has always been a barometer of political weather and in my time it gave stormy readings.

But the prevailing tone in the Society was moderate. At our suppers we continued to drink the King's health. As he was still our King, there was nothing very remarkable in that. But in those years the Cosgrave government, first through Kevin O'Higgins, and later Costello and McGilligan, was trying to whittle the Commonwealth link to a shaving. The Board of Trinity College was still unashamedly Unionist in sentiment and, while it obeyed the law and sent representatives to the Dáil, these usually spoke in the voices of reprieved prisoners. They spoke with the voice of the Board, composed mostly of old men. The Society, an undergraduate body, accepted the new State in spirit as well as in fact. Unionists and republicans alike were minority groups, although the first was far larger and more influential than the second.

The College Historical Society selected as a rule for its highest office one of its sleeker brethren. In 1930 it departed from this tradition and honoured a character, Eoin O'Mahony. He was called 'The Pope' on account of his dogmatic manner of speech. 'The Pope' had a rich Cork brogue and one of the most mellifluous voices in Ireland. Only James Dillon could compare with him in organ power, in copiousness and volume.

At the beginning of his term of office the Auditor (as the person holding O'Mahony's position is called) delivers a written address which is spoken to by a platform of speakers. This meeting is open to the public.

O'Mahony departed from custom by not writing a paper, but speaking without pause for an hour. His subject: 'Canada in Travail'. It was quite incomprehensible and whatever the pains of Canada may have been, the audience, upon whom a twilight sleep had mercifully descended, were oblivious to them long before O'Mahony had completed his delivery.

Auditors attempt to collect as distinguished a platform as possible. They issue invitations to Prime Ministers, Archbishops and Nobel Prize winners, and settle, as a rule, for local celebrities and, if they are lucky, a 'name' from across the water. Some auditors have better luck, some try harder than others. The principal attraction of O'Mahony's platform was the leader of a separatist party in Canada. The party consisted of himself: and his surprise at being invited to express his views in public must have put his health in considerable peril. For he was very old.

O'Mahony, at least, made a delightful, if too prolonged noise; the Canadian separatist addressed his boots in a mumbled monotone. He went on for hours. It was for him the opportunity of a lifetime. The meeting was a flop. O'Mahony's unconventional gesture would have only been justified if it had succeeded.

As we were going in to supper at the beginning of his term of office he announced briefly that he would not toast the King. His officers, of whom I was one, were as panic-stricken as if he had elected to sup in the nude. 'Would he object if someone else proposed the toast?' He expressed indifference; but put an end to that possibility by jumping up at coffee and proposing the toast of 'Ireland'.

The rest of the year was one of fierce political excitement. A motion of impeachment of O'Mahony was proposed and debated for a whole session. Champions on his behalf were not lacking. Most prominent was Owen Sheehy Skeffington whose father had been murdered by Captain Colthurst during Easter Week 1916.

O'Mahony had brought our proceedings into line with the policy of the

Irish government and away from the sentiments of the then Board of the College. I thought, and still think, that he went about it in the wrong way and by his precipitancy (or policy) made the gesture in an undignified manner. He was much older than the rest of us, and if his attitude to life was not in general sagacious, he was more in tune with the times than we were. His action had the effect of shaking us into politics: some found themselves more on the right than they had expected: some more on the left. But all were forced to discover that man is by nature a political animal. We owed him more than at the time we realized if only for teaching us this ancient lesson.

To the College Historical Society I owed a great deal. It gave me trips to Cambridge and Edinburgh and an opportunity to measure myself against the men in those places. Of Edinburgh I have only the foggiest memory. We were given so much to drink before the debate that when we arrived at the rooms of the Edinburgh Speculative Society (in which Robert Louis Stevenson used once to speak) I had forgotten the subject for debate and the fact that I had to speak first. When called upon, I put up my hand and found some firm projection by which I was able to pull myself to my feet; then, with as much dignity as I could muster, I asked the Secretary to repeat the motion which I had come to propose. He did so. Whatever my oration lacked in formal preparation, it made up for in a total release from inhibitions and I burbled on without let or hindrance for half an hour about anything that came into my mind.

A horse that was grazed on a prairie will be fretful in a paddock; and there is something about Ireland, not only in respect to size, but in the prevailing spirit which creates a feeling of mental enclosure.

I had my first experience of this when, following in O'Mahony's footsteps, I started to collect a platform for my inaugural meeting. A sympathetic friend, trying to help me, had driven me up to the Governor General's house (now Áras an Uachtaráin) to meet G. K. Chesterton. The great man was staying in Dublin for the Eucharistic Congress. We went into the garden and walked around. It was a very hot afternoon. Chesterton sat down and sweat beaded on his forehead. He was extremely fat and rather grey in colour. His fat was of the unhealthy, lardy kind.

He said very little and gave the impression of being shy which increased my own shyness. Whether, even in that weather, we would have become

206

more at ease with one another, remains a speculation: an Indian bishop bore down on Chesterton and spoke with such eloquence and rapidity no problems of conversation remained.

Chesterton promised to come in the autumn and speak to my paper. The news got about and one, Hugh Blackham, published in *The Irish Press* a protest against Chesterton being tricked into a visit to a university which was anathema to the Catholic hierarchy. He also wrote to Chesterton advising him not to give scandal by appearing. After some correspondence Chesterton decided that the game was not worth the scandal and cancelled his visit.

This was a blow. But I felt reasonably satisfied in the end with my bag which consisted of Compton Mackenzie, H. N. Brailsford, Maurice Dobb and Desmond Fitzgerald.

We were handicapped by lack of funds but there were usually kind people who had the way and were pleased to put up visitors on these occasions. Mackenzie stayed with old friends, the Nolans, in Shankill. Diarmuid Coffey put up Brailsford; I asked Dr Lombard Murphy, Director of Independent Newspapers, to give Maurice Dobb a bed.

'Gladly,' said Dr Murphy. 'I am glad you asked me to have the Cambridge man. I was afraid you might put one of your left-wing fiends on me.'

Dr Murphy was a Cambridge graduate. Maurice Dobb was at this date the author of *Russian Economic Development since the Revolution.* As I knew Dr Murphy to have views of particular rigidity on such matters, it was plainly madness to have asked him to give house room to one with the views of Maurice Dobb. No matter how tactful as a guest, he was unlikely to push politeness to the point of disguising his opinions of the platform. Having made my gaffe, I let matters lie.

'I shall expect him to breakfast at nine o'clock,' said Dr Murphy.

The mail boat, in those days, came into Dun Laoghaire at six-thirty. I was on the pier with a borrowed motor-car to meet it. Lenin's disciple looked meek and travel-stained and ready for a hot bath and comfortable breakfast: but dread of my impending doom rendered me too craven to risk adding injury to insult by arriving before the stated hour. Torn between the claims of capital and labour, I plumped for capital. I did not let myself see the expression I imagined on Dobb's face when I announced: You must see the view of the Bay before breakfast. You will not have another chance.

Was it a moan, or the slumped figure in the back seat with hunched shoulders and fallen head, that made me weaken, that caused me to pity the foreigner sufficiently to brave the consequences and turn back from the sight-seeing expedition in the wreathing November mists? I cannot remember now.

It was a pity that Mr Dobb had to endure such a Siberian introduction to Dublin, because Dr Murphy never breathed a word of complaint or taxed me with my inconsiderate abuse of his hospitality. It would be pleasant to think that, exhausted by two hours of oratory he had reached a comfortable somnolescent condition when Dobb rose to speak, that he heard not one of the shrill arguments on behalf of the Soviet, but saw only a radiant figure on tip-toe with hands outstretched El Greco-wise: noted with approval the accents of Charterhouse and Trinity (Cambridge); and nodded in nostalgic reverie while his guest proposed the destruction of his host's class and the ruin of his host's world.

Under the spell of Compton Mackenzie, whom I met for the first time, I became oblivious to my duties and my trials. I now remember with shame that I sat between Mackenzie and Douglas Hyde at supper and had ears only for the stranger.

Extract from A Fretful Midge *by Terence de Vere White, London 1957.*

CONOR CRUISE O'BRIEN – ELECTED PRESIDENT 1983, GOLD MEDALLIST 1938–39

I remember the Hist of my day (1936–40) as an institution of almost preternatural decorum — at least during public business — in which the style of an idealised Victorian Parliament was preserved, or created. However distasteful their opinions, or — much worse — however boring their style, speakers were heard patiently, with at least apparent respect. The laws of debate were rigorously followed, heckling and interruption almost unknown. The Old Adam, so conspicuous and influential in all real parliaments, was invisible in his rowdier manifestations in these public debates — at least as I now recall them.

On the one visit I paid to the Hist in recent times, the Old Adam was roaring. It is true that it was a special occasion: the subject of debate was the exclusion of Eve. Frequent interruptions, violent language, shouting on the floor culminated in such an uproar that the meeting had to be suspended. The proceedings lacked decorum, sweetness and reason, but they did resemble a bad night in a real parliament much more closely than the public proceedings of the Hist in my own time resembled anything in the real world.

The Hist I remember had a certain style of its own: astringent cerebral, a little musty, quite formidable. The late Peter Allt — whose monument is the Variorum Yeats — was a master in this kind and added, like all masters, something uniquely his own. He had an unusually large head and nose, tremendous natural equipment for the booming style, and he used this resource in strange contrapuntal effects to the blinking of very small red-rimmed eyes to suggest argument of high intellectual power, and enthralling perversity. The strange alliance of the bittern and the ferret, with an undertone of fey, menacing unction never failed to dominate his audience, and lingers in the memory with its own peculiar savour. The Hist I remember is one in which Peter Allt is always speaking — which means that it is somewhat stylised and distorted. Which would have pleased him.

🖤

JOHN ROSS – AUDITOR 1942–43, GOLD MEDALLIST

It is appalling to think that the passage of about twenty-five years either blunts memory to such an extent that all is lost in euphoric fog or sharpens it to an unreality that is positively defamatory.

MICHAEL CAMPBELL – SECRETARY 1945–46, GOLD MEDALLIST

It was twenty-two years ago. I was then Correspondence Secretary, and was, as usual, discussing with friends, late at night, the Meaning of Existence, and whether the cow exists in the Front Square when there's no one about, when there entered into my Rooms — at that time, before linoleum and toilets were invented, consisting of a basin of solid ice and a convenient sink on the landing, both the creation of Queen Elizabeth I — a group of masked men. Nearly all of them looked like Guy Fawkes, and three of them were terribly old Honorary Members, aged about thirty, at least.

We stopped discussing God, and I felt faint. It was the dreaded, forbidden thing, a caucus meeting.

If *I* did this, and everybody else did that, I would be made Auditor. (I couldn't grasp what I was supposed to do)

(The word 'caucus' was invented by John Smith from the Indian word 'caw — cawassough'. He was saved from the Indians by Pocahontas, who married an Englishman and settled down quietly in London.)

Well, I said I wouldn't, because I wanted Peace of Mind; later discovering that an identical caucus, involving my rival, was taking place in the New Buildings.

He won. And *I* had sacrificed a bottle of crème de menthe.

I was then flown to Glasgow in a very small, sickly, biplane with a representative of the Rival University. I had prepared — and learned to the point of near mania — a speech about the decay of the Abbey Theatre. We were met at the Airport by about fifty youths — twenty-two years before Demonstrations became easy — bearing the Irish tricolour. Also banners — 'Freedom for Scotland', 'Freedom for Ireland'. And the question: 'What are you going to say? Will you give them what for?'

By now obsessed with the question as to what Yeats had said to Frank O'Connor and where Sean O'Casey went and what had happened to Lennox Robinson, I walked speechlessly through Glasgow, surrounded by this flag-waving, near hysterical mob of apprentice revolutionaries.

The Rival University and I were placed in a temperance hotel, where he walked up and down the room, reciting *King Lear* with terrible accuracy, for hours.

Tricolours were waving, and shouts for freedom sounded through the hall. I told them, with surprising calm, what Sean O'Casey had said to Yeats and how Yeats had reported it back to Frank O'Connor, who had told Lennox Robinson the whole story.

There was a very hostile hush.

But I treasure the medals. And I loved it all.

H. R. F. KEATING – SECRETARY 1950–51, GOLD MEDALLIST

I came an unlicked cub into the Conversation Room for the first time in 1948. I was older than a good many of my contemporaries because I had spent my portion of years as a British Army conscript, but this did not mean that inwardly I was really much more sophisticated — military life is simultaneously coarse and sheltered — and it was with a good deal of trepidation that I entered into that lofty room. The first sight that struck my eyes was a young buck of a sizar from Cork sprawled legs up wantonly asleep on the old brown sofa that used to stand against the wall under the windows.

I never got to the pitch of sleeping in the Conversation Room in the four years that followed, but I did sprawl. Indeed, looking back I see it is the Conversation Room rather than the debating chamber that most means 'the Hist' for me. The hours I spent there, the things I talked about there, the progress I made there.

The room's lineaments are fixed in my mind's eye forever, though probably inaccurately. I see now its heavy four-square armchairs and settees ranged in their appointed places like regiments of soldiers for ever on parade. I see the two big facing-each-other fireplaces, with in winter generous fires in one or both according to some complex code lodged in the mind of grinningly cheerful Jack, the Attendant. I see the cabal of cold Africans always to be found at the top end.

I see the patterned carpets, honourably worn, and, when I became a Committee member, subject of much dutiful financial calculation. I see the heavy swinging door and remember its sighing wheeze as it closed again after someone had entered. It meant then that likely as not here was some new ingredient for the rich stew that Conversation Room life soon came to be for me.

I see too the notice-board, another source of perpetually renewed excitements. Was it the order of speakers for next week's debate, on one of those small sheets of comfortably thick paper with the old-fashioned print-style? There came a moment when one was chosen for the first time to propose a motion. Was it the announcement of the subject for the President's Composition prize, with its awesome challenge almost as it seemed coming from a voice in outer space (it was like that then, long ago)?

And, a much lesser excitement in those inward-turned days, there was the papers table. I recall its ranged Journals from the politely fought-over copies of the *Irish Times* ('Have you seen what Myles na Gopaleen says today?') to its single decently mouldering issue of *Hermathena*. But I fed from this table too.

This scene is more vivid to me than the debates for which the Society primarily exists. Of all that I heard and said in them, and I bobbed up enough with all the cubbish conceit of undergraduatehood, I can recall only the words 'Mr Chairman, Mr Auditor and gentlemen of the College Historical Society.' With one thing more — strange the selective processes of memory — that I once surmised that one of the little opaque glass lampshades that had been partially broken for years had suffered from the oratorical power of one of my more ebullient contemporaries. Is that shade broken yet?

And indeed I can remember little of the tasks that fell to me when I rose to become Correspondence Secretary. I must have written a lot of letters. Not a word remains. But I do recall one task that fell to my lot. It was the Correspondence Secretary's duty to meet the guest chairman before each debate began and to escort him up to the Conversation Room. I was solemnly warned by my predecessor that the very cornerstone of this task was to warn the distinguished old bod that he was likely to have to sit for a number of hours without it being easy for him to leave his place, and that therefore he might like to make use of the cavernous lavatory facilities of the basement. And on every occasion I had to do this my social courage failed me. How many eminent figures in Irish public life owe me a secret grudge I tremble to think.

And yet I believe that out of that fearful embarrassment I did somehow learn to cope with the similar minor complications life has produced since. Just as from the juvenile hurly-burly of Private Business — when the debate is over my poor chairman had at least managed to right his situation — I learned in retrospect how much sheer gall it needs to bluff a way through public life, although at the time if a bold lie or a bland denial was called for I never somehow managed to bring it off.

But, though I learnt a good deal in these situations — and even by the end of my College days had worn that fearful urge to leap to the feet and speak on any and every occasion — it was the Conversation Room that was by far the most effective and the picture of it will remain with me through the years. If I have yet to put it into a detective-story it is only that the right moment has never quite turned up. But how nicely a body would lie on one of those worn-yet-surviving carpets.

I suppose that in whatever seating accommodation they had in that place downstairs I might have learnt something, but I feel that conversations originating there would have lacked the bite and edge of true Hist talk, talk that might begin under that big, brown-varnished, anonymous portrait over the fireplace but which would often go on for hours after the big fire had become a heap of sluggish embers as I wandered with some choice spirit through the still and silent squares outside — 'I think we'll take just one more turn' — and absorbed like a column of walking blotting-paper.

Learning of this sort, learning not what life is about (which comes later) but what life is, this is supposed to be the great gift a university education gives you. Oddly enough, looking back, the dear platitude turns out to be perfectly true. And of all this kind of learning that I acquired at College, the bigger part came to me in the battered dignity of the Conversation Room.

MAURICE ABRAHAMSON – AUDITOR 1951–52, MEDALLIST

The sight of the Auditor walking round and round the streets of Dublin in the early hours of the morning mumbling to himself about points of order and points of fact might seem to reflect the result of recent events and turmoil. In fact, the memory of making such a tour is the first thing which always springs to mind when asked about my own experiences of the Society. Assurances from kindly Elder Statesmen that the world had not come to an end, that officers before had experienced their trials and tribulations and would do so again, probably for similar reasons and in similar manner, did little to console one at that time, but the truth of these comments were fully evident in later years and have been passed on since with some success. For the sad story of the failure of a by-election due to the theft of a ballot box was received with much relief recently by a sorely-tried Auditor facing the same complications, whilst many have been

Corresponding Societies Debate 5 March 1952. (Front left to right) *I. W. S. Wilson Edinburgh Speculative Society, E. K. T. Coles Durham Union, Senator Professor W. B. Stanford Vice-President, G. Janner Cambridge Union, P. Mayhew Oxford.* (Back left to right) *J. F. Wood Correspondence Secretary, M. Abrahamson Auditor, W. L. K. Cowie Edinburgh Speculative Society, J. W. Flegg pro-Record Secretary, D. Hurd Cambridge Union, M. J. Jaffer Treasurer, R. D. F. Kimmitt Librarian. Photo courtesy of the* Irish Times.

heartened to learn that the roar from the Opposition demanding immediate removal from office is not necessarily matched by the voting on such an issue.

The question of admitting women was certainly not an issue in the 1950s but the swing back towards a closer involvement in matters Irish was beginning to show, with the end in sight of the post-war influx of students from Great Britain and abroad. Indeed, the early morning walk was caused by events which reflected a desire to give concrete evidence to this tendency. The ruling monarch of the United Kingdom passed away during term time and a hasty examination of the precedents indicated that the House had been adjourned previously on such an occasion. But that had been in 1936 and there had been certain changes since, not least the Act of 1948, with its new status for the country. Not for the first time, the Auditor found himself between two opposing factions and brought the wrath of many on his head by a decision to adjourn public, but not private business and by drafting a Resolution of Sympathy said to satisfy few. Resignations quickly followed, the attempt to fill the empty places being thwarted for a time by the trick of the disappearing ballot box.

Oppositions generally were very lively but always operated within the spirit of the rules and never went so far as to wreck meetings.

PETER HALEY-DUNNE – SECRETARY 1957–58

I was a member of the Historical Society over an important phase of its history — from 1954 to 1960. During my period of ordinary membership the Society underwent several important changes. When I first entered it was in a state of graceful decline, but when I left College it was a vigorous, thrusting, if rather noisy, body which had successfully absorbed — and been re-invigorated by — the intake of students from the levy.

In 1954 it cost two guineas to join the Hist and not very many people wanted to join at that price. The Conversation Room had a relaxed, club-room atmosphere: those were the days when a coal fire blazed at one end, and the long, leather settees were drawn up close on either side of it with their complement of snoozers. More often than not, the buzz tended to be one of snoring rather than talking, with the quiet flick of newspapers in the background.

The decade of the fifties saw not only the transition from a small to a large membership, but also the swing from 'oratory' to what one can only call 'public speaking'. Whether the two trends were more than coincidental is doubtful. The shift from oratory seems to be taking place everywhere. By oratory I mean the calculated use of emotion and modulation of expression to achieve an effect, whereas by public speaking I mean the more or less straightforward and dispassionate presentation of arguments with which the speaker feels he can convince his audience. Of course, I am not suggesting that 'public speakers' do not make some use of emotion and expression any more than 'orators' neglect their facts — but one or other tendency predominates with any speaker.

Again I have noticed that while 'public speakers' will often raise their voices to achieve an effect, they cannot, by contrast, sink to a dramatic whisper, as some of the best orators I have heard in the Hist. Who, of my generation can forget some speeches by the late Noel Hartnett, Hon. Mem? They were virtuoso performances — the thunder of social indignation would give way to the whisper of compassion that was in his heart, and one would leave the building anxious to make an immediate start on setting the world to rights. Unfortunately, very little can be done with the world at midnight on a Wednesday in Dublin, and the daring deeds had to be postponed until the morrow — and here was the snag: by then the immediate swell of emotion which Noel Hartnett had aroused would have gone and the world would once again be an ordinary place. But if only Noel Hartnett had delivered himself of his speeches at midday! What extraordinary social upheavals might not have taken place in the streets of Dublin then! I've never heard oratory such as Hartnett's again in the Hist or anywhere else: people like him aren't made anymore. It was from Hartnett's lips also that I heard, at an after-dinner speech at the Honorary Members' Supper, one of the best definitions of the spirit of the Hist. Certain of his words stick in my head even now: 'We are', he said, smiling round the room, 'a goodly company!' People who had been at each other's throats an hour ago in Private Business looked at each other, and found it was true; when the words were said as Hartnett said them, they were indeed a goodly company.

In this same period another man who did not fail to provide us with a striking oratory was Frank O'Connor, who came one day to the 'Hist' to belt with his own wild indignation Ireland's petty censors. His condemnation of those who had hounded *The Tailor and Ansty* was full of a particular horror, which is not in one whit abated by knowing that today *The Tailor and Ansty* are the subject of a play at the Abbey.

In the 1957–58 session Hartnett's 'goodly company' was swelled by many new members who, having paid the new Societies' levy, were entitled to join the Hist for a mere five shillings as against the former two guineas. Some of the older members resented the influx: there was often no room to sit down in the Conversation Room and people were actually talking loudly and argumentatively. The new arrivals were nick-named the 'five-shilling Englishmen': Englishmen because so many were part of the prodigious English intake which Trinity absorbed at that time. But in fact they saved the Hist, which I am convinced could not have continued for much longer as it had been doing.

But one trend — and it has since much accelerated — was becoming more noticeable in my last years: the decreasing cosmopolitanism of the Hist. This was but a reflection of the decreasing cosmopolitanism of the University — but it must be noted and deplored. One of the factors in Hist politics in my earlier days which one heard quite openly talked about was 'the African vote'. Candidates for office would actually wonder which of them might be more acceptable to the Hist's many African members. Whether the Africans did vote in a bloc, as some suspected, or not, I don't to this day know: personally, I doubt it. And I rather disliked some of the calculations that some members made about them. But the fact that they were made is a pointer to what a cosmopolitan body the Hist was in those days — and a glance around the Hall on my more recent visits has shown me that it is no longer. This is a loss for all concerned: I shall always myself feel privileged to have worked, debated and argued with many excellent people who under Trinity's present admission policy would never have come to Dublin at all.

৵

ERIC LOWRY – AUDITOR 1963–64, SILVER MEDALLIST

It was in Mulligan's pub. Just a few minutes after plunging in out of the air, the exile returning, for the Bicentenary celebrations. We stood solidly sinking the inevitable. Before long, the *subject* was mentioned. The fermenting gout of this age. Violence.

And sure enough, Senator Kennedy's first words that evening told of an anonymous telephone call which had warned that a time bomb was set to go off in five minutes. 'I couldn't think of nicer people to go up in the air with,' he said. The only time bomb that blew up was the chant of a Maoist. After a thirty-second life this counter-attraction, true to the spirit of his red book, was eliminated. But, combined with the action of a few who tested the strength of the Senator's car roof as he later drove away, this was enough for the *Irish Times.* 'One Arrest in Protest at Kennedy. Students pound on car after T.C.D. address' was the front-page headline the next morning. Thus were the *significant* facts of the meeting conveyed and we are left to ponder how much of our view of the prevalence of violence in the world results from the flair of sub-editors' pens.

At least ex-Auditor David Ford consoled us in an article published on the same morning in the same paper. This 'violence' is nothing new. The Society has survived such mighty assaults before. He quoted from the *Freeman's Journal* description of the 1874 Inaugural meeting when an apparently unpopular politician called Miller was on the platform: 'The undergraduate element was conspicuous, collarless, stick-bearing, up-roarious, and spilling for a fight. . . . There was a wild scene of tumult, uproar and riot, which raged for two long hours. Whistles and bugles added to the din, while on all sides were heard the sharp cracks of the explosive fire-works known as Ashantee bombs. The undergraduates yelled, screamed, roared, brayed. The seats were broken in the body of the hall. . . . For nearly an hour Mr Miller stood his ground, and all this time the riot grew worse and worse . . . the meeting was adjourned.'

This recalls memories of the ordinary meeting only a few years ago at which the late Randolph Churchill spoke. At the end of the debate as the chairman was about to speak, some firebrands, with the daring, cunning, courage and initiative for which the Irish are renowned, fused the lights. That meeting, too, with at least a couple of hundred people present, was adjourned — to the Hist conversation room.

It must in truth be admitted that the night Kennedy spoke a security operation was mounted in the university that would have gladdened the heart of the F.B.I. As a result of the sight of placards and the gathering of bodies outside, Front Gate was shut — even to those of us with tickets. As I touched the ground inside the railings just by No. 20 I looked a newly-arrived policeman on the other side straight in the face and bade him 'Good evening'. Word was passed to the security squad inside the university that a breach in the defences had occurred. Alas, a quickly amassed hunt for me proved fruitless. (This 'inside' information was learned with mutual amusement at the Bicentenary dinner on the Thursday when I was sitting beside the university's head of security!)

DAVID J. McCONNELL – AUDITOR 1964–65, GOLD MEDALLIST, VICE-PRESIDENT 1977–

The courageous and distinguished radical, Owen Sheehy Skeffington, Hon. Member, was a Governor of Sandford Park School. He taught us how to debate at the founding meeting of the school debating society. Under his continuing influence, and that of the Headmaster, Trevor Dagg, also of the Hist (nephew of T. S. C. Dagg), it was inevitable that I should join the Hist in Michaelmas Term 1962. The Auditor, the urbane Lancastrian, J. Michael Newcombe, gave his Inaugural Address on 'Christ, Class and Communism'. The final speech of the evening by Rev. Dr A. A. Luce,

Vice-President, the austere Berkeleyan scholar, was brilliant and humorous, contrasting well with some dull stuff from the Secretary of the British Communist Party. It was an impressive College triumph. I hardly missed a meeting for the next three years and I look back on the time spent with affection and gratitude.

The College and the Society were reforming. Dr Albert McConnell, the Antrim Protestant was Provost, and the College Board was composed of men (exclusively) who were intent on modernising Trinity and integrating it with Irish life. This was not easy. The infamous 'Ban', repeated dutifully in each Lenten Pastoral by the enthusiastic Archbishop of Dublin, Dr John Charles McQuaid, threatening mortal sin, admonished parents not to send their children to Trinity College. Irish Catholics thankfully did not always obey, and the English did not; places in College created by the 'Ban' were filled by numerous students from all corners of these islands. Skeff mischievously argued that the Ban was a filter — the best came through — but in fact it was pernicious and damaging to Ireland and the College; the effect of John XXIII was still to come. The public school and northern influences were strong and the UK grants gave some British students unusual opportunities for exuberance which they happily and noisily accepted. The southern Irish students were probably in a minority, most of them were nominally Protestant and they were keen if moderate nationalists, quoting Tone, Emmet and Davis with pride, but not Pearse. The Fabian Society, the Cumann Gaelach, Choral, Singers and Players were active, *T.C.D. Miscellany* and *Trinity News* flourished, the sports clubs were in the top leagues and some students were international players. There was no Student Union; students cared little about the Board provided the Board minded its business which it always seemed to be doing.

The Hist, the Other Society, the Eliz and the Theo, as the Major Societies, all did well from the Capitation Fund — the Senior Dean, La Touche Godfrey, knew the pecking order, and preserved it. The quintessential Junior Dean, Brendan McDowell, a Hist man, was quietly relaxing College rules, and he could be relied on in nearly all crises. W. B. Stanford and David Greene were other Hist men, prominent in College, who spoke often at debates and stepped in to take the Chair at short notice. K. F. G. Purcell (affectionately known to his numerous friends as 'The Gink'), Vice-President, came to College nearly every week to ensure that the Hist accounts were kept meticulously; his devoted service to the Society for decades should be recorded.

The Hist, the largest society, reflected the great cultural diversity of the College, and debates on politics, ethics, and philosophy were vigorous. Michael Newcombe had an excellent year, and was followed by Eric Lowry. Newcombe's style gave way to Lowry's intention to make the Society more Irish. He ran it with a sure hand, showing that decisiveness which has marked him in his business career, and he spoke convincingly and often. Private Business was a serious matter with the Committee fighting off the persistent attacks of the 'opposition' who brandished the light blue copies of the Laws with glee, and sought to amend them as much as possible. David Segal was mainly responsible for introducing proportional representation for elections, by far the most complicated of the changes. But for the most part the session was without major controversy as I remember it. Jeremy Craig, the Treasurer, was already showing his skills in diplomacy, and his delight in principled intrigue, which were to lead him to a distinguished career in the Department of Foreign Affairs. Patrick Evershed, a delightful and impish Englishman, was Correspondence Secretary. An ardent Tory, with an interest in making honey, he made sure of a stream of British politicians to the Hist (Hogg, Douglas-Home, Randolph Churchill). Robert Ervine-Andrews, Record Secretary, was the funniest speaker for many years, he played bridge, ran a riotous rugby team and generally did everything he could to conceal his native talent, which in spite of all his efforts surfaced in his role as the hugely successful and genial grocer of Waterford and Captain of Tramore Golf Club. Michael Morgan, a biochemist, who was to become a leading figure in the Wellcome Trust, was Censor. He was one of the few truly 'sixties' persons in the College, liberated and liberal in his views about women, and deeply committed to such matters as family planning. I think that the Board allowed us to debate his suggested motion on contraception 'in camera' — members only and no press. As Librarian, I ran the Conversation Room, organized the papers and the small but useful library, and spoke for the first time in the *Irish Times*. Lowry and I were up against Anthony Clare and Patrick Cosgrave of the L. & H. who won for the second year running and then took the *Observer* Mace. Clare was outstanding, Cosgrave was learning how to become English and never looked back.

Evershed, Ervine-Andrews and I ran for Auditor. PR was used and it went to a second round if I remember. The 'scientists' took over: Michael Cameron (Treasurer) was a chemist, Cian Ó hÉigeartaigh (Record Secretary) a mathematician and Hugh O'Neill (Censor) a medical student. Only Ed Liddle (Librarian), an historian, kept the arts flag flying among the officers. I spent the summer assembling my inaugural address, entitled on Liddle's suggestion, 'A terrible beauty'. I failed to get Brian Faulkner or Charles Haughey. I asked Father McDyer, the renegade, reforming curate of Glencolumcille, whom I had met at the Irish student work camp in 1964; the Bishop would not let the greater man come. Peadar O'Donnell, his fellow Donegal man, then quite old and mellowed with the years, did speak, most thoughtfully. Brian Lenihan stood in for Haughey (portent of things to come), General Costello (another keen supporter of Father McDyer) spoke to my interest in Irish industry and Owen Sheehy Skeffington to my hopes for a radically different Ireland. Mr F. H. Boland, President of the Society, presided.

The year seemed very busy. Public debating went well, but I found Private Business irksome and often trivial. I do not know whether my colleagues ever realized the depths of my ignorance of the Laws, which of course dominated Private Business. I did not particularly enjoy the jousting which was contrived, but in retrospect I see Private Business and the Laws as the essence of the Society. They kept the Officers and the Committee in check and provided the continuity.

William Bateson, the founder of genetics in Britain, and the first Professor of Genetics at Cambridge, noted that one should treasure exceptions. The Hist was truly an exception, a very odd place, nearly as odd as the Speculative Society of Edinburgh. It was full of character and as Lord Jenkins remarked in 1992 (at the dinner in the House of Commons hosted by Sir James Kilfedder, after the Quatercentenary Service, 23 November), remembering a visit to the Hist, Trinity made Oxford and Cambridge look 'decidedly red brick'. The Society had wit, style and talent to spare and it was certainly different. No one forgot a visit to the Hist with the officers in tails and the Committee in dinner jackets, all in gowns. Part of the strangeness in its character was that the Hist was a male society.

There was a strong move to admit women in 1964–65. The question was very controversial and I set up a Committee to investigate it. Cameron was chairman and it deliberated for the whole year. A report was presented, the Society voted, and women were not admitted that year. Ó hÉigeartaigh, my closest friend in Hist circles, had won the Committee nomination for Auditorship. He and I had won the *Irish Times* and he had won many admirers, even among the Tories (who had tried to impeach him for writing the minutes in Irish). They respected his intellectual brilliance and his vivacious, combative character. Though not tall or large, he had a Churchillian approach to life. Having entered College with a scholarship in Maths, he dropped that subject and promptly got Foundation Scholarship in Early and Modern Irish. He was widely read, he played the cello and the tin whistle, and could speak about anything at all, *ex tempore*, for as long as he was let, and he was always scintillating. When the Hist voted against women, he stood up at the end of an electrifying Private Business, and shaking with emotion, he said he was withdrawing from the imminent election. I seem to remember him walking out, grim.

I met him as soon as possible, and after several hours sitting in College Park by the Museum Building, I persuaded him that he was not entitled to withdraw. The Committee had nominated him for Auditor, and only the Committee could withdraw its nomination. He demurred, the Committee did not withdraw its nomination, but he was not elected. The Tories, who I believe were going to vote for Ó hÉigeartaigh, deserted him for the perceived safer hands of the laconic Cameron, then a socialist. Next year, during Cameron's auditorship, Ó hÉigeartaigh and I took the *Irish Times* and the *Observer* Mace, the question of women was debated once again, but they were not admitted. Mícheál Ó Siadhail, who was the most impressive of the new debaters, became more serious, and left too quickly to follow his muse. I pursued Genetics and Ó hÉigeartaigh has entertained us with wonderful productions on radio and television.

Looking back, we were all serious. We would change the world, we would debate with the leading figures in any subject, and visiting speakers and Chairmen were politely but firmly assessed. The Hist knew it was important. The Society, run by the Laws, was training us in how to manage complicated organisations; Private Business often went on to the small hours of the morning, though never finishing after the Librarian's watch passed midnight; officers were impeached; the Officers' Conduct Report (O.C.R.) could be hard and the phrasing of the final sentence of any O.C.R.

needs to be read with all other phrasings of the period to discover the real weight of the judgment. The Hist went to some trouble to be fair-minded, it had high standards in all its doings, and because we were a diverse lot — Alan Craig and Francis Sheehy Skeffington from Dublin, Ross Hinds from Laois, Bryan Rose from Cork, David Wagstaff from Wexford, Martyn Lewis and Leo McCloskey an unlikely pair from the North, Paul Thompson, Chris Knox, Brian Williamson and Jeremy Lucas from various parts of England — we learned to respect differences in a way which laid the basis for long friendships and we sharpened each others' minds for later and more serious tests of will.

Many of us, gathered for the Bicentenary, celebrated a memorable week in 1970. I was based in Pasadena at the time, but I happened to be in Trinity, lecturing for Hilary Term. Declan Budd, Ross Hinds and others conspired to put me in charge of Security and the Press, an appropriate pairing. I seem to remember that a journalist (was it Mary Holland?) was keen to attend, representing a British paper as if London was still the centre of the universe — that carried no weight with me after four years in the USA. The Maoists were active, and though we had invited Andreas Papandreou and Eugene McCarthy, who could be said to be 'on the left', the Maoists had no respect for them, much less Edward Kennedy at a time when the Vietnam War was at its height. They were intent on disrupting Kennedy's address on Burke. Gerald Giltrap, the College Secretary, believed they would try to drown out the meeting with amplified music and slipped me a pair of pliers for cutting the Maoist electricity cables. I did not need the pliers but I did need other help. I asked William Tector, Alwyn Williams, Brian Wilkinson and Malcolm Johnston, old friends from Sandford Park and rugby, who knew the Hist through Skeff, to help by placing themselves around the Examination Hall. Kennedy was in full flight when a voice from the gallery started *'Down with Ted Kennedy — agent of American Imperialism'* tailing off as Malcolm Johnston had him in a half-Nelson; he was gone in seconds but re-appeared the next morning politely asking for his coat. It was a great occasion in every respect, with the Hist showing the College that it knew how to do things.

EDWARD LIDDLE – LIBRARIAN 1964–65

We were sending out our Annual reports — the Green ones 1961–63, and did not have a complete list of the addresses of all the Honorary Members and Medallists. Jeremy [Lucas][16] undertook to find them. To do this, he acquired both Republic and North of Ireland telephone directories and a copy of every one in England, Scotland and Wales. He took these to bed with him meaning to work through the night. I was out late, whether at a party or pub or what I can't recall and came into Jeremy's room to see how he was getting on. He was lying asleep, his light on, a blissful smile on his face, and a copy of every telephone directory in the British Isles locked in his deadly embrace.

W. A. C. (GULLY) STANFORD – AUDITOR 1967–68

No blazoned banner we unfold —
One charge alone we give to youth,
Against the sceptre'd myth to hold
The golden heresy of truth.

On Behalf of some Irishmen
not followers of tradition — Æ

Given family traditions and a fondness for debate, my involvement in the Hist, as it approached its Bicentenary, was somewhat

---

[16] Jeremy Lucas donated the Lucas Impromptu Debating Trophy to the Society in 1968 and the first Lucas Impromptu Debating Competition took place on 16 April 1969.

inevitable. In fact, my first T.C.D. speech, as a nervous freshman, was to the Elizabethan (where my sister Melissa Webb presided in the drafty vastness of Regent House).

In 1964 the Hist was enjoying spectacular success: the *Observer* Mace era of McConnell and Ó hÉigeartaigh fostered high standards of competition and eloquence. The lively issues of Ireland's national identity brought sharpened focus to the discussions in the G.M.B.: key figures from North and South, as well as from England, felt it worth their while to address the Society's well-attended meetings. And the media covered the debates scrupulously; it was a far cry from the stuff and nonsense we endured on our trips to Oxford, Durham and the like, and a sane, balanced forum compared with the posturings and rantings of the L&H, Galway and Cork (where they still, in those reckless days, hurled (old) pennies at stumbling speakers).

We believed, as Ireland approached her half-century, that our debates should address issues of national significance and should influence the national consciousness: after all, the Hist offered — and occasionally respected — opinions from members hailing from the North and England. Under McConnell's Auditorship, it was heady stuff indeed.

Curiously, of course, the anniversary years of the Easter Rising were marked by a resurgence of English leadership in the Hist, with Socialist Michael Cameron and Young Conservative Brian Williamson, both of whom, endowed with more than their share of political aspiration, leading serious discussion of more global and European interest.

The presence of Irish Officers kept patriotic considerations alive, however, as did the curious case of the disappearance of the Minutes of Burke's Club — missing for two years — from the night of Cameron's election in 1965 till their mysterious reappearance on the morrow of my own election in 1967.

A couple of events stand out from those years, however, as the Hist played an increasingly engaged role in the affairs of the College and the City: a group of Young Conservatives invited the radical English isolationist Enoch Powell (coincidentally a fine classical scholar) to speak at Trinity, a move calculated to arouse the ire of the Irish: after much debate, the organizers were informed that Mr Powell was not welcome in Trinity. As one who supported the opposition to his visit, and since then a frequent champion of the First Amendment to the American Constitution, I have often revisited this landmark decision (for Trinity has always been proud of its open-mindedness): I conclude that the decision was just, insofar as Mr Powell's stand was notoriously confrontational and inflammatory, at a time of great tension on issues of immigration and empire.

It also marked a turning point in the College's involvement in political affairs: unlike the Oxford Union's 'King and Country' debate, we were learning to accept responsibility for our choices, that — whatever the academic value of oratorical sophistry — we could not choose our moments of (dis)engagement.

Much of this was emphasized by the ongoing Fianna Fáil campaign to abolish the Proportional Representation electoral method: I remember well that the *Irish Times* Debate final in 1968 addressed this subject, and I remember that those of us opposed to the abolition cared far more about the House's support for PR than about the outcome of the competition. The training in considered persuasion learned in the Hist stood me in good stead as I campaigned in Waterford for defeat of the proposed changes.

Other elements moving us out of the ivory tower at the time included the emergence of the Internationalists (a loud, implacable — if entertaining — mouthpiece for Marxist-Leninism), the student rebellions in the United States (where my father witnessed first-hand the Berkeley phenomenon, and (then) Regent Ronald Reagan's heavy-handed response), growing concern with the Vietnam War, issues of inequity in housing, jobs and education in the Republic, and the worthy, if fragile, efforts to negotiate peace with the North.

References to the College Societies' 'rearranging the furniture on the Titanic' were common, and, within Trinity, there was increased pressure to replace the old, paternalistic hegemony of the 'Major Societies' with a more democratic, professionally staffed Student Representative Council.

And then, there were the Bourkes — led by one articulate, persuasive and (easily said now) visionary female (one of whose speeches on political cause and effect to a packed attentive L&H house I keenly remember) and enforced by a remarkable pair of brothers, who balanced their fondness for student power-brokerage with a realistic sense of connection to political imperatives outside the College gates.

Loud emphasis was provided late one night in the spring of 1966, when a group of us were playing bridge (a Cameron obsession) in Botany Bay, and heard a muffled explosion from not far away. It was, of course, the demolition of Nelson's Pillar, verified next day to have been a very efficient job (leaving the General Post Office unscathed): one or two of our more lively firebrands were missing from the usual traffic through the rooms that night, and I've often wondered how much more they knew of this breath-taking plot.

With 1967 came the responsibility to offer my own Inaugural Paper, and I chose the subject of Church and State in Ireland since 1922. Among those invited to speak were Cardinal Conway, Archbishop McQuaid (the author and enforcer of the notorious ban on Roman Catholic students attending Trinity), Brian Faulkner, William Craig, Ulster M.P. Phelim O'Neill, Education Minister Donogh O'Malley, George Simms (Protestant Archbishop of Dublin), Rev. Dr Patrick Corish of Maynooth College, and Sir John Wolfenden, Chair of the British University Grants Committee. The speakers in the end were Dr Simms, Dr Corish, Wolfenden and O'Neill. The event was well attended and covered in the media, and sent — I hope — a message that the Hist was indeed an Irish Society concerned with Irish issues, and prepared to be accountable for its opinions.

Perhaps the most interesting souvenir of the event, however, was my correspondence with Archbishop McQuaid, who wrote (4 July 1967) that 'I fear that I am not competent to speak on the relations between the Anglican Church and the Irish State'! When I replied that I proposed to address the relations of the 'majority, Catholic church with the state' — pointing out that President de Valera had recently spoken of Trinity as a cherished part of the Irish heritage and essential to the nation's progress, whereas in 1934 Mr de Valera had told the Hist how anathematical the College was to Irish interests, the Archbishop wrote back (28 July — in his own hand):

'There is no doubt that you describe well your paper when you call it ambitious. With respect to your scholarship, I venture to believe that you have not, and cannot have, the evidence, that would allow a full and just estimate of a thesis so vast and so complex'.

'The ban' lingered for some more years; but the ecumenical seeds were sown, and the Hist had played some small part in confronting and eradicating yet another divisive wedge from our community.

All the while, the Hist was wrestling with its own systemic inequity, the exclusion of women from debate and membership. The topic dominated the internal affairs of the Society throughout my year as Auditor: my own conversion to the admission of women was not enough the win the day. But I was delighted to see that the following year — just in time for the Bicentenary — David Ford led the Hist Joshua-like into the promised land. My vintage enjoyed one small victory, however, when women were admitted to Commons for the first time, an event celebrated in the Grace After Meat by the Scholar of the Day, who inserted, after duly acknowledging 'ceterisque benefactoribus nostris' (our other benefactors) the (rather unCiceronian, but perhaps adequate) phrase 'inter quos hodie nominamus Praepositum nostrum, quia feminas ad mensam appellavit' (among whom today we name our Provost, as he has invited women to the table).

Through a curious coincidence, the *Irish Times*' report of my Inaugural Address appeared on the same page as a story 'Professor is Confident of T.C.D.'s future in Merger': the same day as I opined that 'The theory of reorganising the university system in Dublin is welcome . . . the new Universities of Ireland one hopes will be non-denominational', my father, W. B. Stanford, was reassuring the Diocesan Synod that Trinity's values would not be betrayed. This proposal of Education Minister Donogh O'Malley — to merge Trinity and U.C.D. — spawned what the *Irish Times* called 'one of the best debates held by the Society in recent years': on 28 February 1968, after a furious and intense debate the Hist voted by 108 votes to 32 that 'Merger means Murder'. Eloquent for the proposition was Wodehouse scholar R. B. D. French. Courageous for the opposition was U.C.D. Latin Professor John O'Meara. Several Honorary Members attended, including 'The Pope' O'Mahony, no stranger to lively debate. Off to one side, but not participating, was the Minister for Education himself, incidentally providing us with a front-page picture, which — for me — sums up the Hist of that time: aware, engaged and passionate about the issues of the day, and at the same time free to reject traditional wisdoms and explore new paradigms and solutions to age-old problems.

Summing up the debate, Mr Justice Kenny put it thus: 'May I say how sorry I am that this great society representing the undergraduate opinion of this College should have decided what it did? Let me say also that that it is much better that, if the graduates and undergraduates connected with the university have this view, that it should be expressed.' There is no better epitaph on those years of transition and coming of age.

A TIME OF CHANGE

The Hist changed more rapidly in the late 1950s and 1960s than at any time before. This was a reflection of the changes which were running through the whole of Irish society and perhaps across the developed world too. Alan Craig Treasurer and Ross Hinds Librarian 1966–67 researched these developments in 1970. Their conclusions are given below.

Alan Craig   *Ross Hinds*

The present era in the Society began with the introduction of the Capitation Fee for clubs and societies by the College in 1957. This brought about a period of very rapid change in the Society, and few would doubt

233

that the change was for the better. A glance at the accounts of the Society shows that annual membership increased from 83 in 1956–57 to 535 in 1959–60. Lest it be suggested that this represented merely an increase in the number of people using the facilities of the Society without participating in debates, a similar change in attendance can be shown. In 1956–57 the average number of votes in the division at the end of the debate was 28. By 1959–60 this figure had risen to 67. These figures are only of relative significance; they seriously underestimate the total attendance at debates.

There have been further increases in membership since, but these are related as much to increasing numbers in college as to any other factor. But there have been other changes in the Society, changes which cannot be demonstrated by statistics. The most important of these changes was the decision in 1968 to admit women to membership. Whatever about the effect of women since then, their effect on the Society in the years before they were admitted was profound. The topic of their admission was without doubt the principal topic of controversy during this period. It lay not far from the surface of all the politicking, in the house as well as in the 'cliques and cabals' of the middle sixties and the 'caucuses' of the last couple of years; and it was the ultimate cause of most of the memorable occasions of the decade. Prominent among these memorable occasions were the numerous times when the subject of the admission of women was actually debated by the Society. The chronology and factual details of these meetings are recorded in the table on the facing page.

The changes in voting and in the extent of the proposals during the decade can easily be seen. On all occasions the subject provided an exciting debate, with great emotion shown by both sides.

But these debates and the topics discussed sparked many other incidents. On 14 November 1962 C. J. Lester tendered his resignation as a member of Committee because he was told by the Committee that his organisation and signature of a circular advocating the admission of women to meetings was incompatible with Committee policy. He could perhaps be regarded as the only martyr for the feminist cause. The debate of 14 April 1965 followed the report of a sub-committee that had been set up to ascertain the views of members on the admission of women. After the vote in the debate a dramatic moment ensued, when the Record Secretary, Cian

Table 1 Debates on the admission of women

Date	Motion	Meeting	Ayes	Noes
28/11/62	That this house would not admit women	Public Business	173	39 (negative motion)
14/4/65	Admission of women to opening meeting	Private Business	19	26
1/12/65	Admission of women to debating membership	Ordinary private business (all evening)	57	159
23/1/68	Deletion of auditorial rulings to admit women to full membership	Extraordinary private business	85	87 (later declared invalid)
17/4/68	Deletion of auditorial rulings to admit women to full membership	Ordinary private business (all evening)	70	71
27/11/68	Deletion of auditorial rulings to admit women to full membership	Ordinary private business (all evening)		
4/12/68	(continuation of previous week's debate)		82	67

Ó hÉigeartaigh, announced in a choking voice that he was withdrawing his candidacy for the office of Auditor as 'he did not now feel that it would be possible for him to pursue in the coming year what the Society evidently felt to be its best interests'. Subsequently he withdrew this decision. However, the incident may have cost him the Auditorship, which he lost by three votes in the ensuing election to Michael Cameron, another noted proponent of the admission of women.

In the session 1966–67 the topic of the admission of women was never

Sir Alec Douglas-Home and Brian Williamson in College for the debate on the motion 'That in politics, principles should give way to pragmatism' on Wednesday 4 May 1966.

discussed per se. However, there were several occasions when women were introduced to meetings, and there were other attempts to circumvent the fact that apparently only three auditorial rulings prevented women from being members. The most remarkable of these occasions was on 1 March 1967, when privileged motion No. 1 was proposed 'that the house do adjourn to the usual night of meeting to permit the Auditor (1) firstly to rule that ladies be admitted to the debates of the Society, (2) secondly to prepare satisfactory legislation to be submitted to the Society to reinforce his ruling'. The members present on that occasion were more than usually favourable to the feminist cause. The Auditor, Brian Williamson, in a hurried note requested the Librarian, Ross Hinds, to call the hour of midnight and thus end the debate. The Librarian while acknowledging that his watch was somewhat flexible declined to allow that much flexibility. The Auditor then adjourned the meeting, being of the opinion that the course of action proposed would not be legal, and that it was accordingly not advisable to discuss the motion. He then left the chamber, accompanied by the Chairman, the Correspondence Secretary, four members of Committee, and a few ordinary members. The other half of the Committee, including four officers, and most of the ordinary members present remained, being of the opinion for the most part that the Auditor had no

Mr Gerry Fitt (centre) *with Brian Williamson Auditor on his left and Alan Craig Treasurer on his right on 30 November 1966.*

right to adjourn the meeting. The Treasurer, Alan Craig, having first tried to prevent the Auditor from leaving, then with assistance of other members persuaded a reluctant Senior Member of Committee to take the Auditor's chair, and a new chairman was installed. The adjournment motion was duly passed, and the 'rump' meeting came to an end. Lengthy and heated arguments ensued, and old minute books in the Victorian workroom were searched for precedents. The vacation intervened before the Society as a whole could take any further decisions. At the next meeting a motion was passed regretting the Auditor's departure but it was concluded that his conduct was legal and that the meeting after his departure had not been a meeting of the Society. Subsequently the Auditor ruled to clarify the situation about adjournments for the future.

Other disputes in these years hinged on the attitudes of prominent members to particular matters and sometimes to their fellow members. One of these occurred during the annual elections in 1963, when the Auditor, Michael Newcombe, was accused of canvassing for one auditorial candidate, Librarian Eric Lowry, and of disparaging his opponent, Correspondence Secretary Antony Harrison-Barbet. Feelings ran very high, Newcombe's conduct was alleged to have been 'embarrassing, untraditional and unwise', and Lowry defeated Harrison-Barbet by one vote. However,

Newcombe was defended from impeachment and was in due course awarded the Marked Thanks of the Society and elected to Honorary Membership.

Although an Auditorial Ruling of the 195th session obliged the Society to hold a candlelight meeting once every 194 years, it did not have to wait that long to see candles in use again. The Committee of the 197th session were following a well worn path when they planned a debate on the motion 'that a nation without a language is a nation without spirit', for similar motions had often been debated before. But this time it was different. The Language Freedom Movement founded by Christopher Morris had just emerged, and had provoked active opposition from Irish speakers around the country. Angry and even violent meetings had been held. When the Committee invited Morris to speak, a group of members to whom he was anathema tried to persuade the Committee to withdraw the invitation. The Committee remained adamant, and attempts were made to pressurise them by suggesting that it was not in the interests of the Society to hold a meeting which was likely to be broken up. Rumours of the intentions of the group to break up the meeting, or to have it broken up, circulated freely in the days before the debate, and were confirmed by a fifth columnist in the group who revealed the plans to a member of Committee.

The Committee drew up contingency plans, including guards on the fuse box and two candles and a matchbox for each Committee member. On the night the Records and Library Committee formed a rota to guard the fuse box, and the debate began without incident. Then at about 8.45 p.m. a stranger posing as an electrician, complete with tools, came down the steps towards the fuse box in the basement. There was a struggle but he managed to rip out the fuses and smash them on the floor. Moments before, a group of people headed by some girls had burst into the debating chamber. Members at the door resisted them. Then the lights went out. Amidst the confusion the Auditor was heard to adjourn the meeting, and somehow the chairman and guests were ushered from the chamber. The audience spilled out into the hallway, their way lit by the few Committee members who had managed to light candles, and milled around wondering what would happen next. After a while they filtered into the Conversation room where the meeting resumed in a much less formal atmosphere than usual; there were no more interruptions. Speaking at the end of the debate

*Ross Hinds, Librarian 1966–67, addressing the House on the motion 'That this House regrets
the Offences against the State Act' on 16 November 1966. Seated at the table from his left:
Cian Ó hÉigeartaigh, Asaph Maradufu, David Maxwell Fitzgerald, Eoin Ó Murchú Censor,
W. A. C. (Gully) Stanford Record Secretary, Chairman Alfred Hinds, Brian Williamson Auditor,
Alan Craig Treasurer, Eoin Mac Aogáin pro Correspondence Secretary in place of Jeremy Lucas,
David Reid, Martyn Lewis, Ronald Farmiloe.*

the chairman, Professor David Greene, although in utter disagreement with
Christopher Morris, deplored the events of the evening and apologised to
the guests.

The fuses having been replaced, Private business was held in the debating chamber. The sub-Committee set up then to investigate the incidents concluded that Cian Ó hÉigeartaigh, Honorary Member, had played a major part in organising the disturbances. Accordingly they recommended that he be relieved of all privileges above those of ordinary membership for the remainder of the session, which recommendation was endorsed by the Society on 15 February 1967. The question of whether Ó hÉigeartaigh now had to pay the annual subscription was a moot point. However, a formula was found to avoid a demand for payment. Shortly afterwards he won the Liverpool Impromptu Debating Competition, and the issue faded quietly.

Another controversy, in Michaelmas term 1967, concerned the *Irish Times* Debating competition. It was suggested that the trio of Hist, Phil. and Eliz. had an unfair monopoly of participation in the competition on behalf of the College. The Law Society in particular was aggrieved. In return it was claimed that it was too late to alter the status quo that year. Accusations of vested interest and deception were made and a period of deep intrigue ensued, involving the Auditor, William Stanford, the Law Society and its Auditor, the S.R.C., the Debates sub-Committee of U.S.I. and the President of that body. The problem has since been settled, and other societies can, and the Law Society does, participate in the competition.

The greatest controversy of all was also the most recent. In November 1968 the Committee took the unprecedented step of expelling the Censor, Joe Revington, from the Society. This resulted in the resignation of two officers and three Committee members who could not support the decision. One side felt that Revington was a purely disruptive and destructive influence who had to be removed to save the Society from chaos. Those on the other side felt either that Revington was within his rights and was merely expressing his disagreement with the structure of the Society, or that more consultation was needed and expulsion was extreme, even if his conduct was insupportable. Most of the discussion was about the morality not the legality of the steps taken although there was controversy about the meaning of 'a clear majority' of the Committee in the Laws relating to expulsion. An impeachment of those who remained on the Committee was defeated by one vote in a house of over 300.

However, the Auditor, David Ford, was defended from impeachment the following week by a majority of over 100 votes. Although the Society was

Richard Clarke, Record Secretary, reading the minutes at the debate on the motion 'That Female Government would hasten World Peace' on 12 November 1969. On his left are Hilda O'Malley, Chairman, Ian Ashe, Auditor and Nicholas Fitzgerald Browne, Treasurer.

deeply divided at the time, more normal conditions were quite soon restored. This is indicated by the fact that the three ordinary Committee members who had resigned were elected to office for the Bicentenary session, two of them without opposition.

It would be a mistake to imply that the sixties were years merely of politics and intrigue, that the meetings of the Society consisted of nothing but a series of disputes. There were more peaceful events of note. The Burke's Club Minute Book, the most treasured possession of the Society was found to be missing in 1965. Prolonged searches and advertisements produced no result. However, two years later, in April 1967 the book was mysteriously returned to the private letter box in No. 16 College of the Correspondence Secretary. The precious minute book was undamaged, and the only long-term effect was that many valuable records of the Society were removed to safe keeping in the College Manuscript room.

A number of important changes were made in the laws of the Society during these years. On 8 March 1961 the office of Censor of the Society

Prior to the debate 'That Trade Unions have forgotten the Working Man' on 17 January 1968 the Chairman Sean Lemass on the left with Declan Budd, Record Secretary, on his left and Gully Stanford, Auditor.

was created, after lengthy meetings and much drafting of laws. The office was created primarily to remove some of the Treasurer's burden. Since then some of the more bureaucratic of these duties, in connection with membership, have been abolished, but the Censor has been given other duties such as being responsible for tape recording debates. Other major changes include the elimination of balloting for membership of the Society, the introduction of the transferable vote in elections to office, and the introduction of provision for medal winning essays to be read to the Society and for an impromptu debating competition among the members. One change which was not approved was the introduction of points of information in debates. This proposal was on one occasion passed for the first time, but was defeated on the second reading after a heated debate.

These changes were the most important of many that resulted from widespread reforming zeal among the members and that were facilitated by a high degree of organisation in the Society. The concept of Committee solidarity, which has come in for much abuse of late, was not a barren one. When the Committee agreed on a united policy in advance and then presented it to the house, they elicited a response. The ordinary members of the Society formed an organized opposition which met regularly while the Committee was in session and also discussed policy. This system, which broadened participation, was particularly well developed in the session 1963–64, but persisted in some form for about four years more. Unfortunately the concept of 'the Society's loyal organized opposition' seems to have faded away. Another feature that helped progressive legislation was the high regard for laws and established precedents shared by radicals and reactionaries alike. Changes in this respect seem to be a feature of society as a whole and not merely of the College Historical Society.

Nor did the Society forget that its main function was debating. Many great debates were held. Attention at some of these focused on distinguished guests, among whom British Conservatives Randolph Churchill, Quintin Hogg and Sir Alec Douglas-Home attracted the largest crowds. Whether the attendances were a measure of the popularity of the guests or merely of their fame cannot be determined. Early in 1968, when the topic 'That merger means murder' was debated, the packed house was interested primarily in the issues involved in the University question in Dublin, but the presence of the Minister for Education, Donogh O'Malley, sitting discreetly observing the debate added greatly to the occasion. Another historic debate was the first debate with women present, in January 1969, on the motion 'that this house reveres the memory of Mrs Pankhurst'.

On less historic occasions also, fine speeches were made. It is hardly invidious to pick out the oratory of Cian Ó hÉigeartaigh, whose capacity to hold an audience spellbound for many minutes, with passionate yet lucid conviction, was unequalled. The passion of Ó hÉigeartaigh was complemented by the calmer, more methodical, yet likewise convincing oratory of David McConnell. Together they formed a magnificent debating partnership, as was shown by their victory in the competition for the coveted *Observer* Mace. This victory was only one of many won by the Society's members in competition. The accompanying table lists the major competition victories of these years.

Table of trophies won in Competition

Trophy won	Winners	Year
Irish Times Debating Trophy	D. J. McConnell C. S. Ó hÉigeartaigh	1965
Scots-Irish Debating Trophy	C. S. Ó hÉigeartaigh M. L. Ó Siadhail	1965
Irish Times Debating Trophy	D. J. McConnell C. S. Ó hÉigeartaigh	1966
Observer Mace	D. J. McConnell C. S. Ó hÉigeartaigh	1966
Scots-Irish Debating Trophy	R. B. Williamson S. G. Harris	1967
Liverpool Impromptu Debating Trophy	C. S. Ó hÉigeartaigh	1967
Oscar Wilde Impromptu Debating Trophy (Queen's University)	J. R. Lucas R. Lescher	1967
Liverpool Impromptu Debating Trophy	D. F. Ford	1969

Other fine orators will be long remembered too, each with his own distinctive style. The fire of Neville Keery, the authority of Michael Newcombe, the rhetoric of William Stanford and the clarity of Alan Matthews are but examples; the various qualities of these men and of others like Michael Cameron, Brian Williamson, Mícheál Ó Siadhail and Eoin Ó Murchú all contributed to a flourishing tradition of great debating. Another important tradition is that of humour in debate, a tradition well maintained by Robert Ervine-Andrews, Hugh Grange and Steven Harris. Such speakers gain fewer conventional honours in the debating world, but the standing ovation given to Ervine Andrews on one occasion was a sincere tribute.

With the Bicentenary celebrations in March 1970, the College Historical Society begins its third century. During the seventies and afterwards, the attitudes of members will go on changing, laws will go on being amended,

Donogh O'Malley, Minister for Education, seated top left, at the debate 'That Merger means Murder' held on 28 February 1968. On the left of the Chairman, Mr Justice Kenny, is the Auditor W. A. C. (Gully) Stanford. On his left are Rupert Lescher, David Reid, David Ford, Eoin O'Mahony, David Butler, Ian Ashe, and Joe Revington. On the right of the Chairman are Declan Budd, Alan Matthews, Prof. John O'Meara of U.C.D., Victor Allen and David Watson. R. B. D. French is addressing the House.

and new traditions will appear. But there are certain essential features which have remained changeless and must continue to do so. The most important tradition is surely that of bringing together people of widely different views. A Society that takes its inspiration from Burke, that constantly pays tribute to Tone, Emmet and Davis, that yet produced Carson, a Society that within the last few years has accommodated together conservatives and socialists, liberals and revolutionaries, unionists and republicans, must not allow its vision to be narrowed. Long may political antagonists continue to meet one another in the Hist.

March 1970

Bicentenary 1970

The Society has celebrated its origins at each opportunity. In 1897 the Centenary of the death of Edmund Burke was marked by the Burke Memorial Banquet. His birth was commemorated in 1928, and the founding of the Club was celebrated on its Bicentenary in 1947.

W. A. C. (Gully) Stanford, Auditor for the 198th session, took the initiative to ensure that the Bicentenary of the Hist would be celebrated in 1970. A Bicentenary Committee was established under the Chairmanship of Mr K. F. G. Purcell, Vice-President, to plan the event.

The Bicentenary was celebrated in the week 2–7 March 1970. The proceedings are recorded in the following pages.

BICENTENARY ADDRESS

The Bicentenary Address was delivered by Edward Kennedy, Senator for Massachusetts in the United States of America, in the Public Theatre of the College on Tuesday 3 March 1970

CHAIRMAN: MR F. H. BOLAND, PRESIDENT AND CHANCELLOR

'Your Excellencies, Ladies and Gentlemen, it is my honour to ask Senator Edward Kennedy to deliver the Bicentenary Address.'

SENATOR EDWARD KENNEDY

Let me say that before coming in this evening I overheard a telephone call that was made to one of the members of the Society to indicate that there was a time bomb that was planted in this hall tonight and I recall the words that my brother Bob said out in Salt Lake City, 'I couldn't think of a nicer group to go up in the air with.' In any event, it is set for about five more minutes supposedly, so we will know very soon what kind of shape we are in.

I was most pleased to receive the invitation to deliver the Bicentenary Address of the College Historical Society. I consider this occasion one of the greatest honours of my public life, as well as an opportunity to express myself on matters that I feel are vital to our time.

Candidly speaking, your kind invitation also forced me to take time off from my public schedule to reacquaint myself with Edmund Burke. In my student days I was of course aware and impressed with his eloquent speeches but I knew little of his personal life. Now that I am a politician I thought I should talk about the politician Burke to learn whatever lessons I could for myself. Well, Burke fought to lift the taxes on the American Colonies, and lost. He fought to give Ireland the protection of the English Constitution, and lost. He fought to bring relief to the Catholics of Ireland from the Penal Laws, and lost. He fought to reform the abuses of Royal Patronage, and lost. He fought for years to impeach Warren Hastings and won it below, but lost it in the House of Lords. He won the coveted Seat in Bristol and held it for a short time, and lost it. And spent, with the exception of a year and some days, all the twenty-nine years of his public life out of power and in the opposition. Now from this study I have come to the conclusion that Burke's speeches were better than his politics.

The College Historical Society has been called the greatest of all the schools of the orators. Fitting, then, that Edmund Burke was instrumental in its founding.

And this Society carries the tradition of open debate — barring no point of view — a centre of controversy and discussion. It has heard the voices of Irish nationalists — Wolfe Tone, Robert Emmet, John Blake Dillon, and Thomas Davis — as well as those who opposed their thoughts and actions. Men of letters, science, and government passed through this Society, as light through a prism, to go on to form their own colours and patterns in life. This, too, is fitting, for Burke was not so committed to his own thoughts and pursuits that he could not delight in, or learn from, the voices of others.

At first glance the public career of Edmund Burke seems laced with inconsistencies. He was dedicated to the established order and institutions of his time, yet was sympathetic to the demands and complaints of the colonies that formed my nation. He was devoted to the wisdom of the past, yet was a leader in forming the basic structures of government. He was an intensely pragmatic realist who heeded the facts of political life when proposing policies, yet he was dominated by powerful moral values and the hopes that flow from such values.

Still Edmund Burke was not an inconsistent man. Rather he reflected the inconsistency of society itself. What appeared to be Burke's conflicts of views and temperament were, in reality, the product of his unwavering human scepticism, the great gift of your experience to Western political thought, and to my own country in particular.

For every society is a mixture of stability and change, an irrevocable history and an uncertain future. We are both what we have been and what we desire to be. We are creatures of memory and hope, struggling with uncertainty as we try to fulfil the promises that we know we must keep.

Thus our society is constantly in flux — different today from what it was yesterday — a continuation of the past, part of an organic process with roots deep in the history of our nation and of our common ancestors. Societies are like rivers, flowing from fixed and ancient sources through channels cut over the centuries, yet no man can ever step into the same water in which he stood only a moment before. This view of society as a process, its new growth sustained by ancient roots, was the essence of Burke.

Burke, the conservative, believed that values and existing institutions reflected the accumulated wisdom and experience of a people and could not be discarded to satisfy every transient impulse without rending the fabric of the society. Burke, the sceptic, believed that no one man or group of men could claim a monopoly on revealed truth, and, so armed, undertake the destruction of what generations had built in order to impose their own personal visions of a utopia. Burke, the moralist, believed it was man's first duty to defend the values of decency, tolerance, reason and respect for freedom against all onslaughts. And Burke, the realist, understood that we could only hope to preserve tested values and institutions if we were willing to undergo sometimes painful adaptation to new facts and relationships in a constantly changing world.

Edmund Burke was a complex man and he was a moderate man. His moderation did not consist in automatically taking the middle position between left and right, radical and reactionary, one extreme and the other. He was a moderate, not because he lacked passion or conviction, but because he combined an acute sense of human limitation with a deep reverence for the moral values essential to human liberation. To him a lifetime of thought and action, consumed by the slow labour of improving the human condition, was more valuable than all the rhetoric of destruction and impossible visions. He was not in the market of human and political affairs for the windfall or the notoriety that history soon buries under its chronicle of real achievement.

Thus, Burke sets an example for all of us in an age when, in all our countries, the forces of moderation are on the defensive. We live in a time of change — huge and tumultuous and filled with danger. Any society that is rigid or entrenched in the face of this change, or that heeds those who constrict liberty by calling upon fear, mistrust and hate, will shortly be overwhelmed. That would threaten the destruction of everything worthwhile that prior generations had managed to create. Any society that yields to those, who in some mindless fury seek to tear down completely the old structures, will also lose the values and wisdom accumulated over the centuries.

Western society is in ferment. If my own country appears to be more tumultuous and dangerous than others, it is only because we are further advanced along the course of modern life; and we have less of a common heritage to guide us, or help absorb the blows. Our travails are also more visible because we are large in numbers, varied as a people. In addition, a nation — rich and powerful as my own and so fortunate in its history —

is tempted to believe that all problems, no matter how complex, can be solved by pulling on the levers of power or pushing the buttons of solution. But the truth is that the problems of man cannot be resolved so mechanically. For the human condition has changed less than the world we have created. We are frail, limited and plodding in constructing the relationships between men and nations despite the comforting and boastful facade of speed, chrome and capsules on the moon. Yet all the nations which can call themselves advanced or developed are menaced by the clash between the sustaining past and the troubled future. For all of us, the institutions and ideas of the old age are buckling under the drive of new concepts and relationships.

The challenge to men in Burke's tradition of moderation is to find the strength to lead the drive for change and adaptation, to satisfy the real discontents and just grievances of our time so that we may conserve the reasoned and humane legacy of our past.

I wish to suggest to you this evening that the two greatest dangers to peace and the future existence of mankind in this age are the continuation of human oppression, whether conscious or unconscious, and the toleration of weapons that can destroy our earth.

[Heckler: 'Down with Ted Kennedy — agent of American Imperialism.'

Scuffle!! A supporter of the Maoists had hidden in the organ of the Examination Hall, and emerged to shout slogans. The Bicentenary security team, in the person of heavily built sportsmen, went smoothly into action, and quickly presented the interrupter to a waiting Junior Dean, Brendan Kennelly.

Kennedy: 'There goes one of the great debaters now.'

Scuffle again!!

Kennedy: 'He can come tomorrow night.']

These basic problems must submit to the control of humane and reasonable men if we are ever to be optimistic about the future of the world. And so I feel this is no time for moderate men to be in retreat. The successful charting of human affairs is too important a matter — failure, too ghastly a matter — to be left in the hands of those who discard reason for passion.

What follows will be limited in large measure to the condition of my own country. This is the land I know and my doubts and criticism are tempered by love. Still some of our problems of today are also yours — the others will be upon you tomorrow.

The greatest threat to a progressive and peaceful society anywhere is the existence of oppression. For the conscious oppression of one group by another within the family of a nation, or of one nation by another, produces abuses and rages that strike at the heart of a nation itself. The immorality of the act is so pervasive that no part of the society escapes it, and the continued existence of oppression and its mentality cannot help but foul any attempt of a people to be great.

This ancient form of tyranny exists between nations openly — as in the political situation of Eastern Europe — or subtly, as in the economic situation of many of the under-developed countries. Oppression exists internally in a blatant fashion, as in South Africa, or with greater sophistication, as in Northern Ireland. *(applause)* However it exists, it is detrimental to all men and peace.

In my country black people are oppressed. We live with this fact despite the effect it has had upon them, our history, and modern life. Rebellions, uprisings, civil war, the degrading effect of this oppression on blacks and whites alike — all this has been suffered rather than adjustments that would rid us of this strain.

Some advances have been made — but that is faint praise at this late hour and in a nation that prides itself as the light of democracy. 'Liberty', said Burke, 'is a general principle and the clear right of all . . ., or of none. Partial freedom seems to me a most invidious form of slavery.'

In America we live with a form of partial freedom.

Over the past twenty years there have been assaults on racial oppression with the initiative coming mainly from the black community. Working through the institutions of our land — the courts, legislature, and Presidential leadership — it appeared as though one barrier to equality after another was falling. Men of concern from the white population joined the surging effort, anxious to participate, inspired by their instincts for good, and the courage and selfless dedication of black men in the front of the movement.

But the changes did not come so rapidly. The barriers only appeared to fall, giving the illusion of progress. In matters of minority housing, employment and public education, reasonable expectations were far from realized. Passage of laws was one thing, their execution quite another. Delays, exceptions, studies, administrative apathy — all sapped the hope of the waiting minority. The resulting frustrations and impatience gave rise to a new militancy, of harsh rhetoric fearful to many, and these fears were played upon by forces of reaction.

Over the last few years of decline in the civil rights momentum the voice of the moderate man was not clear. Though many such men remained, many others left the field. The attention of some was diverted by the war. In the heat of the struggle some were afraid to speak out against the excesses of the extremes, and many leaders upon whom we depended — both black and white — were lost to violence. Whatever the cause, the tide shifted in America away from progress and equity.

Change causes disruption and discomfort. The lessening of the intensity of that change brings back the warm security of the past. So it is that for the moment many still find comfort in this turn of events. But this sense of well-being is false, the mine has merely been closed, the fire still rages within. Burke's warning that '. . . nothing is security to any individual but the common interest of all' still holds.

Whenever oppression exists, those who truly love their land, its history and its values, will press endlessly for its elimination. Men of reason, men of Burke's moderation, have no choice but to persist, if not for moral reasons, then simply to guarantee the future.

Yet oppression is not always a conscious act — people pitted against each other out of twisted racial or religious views. We have found that society itself can oppress, unconsciously, blindly, but with equal cruelty.

So do the sources of man's discontent change with time. When this Historical Society was founded the great majority of people in the Western World was concerned with mere subsistence. Daily life was physically more difficult, the elements were harsh, and the rewards for a life of work meagre. These conditions created the problems and affected the institutions of the day. Revolutions, civil strife, and discord resulted when societies and nations were slow to adjust.

Within Western society today perhaps the universal and overwhelming source of discontent arises from the increasing dehumanisation of life. There is a sense of powerlessness, not simply among the young, but among all who feel their lives are spent impersonally in modern societies. More and more, the things that vitally affect us do not submit to control. The institutions created to support us in meeting the responsibilities of our lives — whether religious, political, or educational — no longer respond to the individual's changing needs. There is no feed back. The machines of society take on a life of their own. They run themselves, perhaps efficiently, perhaps productively, but seemingly with less and less concern for the desires of the individual human being they were designed to serve.

Our large cities, totally impersonal, crank human beings through their daily activities. Our large universities, totally impersonal, stamp our people with fixed credentials. Our large industries, totally impersonal, employ people in repetitive tasks seemingly devoid of some sense of social value. Our large units of government function more for their own sake than for the people they serve. And all these institutions seem unresponsive to the individual complaint or desire. This creates a general sense of helplessness, a feeling of uselessness, that can result in unchecked national or institutional behaviour, or in individual aimless rage that seeks to destroy.

It is responsiveness that the new voices, the oppressed and the powerless, seek. Governmental systems capable of growth and adaptation. An opening of the channels to participation and elective office, and political units close enough to the people to reflect their concerns and aspirations.

The political forces of such change have been most apparent in my land, as they have been on this side of the Atlantic. But whether or not they will be successful depends on their ability to release their frustrations with the restraint necessary to bring the majority with them. If the position of the established interests is viewed as rigid, if the arguments of the militarists are considered radical and abstract, if governments and institutions are unresponsive, then those seeking change surely should not be rigid, radical or abstract. Unfortunately, this is not always the case. The young have their own harsh rhetoric. They often consider the compromise position to be a 'sell-out', and their ability to be disruptive and take to the street — no longer an ability in question — is now becoming a mechanical act. The result is less and less effectiveness. And as one who shares many of their hopes and aspirations for the future I feel constrained to warn that history is a harsh judge of those so caught up with revolution that they forget reformation. As Burke said to the French: 'You possessed in some parts the walls, and, in all, the foundations of a noble and venerable castle. You might have repaired those walls; you might have built on those old foundations.' But if we have the sense of being overwhelmed by the institutions and machines we have built, is it not even more incredible that we have the premonition that we could be destroyed by them. From the threat of nuclear weapons there is no safe haven. To the individual this represents the ultimate in total lack of control over life and environment. The presence of these weapons, and the will to use them removes the essence of life. Why seek to perfect, why struggle for orderly change, why look for the meaning of life, when without any consultation, all life can be immediately ended?

In America we know what our weapons can do to another country and the world. And we know that the same can happen to us. But, as in some mad chess game, the continued expansion of such strength goes on. Men considered reasonable can coolly calculate and compare millions of deaths with millions of deaths, megatons are matched against megatons in earnest debates over national security, and overkills of four to nine times the population of a country are discussed as though there is some sense to it all.

The new generation has been raised in this atmosphere. To them the ability to destroy the world, and at the same time not treat this ability day and night as the first matter to be solved among the nations, goes beyond the limits of the human mind. Can any society view their visions and thoughts as radical or extreme when the visions and thoughts of men in power include the real possibility of final destruction?

How did our world get swept into this position? What future was so dismal that rather than face it we elected to hold open the final option of ending everything, and taking everyone with us? And if we have arrived at this point through the failure of moderation, what faith can we put in the power of reason to now rescue us?

There will have to come other ways for nations in the last quarter of this century to resolve the problems of the planet without reliance on arsenals that could obliterate it. For too long this position has been considered naive, for too long men in public life have feared risking their reputations as realistic men by avoiding this conclusion. If the world is to continue it

257

must not only control nuclear weapons but eventually destroy them. 'How much' and 'when' are matters that can be solved once real agreement is reached in reversing the trend. To date, I do not believe that any real attempt has been made to reach this basic agreement.

It will take men like Burke, moral but realistic, committed to their own nation but responsible for the condition of all men. When he spoke of meeting the challenge of the American colonies, he was not matching the first strike capability of George III against the retaliatory power of the Lexington farmers. He was measuring the future possibility of colonialism in the new world against the continued existence of a community of men known as the Empire, and Burke argued for the latter.

Who today will measure the future possibility of international relationships built on arms against the continued existence of the community of the world — and argue for the latter?

Must we wait for the newer generations to assume their places in power, indeed, can we wait, or must we exercise the responsibility that falls to moderate men? Clearly it is our task, and we had better be about it.

So we live in a time demanding great change, and a time when survival is a real question. And how we will succeed cannot be predicted. But we will never succeed if men of reason abdicate to those consumed by passion or by fear. Change within Western nations will not come about through random actions of violence and disruption, for sheer violence cannot compel fundamental change. Rather it helps defeat those who are serious about change — the forces of humane moderation. So I fear that the present reactions — the words law and order, the trials and gaolings, the public statements and name calling by men in high places — are only the touch of a giant. Aimless and frivolous acts will turn the millions of citizens, whose fears spring from shared anxieties and frustrations and discontents, against progress and reform. Some argue that intolerance and violence are justified because modern society is violent and intolerant. Even if that were true, the argument is pure demagoguery. The objective of the discontented should not be revenge, but change. The only question for the serious man is whether these acts are effective tools of liberating change. They are not effective and they are not moral. And thus the use of violent acts is self indulgent and, worse, the unwitting instrument of those who seek to impose oppression from the right.

And, in the world, war can no longer be considered an instrument for change. We are too close to the edge of oblivion for that — and the final realisation of this fact will demand adjustments and innovations in the affairs of men unparalleled in history.

We are, then, engaged in a profound struggle for the future of our common civilization. The discontent and the ferment are realities. Only by reasoned change amid a changing world can we hope to preserve those human values which Burke struggled to protect and which were summarised by the founders of my own nation in the phrase: 'pursuit of happiness'. We may not yet understand the complexities of our dilemma. We do know that the future will either be one of increasing justice for our fellow man and the liberation of the individual to enrich his own destiny — or it will be a future of increasing repression and control, if a future at all. Discontent must either be met or suppressed. To meet it is liberation. To suppress it is the end of liberty. It was my genius countryman, Benjamin Franklin, who said, 'They that give up liberty to obtain a little temporary safety deserve neither liberty nor safety'. Nor, may I add, will they have them.

What will the outcome be? No man can know the future and Burke first of all would scorn one who tried to predict it rather than shape it.

It is now almost seven years since the President of the United States came to this city — not to the land of his birth, as he said, but the land for which he held such great affection.

John Kennedy referred to the age in which we live — an age when history moves with the tramp of earthquake feet, an age when a handful of men and nations have the power literally to devastate mankind. But he did not speak in despair or with a sense of hopelessness — those feelings had no place in his Irish heart.

'Across the gulfs and barriers that now divide us', he said, 'we must remember that there are no permanent enemies. Hostility today is a fact, but it is not a ruling law. The supreme reality of our time is our indivisibility as children of God and our common vulnerability on this planet.'

I choose to believe that Burke would have agreed with that view of reality and I can only hope that we who remain will choose to work from it.

The Bicentenary Address was broadcast live on RTE television, and recorded by both the BBC and Boston TV. Closed-circuit television relayed it to other places in the College for those members who could not obtain tickets for the Examination Hall.

BICENTENARY INTERNATIONAL DISCUSSION

'That the only liberty is . . . a liberty connected with order.'

*Edmund Burke's statement quoted above provided the topic for the
International Discussion, which was held on Wednesday, 4 March 1970 in
the Public Theatre of the College*

CHAIRMAN: AN TAOISEACH, MR JACK LYNCH

'I propose to introduce the speakers to the International Discussion of the Bicentenary Meeting of the Historical Society. The first speaker will be Senator Eugene McCarthy, Junior Senator of Minnesota, of the United States.' *(applause)*

SENATOR EUGENE McCARTHY

Prime Minister, Chancellor, fellow participants, students of Trinity, and friends:

I very much appreciate being introduced by the head of the government. I don't see the head of government in our country very often; *(laughter, applause)* I'm not often introduced by him in any case. *(laughter)* I'm pleased to be here — to be in Ireland. I was asked why I had come, and I said I didn't know you had to have a reason. I never thought it necessary. But I did use this invitation, not as an excuse for coming, but as a kind of an explanation for those back home who seem to insist that you explain any departure from the Senate.

We've worked down through some rather fine points in the Senate. As you might know here, we have a regard for the language. We've had votes in the last two months — one on an adjective in the Senate, and that's a refinement, and one on whether we should use the form 'may' or 'will' as an auxiliary verb. So even though we've kind of left Latin behind, we feel we have concern for the refinement of the language. This was a question of liberal and conservative position; I won't go into the more complicated one of the verb, that takes more explanation, but the adjective was relatively simple. It had to do with cigarette advertising. We require a slight warning — that cigarettes have an effect on cancer, or may have. The conservatives' position was that the notice should say that 'Excessive smoking may cause cancer' and the liberal position was to say simply that 'Smoking may cause cancer'. We didn't have a radical position either way *(laughter)* on that particular issue.

In any case, the theme here tonight is a theme from Burke, which I think was stated to you last night and very well presented — the question of liberty and order, as to whether or not one can exist with or without the other. And to raise that proposition, of course, is to say a great deal, and to say very little. The really great controversies in public business are not, as we like to think sometimes, about the ends or the objectives that we're seeking, but rather about the methods, and the means, and the devices, by which we seek them, the laws and institutions and practices, the things that generally fall under the name of order. And the same is true with reference to the question of liberty and order. This is not a matter really of confrontation; there's not much dispute about what one seeks by way of liberty or what constitutes liberty when you've achieved it. But rather great dispute as to what the order must be, or which order one would like to have, within which to seek freedom and liberty. Not one against the other, but one somehow living within the other. I was reinforced in my general judgment about this in talking to my daughter and she said, 'You don't really have a choice of freedom and order; all you have is a choice of which order you want.' And I am prepared tonight to talk about what I think has to be at least the outline of the order within which we must seek freedom and liberty and some kind of individual and social fulfilment in these, the last stages of the twentieth century.

There are those who propose for us what they say is a very carefully worked out, rationalized, and logical political order in the field in Marxism, and we have neo-Marxism being advocated here. When I was in college, the Trotsky-ites were the purest. *(laughter)* They've lost the crown since. *(laughter)* Those who advocate that we simply pay attention to the ancient liberties and the precedents, and those things which have been handed down to us, are somewhere between rationalization and a kind of acceptance of reality without question.

There is a form of order, which could be arrived at by arbitrary acceptance of some sort of 'social contract', in order to avoid complete chaos. Well, this is a classical position, one that is being restated by philosophers of politics and of society in a million different terms today. One on which Stephenson says he has written a book called *The Rules of Chaos*. It's a rather curious approach; it's something like the negative income tax we're talking about in the United States. It's supposed to be painless; it's another way of getting to the same point. But he says that since we live in chaos, and this is temporary, we try to establish something which is permanent, and since the world is changing, we insist that order is something which is unchanging.

And I don't know if it really profits much to approach the problem from his point of view because the whole matter of order and freedom and authority and liberty is one where you do reach a point where there's a kind of 'No Man's Land' which might be described as chaos. And you can start from the acceptance of chaos and build around it, or you can start from outside and build in to it, as long as you accept that there is an area in which the freedom of choice on the part of the individual must somehow be protected. And it's most important that you protect that area as you move from the rather lower order of things that man needs to the higher order things of the mind and of the spirit.

We've had a rather strange reversal of thought, reflected in many ways in the United States now, working on down from the acceptance certainly, of theological revelation to the questioning of philosophy, to the point now where many would say that the proper study of mankind is animals. There's a lot to be said for it. There are two or three rather popular books: *The Territorial Imperative*, a book on aggression which many people have taken up as a way of explaining all forms of social behaviour. There are, I think, some things to be said for these studies, but they have been applied unusually as a concern over animals. We find, especially among women in the States now, a refusal — I know one who won't wear the fur of an animal that has reflecting eyes. *(laughter)* She hasn't explained it yet; others will not wear the fur of animals that have not been domesticated. If you've a domesticated mink, you're in trouble. *(laughter)* If you can remain somehow wild, you can die a natural death under difficult circumstances.

These distinctions do not grow necessarily out of reflection on the animal and its social behaviour, but are a rather strange and extreme turning away from the somewhat reasoned judgment within the context of history. And it's within this context I think we have to seek to establish some rules of order today, not by old precedents, not necessarily by what's handed down, not any kind of complete and certain order that fits together, but a kind of moving determination of what the rules are and what the principles are and what the confines of order are, in which we can move towards independence and personal realization. And, as we attempt to do that, I'd say that there are two or three observations that are important. We're operating under a somewhat different time scheme, I think, from any that was accepted in the past. There's no one seriously talking, excepting some of the astrologers, about the second millennium; I think an encouraging sign. We've more people worried about 1984, and some in our country worried more about 1972, but *(laughter, applause)* 1984 is a more seriously important year than the year 2000.

Also there have been some changes in our general conception of space, and this, I think, is quite unrelated to the moonshot. No one talks about Utopia, really, as being some place in space or El Dorado or Shangri-La. No searching in space, really, for the good life and fulfilment and even the theologians are now saying that heaven is not a place. This was really more disturbing than when they said God was dead because there were some people who really weren't as concerned about that as whether heaven was or not. Heaven without God might be better *(laughter)* — it would be under some jurisdiction. I mean the question of liberty and freedom *(laughter)* without authority which would be more appealing to some of them. Well, I hesitate to give this condition a term to try to say it means this, that this is existentialism, because that would be to fix it but rather to say that we accept that it is a kind of moving game. We've accepted it in the physical sciences. The old certainty of Newton, and even the relative certainty of Einstein and his theories, have not been altogether discarded. They're still somewhat useful, but not accepted as giving a full explanation within which analysis and experimentation in the area of physics must be carried on.

And so, in history, two things to recognise: that the movement of what we call history is faster than it's ever been before, and secondly, that what one might call the volume of it is greater than ever, in that in every part of the world now, people are concerned about things that are happening in every other part of the world. The old idea was that Africa was simply a dark continent that need not concern us, China was the 'sleeping dragon', and so on. This has all been set aside, and all of these continents and peoples and nations demand some attention from us, and not just attention, but almost every day some kind of a judgment, and some commitment. So within what framework do we make that judgment and within what framework do we make that commitment? We say that generally it must be a more flexible order, it must be one which is more ready to change, and one which must allow much more for personal determination and for the definition of individual responsibility.

I'd like to cite two or three examples from the United States to indicate the complexity and the need for, not an easy, but a quick response. In our

Bill of Rights we speak of the freedoms guaranteed to Americans. The notion of freedom of speech is quite a simple one and it's easy to declare. And we have a rather good tradition of it in the United States. What people had in mind when that amendment of the Constitution was drafted was a society very different from ours, and very different forms of news communication, and a pretty different kind of educational system. And to simply say that to guarantee to everyone the right to say what he thinks was perhaps the best way to ensure that at least what people had by way of truth would get to those who were interested in it.

But today, with the kind of concentration, control, and domination we have, the idea of simple freedom of expression has to be explained in terms really not of the right of man to say whatever he wants to say when he has no means of saying it, but what is probably even the more fundamental thing, the right of a person to hear the truth. And so you say, well, how can you guarantee that? And there's no real way to do it except to ensure, within a kind of pressing if not oppressive system, that more people will be free to speak. And in consequence of that, you would hope that more of those who are in need of the truth or are seeking it will hear it, because unless you can determine in advance what the truth is that is to be heard, you can't really say who is to speak and who is not to speak.

We find this conflict running in our country, and not only there, but in other parts of the world as to whether you should move toward some kind of carefully determined programming, especially as we have it with television now in the United States, or whether you ought to allow it to be run individually and separately. And I have a feeling we're moving in one way, since we started out with rather free radio and television to an advocacy, at least, of more control; whereas here, in Ireland and in England, where you started out with control, you're tending to move in the other direction. I think it indicates there's no real solution to it, that you move it around in the hope that somewhere you strike a kind of balance between the freedom of the individual to speak and to hear, and the kind of social control which is essential.

Another area of special problems for us is that of freedom of assembly, which was a very simple consideration back in 1789 or earlier. But now it's not so much a matter of meeting in a room to discuss things as it was then, or even a street corner meeting (although we do have some problems about those), but things such as demonstrations, for example, and mass protests, which were not anticipated, and the somewhat more sophisticated form of assembly, that of organizations, even though their members may never meet.

We have in process now rather interesting court proceedings on the question of conspiracy. In the case of the trial of Dr Spock, it was decided that if he and Mr Coffin had done separately, what they supposedly did after conspiring, it would have been all right. But it was their conspiring to do something which was not wrong that created the difficulty. And more recently, it was decided in the Chicago Trial — it's not ended yet — that they had not conspired, but that if they had not crossed the State line to do what they did they would not have been subject to prosecution. To stay within one State and provoke a riot is all right, *(laughter)* but if you step over the line into another State with the intention of provoking a riot, you're subject to prosecution.

These are not really decisions that are fixed in the law of the United States yet, but they are a reflection, I think, of the great difficulty and stress under which we try to define the areas of freedom and the areas within which individual action is allowed. I suppose we could list nearly all of these: the question of privacy when the Constitution was adopted had to do with the quartering of troops and whether the house could be searched without a warrant. To all of the really difficult, really technical questions now, wire-tapping, eavesdropping, and various kinds of electronic devices for spying on people, we've made some fine distinctions, such as sometimes a tap on a telephone line is not to be allowed, whereas if you pound a nail in the wall and pick it up in proximity, it's not really a violation of privacy. I don't think this has quite been settled very clearly yet but we've been moved to make distinctions that make those that are attributed to medieval moral theologians and canonists really look like rather crude operations. *(laughter)* Ours call for not only refinement of thought, but for great mastery and distinctions in technological and scientific devices.

Altogether, this I think should make clear to you that the question of order and liberty is one which is never quite fixed and is perhaps less fixed today than it has been. And as we proceed, it means that the individual more and more is called upon to make his own particular decisions. This does not mean that he makes them in a vacuum and unrelated to any standards, but that he must be prepared to establish the standards himself, and then to be responsible for his decisions. It's not really a permissive society in which you're growing up, it's one in which there is a great deal of freedom. But along with that freedom goes a greater and more pressing burden of individual responsibility.

If I could cite an example or two: the monk, Gregor Mendel experimenting with genetics in beans and peas and other things of that kind and dominant and recessive traits, and what a free kind of activity it must have been. Now, contrast with that the modern nuclear biologist, who has begun to learn things about human genes and how he has to consider the potential application of his knowledge. In contrast with that, Mendel's genetics appeared to be interesting, also something which had a practical rather easy kind of application to human good. The nuclear biologist case is one having some of those aspects, but also creating the most difficult kind of philosophical and moral, and not only that, but political problems. It is a fact that nearly every major philosophical and theological problem that has application to human behaviour does eventually become a political problem.

Or someone like da Vinci, who I'm sure had the most exciting time theorizing about aerodynamics, working out those relationships, and never having to give a thought to how his knowledge might be taken up in a new and vast technology, and made the basis for inter-continental ballistic missiles and other forms of weapons which we have today. Or Descartes and the earlier mathematicians talking about mathematics as pure science meaning that no one was responsible for it, in a way. With mathematicians today who have to face the fact that mathematical knowledge can almost immediately be taken up by the master of technology, incorporated in nuclear bombs and all the other new devices and new knowledge that emerge almost every day. Men like Oppenheimer, for example, had to make the most difficult personal and very lonely decisions.

I can take the somewhat more practical example of some of the men involved in our military activities in Vietnam, who might have been expected in another age to proceed with a rather simple rule: if captured, give your name, rank, and serial number; in contrast with the captain of a ship like the Pueblo, for example, or men in the Green Berets, and some of the other military missions which we and other nations have abroad in the world. These men have to make decisions in a very personal or intense way, sometimes by one man alone and sometimes by those who may lead a special profession, and sometimes of course, brought even to the point where the politicians are called upon to make them. I hope that in many of these areas that the professions that are immediately involved can be moved to make acceptable decisions and I hope that in some areas that the moral theologians, those that are left with some reputation, will be prepared to move somewhat ahead of political decision. When this does not happen, then eventually some kind of social determination must be made and that determination is made largely within the context of politics, the area within which Edmund Burke worked throughout his life, the area in which I have been involved, as have many of the men who will speak to you here tonight.

So I end with the plea that you be understanding of the politicians in action and also as they attempt to explain what they have done or what they may do. Because they're caught as the moralists are, somewhat. If they lay down absolute rules by which they say they will act, they are accused of being unrealistic, and I've been accused of that. Or if you propose some kind of adjustment or some kind of compromise in the context of the rules or practices or even within the context of history, you are accused of being morally irresponsible, or the advocate of expediency.

So it is not a question of liberty versus order, but of liberty and freedom within an acceptable set of rules which can be arrived at only by two considerations: that of philosophical enquiry and some reflection, and on the other hand, by a study of man in society and society in history. If we do not accept that these must be our guides, we necessarily surrender ourselves to a kind of total ignorance and false fear. The alternative to that must be to assert the power of reason, knowledge and human judgment to give some direction not only to life but some modest direction also to history itself.

CHAIRMAN: AN TAOISEACH, MR JACK LYNCH
'Thank you, Senator McCarthy. I'm not introducing the speakers at any length as I think it would presumptuous of me to try; it would certainly be superfluous to give any account of their careers and their very names are sufficient for us. And therefore without delay I propose to call on the next speaker, Professor Andreas Papandreou.' *(applause)*

PROFESSOR ANDREAS PAPANDREOU

Mr Prime Minister, members of the Historical Society, Ladies and Gentlemen:

I feel very honoured to be here tonight and speak about as important a topic as this. I have just told Senator McCarthy that his very quiet words belie strength. And while my words may not be so quiet, maybe this will be understood in view of the fact that our experiences, or recent experiences, may be somewhat different. *(laughter)* But I have great respect for Senator McCarthy and for his courage, for what he is trying to do in his country, and anything I say about his great country comes from the fact that it is so critical to all of us, and it is a country in which I lived myself and worked for over twenty years.

Two quite distinct notions, popular sovereignty and personal liberty seem to vie for recognition in the concept of democracy. Logically, the two are unrelated. The Bill of Rights is a legislative monument directed to the concept of personal liberty, while Lincoln's epigram, 'government of the people, by the people, for the people' sums up the case for popular sovereignty. So it should not be really so surprising to discover that Edmund Burke condemned popular sovereignty in the name of personal liberty.

As he says, 'No experience has taught us that in any other course or method than that of an hereditary crown, our liberties can be regularly perpetuated and preserved sacred as our hereditary right.'

For Burke's king did not exercise arbitrary power. He was constrained both by custom and by Divine Law, while the revolutionary Assembly in France 'since the destruction of the Orders had no functional law, no strict convention, no respected usage to restrain it. Instead of finding themselves obliged to conform to a fixed constitution, they have a power to make a constitution which will conform to their designs'.

And he continues: 'For if civil society be the offspring of convention, that convention must be its law. That convention must limit and modify all the descriptions of constitution which are formed under it.' This is Burke.

It is clear that he, as many of his contemporaries, thought of sovereignty as limited by convention, in the context of a nominalist concept of society, and thus capable of providing guarantees of personal liberty.

In the sweep of the French Revolution, the concept of popular sovereignty, having taken the place of Divine Sovereignty, merged with that of the nation and national sovereignty. In this new context, the legitimacy of the State's commands derived from the fact that it is the mandatory of the nation. And the beneficence of the State derives from its supposed service to the goals of the nation. This radically new perspective is essentially organic, expressing an image of society as a purposive, wilful whole, rather than as an assemblage of individuals.

For the critics of popular or national sovereignty, as the basic legitimacy for the State's actions, two questions emerge: first, will the mandatory of the sovereign people be the executive or the legislative branch of the government? Deriving, as it does, 'of the people and by the people', will it also act for the people? What are the guarantees? The second question is equally important: what is the fate of the minority, the fate of dissent in the context of popular or national sovereignty? Certainly, if the rules of the game are fixed by a majority, in the interests of the majority, there can be no protection, in principle, for the minority. The concept of popular sovereignty or rule of the people by the people, and for the people makes no provision for the fate of the minority. Admittedly, the Bill of Rights does. But in the context of popular sovereignty, what are the guarantees that they too will not be swept away by the majority's interests?

It is clear that the concept of democracy as we understand it should make provisions both for effective popular sovereignty and for personal liberty. It seems then that the necessary and sufficient conditions for a democratic process are as follows:

1. A set of rules that make it possible for the majority to govern; that is to say to make decisions in the name of the whole.

2. A set of rules that permit the members of society to exercise continuous, uniform control of it.

3. A set of rules that permit the minority to become a majority under terms that are equal for all.

4. A set of rules that specify the limits of unfavourable effects or actions on the parts of the governing body, actions presumably taken in the interests of the whole on any segment of the society in question.

5. A set of rules that specify the limits of unfavourable effects of action taken by any group or person on any other group or person in the society in question.

The first three sets of rules encompass the democratic concept of popular sovereignty. The remaining two define the concept of liberty. This much can be said on purely logical definitional grounds. On historical grounds we are bound to recognize that the enactment of such a set of demanding rules of a liberty-preserving order presupposes a rather unusual distribution of the structure of power. For no rules will be enacted, or observed even if enacted, unless they correspond to the prevailing structure of power.

Our purpose then must shift to an examination of the prevalent structure of power in our contemporary world, in order that we may judge the extent to which the order under which we live supports liberty or suppresses it.

Let us define political power as the power to influence directly or indirectly the instrumentalities, the organizations that make up the apparat of the State. Do the citizens exercise such power in the contemporary representative form of democracy? The truth of the matter is that in contemporary society and especially so in its most advanced form, the citizen has been alienated, not only from all power, but also from a reasonable, sensible understanding of the processes that hold the key to his future and to the future of his children. *(applause)*

Who then, holds this power? The answer is that it is held by a limited number of power enclaves, of power oligopolies. These forces of power exercise influence over the State by reason of the strategic position they occupy in the social process. Some are visible, legitimized spokesmen for sectional interests. But power, substantial power, is exercised on a huge scale by non-legitimized enclaves of power. The large firm, the modern multi-national corporate conglomerate leans to mentalities that make up the apparat of the State. That is to say that bureaucracy, and especially the modern military bureaucracy, all exercise substantial political influence; They constitute today the new ruling coalition, the new establishment.

The apparat of the State, the organizations that make it up have always had a place in the establishment. Their importance has varied with the role played and the power exercised by the State. The modern State, whether we look at the advanced industrial society of the West, or at the socialist republic of the East, is now approaching its climax of power, and it is evident that the apparat associated with it, especially the bureaucracy, is not merely a member of the contemporary establishment, but conceivably its most important and dominant component. Hand in hand with the ascension of the bureaucracy to a dominant position within the contemporary establishment, and the expansion of the area of competence of the Modern State, goes the alienation of the citizen from any effective exercise of his sovereignty. Elections increasingly take the form of a plebiscite for or against the party and the program. With his vote the citizen delivers to a party both legislative and executive functions. He is a sovereign citizen for just that day, returning to his role as a subject the moment after he has cast his ballot. *(applause)* But even his vote is, typically, not the expression of his mature judgment, or of his unfettered will. For political machines have taken on the role of delivering the vote to the candidate of their choice, just as they have taken over the task of developing the image of the candidate. And, to a large extent, he stands on public issues. For what matters in the end is not that he wins, but that the machine's candidate wins the seat. *(applause)*

Thus, popular sovereignty as exercised in the modern, industrially advanced society is but a shadow of its intended meaning. Elections have become a formality, a necessary ritual, for the legitimisation of a State which, while acting in the name of the people or of the nation, is in fact committed to serving the interests of the establishment. *(applause)* In the democracies of the West, this establishment consists primarily of the corporate managers and of the public bureaucrats, but especially, and increasingly so, of the military caste. In the republics of the East, the establishment represents a varying mix of the State, industrial, and Party bureaucracies along with, inevitably, the military caste. This new order, this new structure of power, constitutes a true menace to liberty.

Liberty, in two senses, is the self-determination and independence of nations and the basic freedom of the citizen within them. It is only now that we are becoming aware of the fact that since the last World War, a new elite has been ascending to power. A new elite that threatens de profundis whatever remains of our liberties. The modern military man in contemporary society is the technocrat planner par excellence. His speciality is the management of national security. His power is measured not only by the size of the budget that is devoted to national security, but also by the fact that he holds under his control a power of destruction never before perceived by Man.

Side by side with the military technocrat is his indispensable associate, the intelligence specialist. The circle is rounded out by the foreign relations bureaucrat and the scientists who specialise in war technology. The expansionist dynamic of the modern military caste, of the modern national security managers, has not been fully understood or appreciated. For the modern military man is quite different from his predecessors. He deals with awesome technologies. He commands spectacular resources. Given modern war technology, the geosphere, necessarily, becomes his oyster. As a planner, he must consider the long run. He must anticipate new weapons systems. He must anticipate political, social, economic developments, not only at home, but on a world-wide basis. And since war preparedness, which is the basis of national security, requires total mobilization of human and material resources, he must expand his control. In the end, he must control foreign policy, domestic policy, and education. Nothing less will do. Effective popular sovereignty is a direct threat to his position. Liberty and dissent are disruptive, dangerous luxuries at home, and assertion of national independence of a morally equal voice by nations within alliance systems is subversive arrogance.

This is especially relevant to the national security managers who occupy the seat of either one of the two great centres of power — Washington and Moscow. The military establishments of the two super-powers are quite similar. Indeed, as Richard Barnett has put it, the competition between the national security managers of the USA and the USSR resemble that between Ford and General Motors. Certainly, one can point to a difference. In the USA the national security managers share their power with the managerial elite. And legitimately one can speak of there being present two expansionist dynamics, one emanating from the business system, the other one from the security system. In the Soviet Union the business dynamic is very present indeed. And since it is true that the economic dependence of a Warsaw Pact member on the Soviet metropolis furthers its political and military dependence, it can be counted upon that the bureaucratic and militaristic dynamic of the Soviet Union's establishment will impose a similar pattern on its managerial economic component. Even if one were to grant that the Soviet Union's policy is essentially consolidationist, one would still be forced to admit that the distinction is of no great practical value, because, while world consolidation is different technologically from expansionism, it is not so in terms of instrumentation.

There is the old saying that the best defence is a good offence. The shape of our world today and its pattern of change can best be understood in the context of a global conflict dynamic in three dimensions. There is, first, the conflict of the two super-powers for world domination, for the propagation or the consolidation of their systems. There is, second, the struggle of the post-colonial Third World for emancipation and self-determination, a struggle that leads to revolution or insurgence. There is, third, the ceaseless struggle between the ex-colonial powers, the middle-range powers, as they are called today, to achieve a collective identity in the context of a United Europe and the super-powers, which have every reason to maintain a Europe divided, tamed, and subjugated to their own military and economic interests. *(applause)* So far as it concerns the super-powers, the deadly chess game is being played in the context of peaceful co-existence, according to relatively well-observed rules. These rules include: mutual respect of each other's supremacy *(laughter)* within its well-defined sphere of influence; prevention of the rise of another super-power; elimination of neutralism. *(laughter)*

Naturally, the stability of this evolving system of rules is threatened both by centrifugal tendencies within the Blocs and by extremist tendencies within the establishments of the super-powers when tensions between them becomes high. For Europe, East and West, what is especially relevant is the revolutionary change that has taken place in the role of the military commands of NATO and of the Warsaw Pact. NATO, initially conceived as a defence ally among morally equal partners, an alliance intended to defend the democratic institutions and traditions of the West, has developed into an hierarchical, international military structure — a pyramid of command that finds its apex in the Pentagon. This Pentagon-dominated military structure constitutes a network of power that has spread its tentacles throughout the nations of the West. It commands the allegiance of national armies, in at least one instance — Greece. The national army toppled the government on the basis of a NATO-elaborated contingency plan in order to protect the so-called strategic interest of the USA in the Eastern Mediterranean. *(applause)*

Thus, national sovereignty, and by implication, popular sovereignty, and freedom have been cynically sacrificed on the altar of 'Bloc Security'. Nor is it different in the East. The flagrant invasion of Czechoslovakia by the Warsaw Pact nations parallels the death of democracy in Greece. The Soviet Union has discovered too that it is much simpler to control the governments of its allies through the armies of the Warsaw Pact that through political or economic means. The division of Europe and the support of this division through the pressure of the two military bloc commands constitutes a clear and present danger, not only to national self-determination, but to democratic institutions as well, in every European nation.

The tragedy is, of course, that freedom is either non-existent or mortally threatened in the Bloc metropolis. For this is a sure sign that militarism is growing deep roots. The process is especially striking now, dynamically speaking, in the USA where, despite the valiant efforts of many members of Congress, one of them here, *(applause)* of many distinguished journalists and intellectuals, and of a conscious, vibrant, youth movement, the Pentagon is still impregnable. New legislation, new court decisions (the case of the Chicago Seven), new pronouncements by the administration, *(laughter, applause)* presage a totalitarian spirit quite novel in the USA. As for the Soviet Union, ever since Khrushchev's disappearance from the political scene the structure of power, and along with it the spirit, has been moving towards a much more clearly defined totalitarian direction. The democratic vision is getting dimmer by the day.

Popular sovereignty, having practically become the universal basis for legitimacy for the modern State, is rapidly turning into a mere slogan and liberty is on the retreat. The new mushrooming order is the law and order that appeals to the silent majorities and to the very vocal minorities of the establishment which hold the key to the gates of power.

This, no doubt, is a reflection of a highly dynamic process. A process set in motion by the thrust of the two new empires to consolidate or expand their spheres of influence, to divide, solidly and permanently, the world into two air-tight compartments, to subjugate the new nations of the world in the context of a new imperialism, no less awesome that its older, classical form. For my democratic, progressive and peaceful world, it is not easy to contemplate a new totalitarian era. And it is our supreme duty therefore, to act and act now.

The struggle for human freedom today has two meaningful dimensions. Globally, we must act to strengthen the United Nations. We must act to support every genuine national liberation or national independence movement *(applause)* — we must support every movement to break the vice of bipolarity. Always mindful of the fact that the road to genuine internationalism goes through genuine national independence. *(applause)* At home, wherever that may be, we must resist every invasion of our freedom and we must act forcefully to reinstate or to assert democratic, popular sovereignty through new political institutions that make possible the active participation of the citizen in the social decision-making process. *(applause)*

Above all, we must have the courage, the courage to listen carefully to the quests of the new generation, on whose sensitivity, awareness, and determination depends the outcome of the great confrontation between the forces of totalitarianism and freedom. *(applause, cheering)*

CHAIRMAN: AN TAOISEACH, MR JACK LYNCH
'Thank you, Professor Papandreou, and I now call on Mr James M. Dillon.'
(applause, cheers)

MR JAMES DILLON T.D.

A Chathaoirligh . . . *(applause)* There's no need to get so excited about the Irish tongue. *(laughter, applause)*

A hundred and thirty years ago my grandfather, as President of this Society *(applause)* used this platform to commend the virtue of peculism to his audience. It wasn't a universally admired virtue in 1840 or 1841. In fact, I think the Society's acceptance of it involved their expulsion from Trinity College, Dublin. *(laughter, applause)* I know the meeting at which he spoke had to be held without the precinct of this University. But though the Young Ireland movement of which he was a leader seemed to end in fiasco in 1948–1848 *(laughter)* — something else happened in 1948. I became a Minister of an Irish Government! *(laughter and applause)* And those two events are not disassociated! *(laughter)*

Because of the events, 1848 may have looked like fiasco, but probably they're the reason that we here tonight are proud to call ourselves Irish and not British! *(cheers, applause)* I'm concerned to commend to this audience in 1970 — freedom. I admit that my observations are mainly directed over the heads of your distinguished guests, but to the students of this generation, astonished as they may be to hear that information. *(laughter)* I'm concerned to commend freedom and to ask those who share my concern for freedom to read two books about it. Particularly my friends the Maoists, I would ask them to consult the Librarian and have access to George Orwell's *Animal Farm. (cheers applause)* And the next time they wave the little red book, or are sent out to say 'Ho, Ho, Ho Chi Minh' *(laughter)* I'll ask them to remember the animals who were at one time allowed to say, 'Four legs good, two legs bad', until Napoleon Pig took to wearing a bowler hat, smoking a pipe and walking on his hind legs, and then they were allowed to say only, 'Four legs good, two legs *better.*'

I say, despite the criticisms I've heard tonight of the rival powers of the world, 'Thank God for America!' *(boos, cheers, applause)* But for America you wouldn't dare to boo, or you'd be hung in the morning! *(applause)* Anytime you boo, thank God for America. *(boos, cheers, laughter, applause)*

I say freedom has two irreconcilable enemies: one is inflation *(laughter)* — you see, I am a pragmatical politician, *(laughter)* with respect to my two distinguished predecessors, both of whom are great politicians. I'm quite simple and down to earth. *(laughter)* The first is inflation and the second is anarchy. Both of these are infinitely seductive in their initial stages. They are the opium and the heroin of a free society. They are never static. They always develop in a dialectic which leads inevitably to a dictatorship of the Hitler or Stalin variety. The only effective safeguard against that kind of slavery is parliamentary democracy, *(applause)* which has been so rightly described as the worst form of government known to man, except all the others. *(laughter)*

Each of these propositions I respectfully submit to this Society as Truth. I want further to suggest that active participation in parliamentary democracy is politics. Your whole approach to politics hinges largely on the question of whether on the one hand you prefer to be free, with all the perplexing responsibilities involved in being free, or, on the other hand, to be one unit in an authoritarian society where you're told what to do and what to think, and effectively disciplined in a concentration camp or by an execution squad if you fail to conform. When all irrelevancies have been eliminated, the purpose of politics ought to be to secure that each one of us shall remain free. Free to think whatever we want to think. Free to protest against anything we believe to be wrong. Free to organize, to take over the government by the consent of the majority of our fellow citizens if we can persuade such a majority to agree with us and consequently, by their votes in a general election, to give us the authority to govern under the supreme authority of God.

If you don't want to be free, there really isn't any need to bother about politics. You'll be told what to do and what to think, and that will be that, as far as you're concerned. You will, in all probability, be adequately fed, and clothed, and housed, so long as you continue to be a well-oiled cog in the State Machine, because like every prudent slave owner in history, the State, which owns you absolutely, will take all reasonable precautions to ensure that its property is kept in working order. And you will never need to feel the agony of making up your own mind between right and wrong and having to act accordingly, whatever the social consequences for yourself may be.

You will always know that to conform to the dictates of authority will involve no blame and no misunderstanding. And that so long as you are content to be eyeless in Gaza at the mill with slaves, you need never apprehend either ecstasy or despair. You can look forward, and here I am speaking far above the heads of your distinguished guests, *(laughter)* you can look forward to your three score years and ten of uneventful living, no better and no worse than any horse or cow or camel *(laughter, applause)* in the name of a prudent, if exacting taskmaster, in your case the State. If, on the other hand, you believe with me that to live unfree is worse than death, you must prepare to play your part in the society to which you belong, keeping eternal vigilance if necessary, to ensure that the flame of freedom is kept alive.

Your part in that vigil is politics. You may well ask, 'what is politics?'. And for an answer to that supremely relevant question, I must refer you, and I do refer you to a source by which I stand, the late Thomas Kettle, M.P., an Irish nationalist who laid down his life on the battlefield in Flanders in defence of the sacred principle of freedom, as he saw it. God be good to him. When he was twenty-one years of age, he addressed the Young Ireland branch of the United Irish League in 1905. The title he chose for his inaugural address was the Philosophy of Politics. The average age of his audience was about twenty-three, and they were all on the threshold of active participation in the public life of Ireland. It is reported verbatim in his collected essays published under the title of *The Day's Birth* and if you're serious in your enquiry, you must read this essay from the first word to the last. Every word is significant; none more so than the final paragraph which I read and re-read on countless occasions during my long political life, whenever the going appeared to be impossibly tough and unrewarding; it always gave me fresh courage and inspiration to carry on, for which I shall be eternally grateful.

Looking back on fifty years of political life, which I began in 1918 at the age of sixteen, I've never regretted a single moment of my political activity. And in politics, I have found what I am convinced I was meant by Providence to attempt in life. Politics certainly gave me ample scope to use whatever gifts I was endowed with. Whether I adequately availed of that opportunity or not is irrelevant, because if my performance was unsatisfactory, the fault was wholly mine. It was not for lack of opportunity. Happily for me, those fifty years of politics gave me great satisfaction, and it can do the same for you *(laughter)* in the half-century that lies before you, if you observe some simple but inflexible rules of conduct, some of which are obvious, and some not quite so obvious until you've had time and experience to learn their wisdom.

The first relates to wisdom itself, and I want to suggest to you that wisdom can't be acquired from anyone, no matter how wise he or she may be. It is available only in the hearts of those who have experience, for you must learn it by trial and error.

The second rule is that in the long run, quite apart from the moral aspect, it never pays to tell lies. *(laughter)* Ephemeral success may be secured by a liar, but sooner or later he'll be found out and judged accordingly. *(groan from a member of the audience)* Don't groan about that, simply reform! *(laughter, applause)* You still have time. *(applause)*

The third rule in politics is, avoid becoming a chronic resigner, *(laughter)* that universal pest. Every politician must satisfy his own conscience on the question of whether an issue is a fundamental matter of principle or merely a question of expediency as to how best a desired end can be reached effectively. If fundamental principle is involved, and this is rare *(laughter, applause)* I say that deliberately. And this is rare. I found one once in my public life. Then your only course is resignation from your Party, if your view doesn't prevail. But on questions of expediency, you should accept the opinion of the majority and work with your colleagues to make the best that you can of the policy agreed on.

The fourth rule is, don't allow your inexperience to make you simple. Tom Kettle has said all that needs to be said on this subject in his philosophy of politics. Read it carefully, and you will never be guilty of this last treachery, this irredeemable deceit.

The fifth rule is, be on your guard against Utopianism. And by that I mean that you should realize that you can't make heaven on earth by passing laws. You can always be on the lookout for possibilities to do this through appropriate parliamentary action. But keep on trying are the important words.

The Duke of Wellington is reported to have said to his officers at the most critical moment of the battle of Waterloo, 'Hard pounding, this, gentlemen. Try who can pound the longest now.' It's good advice for a young politician. I don't think, Taoiseach, after fifty years, that I should secede from this distinguished company. I still retain some of the romance of politics and some of the faith that brought me into it. And so, I dare to say to you 'God Bless America'. *(laughter and applause)* By Heaven, they wouldn't do it in Moscow or Peking! *(laughter, applause)* So I say, if you believe in what you're trying to achieve in politics, never lie, never give up. Remember always Arthur Clough's splendid affirmation of faith:

> Say not the struggle nought availeth,
> The labour and the wounds are vain,
> The enemy faints not, nor faileth,
> And as things have been they remain.
>
> For while the tired waves, vainly breaking,
> Seem here no painful inch to gain,
> Far back, through creeks and inlets making,
> Comes silent, flooding in, the main.
>
> And not by Eastern windows only,
> When daylight comes, comes in the light,
> In front, the sun climbs slow, how slowly,
> But Westward, look, the land is bright.

(During this recitation, people in the audience are chanting but the words are not clear.)

Lastly, young politicians would do well to remember the precepts of an Irishman whose fame is world wide as a great statesman. His words will suitably conclude this affirmation of faith in freedom. *(chanting, and interjections)* The first is, falsehood has a perennial spring. And that means that you must be prepared to cut down falsehood year after year, just as a farmer cuts weeds, which unlike crops, can grow and flourish no matter how often they are cut down. He goes on to say: 'All that is necessary for evil to prevail is that good men should do nothing.' And then he adds:

'When bad men combine, the good must associate; else they will fall, one by one, an unpitied sacrifice in a contemptible struggle.' And when the radio *(chanting)* and the television and the press and the Maoists *(laughter, applause)* combine to tell you what ought to be done and how far short of their expectations they think you have fallen, you can turn again to Edmund Burke for the appropriate reply.

'Applaud us when we run; console us when we fall; cheer us when we recover; but let us pass on — for God's sake, let us pass on!'[17]

(applause, cheering)

CHAIRMAN: AN TAOISEACH, MR JACK LYNCH
'Thank you, Mr Dillon. I now call on Mr Michael Foot, M.P.' *(applause)*

MR MICHAEL FOOT M.P.

Mr Prime Minister, Members of the Historical Society, Ladies and Gentlemen:

May I first of all thank you for the invitation to come and speak here at this debate. I appreciate the honour greatly and I do so the more because I believe that many of us feel it is a privilege to appear on the same platform with two of the visitors from other countries, Professor Papandreou and Senator McCarthy. *(applause)* I will seek to make some comments on what Professor Papandreou said to us, but of course all of us must, on this subject of freedom, speak with some diffidence in the presence of a great Greek patriot and democrat. *(applause)*

To Senator McCarthy I would wish to say, I believe on behalf of great numbers of people in England and in Wales as well as, I am sure, many in Ireland, that some of us regard the political initiative which he took prior

17   Speech at Bristol previous to the Election, 1780.

to the last Presidential election in the United States as the boldest political initiative taken by any politician in the Western world since the end of the Second World War. *(cheers, applause)* When the fighting at last ends in Vietnam, when the killing and the burning and the maiming have all ceased, there will be no man I believe who will deserve greater credit for that achievement than Senator McCarthy and therefore, that is the reason why many of us find it such an honour to meet him and to hear him.

As far as some of the other speakers are concerned, I say nothing about my friend who was to speak later. We maybe will approach some of these matters from a similar angle. I had hoped I may say, and I hope it won't be thought parochial of me to mention it, that Mr Quintin Hogg was to be present here on this occasion.[18] I had hoped very much that he would be because he is an authority on the subject of law and order. *(laughter, applause)* I wished to say something to him, more directly on the subject than we sometimes find possible in the British House of Commons. *(laughter)* However, in the absence of Mr Quintin Hogg, I think that all I can say is, 'Thank God for Dillon!' *(laughter, applause)* 'Thank God for Dillon, the Quintin Hogg of County Mayo!' *(jeers, laughter, applause)*

We are extremely grateful to him for putting the case for the motion, as I understand it. Now I hope it won't be regarded as an intrusion in this debate if I refer to the motion which is being proposed. *(laughter, applause)* He says that the only liberty is a liberty connected with order. And I suppose that in a certain sense that everyone could agree with that. Indeed, it is almost to reduce the paradoxes of Burke to a platitude. But obviously, we haven't assembled here tonight to discuss a platitude *(hear, hear! interjected by Dillon) (laughter)* It is a . . . I'm glad that my remark was not over the heads of everybody! *(laughter, applause)*

It might be thought that the proposition is almost incontestable. But in my judgment, there is something wrong with its tenor — that the only liberty is a liberty connected with order. I realize that it is a very risky proposition for an Englishman, even though I'm only partly an Englishman — I say that as an excuse — and I'm an honorary Welshman. I hope that will appeal to some! *(laughter)* But even so, I hope it will be —

---

[18] Mr Quintin Hogg had accepted the invitation to speak, but in mid-February had been obliged to withdraw to take a case in the Court of Criminal Appeal in London.

and it does require some temerity to speak on the subject of Edmund Burke. I suppose it was thought that because the only reason why they only had one speaker in favour of the motion was that they thought that Edmund Burke on his own was sufficient to make the proposition acceptable. Particularly when Edmund Burke himself has been made respectable by Conor Cruise O'Brien. *(laughter)*

However, in having to discuss Edmund Burke at a meeting such as this in Trinity College, I feel a little as if, having arrived in the Kingdom of Heaven, I were called upon to give a short address on the Ten Commandments *(laughter)* before an audience composed of Moses, Aaron, and a representative selection of the major prophets. *(laughter, applause)* So it is in that spirit, coupled with my natural modesty anyhow that I approach the subject. *(laughter)* As I say, I missed Mr Quintin Hogg very much. I had hoped he would explain to us exactly how law and order had been operating in the other part of Ireland during these fifty years.*(applause)* The longer I remain in political life, and the more I see of the varieties and discrepancies of political experience, *(laughter)* the more I am coming to recognise that it would be neither unwise nor an exaggeration to say *(laughter throughout, due to his imitation of his Prime Minister's inflection and speech)* that on all subjects there is much to be said on both sides of the question. *(laughter, applause)*

And this is what the champion of order, Edmund Burke, had to say about the situation in the Six Counties: 'On the right side, there is a time when men will not suffer bad things because their ancestors had suffered worse. There is a time when the hoary head of inveterate abuse will neither draw reverence, nor obtain protection.' And I was hoping to have commended that to Mr Quintin Hogg in person but I will pass it on to him when I see him in London. And I must say, I think it was a very daring — I'm not talking about England; of course we have to discuss law and order there because there is an election coming up — but I say any Tory who dares to talk about law and order in Ireland after the past fifty years in the North, I think is a very daring politician indeed. *(cries of hear, hear!, applause)*

There is of course a strong philosophical ground for what I'm saying as well. I don't need to deploy the case in any great detail, because I don't think that any of the speakers, including Mr Dillon, has attempted to sustain in its full force the proposition that the only liberty is a liberty connected with order. It would be an extraordinary proposition for anybody really to say that the only liberty is a liberty connected with order. I was named after an Irishman, Michael Davitt, who spent many years in an English gaol. The only liberty a liberty connected with order? He wouldn't have appreciated the remark. *(laughter)* If we delve a bit deeper back into what I understand is regarded as a notable event in Irish history — the invasion of Oliver Cromwell and those who came with him — he represented order, but way back in England there were people who represented liberty — the first opponents of imperialism in modern British history — the Levellist men from Cromwell's army who refused to serve in Ireland. They rejected the demands of order and stood for the cause of liberty. And so you could go through the whole of British history and see that there have been voices raised for liberty, sometimes against the whole serried power of order. Charles James Fox denounced those who were prepared to tolerate a large amount of injustice rather than risk a small amount of disorder. And therefore, we don't have to search very far, I believe, to see facts in our history which deny the proposition which Edmund Burke has stated, or is held to have stated in this proposition.

Or we can quote statements that have been made of a much more recent character. I'm not quite sure if I quoted this one when I came to Trinity College before, but whether I did or not I think it will serve again because who said this — what champion of order was it that said this: 'I am sorry to say that if no instructions had been addressed in political crises to the people of this country' — he was talking about England, but I have no doubt it applies to Ireland — 'except to remember to hate violence, to love order and to exercise patience, the liberties of this country would never have been attained.' That was said by William Gladstone, no Maoist as far as I understand and not a revolutionary in any sense at all. But that was his description of how the liberties of English people and of Irish people had been established. It was not established only by people who loved order or who said that the only liberty was one connected with order. If Gladstone is thought too respectable a figure to be commendable to an audience of Trinity College, let me take another statement:

'What is said by great employers of labour against agitators is unquestionably true. Agitators are a set of interfering, meddling people who come down to some perfectly content class of a community and sow the seeds of discontent among them. That is the reason why agitators are so absolutely necessary. Without them, in our incomplete state, there would be no advance toward civilization. Disobedience, in the eyes of anyone who has read history, is man's original virtue. It is through disobedience that progress has been made, through disobedience and rebellion.' I wouldn't have thought I would have to stress these matters at all in Dublin but the motion on the order paper persuaded me that it was necessary to come and quote Oscar Wilde as well as Gladstone in order to . . . *(laughter, applause)*

So those of us who take the libertarian side of the argument I don't think have to press our case very strongly. Tonight, nobody looking out on the world at the present time could say that surely there is too much liberty. I know that some people are extremely panic-stricken about the expressions of protest and demonstration which happen throughout the world, and sometimes these demonstrations do occur at inconvenient moments for speakers on platforms. But even so, nobody looking throughout the world can surely say that there is too much liberty. Much too little, too little!

As Professor Papandreou has said to us, surely this is the major issue in the debate. Is it true, as he says, that we are heading for a new totalitarian era? Is it true as he says, that we have — or as he implies — that we are so caught between the hammer and the anvil of the superpowers that there is no escape for all the other nations middle and small? Is it true that the military bureaucracy and the military caste have become so powerful that democracy itself is being strangled in the process? As I said at the beginning, anyone who speaks on a platform today in the presence of someone who comes from Greece, particularly those who come from the Western powers, they have to speak with some diffidence, and indeed with some shame in this matter. Because it is a fact that democracy has been destroyed in Greece *(applause)* not as I say by the deliberate action of the Western powers, but at any rate with their shameful connivance; *(applause)* and subsequent apologies which every democrat should scorn.

So, in the presence of a spokesman from Greece, in the presence of Senator McCarthy who reminds us by his being here of what is happening across so much of the Asian continent, when we see what has happened in Czechoslovakia, where what some of us believed to be one of the most hopeful developments in the whole of Europe and indeed in the whole world for the last twenty years, was snuffed out by the brutal military power of the Soviet Machine, is it true that there is no escape from this oppressive new totalitarianism? Well, as I say, those who come from these countries and those who have witnessed these events must necessarily feel a deep pessimism. And anyone who fails to face the pessimistic characteristics of the situation would be guilty of dereliction. Of course it is not possible for civilized people to look optimistically on the situation, but I do believe, whilst acknowledging that it is equally the duty of those who believe in democracy, and indeed think of that democracy as a plant that has rarely been tried in most places, that we should realize what are the forces ranged against the possibilities of the new totalitarianism. And I believe there are forces in the world which can prevent the catastrophe and which can turn back the power of totalitarianism.

I shouldn't have to say it in Dublin, but empires don't last forever! I believe that the American empire and the Soviet empire — I believe they have passed. Many millions of people may suffer agonies before they've passed completely. But in some respects they are passing. I don't believe that in the United States of America, although I say it again with diffidence in the presence of Senator McCarthy, I do not believe that those who hold power in the United States of America today — they may be mystified, they may be uncertain as to where they are to turn and what steps they are to take — but I do not believe that their arrogance and their brutal arguments of a few months ago still reign there. I do not believe they do because they have met forces that are more powerful than they are; forces in Asia, forces in the United States itself, forces in the universities, forces which have shown that they refuse to accept the orthodox doctrines laid down by the Pentagon and by some of the other authorities in the United States. In my opinion, much the most hopeful characteristic of the last five years — which as I say and said earlier, I believe Senator McCarthy so bravely expressed in 1968 — is the revolt of the American people themselves, or great numbers of them, against the new totalitarianism. Against the power of the military bureaucracy.

Similar things are happening in many other parts of the world. Despite what has happened in Greece, smaller nations can play a very big part in world affairs. And I conclude by saying that I hope that the two smaller nations in this part of the world will play their part too. We should recognize that those who have the privilege of being born and bred as I was in the British democracy and you here, in the Irish democracy, democracies built for us by the world of trade union movements, the activities of democrats who fought for parliamentary rights and all the other rights that we possess, rights to speak and to argue and to associate, those of us who have been brought up in such societies — and we can look throughout the world and see what a privilege it is — we have indeed a great responsibility to assert the power of democracy and how it can turn back the forces of totalitarianism. We can see how it has been done in the past and we must combine to do it in the future, rejecting the idea that only the nations that can speak to the world are the great nations. The great nations are losing their power, partly because they cannot provide the answers which civilized men and women demand. And I trust that in these years and decades to come — Senator McCarthy referred to the period of the next thirty or forty years — I trust that the smaller nations, amongst whom I include the one that I come from, will combine to tell the world of a doctrine different from that which the great nations have taught us.

And I must say that I was glad to see in my Burke researches — before the expert speaks — I was glad to see that Edmund Burke, wisely looking forward to this occasion, foresaw exactly what should be said at the end. He said that — these are not his words, but he was indicating how liberty and order could flourish together — and he said, that England and Ireland may flourish together and I hope as an Honorary Welshman you'll let me include Wales too. But England and Ireland may flourish together. The world is large enough for us both. *(laughter)* Let it be our care not to make ourselves too little for it.

The danger for Ireland, having expelled the English, and the danger for England, having lost her empire I'm very glad to say, the danger for us both is that we should become too parochial, too obsessed with our own immediate problems and unaware that England and Ireland and Wales have something to say to the whole wide world and we should say it more forthrightly than ever. We should say it in the language of Burke which I have quoted at the end, instead of the motion that was put at the beginning. *(applause)*

CHAIRMAN: AN TAOISEACH, MR JACK LYNCH
'Thank you Mr Foot. I now call on Dr Conor Cruise O'Brien.' *(applause)*

DR CONOR CRUISE O'BRIEN T.D.

Taoiseach, Chancellor, Members of the College Historical Society, *(cough)* Ladies and Gentlemen: *(laughter)*

The cough wasn't at all humorous, at least it wasn't meant that way. I should begin by explaining that the garb I am wearing* is not intended to be expressive of any disrespect towards this most distinguished gathering or this honoured Society. As a matter of fact, all unbeknownst to myself I have been engaged all day in following the advice of Mr James Dillon. *(laughter)* I have been participating in the process of parliamentary democracy. *(laughter)* I have been out in Dublin Southwest where there is a serious outbreak of democracy. *(laughter, applause)*

I notice that Professor Papandreou, in his brilliant address, with almost all of which I would find myself in agreement, said one thing I have little doubt about. He said, 'Elections are a formality — have become a formality'. Of course I may possibly feel like that tomorrow if Mr Matt Merrigan has not won *(laughter)* but I have still entertained some doubts about it. At the same time, I can't quite share the moving and finely expressed but absolutely unconditional unbounded enthusiasm of Mr Dillon on this subject. *(laughter)* Incidentally while I speak of Mr Dillon, there's one thing also that worries me a little bit about him, and I hope he won't mind my saying it. I am seriously perturbed about the possible effects of his repeated invocations to the Deity to bless America. *(laughter, applause)* I'm afraid that these may create some serious imbalance some

---

* Dr O'Brien had been unable to change into formal dress due to his involvement in election campaigning.

shift in the, shall I say the charismatic ecology. *(laughter)* And I would urge him from time to time to say God Bless Albania *(laughter)* which, from his point of view, surely stands in at least as much need of blessing. *(laughter applause)*

I think the wisest expression on the subject of parliamentary democracy was that of E. M. Forster: 'Two cheers for democracy.' Not three, just two. *(laughter)* And I think it's important that the two cheers be delivered. Elections may be a formality, but if they were a formality that we were suddenly to be deprived of, I think we would have some reason to feel uneasy. Before I pass from the subject of Mr Dillon, in this gathering, I should like to pay tribute to the disinterested nature of his deep and sincere affection for democracy, since he belongs to a party that has been out of office for so many years. *(laughter)* If he feels that way, what a passion for parliamentary democracy must seethe in the bosom of our Chairman. *(laughter, applause)*

When I said I was passing from the subject of Mr Dillon, I was premature *(laughter)* but this is something rather more serious. Mr Dillon attacked the systems of government of the Soviet Union and of China. I am sure that it's a very meritorious thing in this country to attack the government systems of the Soviet Union and China. And I think that these governments and systems of government do indeed deserve the most serious criticism and even, sometimes, attack. But, if this attack is made in terms of a defence of parliamentary democracy, and it was in those terms that Mr Dillon delivered it, then it was, it seems to me, singularly inappropriate to deliver such an attack based on the principles of democracy in the presence of Professor Papandreou, and fail to refer to the case of Greece. Because, in Greece, democracy, or parliamentary democracy of a kind, with all its faults, has been swept out of existence and swept out of existence not by the Communists, but swept out of existence as a result of the operations of a system of States which are themselves democratic, which belong to the order which Mr Dillon upholds.

There are many countries in the world, I think even a majority of the members of the United Nations, whose relation to the democratic process is a very peculiar one. This is to say their governments may be changed as the result of free elections which take place in another country. *(laughter, applause)* I lived in the Congo when the system of government of that country was changed, not because of anything that had happened in the Congo, though many strange things had happened there, *(laughter)* but because, in Washington, the Republicans had gone out and the Democrats had come in. And politics in the Congo and in all the underdeveloped countries of the world changed overnight. Often, slightly, for the better. One would be tempted to follow Mr Dillon in an invocation to the Deity at that point, but I tremble for the consequences, so I . . . *(laughter)*.

The terms of our debate — I shall not take you very long — following so late on what was intellectually, I think, up to my coming in, a most rewarding and somewhat strenuous evening. Liberty and order in Burke's phrase, constitute, I'm afraid, almost an eighteenth-century cliché, that part of Burke which the eighteenth century heard, missing many other tones and strains in Burke. They represented both liberty and order, represented in terms of that phrase, different facets, different aspects of oligarchic rule. They had oligarchic rule, you remember, in those days. We still have it, but, of course, the oligarchy has changed. The composition of the oligarchy has changed.

Liberty and order expressed the achievements of the glorious revolution, the kind of privileges and the kind of authority that was held by the 18th century Whig magnates, and to a lesser extent, their subordinates within that system. Today, the term has become almost infinitely elastic, so that one could defend or oppose this motion on grounds which would have no connection, the defenders being more divided among themselves than divided from the opposers, which indeed often happens in various conditions. One could have a definition of terms under which, as often happens, liberty was no more than a code word for unrestricted free enterprise, and the sovereignty of the profit motive.

Did the American Revolution entail no fundamental change? Or no violence? Or did it contain the two? Is the same true of the French, the Russian, the Chinese Revolutions? Certainly, violence was a part of all these events which we are accustomed to think of as having brought about fundamental changes in the ordering, in the system of thought in our society. The same was true of the 1916 Rising, and the subsequent events in our country, a matter of which our statesmen sometimes lose sight, when they make unconditional condemnations of violence in all circumstances.

That is a defensible position, but it is a pacifist position and one that cannot be consistently or logically held by persons whose own power derives from an act of violent revolution. Yet, one can see, and I don't know whether this was the sense in which Senator Kennedy meant it, a sense in which there was not, after all, fundamental change as a result of these events — the sense in which the world goes on much as before. It is a pessimistic line of thought in which, in spite of the Russian Revolution, the Soviet Union continues essentially the policies of the Czars in relation to Czechoslovakia and other parts of the world, while the United States carries out in Vietnam and elsewhere policies of which George III would heartily approve. *(laughter, applause)*

Where Senator McCarthy has referred lightly but astringently to those figures and popular writers who are pursuing the idea of man understood in connection with the behaviour of other species of animals, I would like to differ slightly, in emphasis only, with my friend Eugene McCarthy here. It seems to me that it is good for men, good for us as a species, to think of ourselves in connection with other species, to think of ourselves as a part of the fauna that cover the planet and not as entities wholly distinct and above them. I think that form of thinking, to which we have been adapted for so long, has a connection with the arrogance which we show in our behaviour towards other varieties of the human species. And I think it also encourages our irrationalism and our pride generally, and that therefore this tendency — and I agree with Eugene McCarthy that it can become a fad and a silly fashion, and can be pushed to peculiar, almost Fascist lengths as in the writings of Robert Ardrey — has a function, and to a considerable extent, a cleansing tendency. These writers, at any rate, whatever we think of them, remind us that man was a hunter for 98 per cent of the history of the species. They like to claim that predatory habit is part of his nature. And insofar as this is true, insofar as it is an abiding, insistent, consistent pattern in human behaviour, then terms however noble, such as liberty, order, and even peace will contain their predatory element as when people say, for example, that the United States army is protecting the liberty of Vietnam, or that the Red Army has restored order in Prague, or, as the French army used to say, Algeria has been pacified. *(applause)* Three noble terms, all used in the interest of the opposite.

George Orwell has been quoted and this is a trend whose development he observed. Insofar as it is a trend and not a permanent thing because, in

Burke's day too, noble language was used in the same way. The idea that human nature continues to behave in much the same way with the same greed and aggressiveness under changing slogans and systems is obviously a pessimistic one. It becomes more pessimistic still if one compounds it by introducing a sinister reflection of Francis Bacon's, a sinister reflection that I think should be inscribed on the walls of all legislative assemblies, whether parliamentary democratic, non-democratic, or whatever. What Bacon said, and he said it rather cheerfully, in that cheerfully sinister manner of his time, he said that those who choose a political life — are you listening, gentlemen? *(laughter)* — those who choose a political life are those who do least affect the common good. *(laughter)* There may be something in it. *(laughter)* I should explain to the quite many of you who probably don't know me that I am myself a politician, so I'm not attacking politicians. *(laughter)*

On this view of life 'man is a predatory species within which the most predatory specimens seek, get, and wield power' and how they wield it, we see. Well, this is not — this thought, this line of thought — is not alien to Burke. I think the view of Burke presented by Senator Kennedy was misleadingly sunny, a smooth sort of Burke, processed if I might say so, by Madison Avenue. *(laughter, applause)* There was a dark, tragic, stern, bitter side of Burke underneath that smooth eighteenth century surface, and this is a large part of what makes him interesting. Burke was not notably tolerant, though that attitude was used about him by Senator Kennedy. He favoured banning the meetings and imprisoning the persons or people whose opinions he disliked. He might have approved the Criminal Justice Bill. *(laughter, applause)*

Burke believed that war was a necessary and permanent part of human life. Nor was he even as opposed to violence in change as he is suggested to have been. He is a very complex writer indeed. He distinguished between revolutionary movements arising from what he called wantonness and fullness of bread and those who draw their sustenance from the bottom of human nature. And those which draw their sustenance from the bottom of human nature he reluctantly condoned, as in the case of Ireland. I think that if he were around for the demos of the last few days, he would have been likely to say that the demonstration, which took place here in the Front Square, was one springing from wantonness and fullness of bread, *(laughter)* and that such a demonstration as was that which was staged by the neglected and oppressed tenants of this city in Belfast Road last night arose from the bottom of human nature and represented a force which had to be taken into account. The problem of giving liberty and order the kind of content in practice, that we associate with them in theory, is a problem of coping with human aggressiveness. And this is, in fact, our greatest problem, our greatest problem within ourselves and within our society.

The problem is not the weapons, the problem is the people who will use the weapons — the people who are sufficiently bent upon their purposes to do so. Is man, as some of these writers say, an incurable predator? Capitalism is then, an appropriate system. It is a system based on some such hypothesis. Also, imperialism is. Is it more reasonable to assume, as I do assume, that man can bring his predatory impulses under rational and social control on a planetary scale, as he has already to some extent within the limits of a few communities, mainly small communities, which try to work under a rule of law?

I think if we are to go on living with any hope, we must be making that kind of assumption and trying to work in that direction. This is one manner, and is to me the most acceptable manner, of interpreting the idea of liberty connected with order. And it is in that sense that I support it. It is not unobtainable; man is an intelligent as well as an aggressive being and can inhibit tendencies which threaten the survival of the species.

I'm sorry if I use a jargon which must jar on the ears of my friend, Eugene McCarthy, but I think, as I say, that it has some relevance. Capitalism, authoritarianism, bureaucracy and imperialism represent clumps of such tendencies, and their elimination is possible. On a planetary scale, this is a long way off — a very long way off. We are not likely to see it, nor are our children likely to see it. The world is a result, in the main, of what kind of people we are, and particularly those who wield power on the planet, and in part because of overcrowding, the so called population explosion. The world population is heading towards enormous disasters. And here I would like to protest against the irresponsibility of those who argue against rational control of population growth, *(applause)* those who are telling us in effect that the only checks on population — they never say it in words, but the logical implication of their words is that the only checks on population must be the well-known natural checks of famine, plague, and war. On a planetary scale, it is a long way off. We can work for it locally, now. We can study and promote the study of the workings of greed and aggression in ourselves, in our institutions, and in society.

These are the tasks of the psychologists and the sociologists, the economists, and the zoologists. We can try to bring these manifestations under a greater degree of democratic social control. These are tasks of the citizen and of the politician, hoping always that the politician will bear in mind Bacon's remark about his own nature. We should try to understand the role of myth, ritual, and drama in our personal lives and in society, and to release the creative, instead of the destructive, potential in these. These are tasks which involve artists, writers, and religious thinkers as well as other citizens.

Socialism — not a nineteenth-century form of socialism but a form suitable to the knowledge, capacities, and problems of the twentieth century, an idea of Socialism which could draw on the insights not merely of Marx but writers as remote from Marx as Edmund Burke — this could be a Socialism preparing within the twentieth century for the twenty-first century. It is in that sense that I would support the view of favouring a liberty connected with order. Thank you. *(applause)*

AN TAOISEACH MR JACK LYNCH

It now calls for me, according to my instructions here, to sum up. But before I even attempt to sum up I would like to congratulate you, Mr Auditor, and your colleagues in the Hist for the quality of the platform that you have put before us here. *(applause)* And it's not my intention to refer to them individually. All of them have referred to some extent to demonstrations, insurrections, and invasions. At least we have witnessed here tonight what I can best describe as an intellectual upheaval for many hours. I am speaking of intellectuals; we know that the Hist has had its quota of them, of intellectual giants. I have been sitting here in this huge chair for the past two hours and a quarter with my legs dangling!

There are many people today, particularly amongst the young, who regard the theme of tonight's debate as being thoroughly reactionary, and who take Burke, as indeed many people have done, as being none of our concern. To them liberty connected with order stands for establishment, for received opinion and for official channels. Such a view is, of course, extreme but perhaps its extremism is part of its effect, living as we do in times when the individualism often excludes eccentricity and when each man not only does his own thing but must be seen to be doing his own thing. *(laughter)* I suppose it seems to many of young blood that the only way that he can go one better than his fellow man is by going one worse than him. Consequently he is looking for a liberty connected, not with order, but with disorder.

I don't wish to talk or imply that the motives giving rise to such disorder are not often based on righteous indignation and high moral purpose. The contemporary implication of Burke's dictum is that this whole question of liberty and order is no longer a simple or a formal matter of a gentlemanly set-to between government and faction, fought out over its own set of Queensbury Rules, with the rest of the body filling the role of spectators. 'The liberty and source of freedom', so says Edmund Burke, 'is that state of things in which liberty is secure by the quality of restraint, the constitutional things in which the liberty of no one man and no body of men can find means to trespass on the liberty of one person or any constituent persons in the society.' Here Burke touched on the delicate agreement that is so easily disturbed when liberty is used as a blunt weapon rather than as a reasonable argument.

Manifestly, liberty must include the right of protest but when it is equated with an alleged right to spell disorder, then, just as patently, any responsible government, and here I mean a democratically elected government, must move to contain that disorder. If they do not, one could quickly have a situation that is not only chaotic but also anarchic, and from the disorder will emerge not liberty, but licence. Of those who incite such disorder, Burke said: 'If it should be character rather than accident, then that people are not fit for liberty.' Men must have a certain fund of moderation to qualify them for freedom, or else it becomes noxious for themselves and a perfect nuisance to everybody else. I appreciate that it is easy to stigmatize safeness as trite and regard moderation used in the name of government as a means of retarding social revolution. But such an assertion must surely be disingenuous.

A democratically elected government is a government of and for the people. It is too, a government, not just for the people but from the people as well. It exists and operates to make possible the desires and aspirations of all the people, or in any case, the majority of them. I know very well that minority opinions, minority demands, often in the course of time obtain majority backing. But it is the obligation of public opinion, majority and minority, to influence and convince the government. If they fail to do that, then let them convince a majority of their fellows, so that they can put out the government with which they disagree, in a democratic way. This is how the order with liberty is based. A democratic government must respond to a majority opinion with backing and to minority opinion with consideration. It is difficult to respond with consideration when the announcement of grievances is accompanied by force. A government has to act as custodian of all the people so that the liberty of all its country's citizens can be assured. In this context, I should like to add that I take order to mean, not only physical public order, but also economic order, industrial order, and social order.

One of the manifestations of liberty, indeed its most precious possession, is the right of its own people to elect its own government in free, democratically held, elections. This, as must be patently obvious if we look about us in some other countries, is the real test of a genuine liberty. It cannot be claimed that such a right can be exercised in an atmosphere of disorder. If it can, then of course the only liberty would not be a liberty connected with order, but if such a claim be impossible then Burke's words become incontrovertible. It is for those who really believe in liberty, and are concerned not only with liberty for themselves, to take a firm stand against excesses of the kind that inevitably provoke the so-called backlash. It is the abuse of liberty, the attempt to have liberty without order that paves the way for dictatorship. But we should never forget that there can be no liberty without order. But there can be order without liberty. There are some perhaps who want that. It behoves us to be as vigilant as we can to see that the conditions are not created in which they can achieve their aim[19]. *(applause)*

---

[19] It is worth noting that two months later Mr Lynch demanded the resignations of a number of his Ministers, in circumstances which led to the 'Arms Trial' of 1970.

PERSONALITIES
IN THE HIST

Professor R. B. McDowell, Secretary 1936–37, Gold Medallist, delivered a dissertation on those who had been members of the Society in the past, on Thursday, 5 March 1970 in the Debating Chamber of the Graduates' Memorial Building. The address was followed by the Bicentenary Dinner, which was held in the Dining Hall.

CHAIRMAN: MR K. F. G. PURCELL, VICE-PRESIDENT

'Mr Chancellor, Mr Provost, Ladies and Gentlemen of the College Historical Society, Ladies and Gentlemen, I know we are all looking forward to Professor McDowell's address. It is my pleasure, therefore, without further introduction, to ask him to deliver the address "Personalities in the Hist".'

PROFESSOR R. B. McDOWELL, VICE-PRESIDENT

Mr Chairman, Mr Auditor, and Members of the College Historical Society:

I am glad I have been able to pronounce all those words, I was afraid that I might suddenly, overawed by the importance of the occasion, be rendered speechless. *(laughter)* I'm sure that seems to have aroused immediate expectations.

Now, there is more than one reason why tonight I rise somewhat embarrassed. To begin with, the rules of rhetoric give no guidance on pre-dinner speaking. *(laughter)* We all know that after-dinner speaking is supposed to provide a smooth accompaniment to the digestory process, but as far as I can see, my role at the moment is that of barrier, or given University conditions at the moment, perhaps I should say barricades between you, your sherry, your conversation, your wining and dining; Secondly, of course I have been bothered by problems of time and taste. Well, to begin with, the problem of time, that's the chronology of my own remarks. I will come in a moment to the extent of them, the chronology of my own remarks. I decided on them when I decided one question long ago, and I decided it very quickly. I was going to keep well away from contemporary or recent events in the Society, and that of course I hasten to say means a very wide margin.

When I entered this Society I entered it under the presidency of Douglas Hyde who presided magnificently over our proceedings, I think his (I hope it's not irreverent to call them) 'Walrus' moustaches giving a melancholy frame to what were often superbly humorous remarks. Well you see a Douglas Hyde who presided over my youth in the Society had been a vigorous speaker in 1885. *(laughter)* So in a sense the contemporaneous world when you reach my age carries one well back, I'm afraid, into the nineteenth century.

Incidentally, I needn't say I wasn't afraid of slander actions in case anybody thought I was codding. The members of this Society are far too tolerant and tough to object to comments on their own doings. What I did not want to undergo was, after dinner being tackled by man after man with, 'I'm sorry, McDowell, it's funny you overlooked that little episode in 1920 when I tackled the Auditor so well; you could have made it sound rather amusing.' *(laughter)* I tried to steer a way through that sort of thing.

Regarding the other form of time, I gather I am in a delightful position this evening of not being under, owing to the rather extraordinary nature of the proceeding, of not being under the jurisdiction of the Auditor's bell. But I want you to understand that the members of the Committee have been instructed to give a violent coughing attack if I go on after four minutes. *(laughter)* What is really unknown is taking any part in such a rhetorical feast as the Society has been undergoing in the last few days. I mean it seems almost presumptuous to open one's mouth at the time the Society is celebrating two hundred years of debating — two hundred years devoted to the exchange of ideas, analysis of argument, and the study of persuasion. I may add that in its earlier years the Society devoted, perhaps, rather more time to the last aspect of its life than to the serious exchange of ideas. The Society delighted in form as well as in substance for the first, anyway, century of existence.

Now, as we look, the eighteenth century was an age of reason and reasoning. And it's not therefore surprising that an immensity of interest was taken in the subject of oratory in Trinity College. I think it's of some little significance that in 1762, just eight years before the reconstitution of the Society, the Chair of Oratory was separated from the Chair of History, and a Professor of Oratory was appointed. Now, our first Professor of Oratory, Lawson, was a well-known preacher. It is said pathos and energy compensated for his weak voice. And unlike most eighteenth-century professors, he actually lectured; and unlike many professors, he had the courage to publish the lectures. *(laughter)* I admit that the only part of his lectures I have read with attention is the preface. *(laughter)* The preface I should say is a vigorous defence of the lecture system already criticized, and Lawson points out how extremely stimulating it was for young men to listen to an esteemed person expounding the subject and impressing the truths on their mind. He said it wouldn't stifle intellectual initiative because, as he said, after the lecture it would form a subject of conversation among the undergraduates. He was an optimist. *(laughter)*

I may say that his book, which I have attempted, I have made an effort at, is the sort which is usually called 'exhaustive' by reviewers and found to be 'exhausting' by readers. *(laughter)* It ran, I may say, to a second edition, and shortly afterwards his successor in the Chair of Oratory, just before the Society was reconstituted, his successor Leland, Burke's great friend, also published a work of oratory in which he deals with certain, I may say typically of the time, real techniques of oratory, certain technical problems. I think his line of argument is that the Apostles would obviously be good speakers if . . . certainly an English Bishop criticized them as men lacking in taste. Leland seems to think that they had the makings of quite good orators. Well, as for those who found merely studying the theory rather dull, any Trinity undergraduate could put on his gown and cross College Green, and with the gown as a passport enter the galleries of the House of Commons. And when, owing to architectural changes, it was decided to take away this privilege, Hutchinson, the Provost, made a magnificent speech in defence of it. He pointed out how good it was for the legislators to know that ingenuous youths were watching them and how good it was for the young to see wisdom and virtue in action. *(laughter)* If the young men had had an opportunity to read Hutchinson's private correspondence they would have learned even greater lessons. *(laughter)*

When I first meditated these words, this address, I thought of playing a rather vulgar historical trick. I would go to the newspapers and I would see what was happening on the 21 March 1770, and I would manage to put you into the picture, so to speak, by a few vivid and well selected details. Any historian knows the trick. Well, I went to the only paper I could lay my hands quickest on, which I regret to say was a liberal newspaper, and I found that it was one of the dullest months in one of the dullest winters that Dublin had had. The only thing that seemed to be arousing conversation in Dublin the night the first twelve members of the reconstituted Society gathered together, the only subject that managed to get widespread conversation was a Ball, which the Viceroy had given on the 18th in Dublin Castle, and according to my paper the quality of the guests was low, and their behaviour when supper was served was disgusting. *(laughter)* As I point out . . . *(laughter)* . . . stormed in to the banqueting room. I hope you realize that this was what our predecessors were talking about after the meeting.

But much more exciting things were happening in London. In London, the Corporation presented an address to the King asking for the dismissal of his Ministers. King George III received them rather tartly and, having answered the deputation in a few brusque words, he turned around and started to laugh and to chat with the Lords-in-waiting. My paper added in italics Nero fiddles while Rome burns. Now I am quite aware that there are many differences between the household life of Nero and that of George III, *(laughter)* but nevertheless, Rome was beginning to burn. In the seventies you had Revolution in America, at the end of the eighties a Revolution in France followed by a European war, and if you root through the list, I think it's now in the Exhibition, the rules which the members of the Society signed for the first two decades, you see name after name of men who played their part in sterling times.

May I just relieve those members who are worried about continuity: at least three of the names are those of men who certainly met Burke: Matthew Young, who was Tone's tutor in college; Gould, a young barrister who wrote a rather dull pamphlet in support of Burke's views and got a very good reception when he went to Ecclesfield — Burke cried for what older members of the Society ought to do for the younger, and Burke tried to get the Lord Lieutenant — and lastly, of course, Tone, I'm sure they discussed the Society's fate.

Well, I rather claim to dwell on Tone for three reasons. First of all, as we know, this Society lives from crisis to crisis. I think it's fair to change in fact the preposition and say 'lives *on* crisis to crisis'. Without a crisis the Society would find life somewhat monotonous. Now on the other hand there is one great fact about a crisis in the College Historical Society: it mustn't go on too long or it becomes boring, *(laughter)* and this was the cause for putting an end to one of our early crises. And secondly, Tone was an embodiment of two types of man which the Society prides itself on producing. He was a man of action and a man of ideas, he was an able politician and soldier, and he was a very successful writer producing, I think, in his diary, one of the great masterpieces of the eighteenth century. Thirdly, he was one of a very interesting circle, brilliant and all, I don't want to repeat this term about all of them, surprisingly fine speakers.

Now let me just remind you — I'm sure many of you are familiar with the names — let me remind you of the members of Tone's circle. There was

Miller, there was Plunket, there were many, just to take a few. Now Stokes was one of those amiable and somewhat eccentric men who from time to time appear in academic life *(laughter)* and *(applause)* he always tended to be left wing *(laughter)*. He was a United Irishman, but at the same time he strove to make the Irish poor Protestants say they wouldn't object to his activities because we realize he had no intention to hide them. He answered 'pai' on theology, he answered 'hopeless' on population, henceforth he founded the Dublin Zoological Society. When Lord Clare conducted his celebrated College visitation in Trinity, and every member of the College was asked certain questions, Stokes was the Fellow who was asked did he know of any illegal organizations in College, and he answered yes, he believed the United Irish clubs existed, and the Orange societies. He gave him one long look. He was also asked why had he reported to the Lord Lieutenant atrocities committed by the military and not those committed by the insurgents, and Stokes reply was, that the Lord Lieutenant would hear plenty about the latter, but mightn't hear about the former. *(laughter)* However, Clare had the last word; judges always have, *(laughter)* but when it came — when he began to distribute penalties, he simply said that Stokes was silly rather than ill-intentioned, and he was just suspended from Fellowship for three years.

As for Miller, he belonged to a slightly different school of thought, he was indeed, as I will tell you in a moment, he was a strong conservative. He was at school with Wolfe Tone, and they formed a small debating team, but it didn't go on for long, because the members, being honest schoolboys, found that they hadn't sufficient information to support their debates, a fact which has never militated against the activities of this Society. *(laughter)* And well now, Tone and Miller made friends when they both were in College. Miller became a Fellow and on one occasion Tone asked him to take them both into the Fellows' Garden for a quiet talk. And Miller turned to Tone and said 'I'm very surprised that you should claim an aristocratic privilege', and Tone replied, 'Miller, an aristocracy is a very rude thing when you're in it'. *(laughter)* Now, Miller became in time an Assistant Professor of History, then Professor in History, and produced eighty-four lectures covering the whole course of European History. I may say that he started with a small intelligent audience, and then had a very large audience in the end listening. I think as far as I can make out by a cursory glance, the aim of the lectures was to show that there was a providential design over the evolution of European History and one of the strongest proofs of that was the results of the battle of Waterloo. *(laughter)* In fact one could say about Miller what was said about Allison, that in twenty volumes he expounded the view that Providence was on the side of the Tories. *(laughter)*

Plunket, of course, was a master of that style of oratory of which I suppose the last great exponent was Mr Asquith. That is extraordinary clarity, an extraordinarily massive assemblage of his material using a tremendous effect of purity and force. He was an astoundingly impressive orator who from College Green and at Westminster — I'm afraid his critics pointed out that he had one or two defects. For one thing, I must admit that, like myself, he hated the manual labour of using a pen so he was not prepared to write out his judgment. It has been pointed out that his reputation as a lawyer, I mean as Lord Chancellor, suffered because his judgments don't survive. But as he also loathed legal drudgery, it may have improved his reputation that his judgments don't survive. *(laughter)* Another critic, I'm afraid, pointed out that coming from the North of Ireland, Plunket was noted for the fact that while he made magnificent speeches at Westminster, he was very careful only to go to Westminster when the legal term was over so that he wouldn't lose any of the better remunerative rhetoric which he *(laughter)*, which he would indulge in the Four Courts. *(laughter)*

Finally, of course, now Magee became Archbishop of Dublin; there is a superb picture of him in the Common Room, in all the pride of the establishment, and those of you who remember his bust in the Long Room of the College Library will remember the superbly arrogant position of his head. As a matter of fact, Magee's friends always explain that the reason why he carried his head at this arrogant angle, was not pride, but the fact that he suffered from nose bleeding. *(laughter)* He was a very popular member of this Society who was presented with the silver plate when he left College (a piece of silver plate). But he wasn't too popular in Ireland, because on becoming Archbishop of Dublin, he wrote a charge in which he said, 'We members of the Establishment are confronted by two antagonists: the one has a religion without what we would call a church, the other has a church without what we would call a religion.' This somewhat unecumenical sentence *(laughter)* . . . than any other length of words in Irish History. The pamphlets on it stretched for yards.

Now there were of course younger men. I won't dwell on the Emmets; they are too well known. Their associate Corbet who is amusing, and then, may I mention, became a Major-General in France, and a curious or perhaps absurd historical coincidence: Corbet served and I'm not able to recite his military record precisely but he seems to have served in most of the Spanish campaigns with Napoleon and the French Army. Now we have probably got to about the time that Wolfe, another member of the College Historical Society, was writing his celebrated poem about the burial of Sir John Moore.* Wolfe was one of those Keatsian figures which appeared in the early nineteenth century and he had tremendous nervous vitality, very effusive, very poetical, very religious, and in a sense, surprisingly, added the component of a sense of humour. And like so many of the young and brilliant men of the century, he only lived for a very short span.

Now talking about literary men, there were two men in the Society, just at the end of the eighteenth century which I think deserves a word, because they were extraordinarily well known about the 1830s in London, and each had a tremendous reputation, and I suspect only a limited number of people in the hall now would remember both — some people here remember people I think, but who won't even respond to the name of either. One of course, is Thomas Moore, the master of drawing-rooms and sheet music. *(laughter)* Moore, when I was a boy, whenever there were drawing-room parties, you would hear Moore, played or sung and he'd been played and sung in drawing-rooms for a hundred years, from Holland House to the suburbs of Belfast. *(laughter)* But now I've discovered to my horror, that he isn't even on the course in Anglo-Irish literature. *(laughter)* But now Moore was a friend of Croker's or I should say that Moore and Croker were College contemporaries, they were allies and competitors when they got into the social world. But in fact, if I may inflict on you an exceptionally bad pun that is only interesting because it concerns two members of the Society, *(laughter)* on one occasion Sir Robert Peel was admiring a portrait of Croker by Lawrence and somebody said, 'It's a magnificent portrait . . . you can see the quiver of his lips.' 'Yes', said Sir Robert Peel, 'you can see the arrows flying from them.' *(laughter)*

Now I am sorry it's a problem; the humour of the past never strikes the

---

* Sir John Moore fought on the British side in the Peninsular War, and died from his injuries.

right note. But Croker of course was distinguished in two ways. First of all, he became an M.P., and rather typically, this gives you a measure of the man, the very night he entered the House of Commons he made a speech and for the rest of his life, it was going to be the best speech he ever made. *(laughter)* I read another speech he made that appealed to me very much; he was defending the Duke of York who was being attacked by the righteous for allowing his mistress to sell commissions. And Croker by going into his defence in great detail showed that the Duke had supplied his Mistress with quite enough money for the mistress of a royal Duke and that she had no need to sell commissions. I mean he handled the items of domestic economy with brilliant ease.

I may say he became Secretary to the Admiralty and supposing you read the Hornblower novels you should realize that in the last five or six years of Hornblower's sea cruises, he was corresponding with Croker. *(laughter)* Now Croker of course, also became the great Tory publicist. He is said to have killed Keats. I think that was an exaggeration. His literary standards were those of the eighteenth century and he partially applied them to Cockneys — to Cockney versifiers. He also fought the Reform Bill in the House of Commons line by line. I think it's fair to say no other member of this Society every made more speeches on the subject, not even Dr Skeffington. *(laughter, applause)* When the Reform Bill was passed he said he'd never never sit in the House of Commons again and he kept his word. But he did consider to help his party in the press and he is said to have popularised the word 'conservative', but I know this is a word that members of the party sometimes shirk from. Unionist suggests high moral endeavour, Tory is romantic, but conservative does represent what Croker meant to do, it appeals to the middle class vote. But however, this year being Conservation Year and possibly in defence of the general election, it may make the word more respectable. *(laughter)* By the time Croker and Moore were dead we were well into the Victorian age, the Society had been out of the College a couple of times and back again, and perhaps I should just say a word about the man who brought us back into College.

That was Magee, the nephew of the Archbishop with the unfortunate pen. Now Magee was an extraordinary man, tremendous energy, great ability with words and all that, but he had a policy which is not always associated with the Victorian Episcopal Bench. He had a very quick and a dangerously ready sense of humour. He became, I would like to spend more time on him, but time wouldn't allow, he became a Bishop of Peterborough and subsequently Archbishop of York. And he entered the House of Lords the very night that disestablishment was being discussed — the Bill to disestablish the Church of Ireland, and yet he had a parliamentary triumph. He made a superb speech. It really even now stands out, and absolutely swept the peers off their feet. And I may add that all the better, because he didn't think he had the slightest hope of defeating the Bill with the whole of his energies, but he wasn't going to desert his friends. From then on, as he said himself, after one of his rather indiscreet remarks in the House of Lords, 'I couldn't stop it, it came up like a cork in a bottle.' *(laughter)* And he of course was famous for that great phrase: 'Better England free than England sober by act of Parliament.' *(laughter)* Now most people know that he is famous for these last words. Indeed, on occasion, 'drunk' was substituted for 'free'. He was however, a splendid fellow, I mean a first rate Bishop. I mean ran his diocese as well, was a great diner-out, and a man who brought a genial heart and common sense to bear on all issues. I have a great admiration for Magee. *(laughter)*

Incidentally, I heard a snigger at 'diner-out'. He was not a desert father. He was a Bishop of the Established Church. *(laughter)* Now we come to another Archbishop if I may say so, Peacock, who managed to achieve a rather tremendous feat in the Society by sheer oratorical power, combined with intense conviction. He got the Society by one vote to agree to pass a motion in favour of prophylactics. *(laughter)* I'm sorry if that shocks the Society. I may say his triumph was hard won. He secured it because two drunk medical students entered and voted for the motion, *(laughter)* I'm sure that possibly in accordance with their convictions, but certainly not in accordance with their condition. *(laughter)* May I say that if anybody doubts the story, the facts can be found in the blue book.

Now may I just in slight contrast of these Episcopal figures, say a quick word about another very great figure, Bram Stoker. Now I don't know how many people here have read Dracula. In the Hitchcock age I don't think Vampires are very horrifying. I read it myself when in a more unsophisticated age, and also when I was less sophisticated. I seem to remember having a mild thrill when I discovered that this Rumanian or Hungarian vampire, Count or Prince, I can't give you exact details, rather literally lived on his guests. *(laughter)* Now Bram Stoker wrote Dracula in his old age. He had just written his first Book, a manual for petty sessions clerks, when Henry Irving came to Dublin. Bram Stoker was one of the prouder Trinity students to escort him to the Shelbourne. Irving was so delighted by his reception, a thousand students escorting him through the streets of Dublin to the Royal Shelbourne, he asked them all to dinner. When the Shelbourne began to get a bit restless, he said 'Oh can you all come in and have a drink?' At that stage the police and the manager had to intervene. Now Bram Stoker after taking part in this tremendous affair, the next year managed to get into Irving's presence. And they took to one another at once. Well I can give you one reason for that. Irving was cited Eugene Adman, if I've got the pronunciation right, and Stoker said, 'Oh he'd been Auditor of the Historical Society.' Irving burst into hysterical tears. After that it's not surprising that they became good friends. And Stoker of course became Henry Irving's secretary, friend, and wrote one of the most interesting accounts of Irving's life. But I think it would be a mistake, I'm afraid, to think of Stoker as a typical product of our Society in the nineteenth century.

It was a serious century and I suppose the greatest crop of our members were the Lawyers. I mean the number of distinguished members of the Irish Bar who belonged to the Society are literally as numerous as the sands of the sea. Actually, I will have to use my notes at this stage, or I might omit one of them. And I wouldn't like to offend them in the shade as they were an extremely touchy lot. *(laughter)* Now, to begin with, there were Davis, Dillon, Butt, all advocates, better known I think as advocates of a generous, passionate, perhaps somewhat over-doctrinal nationalism. You remember lawyers who were liberals, such as O'Sullivan, Gladstone's great advisor in Irish affairs; Keogh, a kind of Ramsay McDonald of Irish political life, though he was a hard sardonic man, he began as an extreme nationalist, he became a lawyer. When the Liberals appointed him a Law Officer, he became a Liberal, and later when he was on the Bench, he developed those conservative traits which often go with high judicial office. Now he was reported to be at one stage the most unpopular man in Ireland — in the eyes of many people a renegade — because when an election petition from Galway came before him, he chastised in no uncertain terms the liberals and the clergy of Galway. And I may say for years his memory was revered here because on the Campanile, in whitewash, were the words: 'O Bravo Judge Keogh.' And these were renewed every few years by the college conservatives. But at last Unionism is dormant *(laughter)* and I can only by a great effort when I sometimes am strolling under the Campanile when the light is in the right way, I see these resounding, I see thin traces of this resounding phrase.

I suppose the third liberal lawyer who was one of our best speakers, was Hemphill. He had not a very happy political career. He stood as a young man, as a liberal for Cashel, a Liberal seat. But Liberals of Cashel expected to be bribed. Hemphill was a North of Ireland man, and wouldn't bribe; he didn't get in. *(laughter)* I may say he then had the final and most extraordinary achievement, he found that when being a County Court Judge, he found that sitting on any other Bench he became Lord Chancellor. But it's the conservative lawyers I must dwell on. The name Whiteside, oh I'm sorry, I wish . . . the name is always . . . it's like a list of names from the Halcyon days of ancient Rome: Whiteside, Napier, Fitzgibbon, Ashbourne, Carson, Glenavy, David Plunket. All of them members, I believe I'm right in saying, all members for this College, all able Lawyers, all with one exception on the Bench, all strenuous defenders of the Union. *(laughter)* Well, Whiteside . . . I'm sorry, I haven't time to give you specimens of Whiteside's oratory. I find only the best way I can convey it to you is this: think of a mixture of Cicero, Dickens and Gilbert and Sullivan. *(laughter)* I may say that Magee to break the embarrassment when he heard Whiteside was going to be the Principal of the Irish Church in the House of Commons, he said 'From Whiteside's bad jokes, God preserve us.'

Napier was known as 'Holy Joe' — a joke by O'Connell, and it was a timely remark; Napier was a fervent evangelical. In the Young Men's Christian Association in Belfast the other day, I saw on one side, an ornament to Napier, and on the other side an ornament to Kearns, who became Lord Chancellor, but I'm afraid we cannot, as a Society, I think, claim him. But one thing I think I must say about Napier is that he was extremely fond of undergraduate life and a very good friend of the Society in the period when it was establishing itself in College. Fitzgibbon was a member of the group who was a profound lawyer and known for his sociability. And then there was Ashbourne whose picture I hope still hangs in the Conversation Room. I meant to go up but I think it was hanging elsewhere. He is wearing, I think, the extraordinary precursor of cavalry twill trousers.

There were three factors in Ashbourne's life which greatly helped him in his career, the first, he was the son of an Attorney, secondly, he landed an Attorney's daughter and thirdly his hair went prematurely white, which gave him a great air of gravity. I might add, fourthly, that he had the loudest voice in the House of Commons. It was thought that when he was addressing the House, he was also addressing his constituents in Trinity College, Dublin. *(laughter)* I may add though that he had a judicial temper. He had a remarkable awareness of Irish conditions. He was fair-minded, shrewd, and sat for years, and the only Trinity man indeed, who achieved this feat, sat for years in the cabinet. I may say that I have only seen one specimen of his oratory, and it goes something like this. He was referring to one of Mr Gladstone's Land Bills. He said it lacked the frank fairness of honest compensation and proved a kind of direct confiscation. *(laughter)* Now, that is the sort of thing I think that his constituents in Trinity would have liked to hear.

The Lawyer I just want to dwell on for the moment is rather different to the others. And that is a man who is now forgotten. He is one of the two people whose names for years lingered on as masters of oratory. Most inspiring speakers. One of course was Seymour Bushe. The man to whom I am referring is Plunket. Now Bushe's career as an older generation member was simple. Owing to being the second principal figure in a divorce case, he was never able to go on the Bench. His career was ruined. And it shows perhaps the change in life. And I have talked to somebody who remarked to me what a liberal woman his mother was. She was prepared to call on Mrs Seymour Bushe, the heroine of the celebrated divorce case, married at that stage to her second husband. Now he was a man. I'm sure older people here have heard amazing tributes to Seymour Bushe from people who heard him in court.

But the man I wish to talk about had a more distinguished career. That was David Plunket, the nephew of the Plunkets I talked about earlier. Now David Plunket was absolutely a meteor in the Society. He was brilliant and he then went to the Bar, and in five years took silk. But he was impatient. He had an avidity for politics. He entered the House of Commons, and there he established himself as one of the most brilliant speakers of the day.

Again, when you read Hansard, Plunket's sentence will strike the eye. I mean, I remember one of his sentences — something about tackling the Home Rule Bill — 'Why drop the reins on the neck of a mad horse?' But when his friends came into office, he didn't, to people's surprise, get into the cabinet. He was given the Ministry of Works, an attractive but pleasant, but somewhat insignificant ministry at that time. He himself said it was an attractive job, 'I've got the pick of the bag.' And when his party finally left office, he was relegated to the House of Lords with a peerage. And he remained, still a very pleasant guest at countless houses. Company Directors and all his friends lamented that here was a man, brilliant speech, keen on politics, but utterly devoid of ambition. Now on one occasion Plunket and Fitzgibbon went up to climb the Sugarloaf together. And they took with them a third man who had served with them on several Committees in the Hist. That was Lecky.

Now we have a particular interest, and may I say, I declare my interest in Lecky at once. I got a scholarship in History. I couldn't have answered the paper if I hadn't read Lecky for pleasure. But I always feel a peculiar tribute from me is due to Lecky. More importantly, this Society has a tremendous respect for Lecky's career, because he reactified the Society. He loved it. He really took a vigorous part in the Society's life, and then he spent, until he became a member for Trinity at the very end of his life, the rest of his life in an extraordinarily placid way, cut off from any strenuous or angry contact with man. He had a house in Onslow Gardens in London before he objected very much to the disturbance of the peace by Italian organ grinders. If he had stayed in Carlow as a Landlord, probably other things would have shattered his peace more vibrantly. The Society really trained Lecky in political life and painted the necessary background for a Historian. It also trained Lecky, he admitted it, to think, analyse other men's views, and to express his own view. He used to go striding along Kingstown Pier, on his long legs, ungainly legs, working out his speeches. Lecky, in a way, like his friend Plunket, in some instances might be said to have failed. He wanted to be a philosophical historian, and quite frankly Lecky had not the subtlety nor the strength of mind of a philosopher. He rather disliked the moonlight work which a historian had to do. But still he brought out remarkable works. This is the great thing about Lecky, and that is why I think we can pride ourselves on it. He had two or three great virtues. He aimed at precision. He wanted to get things right. He tried to understand other people's point of view. His own spiritual home was the nineteenth century. But he struggled to comprehend the ethical views and political opinions of earlier eras. He was not a natural witch burner or not a natural practitioner in witchcraft, and yet he tried to understand them. Lecky — you can't help feeling a deep reverence for a man who struggles, not only for precision, but for understanding. The result is that anything that Lecky writes diffuses a fragrant air of honest impartiality of balance.

I myself think those are the sedate virtues which today tend to be overlooked. I mean we live in an age where there are sections of the world which pride themselves on the immobility of their convictions, on the fact that they are totally deaf to argument and that they are ready for ruthless action. Now, I must say I feel that the more sedate and less spectacular qualities which the eighteenth century and the Victorian age cultivated — knowledge, reason, persuasion, the capacity to listen and to try to comprehend are of more value than these dramatic qualities which attract, are bound to attract, adherence and attention. And I hope this Society will continue to practice and defend the sedate qualities which were, which are associated with its past, which I believe are the cement of our civilization.

BICENTENARY NATIONAL DEBATE

'That Emmet's epitaph be now written'

The National Debate was held on Friday 6 March 1970 in the Public Theatre of the College.

CHAIRMAN:
MR JUSTICE T. C. KINGSMILL MOORE, VICE-PRESIDENT

As you know, the subject for the debate tonight is *'That Emmet's Epitaph Be Now Written'*.

'When my country takes her place among the nations of the Earth, then, and not till then, let my epitaph be written.' Robert Emmet. *(applause)*

I would now like to call on Deputy Michael O'Kennedy to propose the motion. *(applause)*

MR MICHAEL O'KENNEDY T.D.

Mr Chairman, Mr Auditor, Ladies and Gentlemen of the College Historical Society:

It's my pleasure and privilege first of all to formally propose the motion that Emmet's epitaph be now written. In celebrating the Bicentenary of the Historical Society we celebrate in particular the common purpose for which it was founded and the determination of its members over the last two hundred years that every view should be heard, every cause should be pleaded. If this Society has a peculiar genius to which it owes its survival and strength, it must surely be that its platform through the years was built on the solid foundations of tolerance, though sometimes with impatience, of understanding, though often tested. Right it seems then, that tonight we should honour one of the most tolerant and fair-minded, and consider in particular whether this land has yet realized, or indeed ever can realize his notion of nationhood.

The pledge of the United Irishmen, to which Emmet, even in his teens, gave his allegiance, and very shortly afterwards his life, was to form the Brotherhood of Affection, an identity of interests, a communion of rights, and the union of power among Irishmen of all religious persuasions. Robert Emmet not only belonged to the privileged class of this country in the late eighteenth century, he was related through his mother to one of the most powerful families in England among whom was the Lord Lieutenant of his day, the second Earl Temple. But his privilege and his connection, as so often in the course of Irish history, bred in him a burning conviction of the rights and nobility of the poorest in the land; a conviction that was to lead him with a band of those same wretches to what Pearse later described as the most complete failure. And yet, in Pearse's own words too, he has left us a prouder memory than the memory of Brian victorious at Clontarf or of Eoghan Rua victorious at Benburb. 'It is', Pearse said, 'the memory of a sacrifice Christ-like in its perfection.'

'I have little time', said Emmet, 'to look at the thousand difficulties that still lie between me and the completion of my wishes.' That self-same time, I suggest, may be fast fading from us also. What kind of Ireland did Emmet conceive of? An Ireland, it can be confidently said, where the genius of each strand of our common inheritance would be woven together in one glorious pattern. And here may I say that it is regrettable that all the strands of that common inheritance are not represented on the platform this evening. *(applause)* Is the United States of America, for all its faults, less a nation because it embraces the tradition of the European races and the noble American and African tribes? Are Italy, France, Germany, yes even India and China diminished in their nationhood because of the widely different races and traditions that create their common name? And yet, we in Ireland have so often decreed that what is lorded as patriotism in the one is branded as treachery in the other.

The characteristics of nationhood are surely: sovereignty, equality, and tolerance. And it is particularly the absence of tolerance that has made us fall far short of Emmet's goal of nationhood. The Boyne indeed should be a sacred water. It was consecrated by the blood of all the Irishmen that poured through its stream.

Right it is too that the siege of Derry be honoured as a gallant stand. Right also that the siege of Limerick be cherished as a noble sacrifice. But this small island, for all the nobility of its various sons, particularly in the past, is too often torn by the various traditions rather than built around them.

The Irish Protestant and the Ulster Presbyterian have generously contributed great men and noble ideas to our past. The former continue to give to every aspect of Irish life a contribution far in excess of their proportion. To the latter, shall we not say, 'This land is our land. This land too, is your land.' I recall clearly the reasoned plea, based on what I regard as an elusive economic advantage, of Terence O'Neill to his people, not to risk the break with the United Kingdom. Small wonder that the Ulster Irishman, in the confidence and determination of his own ability did not respond wholeheartedly to the call. It was directed against the highest aim of their great independent and proud tradition.

My task this evening is how now to weigh the practical advantages and disadvantages of integration on this island of ours. Though I think it can fairly be said that in recent times, through planning, and a large measure of hard work, we have unfolded the resources of a country that, even in my school days, was said to have little or no natural resources. We have developed a fund of native capital and personnel that for centuries was being drained from this land. Ireland is a rich nation. Rich in its resources *(applause)* and richer still in its people. Shall we not then work together to achieve our own destiny at home, and among the other nations to earn the status that is so rightfully ours? Must we not determine together to rid ourselves, as Emmet would have us rid ourselves, of the hateful divisions that have been forced into the homes of too many people?

The achievements of our common past are, I hope, the challenge of our common, integrated future. A future that does not imply, as the latest statement of Major Chichester Clarke seems to say it implies, a prior sectarian blood bath. We wish no such calamity to our brothers in the North. Their blood is our blood, and a fully United Ireland will never be cemented by such a precious liquid.

Did Emmet decree that any one mind should plan his Epitaph? If yes, Mr Chairman, it is too soon to write that Epitaph. Let us at least together select the stone. Our common deeds in the future will write the words. Thank you very much. *(applause, cheering)*

CHAIRMAN: MR JUSTICE T. C. KINGSMILL MOORE:
'I now call upon Deputy Erskine Childers, Minister for Health, to speak in the negative.' *(applause)*

MR ERSKINE CHILDERS, T.D.
MINISTER FOR HEALTH

Mr Chairman, Mr Auditor, Your Excellencies, Ladies and Gentlemen:

I thought I might first of all read a little bit more of that marvellous oration by Robert Emmet:

'Let no man write my epitaph; for as no man who knows my motives dare now vindicate them, let them and me repose in obscurity and peace and my tomb remain uninscribed and my memory in oblivion until other times and other men can do justice to my character. When my country takes her place among the nations of the earth, then, and not till then, let my epitaph be written — I have done.'

A marvellous piece of oratory by a very great man.

I want first of all to speak about the circumstances surrounding the United Irishmen. At the turn of the eighteenth century the social and political conditions were so fundamentally different to what they are today, perhaps we had better place the United Irishmen in their true perspective. Although Ireland received the impressions of the French Revolution from abroad, it was a country largely cut off by sea from Europe, dependent completely upon Great Britain for all of its trade and most of its communications.

You'll recall the fact that the French Revolution had inspired hatred for social reform among all the governing classes, partly because of the excesses that had resulted from the first incidents in the Revolution itself. The established religious faiths were separate, ecumenism was virtually non-existent. And you will remember that Presbyterians and Catholics at that time in Ireland had for decades suffered the most severe disabilities, suffered together the same disabilities. And for that reason we may remember the fact that as it was the title of a book that *Ulster went West* and the Presbyterians from Ulster played a great part in the founding of Canada and the United States to the point that there are six Presidents of the United

States of Presbyterian Ulster origin. And they went and ventured forth because they felt that they would have a greater opportunity for a free life at that time because they were suffering like Catholics from severe disabilities.

Even in that age, thousands and thousands of Catholics and Presbyterians inspired by the broad liberal philosophy of the French revolution came together and worked for the establishment of a tolerant society, which is now accepted as right and proper by all reasonable people. They were an advance guard of the present movement for an understanding between the South and the North and for a complete concord between Protestants and Catholics. And we can always remember them as having played an amazing part in an age where tolerance was virtually non-existent in whole nations. And of course, they did teach us to accept our common Christian heritage.

I'd like to remark in passing that there are today in the North, mercifully, hundreds and thousands of Protestants and Catholics who are determined to live in harmony together no matter how much they may disagree politically or conflict politically together. They are silent and uncommunicative. I wish their voices would speak louder. I wish the press, when it has the opportunity would point out this particular group of people, who, under enormous pressure, are still determined to try and prevent a blood-bath taking place in the North. They represent a very large group of important people.

Well I don't believe that Emmet's epitaph should be written, because in the words of Sir James Craig, the first Prime Minister of Northern Ireland, time must pass before unity comes, and I would remind you of Sir James Craig's words. He said,

'In this island we cannot live always separated from one another. We are too small to be apart, or for the border to be there for all time. The change will come. Not in my time, but it will come.'

A very strange prophecy from the first Prime Minister of Northern Ireland, and one we shall never forget, and one of which we should remind the Unionist Party that that statement was made by Sir James Craig at a very critical time.

I might remind you of the poll taken by the *Belfast Telegraph* some two or three years ago, privately conducted I think by the Sir Henry Gallup organization. Its method of assessment wasn't seriously questioned. It found I think that over 40 per cent of Unionists, when questioned privately, said that they recognized that partition must end someday. I mention that in passing.

Now, in a recent debate in the Dáil, from questions being asked and from speeches being made, we must remember that the overwhelming majority of our people subscribe to the Taoiseach's statement that he made in Tralee in September, when he said:

'It will remain our earnest aim and hope to win the consent of the majority of the people in the Six Counties to means by which the North and South can come together in a reunited and sovereign Ireland, earning International respect both for the fairness and efficiency with which it is administered, and for its contribution to world peace and progress.'

Ladies and Gentlemen, until that aim is realized, Emmet's epitaph cannot be written. *(applause)*.

I next want to say a few words about what I believe to be genuine, social, economic, and political advantages in unity. And I say this in all seriousness. I'm quite aware of the economic difficulties of reunion. I nevertheless believe profoundly that when we realize that we will be joining the European Economic Community in two or three or four years, that regardless of our voting power expressed in the terms of the way in which we join, we'll be a minor member. When we realize that we'll be exporting as a people, goods to some two hundred million Europeans, when we realize the problems that inevitably arise for a small Nation as ourselves, I can't help believing that a common constitutional bond between the North and the South would result in better organization for the stimulation of our exports. A specialised organization that should result in more goods being exported if it was designed and carried out, and promoted by an All Ireland Government. I can't help feeling that if we had grievances in the whole of the country, North and South, they'd be far better ventilated by an all Ireland team sitting in Brussels, than by a team representing one truncated part of Ireland, the other having to be represented by the overall interests of the British Board of Trade.

I really believe that advantage could be gained by both sides through that kind of constitutional unity which we all desire. I believe that for our own particular circumstances it would be better to have our own industrial organization, our industrial development carried out by a joint team. That we should have the same tax incentives, North and South, for exports. I believe that when tariffs largely disappear between Great Britain and Ireland, and between Europe and Ireland, it will be all the more important for a country like ours to think together on the problems that face us in the European Economic Community. And I do believe that there is an economy of scale to be considered, when we think of the development of the island as a whole. When we think of the interests that we should share, when we think of the larger home market, associated as I've said with a forceful development of industry, a common approach in agriculture, in regional planning, in the road transport structure of the country, in health administration, in cultural development, and in the inevitable problem whereby we see more and more a policy of regionalization, and at the same time the necessity of preserving the vitality of the smaller unit within the region. I believe in these things and I realize there's an economic price to be paid. But I've always had faith that the country could do these kind of jobs better as a whole than truncated and I always shall believe it.

And then, I also believe that the personality and character traits of the whole Island are complementary to each other. That Ulster needs Munster and Connaught personality for its growth, for its development, for its survival. I believe in that. It's difficult to imagine England without Yorkshire and Lancashire, or without Devonshire and Cornwall. It's difficult to imagine France without Gascony and Normandy. People of the same race, people of the same language, people of the same thought in a great many ways but with variations of personality. I might remark in purely humorous vein that when I go to Cork or Kerry, I always feel that they are, more or less, Federal Republics on their own *(laughter)*. I often wondered if we had the problem of partition in Cork and Kerry rather than in the North, whether the solution, Ladies and Gentlemen, would be much easier. But here I'm speaking purely frivolously.

Nevertheless, I do believe that there is a great advantage in the kind of Northern personality working together with the Southern personality and character that we have. And I know, that if somebody were to do a sort of careful study of the origins of the people who made Dublin a great City, they would find a fantastic combination of Ulster men and Munster men contributing very largely to the growth and the development and the dynamism in Dublin. And so I speak of these things sincerely, and really believing that it would be to the advantage of the whole country if we had unification on some of the grounds that I have mentioned, quite apart from my belief that the unity of Ireland is essentially of historic origin.

Well now, we have to look back for a moment at the prejudices of 150 years of political hatred and oppression that took place and the tragic role that division has taken in the North. And yet when I think of even the present situation in the North, and the difficulties there, and I look at the European Economic Community today, and then I think of the wars, the invasions, the millions of dead and wounded in two World Wars, the opposing alliances in Europe dividing Europe completely until the fifties, and then the partnership of the countries of the European Economic Community proving that at least on some occasions that Nations are not necessarily always the captives of their history. And if these Nations can come together, I believe that we should look forward to a time when these fearful hates and prejudices will disappear in the North, and then we shall be able to think together and work together to common accord. If they can do it in Europe, in so short a period, and after vast and desperate divisions in their midst, why not ourselves? I think of that immortal spectacle of the German and French armies marching, one after the other, in front of Reims Cathedral, in front of General de Gaulle and President Adenauer, and the reconciliation that meant between two totally different races. I hope that that kind of attitude towards solving the problem can be learnt in the North and learned between us all, because the North can make no progress if this lesson is ignored, the lesson we learnt by watching those armies at Reims.

The Irishmen of all creeds have so much in common that my very comparison is invidious. I'm making a comparison of two separate races who came together. My comparison is really invidious and unvaried, yet I'm compelled to cite it when I see the bitterness that has arisen and when I see the result of fifty years of government in the North. And I still say that it should be possible. However, dramatic emotional statements may be necessary but we not only speak about the essential unity of our country, we must face crude realities of where we are to go now. Now it's quite impossible for me to speak about the current situation in Northern Ireland. I would prefer those who speak after me to make what contribution they have. I'm bound, as a Minister of this Government, to assume that the civil rights will be implemented in the North. That the whole of the arrangements will be implemented, that the extremists will be restrained, and that the suffocating effects of fifty years of discrimination will be ended, and that there is some opportunity for a turning point in the attitude of the people of Northern Ireland, both Unionists and Nationalists. It would be useless for me to debate on any other alternative position. It would be fruitless for me to make any proposals as to what we can do in the future unless we can make this assumption and we do hope that civil rights will be implemented, that the campaign will be concluded, and that there will be a new era in Northern Ireland, for both Unionists and Nationalists. And therefore when I speak of what I hope will happen I'm making these assumptions.

I hope there will be far greater communication and more exchanges between our people and the Unionists of the North. We've got to get to know them far better than we ever have before. We've got to penetrate among them. We've got to understand them. We've got to have more discussions with them. The basis of our communication is not simply to harangue them about the necessity of unity, but first of all to understand each other, to see the realities unclouded by blind prejudice, and if the point arrives when we can have this communication, for us to remember the fifty years of the repression of the Nationalists of the North. If our arguments with them will serve no purpose, we must start anew to communicate, to debate with them, to talk with them, insofar as we can and insofar as we can meet them, and that is the only way by which we can bring about unity, by the consent of the Protestants of the North, which is the policy of the people of the whole Dáil and of overwhelming numbers in this country. This observation applies to every nation, in relation to their current social and economic developments. You can say when in any country in the world where there is stagnation and failure to communicate between opposing groups where they stand and glare at each other, there will be stagnation in that country. So I'm saying something which applies to countries other than our own. The people from the South must make a better effort to understand how the people of the North live.

What are the innermost feelings of Unionists? We must penetrate their minds. I know of no other way of doing it. And there are thousands of Unionists who in the next ten years, I think, will be sufficiently alert and sophisticated to be at least able to debate the problem of unification on a cold-blooded basis. At least so that we can understand the real problem that will arise if unity takes place. Formidable problems, formidable social and economic problems that are not being denied by us. But at least, so that there can come to be some kind of debate, some kind of communication free of the clouds of bigotry that have been the case in the past, and to have debate in this kind of manner which can be found in each country of Europe today, among its own people, among parties of different and conflicting views.

And I think it's true to say that the continuation of the fierce irrational political prejudices in the North will delay economic progress in the North. I'm perfectly certain that industrial growth in the North will be delayed if promoters of industry feel they're coming to a country where people are thinking politically and religiously as though they were back in the sixteenth or seventeenth century or living in Ireland at the time that Poynings Law was passed. So that it is tremendously to the disadvantage of the Northern people to permit this kind of conflict of feeling, this fearful cloud of bigotry, particularly once the main issue has been settled, and once there is a real implementation of the civil rights program. I think we can have some rays of hope in regard to this matter.

There has been more communication, as I've said, already; communication between the people of the North and communication between ourselves and the Northerners. And now may I make a few observations about our own position in the South. In the South, the Protestants in this country have fared excellently since the foundation of the State. They have participated in large measure in the economic growth in this country. They are participating in organizations, committees, commissions, and boards under Government and Local Government auspices, freely and fully. There was too much separation in the past, between the Protestant community and the Catholic community in this part of Ireland, largely for historic background reasons. That is ended. And the present climate of ecumenism is so evident that I needn't comment further on this matter. Having said that, I'd like to repeat again that the Taoiseach, when he spoke about the essential unity of this Island of ours, he did indicate that Constitutional changes might be based on a federal system, on a gradualist approach. Mr de Valera as far back as 1936 equally made proposals for a federalist solution.

We have realized that the economic problems must be mastered. We realize that the growing strength of our economy in the South will make a vital contribution towards unity, and I mention these facts because they must be stressed over and over again. I hope that there will be a reappraisal by the Nationalist minority in the North of their position. I hope that once the civil rights program is implemented fully that they will accept the realities of the new political position which is different from what it was before. I hope that they will prepare a policy devoid of extremist influence, a broad policy dedicated to long term unification; of persuading the majority of Northerners that unification has an ultimate advantage for the whole island of Ireland. I think this will be inevitable some day.

And I would like to close by quoting very briefly what William Orr, a man who was condemned to death for his part in the '98 Rising, what he said at a time when there was a great deal of feeling of stress and strain and fighting and arrests, and shooting and espionage. William Orr said at his trial:

'I trust that all my virtuous countrymen will bear me in their kind remembrance and continue true and faithful to each other, as I have been to all of them.'

If the people of the North become true and faithful to each other, and if together, the people of the North and South become true and faithful to each other as William Orr prayed they would, someday, Ladies and Gentlemen, Emmet's epitaph will be written. *(applause)*

CHAIRMAN: MR JUSTICE T. C. KINGSMILL MOORE
'I now call upon Deputy Michael O'Leary, who will continue the debate in the affirmative.' *(applause)*

MR MICHAEL O'LEARY T.D.

Mr Auditor, Ladies and Gentlemen, I am suffering from a severe headache which commenced yesterday at three o'clock. *(laughter, applause)*

I think, had we another member of the Cabinet here tonight, that he could speak very enthusiastically about Emmet's epitaph being written in view of the result in Dublin Southwest yesterday; I can think of one other member of the Cabinet who would think that the epitaph was well and truly completed yesterday. *(laughter)* It's not the present Minister. I think that there's something a bit obscene in politicians gathering here tonight and talking about Emmet's epitaph from the little we know of Emmet and the period he lived in. Going through my head from what I can remember of the lines of Yeats' poem *The Scholars:*

> Bald heads forgetful of their sins,
> Old, learned, respectable bald heads
> Edit and annotate the lines
> That young men, tossing on their beds,
> Rhymed out in love's despair
> To flatter beauty's ignorant ear.
> ...
> Lord, what would they say
> Did their Catullus walk that way?

Similarly I feel that, with no offence to myself or any of the other official politicians present, we are discussing a very extraordinary man here tonight and we, least of all, are equipped to understand the mentality and commitment of that man.

I'm also on the side of the proposition that his epitaph should be written, and of course this isn't a side that appeals to me. All the rhetoric is on the side of his epitaph not being written, and to taking the title of radical or reformer, if not a more extreme title. Surely in these days of exacting rivalry about who is more extreme than someone else, perhaps I may simulate a claim to the title of radical or reformer. It would appeal to me far more to speak against the particular motion, but at any rate I can say that as I look upon his epitaph and the account of his court case, Emmet pleaded for the understanding of his fellow countrymen, for the understanding of the greater Irish public outside the Court house. He said: 'I make a claim on your memory'; and he did make that claim on our memory. Of all the figures of history, Emmet is one of those who has been remembered. I'm sure others of you here who may have relations in the Irish countryside will remember a very familiar picture over farm fireplaces, over the last half a century in this country, of Emmet making his speech at the dock. It may now have been replaced, up to recently at any rate, by trans-atlantic politicians. *(laughter, applause)*

But Emmet at any rate made that claim on our memory. I therefore would say that, considering the part of his epitaph which seeks that the epitaph not be written until his country is placed amongst the countries of the world, I don't think the two Irelands we have would merit the epitaph being written, on that basis. But I think we could ask that it be written; if we mean to understand his motives, and seek further to investigate those motives, to understand the life of this man and the mainspring of his action at that particular period. I don't think, without citing any social welfare payments or GNP as the Minister has done, or this gain, or that gain, or better roads, or better dental condition in the population at large, that judging from the sacrifice, we can see a State deserving of the brave who were the United Irishmen. One could not perhaps ever see a State appropriate to that sacrifice. Perhaps we can never see it. But certainly there is no doubt in my mind that we don't have it, in either part of the country.

Emmet said that, in a conspiracy, you must always seek to go outside the prejudice. He said to his accusers: 'Since men in this period cannot speak freely about my motives', he said, 'don't discuss them at all, let me have the charity of your silence.' Well, we can break the silence about his motives, and to that extent write his epitaph. Now the great object of the United Irishmen was that objective of independence, national independence. In his day there was a greater possibility of this. The comparison, the relationship between here and Britain was far nearer to a population of something like eight million, representing a real threat to that sister island. The relationship is far different today. We are now permanently a very small European country. And we are a small country in a world moving to greater and greater trading relationships, one with the other. And the maintenance of our independence becomes that much more difficult. This does not mean, of course, that one must necessarily throw overboard the whole national sovereignty attempt at economic independence as the Minister's government has, in fact, done in their part of Emmet's epitaph in the twenty-six counties. Emmet left us no writings, so there's nothing to squabble about. *(laughter)* Nobody can say that he's more true to those writings than another. He just left us his life and his action. He was a reconciler in a movement that had a lot of divisions in it. Can we not think of movements today that have a lot of divisions in them? Gerry Fitt and John Hume have come down from a movement that evidently bristles with divisions, and down in our own part of the country, we have our divisions. *(laughter, applause)*

You remember when Emmet went to Fort George and his brother Tom Emmet wasn't speaking to Arthur O'Connor. In fact, they'd already been attempting to have a duel, and they were restrained, not by any great intellectual appeal he made to either party, but by his honesty, and his sincerity. And this is something that contemporaries remark about Emmet: his honesty and his sincerity. And he was no professional politician or revolutionary. He had, we know, a normal romantic interest. Indeed, the governor of Kilmainham on the morning of the execution, remarked about seeing him winding the strands of Sarah Curran's hair around a fork to put next to his heart, a very romantic notion before his execution.

And when, in fact, he was waiting for the hangman's knot, he didn't as the patriots, according to the Christian Brothers saga, always do, step manfully up to be hanged immediately. He waited for a long time, evidently in the naive expectation that he would be rescued. And several times the hangman asked him to step forward and he said he was not yet ready. And what is so appealing to me about Emmet is that I think of a man leaving no writings, a man of undoubted sincerity, a very young man, and of his role as reconciler, and I think of the ideologues of his period who didn't stand the pace. People like Emmet stood the pace. I think of Russell in Downpatrick Gaol, when he looked at the jurors, the people who had condemned him to death, and he saw at least six United Irishmen, who had sworn into the Society of United Irishmen, were amongst those who had condemned him. And we know a lot of these United Irishmen and it's got to do with something very deep in history, the controversy and dissension, and the essential problem awaiting solution by Irishmen North and South. Emmet's attempt to reconcile the forces of that period is still valid and relevant, and it may be a melancholy comment on the progress towards the Ireland of his ideal, the Ireland he sought, a United Ireland which would claim its place amongst the nations of the Earth, that we may still find the arguments of that period valid in our own day.

Well, we have greater understanding of the Northern position but the claim is often made by civil rights people in the North, that the Unionists for years handed out a fairy tale about the Unionist position in the North of Ireland, said to their working class followers, 'We are giving you a better deal than the Catholics.' And now, late in the day, they are attempting to reform. Can we not say of the political parties down here that they, themselves, have sold a false idea of Irish unity. They themselves have given a false version of the Northern problem, because the insoluble, the immovable rock, the real impediment to Irish unity lies in the ancestral fears of about a million Protestant Irish men and women. And there is a great deal on this side of the border that we are responsible for, in the short period of our statehood, for the strengthening of their prejudices over that particular period. *(applause)* And the major political party has fallen for the permanent temptation, a permanent temptation for twenty-six county parties, namely to play for political popularity in the area under their domestic jurisdiction, to play for popularity in that area on this question of the unity of the whole country. I think they have succumbed to that temptation on several occasions.

Now, the judge accused Emmet of ambition, and that is something that most people involved in a difficult enterprise would be accused of at different times, but Emmet had a better alibi than most at his end. But this will remain a permanent accusation of enemies of any particular progressive movement. And if the main thing one brings away from a study of Emmet's character is his generosity and his sincerity, one could say that, on either side of the border, we need a greater generosity in our political organizations. And I'm not making a moral rearmament speech here, but

I'm saying this, that it is quite evident that what we need in the North is a political organization to pick up the gains which have been made — a political coalition, to use that ugly word. A political coalition or alliance stretching from people like Hume right across to Dick Ferguson. That's the kind of working coalition we need in the North. And, likewise, I would say this: that in the South, in the twenty-six counties, we need a broad alliance of forces gathered on the platform of reform right across the board also. *(hear, hear! interjection from audience)* I believe that this is understanding, in our day, something of the generosity of Emmet. Now you began this week by looking at a man like Burke and I think properly you end the week by considering the character, the personality and the very brief life of a man like Emmet. He had no party programme. He took part in something to reconcile differences, gathering Irishmen together, striving for independence, striving for a position with mutual respect with other countries; mainly he was thinking of the connection with Britain. To some extent he annoyed Arthur O'Connor and, in his speech from the dock, he criticized the French republic and its philosophy.

So he made a lot of political mistakes and he was forgiven in the memory, which he sought from the Irish people, because of his sincerity and, I suppose, a lot of attractive features about his particular end. But finally, in thinking of a person like Emmet, you think of another poem of Yeats; you think of that poem of Yeats, 'In Memory of Eva Gore-Booth and Con Markiewicz':

> The innocent and the beautiful
> Have no enemy but time;

That's the only enemy of a person like Emmet. His picture may now be removed from farm houses around the country. But the tantalising question that remains for anybody working in Ireland, North or South, today is this: we cannot be satisfied with anything so ugly, so far removed from the ideals of all those people for whom the hangman's rope was spun. Their names have gone around the world like the wind. We cannot be satisfied with small states here, the concept of two Irelands, nor can we take refuge either in alibis that mean we are disengaged from action by calling ourselves this kind of Left person or that kind of Left person. It's not howling slogans we must be at this time, but taking part in fashioning the Ireland that Emmet and the United Irishmen sought. Thank you. *(applause)*

CHAIRMAN: MR JUSTICE T. C. KINGSMILL MOORE
'I have pleasure in calling upon Mr John Hume M.P. to continue.' *(applause)*

MR JOHN HUME M.P.

Mr Chairman, Mr Auditor and Friends:

I am reminded as I look around this platform this evening and at the breadth of opinion represented on it of a story, about a county Antrim farmer. And, Mr Chairman, a postman took a very long walk up a very long lane, and when he got to the door, he said to the farmer, 'Willie', he says, 'that's a long lane'. And Willie says, 'If it wasn't so long, or if it was any shorter, it wouldn't reach the door.' *(laughter, applause)* And on this platform this evening as I've said, we're going to have a long evening's talk because you're going to hear very many points of view. But as Mr O'Kennedy has said, the absence of one viewpoint on this platform this evening underlines better than any argument on the motion that we this evening are discussing *(applause)* because while they have not said why they are not here, if I am guessing aright the reasons, their very absence, as I say, makes it inevitable that this House this evening must argue against the writing of Emmet's epitaph.

Because while this country has assimilated many traditions, it's a standing reminder not only to their failure, but to ours as well, that we have failed to assimilate into the mainstream of this country people who have been here for three hundred years. And I think, Mr Chairman, that it is most appropriate at the present point of time that we should be discussing such a motion. And indeed, to discuss it in such a place. Because in the past eighteen months in the Northern part of Ireland we've been through a lot. And many of you on this side have observed and have perhaps been confused by what you saw. The struggle, there, was one against injustice and oppression. And in the event of the eventual removal of that injustice and of that oppression one of the great barriers that does exist between the people in Ireland will have gone. Because its removal will assist not only those who have been victims of that injustice but it will help much more those who have perpetrated it, because in the last analysis it has done them far more harm than it has done to us.

It must also be clear today, to everyone, that a state that has been in the North of Ireland and that has survived by using injustice as a political weapon, is bound now to be radically altered by the removal of that injustice. The prospect of a Northern society built on equality and justice is one that is bound to affect the whole country and one which is a necessary prerequisite to the eventual and inevitable marriage of the two parts of Ireland. Recent events also, must, as other speakers have already said, produce radical changes in the attitudes of those traditionally opposed to the existence of the Northern State. Because it goes without saying that those who fight and have fought for civil rights must also be prepared to accept civil responsibility. Because such an acceptance will mean an involvement in the affairs of Northern Ireland that has never existed before among those who are opposed to the Northern State. And it hasn't existed before either because they were prevented or, and this must be admitted, and admitted frankly, because we were unwilling to play a part and we did not wish to become involved.

At this stage of the twentieth century and at this time in this country, we can no longer afford to opt out. In short, ladies and gentlemen, we in the North who are opposed to Unionism must accept that whether we like it or not, and those of you here who are opposed to Unionism must accept that whether you like it or not the Northern State now exists by the will of the majority of its people. All of us who live there must involve ourselves at every level of it in order to ensure a better life, a more prosperous life for all of the citizens who live there. We must do so while keeping in mind the long term changes that we think desirable and that we wish to promote.

At first glance, an immediate reaction from some people might be that such an involvement, in what amounts to making Northern Ireland work, would appear to strengthen and give permanence to the present divisions that exist in Ireland. But if one looks a little deeper at it, the realities are quite the opposite. Remember after all, the North of Ireland is a part of Ireland. If, for the first time, the people there are working together, then for the first time, the real border in this country will be under heavy attack. The mental border of prejudice and distrust that exists between our people can only be removed by the promotion of better understanding and friendship. It can only be removed by spilling sweat, common sweat, rather than by spilling blood. *(applause)*

Such an approach, Mr Chairman, is not very popular to many people because it lacks the dramatic approach of an instant solution, of an immediate and glorious achievement of the old dream. It may not be a popular way, it may not be a dramatic way, it may not allow anyone to wrap the green flag around them and emerge as a glorious saviour of the country, but it is the only way. And it's a way which is not easy. It's hard, and it's difficult, and it's a long hard road. But it's about time we were marching along it. And if we look over the past fifty years of the history of Ireland since the founding of the Northern state, some startling truths are revealed.

Many people have come, and they have gone, protesting their ideal of a united country. Most of them have agreed that the solution should be a peaceful one. Yet, ladies and gentlemen, to my knowledge, never, and I have searched hard, never anywhere have I found a blueprint policy, a programme, for the peaceful re-unification of Ireland. And why is that? I believe, rightly or wrongly, that it's because those, who said they believed in that, lacked the moral courage to face up to the emotional unpopularity of the consequences of that point of view. We have failed to look this problem fully and squarely in the face. We have talked of Ireland, and tears have filled many eyes as people talked of Ireland and as people looked at their flag and so forth. Nobody ever stopped to ask what was meant by Ireland. Was it just this piece of earth that we're all living upon? Or was it the flag to which we all owe allegiance? And of course it's neither of those things because Ireland, purely and simply, is its people. It is not just a piece of earth. It is people of varying traditions and varying backgrounds, who together form the entity that is known as Ireland. And when we talk of the unity of Ireland we really mean the community of its people. And by the same token, when we view our country in this light, the border is not a line on a map to be eradicated by whatever means we can. The border is a mental border that is built on fear and prejudice and on misunderstanding. The only way to wipe that out is by developing understanding and friendship. And this is the real task, ladies and gentlemen, that faces anyone who genuinely wants to solve the Irish problem.

The weakness of that point of view is that it is not dramatic. But its virtue is that it is the only way. And if we look too at the origins, what, in fact, happened? The Orange Card was played. Reaction to it in the North was predictable and understandable, but unfortunate in that it meant that those, who were opposed to a separate State in the North, played into the hands of those who played the Orange Card, by acting or reacting predictably. And it has meant that nationalism and things Irish have become equated with one religious viewpoint. The result has been, arising out of that, that the divisions in Ireland have been strengthened and deepened and have been to the advantage only of those who have been prepared to use sectarianism as a political weapon. As long as sectarianism is used as a political weapon on this island, then so long will this country remain divided. Indeed it's rather puzzling to me, that in spite of the many lessons of history, that this was allowed to happen. And indeed that similar things could even happen today, because the lessons of history are that any person, who wants to achieve a political viewpoint through extreme means, is usually met by an extreme reaction. And in meeting them with such an extreme reaction, all you do is strengthen their point of view and make it almost certain that they will achieve it. That same danger exists in the North of Ireland today. And we must not allow ourselves to fall into the trap.

The extremism of right wing Unionism must not be met with extremism; it must be met instead with firm and strong moderation. The more extreme they become the more firm must we be in our moderation. Extremism, when it breeds extremism, wins out in the end. By reacting extremely to the extremism of right wing Unionists today, either in the North or in the South, we are only playing into their hands. In the last analysis, reason and reason only, will solve the Irish question. Passion never will. And indeed, not only in the Northern part of Ireland have the reactions to the setting-up of the Northern State been unfortunate, what has happened, as a result of the playing of the Orange Card, and as a result of the reaction playing into their hands, we' have now two confessional states in Ireland, neither of which is worthy of the best in the Irish people.

What we must now be striving for is a pluralist Ireland, one which will be richer for the full participation of our different traditions. And it must also be a tolerant Ireland, and tolerant not only in religion and in Constitutional structure, but tolerant of dissent. And it must be clear and made clear that no one person or no one group has the right to claim ownership of the national conscience. There are too many who pretend that they, or their group, are the possessors of the national conscience, or the possessors of all things Irish.

A county Antrim farmer, ladies and gentlemen, is every bit as Irish as his counterpart in Kerry. And indeed his background is the same as that of Tone, Montgomery, McCracken, and Armour of Ballymoney and a whole host of others whose traditions lie buried in the North today but whose traditions are still there and whose traditions must be rediscovered. Part of our task is to rediscover them. In short, to create the sort of Ireland that we seek to create, we need not overcome the Northern Protestant. We need to seek his help and his co-operation. We cannot do it without him. It's as simple as that. How else can we create a country where Catholic, Protestant, and Dissenter can live side by side and work together for the betterment of us all?

Now there are those who will argue that the traditions, represented by the Tones and the Emmets, are traditions that had violence inherent in them, and that violence was an inherent part of their attitude to the Irish question. Basing their views on that, they will say that violence cannot be ruled out today. To take such a view, is to ignore a very significant change that did take place with the setting up of the Northern State. And that is this: that previously those who advocated force as a solution to the Irish question were talking in terms of independence from Britain. The situation is such today that we're not talking about that and we haven't been for fifty years and perhaps we have been mistaken. We've been talking instead about a united Ireland and this has meant that the enemy, rather than being Britain has been a fellow Irishman. And to talk about violence to solve the Irish question today means that we are asking Irishmen to fight Irishmen and I believe that that is a very significant change in the situation before the setting up of the Northern State. And I would venture to say that the very nature of the problem is such that by using violence in this situation we would only increase and deepen divisions which are already bad enough. Problems of human relationships, and indeed the Northern problem is a problem of human relationships, cannot be solved by violence.

In short, ladies and gentlemen, finally, those in this part of Ireland and in Northern Ireland who believe that we must try and produce a situation where we can write Emmet's epitaph must realize that the open hand and the open door backed up by the promotion and development of a true understanding of things Irish is a much better approach to this problem than is the clenched fist. For in the last analysis, the Northern Protestants are our own people and they will discover in time, perhaps in a short time, as we move into larger international groupings that we are their only real friends. There are many who will argue that the pursuit of the attitudes that I am representing to you is an impossible task. There can be no doubt that it represents a difficult task but how can we argue that it is impossible when we have never tried? What we need in Ireland today, ladies and gentlemen, is more statesmen and fewer politicians, and we will solve the Irish question quicker. And we might remember the words of Ghandi that 'wars are declared in the name of humanity but created by personal ambitions'. Thank you. *(applause)*

CHAIRMAN: MR JUSTICE T. C. KINGSMILL MOORE
'I have pleasure in calling upon Mr Vincent Browne, who will continue the debate in the affirmative.' *(applause)*

MR VINCENT BROWNE

Mr Chairman, Mr Auditor, Ladies and Gentlemen:

I'm sure many of you, like me, are wondering what am I doing here tonight. I'm not elected to parliament, I am assured by my political colleagues that I never will be, *(laughter)* but my only connection, as far as I know, with the gentlemen who are speaking with me here tonight is that in the magazine with which I am associated we've insulted each one of them. *(laughter)*

Mr Childers made one his very erudite speeches. I think it was on the length of each sod of turf that had been cut the week before. *(laughter)* He was then Minister for Transport and Power. *(laughter, applause)* Packie Mooney's main stake to his political reputation was not in his parliamentary oratory, or indeed, surprisingly enough in the work which he did for his constituents in political and constitutional matters, but rather in being a tremendous and noteworthy service to his constituents in taking them by car, anywhere, anytime, any place. *(laughter, applause)* One could easily be forgiven for being confused as to which was Minister for Transport at the time. *(laughter, applause)* Packie got up and said — it was the time of the general election — 'Well, yous all know me, I'm Packie Mooney, and I must have taken yous or one of yous families somewhere, sometime. *(laughter)* So I hope yous all vote for me. And now, one final word: if any of yous want a lift to Dublin this afternoon, I'll be going at 2.30.' *(laughter)*

The motion which we are asked to debate tonight concerns a patriot of little significance in Irish history, despite what Mr O'Leary and other speakers have said about him. Robert Emmet merits no more than a footnote at the bottom of a history book. His rebellion was supported by a tiny minority of Irish people. He left no great political legacy in the sense of political tracts and political pamphlets. The only references to him, the only reference to his ideals and thoughts is a melodramatic and much romanticised speech he made from the dock. The speech he made from the dock gave us no real clue as to what his political ideology was, what he actually saw the nature of Irish society to be.

And therefore we can only guess and speculate as to Emmet's conception of Ireland, a free Ireland, an independent Ireland, an Ireland worthy to take its place among the nations of the Earth. But Emmet, largely because of the influence of his friend Thomas Moore, who later wrote a ballad about him and his girlfriend, has come to symbolize, and his epitaph has come to represent, the legacy we have from past Irish patriots, particularly those who died in the struggle for Irish independence. And we feel this legacy and we have continued to feel this legacy in a forceful and powerful manner, and it influences our thoughts on a national level, so much so, that we are often diverted. We often ignore, very greatly, real and actual social problems around us. The Ireland and the ideology of that time could easily have represented the oppression which was very real and very accurate at that time with the British connection. Indeed, this was the representation made by the United Irishmen of which Tone was an antecedent. The kind of oppression which existed then was attributable at that stage to the British connection. But unfortunately the oppression which exists in Ireland now is a far more subtle and a far more sinister kind of oppression and it has very little to do with the British connection insofar as the British connection still exists.

And therefore the concentration on the kind of idealism, which emanated from the United Irishmen and from Emmet, tends only to distract us from the real forces and causes of oppression in our society today. Our society today mainly has oppression within it caused by forces within it and not without it. It is a marvellous form of escapism for Irish politicians and Irish public speakers to latch all the ills of Ireland, all the faults of Ireland, to an external cause such as that of Britain. *(applause)*

For the fact is today, that for both Northern and Southern Ireland the question of the British connection has very very little to do with the conditions of people in both those parts of the country. The old people, the people in poverty, the people out of jobs cannot point their finger with any true validity to what happened at Westminster, to what happens in England. They can more justifiably and more reasonably point their fingers to Leinster House. *(applause)* And therefore, talk of independence, talk of resurrecting the kind of idealism which the United Irishmen personified, talk of Emmet's conception of a Free Ireland, serves only to distract us, both North and South, from the real causes of oppression, from the real ills in our society and, most important, from doing something about it as John Hume has said.

We have, particularly in Southern Ireland, concentrated and harped on this question of national unity entirely to the detriment and neglect of other social problems. You have major Ministers of State telling us, time and time again, that the main problem of Irish society, the only problem in Irish society, is the solution to the border question. Are the 35,000 old age pensioners living on £3.15 per week, are they not a problem in Irish society? Is not the 100,000 people in inadequate and hopeless housing conditions, are they not a real problem in Irish society? Are the problems of the vagrants, both here and the vagrants we've exported to Britain, are they not a problem? Are the emigrants who weekly and yearly stream from our shores, are they not also a problem in Irish society?

It is all very well for these politicians to safeguard and bolster their position in power by distracting public attention onto a level and a plane which is entirely unrealistic and entirely dated in real Irish terms. The fact is that those people who have laid most stress and most emphasis on this question of national independence, and their national freedom, have been those very same people who have most neglected the problems in the Irish community. *(cheering, applause)*

But there's a more real problem and a more pressing problem, and it is in relation to Northern Ireland. It is not just that asserting this question of freedom from Britain, or national unity, is distracting Northern Ireland from the real issues. This insistence on the national unity question not alone distracts people in Northern Ireland from the real issues but actually aggravates the situation there. One of the primary causes for divisiveness, for hostility and bitterness in Northern Ireland, is that the Protestant majority up there feel threatened by the fact that we constantly and aggressively assert our sovereignty over that territory.

And furthermore, there is a sizeable minority in the state of Northern Ireland which uphold that assertion of the South. John Hume has been quite right to say that it would be a painful and agonising readjustment for us to concede that the major and most immediate problem is not one of national unity in Northern Ireland or indeed, Southern Ireland but rather the solution of the problems of both of those areas. And the solution of the social problems of Northern Ireland necessarily demands the abandonment of the Southern Irish claim to sovereignty over that State. Until Southern Ireland can honestly, generously, and openly concede that it now renounces its aggressive claim to sovereignty over that area, bitterness will continue. Hostility will continue to ensue. I look with regret over what has happened over the last year in Southern Ireland. In Northern Ireland you've had the development of a civil rights movement which sensibly and reasonably has avoided the question of national unity, the question of the border. And John Hume and his like have been very largely responsible for this.

But what have we done here in Southern Ireland? What has the Southern Irish politician's response been to this new movement, this new awareness in Northern Ireland? It has been, particularly on the part of two Ministers who need not be nameless, Blaney and Boland, *(cheering, applause)* it has been a continued aggressive assertion of our sovereignty up there. What effect does this have but to heighten tension, to exaggerate the already impossible situation there? The only thing that Irish politicians and we Southerners can reasonably do about the problem, the appalling human problem that exists in Northern Ireland, is to generously renounce our claim to sovereignty over that area. And to convince those people in Northern Ireland who continue to look southward to direct their attention more closely to their own community.

John Hume is quite right in asking the Catholics and those others of nationalist intent and republican outlook to stop looking southward for solutions. We can't solve our own problems, let alone theirs. *(applause, cheers)* The fact is, only after the renunciation of this right to Northern Ireland can we in a reasonable and logical manner begin the kind of reconstruction, begin the kind of co-operation that Mr Childers has so reasonably spoken of. It is no use for Mr Childers, and his like, to talk of co-operation in spheres of tourism or physical planning when others of his Cabinet are vigorously asserting the right of the people up there, not to decide their own fate, not to decide those questions on which we hope to co-operate with them.

I wish to acknowledge the tolerance of the audience. *(laughter, applause)* I have nothing else to say except to repeat this plea: that we now, or within the near future, when the question of the Constitution comes to be discussed again, in other words, when PR is going to be abolished again, *(laughter)* that we revoke those articles in the Constitution which assert our sovereignty, our claim to a thirty-two county Republic. And if necessary, to include in its place, the hope or idealized wish of an eventual Irish unity. Only by such generosity on our part can we realistically hope to in any way better those people in Northern Ireland whom we seek to serve. Thank you. *(applause)*

CHAIRMAN: MR JUSTICE T. C. KINGSMILL MOORE
'I have great pleasure in calling upon Mr Gerry Fitt M.P., to continue in the negative.' *(cheers, applause)*

MR GERRY FITT M.P.

Mr Chairman, Mr Auditor, Ladies and Gentlemen:

At this late stage in the debate I find myself in almost total confusion. *(laughter)* I find myself in almost total agreement with all the previous speakers. *(laughter)* And that is a rather unusual position for me to be in. *(laughter)* I really don't know how to cope with the situation. *(laughter)* Because, Sir, those persons who have opposed the motion have spoken in favour of it, *(laughter)* those who have spoken the other way have taken the other attitude. I think I will try to be as cagey as they were *(laughter)* but I can say, at this early stage in my remarks, that I am not looking forward to the next issue of Nusight.[20] *(laughter, applause)*

Mr Chairman, when we attempt to discuss Emmet and the motives which activated him during his lifetime, I think we must do so in the

---

[20] Vincent Browne, the previous speaker was Editor of Nusight at the time.

knowledge that 150 years, 170 years almost, have elapsed since then. And certainly, Sir, Emmet during his lifetime could not have envisaged the society in which we live today. The world has changed over the period since he died, and more particularly over the period of this last fifty years, since the partitioning of this country. I believe that Emmet, like all revolutionaries in Ireland, like all those who thought during their lifetime to throw off the British connection, was indeed a social reformer. And here I would disagree with the last speaker when he said that Emmet was a rather insignificant patriot. *(applause)* I do not believe there is such a thing as an insignificant Irish patriot. *(applause)*

I believe that what motivated Emmet in his opposition to British domination on this island were exactly the same motives which led James Connolly before a firing squad, a hundred years after Emmet's death. Emmet, during his lifetime, had to face the problem that Ireland had a population of eight million people. The vast majority of those people were underprivileged, were suffering under the heel of British colonial repression. And indeed, forty years after Emmet's death, forty-two or forty-three years, the population of Ireland was almost halved from eight million to four million as a result of the Famine. And one would have thought that with the halving of the population, with the granting of independence in Ireland in 1920, that the government would have taken some cogent steps to build up a society, to build up a nationality that would in some way have equated itself with the ideals of Emmet. But Sir, far from that. This government, in the twenty-six counties and indeed its counterpart in Northern Ireland, has been unwilling to see, what I believe the first speaker referred to as 'the richness of the Irish people', that Ireland was rich in her people.

Well, both governments, particularly the government in the Republic, have been willing to stand by idly and watch the emigrant ships, day after day and week after week and month after month, and to do absolutely nothing about it. I believe, Sir, that if there is one thing which has prevented Emmet's ideal coming into being, the ideal of Irish nationality for the thirty-two counties, one factor that has contributed to stopping it and will continue to prevent it from coming into operation and that is the government's attitude toward emigration. I think that both governments are taking the very easy way out of it. Because once they do not have to deal with a class of people, with a number of people demanding independence, demanding social emancipation, then I cannot see within my lifetime the future reunification of this country. Because what attraction can there be to the Northern Ireland Unionist to come into a United Ireland if he sees a much lower standard of welfare benefits, if he sees a high figure of emigration that is now reigning in the South, that's certainly no attraction. But I would not go so far as to agree with all the other speakers because tonight they have made out the Northern Protestants as being really innocent people, people who are not to blame, people who have been fed on Unionist propaganda.

But the Northern Unionist and the Northern Protestant is not as innocent as all that. He has his faults too. And those faults were very serious in generations past in this country. John Hume has said that we must face the fact that the majority of the population in the six counties now want to maintain the British connection, and do not want to claim their Irishness in this island. But when we talk about a majority we must ask how that majority was contrived. And we must remember that Lord Carson himself, the founder of the Northern Ireland State, said in the House of Lords, after the partitioning of Ireland, when someone was questioning, 'Why did you not take the whole nine counties? Why did you settle for six?' And he said, 'We went into the population figures of every town and village in the Province of Ulster to see if it would be possible to govern Ulster from Belfast. We found that the majority would be against us, so we then settled for six counties.' So if we talk about the majority in Northern Ireland, remember that this was an unofficial majority created by the British government and the Northern Ireland Unionist Party at that time to give them the right to impose partition on this island. *(applause)*

I recognize that the problem in Ireland can only be settled by peaceful means. But I do know that there is a strong body of opinion in this part of the island, who, perhaps, over-enamoured by the official title which is given to this State, which is the Republic of Ireland, they may believe in their hearts that there is such a thing as a Republic of Ireland. To me, I say there will never be a Republic of Ireland until there are thirty-two counties in that Republic. *(applause)*

We are asked tonight to accept the proposition that Emmet's epitaph should now be written. There are many people in the Republic who believe that Ireland has at last found her place, and is accepted amongst the nations of the world. The Republic of Ireland now has a seat in the United Nations and is accepted by the big power blocs. But even though Emmet could not envisage the setting up of such an organization as the United Nations as we know it today, I believe that if he were alive today he would completely reject the United Nations representation, and the voice that Ireland has in the conscience of the world, as grounds that we have in fact arrived at the stage where his epitaph can be written.

I agree that we are not only dealing with what Connolly termed 'a combination of chemical elements' as some people were pleased to call Ireland. We are dealing with the life and blood of every Irish man, woman, and child in this island. And unless we can bring about a state of society in this island, irrespective of the religion or political adherence of those people, then certainly no one can be proud of the task which we have allegedly undertaken, but have completely failed to bring about; the task of uniting the people of Ireland.

If we were to accept this motion tonight we would not only be rejecting the views of Emmet, we would be giving him a kick in the teeth, because Emmet represented that vast body in Ireland, which held such an influence then and indeed, on the reverse side of the coin, wins such an influence now. He represented that body of Protestant Republicans, and he tried at that time to weld the forces of Irish nationalist and Protestant nationalism together, to ensure that the people of this island would have a say in the affairs of this island.

Even though 170 years after his death we find that the Protestant people in Northern Ireland have gone in the wrong direction I believe that he would be the last to say that we should give up hope. His own brother Thomas, when he appeared before a select Committee of the House of Lords, said, 'I declare to God: I think that if Ireland were separated from England, she would be the happiest spot on earth.' That may have been a completely legitimate thought at that time. Since then with the passage of time we find that it is perhaps not as relevant as it should have been.

Emmet, and those who followed him, left us a great tradition that this island must be in control of its own affairs. We in the island must set about creating a standard of living for all the people of this country. I would say that we have signally failed, because the United Nations, set up in 1949 took twenty years, until 1969, before the voice of the Republic of Ireland was heard speaking in that assembly in defence of the one and a half million people in the six counties of Northern Ireland. I don't believe that the fact that Ireland has a seat in the United Nations in any way contributes to stating that we are now in control of our own affairs. Because who would dare to disagree, to say that all those nations that are represented in the United Nations, whilst they may claim their own nationality, are in fact in the hands of the big blocs which control the United Nations, the East bloc and the West bloc? So the fact is that Ireland, this part of the island, has been doing deals behind the scenes with this delegation and that delegation and putting forward motions and making certain extensions on the motions, making certain there will be a lot of talk and there will be bloody little action in relation to what happens in Ireland. I believe that that is very insincere. *(applause)*

I have taken part in many debates in this part of the island, and I do not believe that, by taking part in a debate such as this, we can in any way contribute to the advancement of social progress and social justice in this island. I believe that this government and the people of this part of Ireland will have to involve themselves more and more and more in the affairs of Northern Ireland. That is the only way that communications can be brought about, that the Protestant fears can be erased. I agree with John that the fears of the Protestant population in Northern Ireland are very real. They believe that if the border were to be abolished that they would lose a lot of personal liberties. They believe that they would be dictated to by an arrogant Catholic Church. When someone living on the other side of the border condemns Ian Paisley and then the next morning we read in the *Irish Times* a pronouncement that has been made by Archbishop McQuaid, we don't have to wonder what motivates Paisley and his opposition towards the unification of this country. *(applause)*

Although our people are divided in the island of Ireland now, particularly in Northern Ireland, by the evil sectarian doctrines that have been pronounced and enunciated by the Unionist Party, I believe that the unification of this country will be brought about by social and economic development. It is quite easy to make an emotional speech on the questions of Ireland's past martyrs and what they did. But we are faced with a different problem today. It is only forty-five minutes from here to London. It is only six hours from here to the United States by aircraft. No country, and particularly Ireland, can afford to live in isolation or insulate itself against events which are taking place in other parts of the world. I do not believe that we can lay all the troubles that exist in Ireland at the moment, and here I agree with the last speaker, at the feet of Britain.

In recent years, particularly in recent months, the British government has taken a commendable stand in the field of implementing social justice in Northern Ireland. *(hear, hear! interjected from audience, applause)* But Sir, I believe that whilst we must set about ensuring that the fears of the Unionist majority in Northern Ireland are eradicated, we are unable to point out to them that in a united Ireland they would be in a very advantageous position. And I might say this to Mr Childers, I have absolutely no doubt in my mind that if the industrial workers in Northern Ireland, Protestant and Catholic, were to unite into a common political party in the event of the abolition of the border there would be a complete change of government here in this part of the island. *(cheers, applause)* We may, in fact, arrive at the stage where democracy would seem to be working. There are many people in the Northern Ireland area who believe that the Fianna Fáil party is the Siamese twin of the Unionist party. *(applause)* There are many people who felt that when Mr Lemass met Terence O'Neill, he was asking Terence O'Neill what he should do if he could succeed in abolishing proportional representation and could he give him a few tips on how to gerrymander the constituencies. *(laughter, applause)*

So, as I see it, I believe the proposal here tonight that Emmet's epitaph should be written is, in fact, an impertinence. I believe that if this meeting, this part of Ireland, were to decide that we wanted to write Emmet's epitaph, then we have the means at our disposal, in a very short time, to bring about such a situation, that we in the island of Ireland can unite to ensure that Emmet's epitaph will be written, and that when it is written, it will be written by the whole of the Irish nation. *(applause)*

BICENTENARY
PROGRAMME 1970

Declan Budd (centre) *with Col. Walsh and Michael Heney at the opening of the Bicentenary Exhibition by Charles Haughey, Minister for Finance, at the National Gallery on Monday 2 March 1970.*

Monday 2 March

8.00 p.m.　Opening of exhibition 'Art & Oratory' in the National Gallery, Merrion Square, by C. J. Haughey, T.D., Minister for Finance.

　　　　　　The exhibition brought together a wide range of paintings with an emphasis on portraiture from public and private collections. In the catalogue, the Director of the National Gallery wrote, 'It would not be an exaggeration to say that had it not been for the inspiration of the College Historical Society in its members, the course of Irish history would have been less exciting and less effective. Had it not been for the patronage of Edmund Burke the impulses and ideas of European culture on the eighteenth century would have taken longer to reach our shores. Indeed the whole course of nineteenth-century

"Romanticism" is indebted to Burke for his separation of the concept of the sublime and to James Barry who was the first amongst European painters to illustrate the isolation of the artist from the community. . . .

We hope that the exhibition will . . . serve to draw the attention of viewers to the importance of reassessing the value of those ideas and images which caught the imagination of Burke's Club and led to the debates on "Taste" and the relative importance of "Poetry" and "Painting". Naturally, Burke was for "Poetry" but Barry in his dissertations to the Royal Academy held that "Painting" was the real art of wisdom. Art and Oratory is the title which we have chosen for the exhibition because we feel that it epitomises the idea of the speaker as captured by the artist but even more because it revives these happy days when aesthetics were as highly valued as politics.'

James White

Tuesday 3 March

8.15 p.m.   Bicentenary Address by Senator Edward Kennedy in the Public Theatre.

Chairman: Dr F. H. Boland

Wednesday 4 March

8.15 p.m.   Discussion on the topic 'That the only liberty . . . is a liberty connected with order' in the Public Theatre.

Chairman: An Taoiseach, Jack Lynch, T.D.
Speakers: Senator Eugene J. McCarthy
            Andreas Papandreou
            James Dillon
            Conor Cruise O'Brien, T.D.
            Michael Foot, M.P.

Thursday 5 March

7.00 p.m.   Talk on 'Personalities in the Hist' by Professor
            R. B. McDowell in the Graduates Memorial Building.

8.15 p.m.   Bicentenary Dinner in the Dining Hall.
            The Bicentenary Dinner followed Dr R. B. McDowell's
            address on 'Personalities in the Hist'. The toasts were as
            follows:

Ireland
            Mr Justice T. C. Kingsmill Moore, Vice-President
The College Historical Society
            Senator Professor Mary Bourke
            Mr Justice T. C. Kingsmill Moore, Vice-President

Senator Professor Mary Bourke (now President Mary Robinson), who proposed the toast of the Society at the Bicentenary Dinner. She has since been elected a Vice-President of the Society. Photo courtesy of G. A. Duncan.

The Guests
Ian T. Ashe, Auditor
H.E. The British Ambassador Sir Andrew Gilchrist
The Toast to Dr McDowell Vice-President
Senator Owen Sheehy Skeffington, Vice-President
Professor David Greene, Vice-President

Following the toasts there was a musical entertainment of songs by former members of the Society sung by Tomás Ó Súilleabháin accompanied by his son Donncha Ó Súilleabháin on the College 1803 Broadwood Grand Piano. The songs were by Moore, Curran, Kells Ingram, Davis, Hyde and Graves.

Friday 6 March
8.15 p.m.   Debate on the motion 'That Emmet's Epitaph be now written', in the Public Theatre.

Chairman: Mr Justice T. C. Kingsmill Moore
Speakers: An Tánaiste, Erskine Childers, T.D.
Gerry Fitt, M.P.
John Hume, M.P.
Michael O'Kennedy, T.D.
Michael O'Leary, T.D.
Vincent Browne

Saturday 7 March
10.00 p.m.   Bicentenary Dance in the Dining Hall.

GENERAL COMMITTEE, SESSION 1969–70

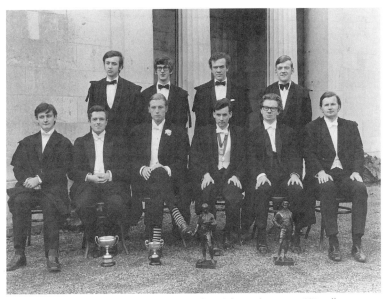

The Officers and Committee of the 200th Session; front left to right: *Fergus O'Ferrall, Jonathon Peel, Nicholas FitzGerald Browne, Ian Ashe, Richard Clarke, William Hamill,* back: *D. Edward I. Smyth, Derek J. Moran, M. D. Woodhouse, Patrick H. P. O'Sullivan. Donnell J. P. J. Deeny and Frank E. Bannister are not in the photograph.*

President	F. H. Boland
Auditor	I. T. Ashe
Treasurer	N. S. FitzG. Browne
Record Secretary	R. L. Clarke
Correspondence Secretary	J. H. M. Peel
Censor	W. J. Hamill
Librarian	R. F. B. O'Ferrall

D. F. Ford, ex-Auditor

D. E. I. Smyth	H. B. Woodhouse
D. J. Moran	P. H. P. O'Sullivan
D. J. P. Deeny	F. E. Bannister

BICENTENARY
SUB-COMMITTEE

K. F. G. Purcell, Chairman

D. N. O. Budd, Secretary

A. J. Craig, Treasurer

D. J. McConnell, Press Officer

F. G. O. Budd, Dinner

D. R. Hinds, Dinner

R. W. Kirkpatrick, Dance

R. R. Marriott, Exhibition

Members of the General Committee also served on the Bicentenary sub-Committee.

Another twenty-seven
years . . .

*In the life of the Hist twenty-seven years is a short time. This book was
originally planned to be published at the beginning of the twenty-seven years
between 1970 and 1997, not at the end. Having waited until now,
there was a need to add to the existing material. Most of the new material
concerns the period from 1970, but some was written by
Honorary Members of a more venerable vintage.*

MY TIME IN THE HIST — 2

A. NORMAN (DERRY) JEFFARES –
AUDITOR 1943–44, GOLD MEDALLIST

Tradition has its uses; that of the helpfulness of Honorary Members, for instance, which I first experienced as Librarian when Dr McDowell taught us how to write a report on the Library; or the traditions of polite, formal writing to be found in the files of previous Correspondence Secretaries; or the traditions of the Laws within which even such personal animosities as those of the late Professor David Greene and the late Prince Alexander Lieven could be contained, despite the former's unmerciful baiting of the Auditor in Private Business — Honorary Members could certainly liven things up. During my Auditorship, some of them generously decided that Auditors be given a year's membership of the University Club, a pleasant and useful privilege.

Preparations for my Opening Meeting became increasingly fraught when I couldn't get an answer from Lord Dunsany, asked to speak at it. Letters, even reply-paid telegrams, elicited only the repeated, cryptic response: 'In my opinion, when the ship goes down the anchor goes with it.' Finally, I included his name on the posters and sent him one. He arrived on the day. At a sherry party, he then terrorized the guests (a very tall man, he was known for his hunting of big game) by pointing fiercely at the standard College light fitting with a large stick, which he also aimed at anyone showing signs of speech or movement, while he denounced mass production. His speech in the Dining Hall began dramatically. Throwing aside the proffered microphone and looming over the audience below, he pointed to the distant doors. Everyone turned to look. 'The wolf', he proclaimed in stentorian tones, 'is always at the door!'

Afterwards at a party in the small hours, Osbert Lancaster (who'd made a superbly witty after-dinner speech) was given a bicycle to ride back to Terence de Vere White's house. 'What do I do with this?' he asked, climbing up one side and down the other. That morning, a damp foggy one, he had arrived in my rooms from the mailboat, speaking, I thought, hoarsely. Concerned for the evening's meeting as well as his health, I enquired whether he had a sore throat. 'No', he replied, 'I always speak like this.'

Daring — when only men attended meetings — was the presence of Kay Miles, a fellow student, disguised in a man's dinner jacket, this causing some eyebrow raising among those who knew of what was then regarded as a (successful) escapade.

Now we have women officers, one of whom tells me how much work the officers undertake, with 1700 members. In my day, there were, perhaps, two or three hundred. Then, administering the G.M.B. was an auditorial chore. When Alexander Lieven handed the books on to me the item Harpic[21] appeared frequently. Asked how we could possibly use so much, he — whose lack of numeracy was notorious (he risked losing his Scholarship by failing maths spectacularly and continuously in 'Little-go'; it was debated whether he finally scraped through by examiners' charity or

---

21   Editor's note: A well-known brand of lavatory cleanser.

friends' prayers) — simply said 'When it doesn't add up I add in Harpic; it's very easy to remember, it's two shillings a tin'.

I met my wife through the Hist, at an Inter-University Debate in Glasgow; she came to it from Edinburgh where I later attended the Speculative Society, making friends encountered subsequently when I became a lecturer at Edinburgh, and again after returning to the UK from Australia, where a great joy was frequently meeting James Auchmuty, ex-Auditor and Honorary Member, at meetings establishing the Australian Humanities Research Council. James became the first Vice-Chancellor of the University of Newcastle, N.S.W. He chaired the University's first public lecture which I gave; a knockout performance between Chairman and Lecturer, much cheerful badinage, and references to and explanations of the Hist given by James in expansive educational mood. He, too, had met his wife through debating — she was reputed to be one of the characters in Mary McCarthy's *The Group*, but he never told us which!

Long live debating in the traditions begun by Edmund Burke, and all the friendship it can create.

NEVILLE KEERY – SENIOR MEMBER OF COMMITTEE 1959–60, GOLD MEDALLIST

The text below is a chapter from a work-in-progress. It focuses on the year 1958 and the central character is called 'Ben Simms'.

While much of the formal and informal student life in the T.C.D. of the Fifties was modelled on Oxford and Cambridge, Trinity has never had a 'Union' as the one single source of undergraduate prestige for students with an interest in debating and politics. There was, and still is, the choice between the College Historical Society, claimed to be the world's oldest university debating society because of its foundation by Edmund Burke in 1747, and the

University Philosophical Society, a debating and paper reading society with little to do with philosophy. Both societies shared the central hall on the ground floor of the Graduates' Memorial Building off the 'Phil' Conversation Room. The Hist had its Conversation Room on the first floor. (Any reader who has seen Michael Caine and Julie Walters in the film *Educating Rita* will recognize the G.M.B. ground floor as providing the large room in which Rita meets her tutor.)

Ben chose to join the Hist, going to the Conversation Room every day to read the newspapers and looking in on the occasional Wednesday evening to watch the public debate and to learn about the Society's Private Business sessions which were restricted to members and followed the conclusion of the debate. The organization of the debates was very much on the lines of the Westminster House of Commons, with speakers addressing the audience from a ballot box at the head of a large table, across which Committee members, wearing gowns and dinner jackets with black ties, confronted each other. The Chairman for the debate faced the ballot box from across another table raised slightly higher by a low dais. There would be a different Chairman for each debate, normally an invited personality of some renown, and while he — the Hist was then a 'Gentlemen Only' society — would announce the name of the proposer and seconder and other speakers for and against the motion, the real responsibility for order lay with the Auditor, the chief officer of the Hist, elected annually with the other Officers and Committee, who always sat to the Chairman's left. By tradition, the Auditor and the other officers — a Treasurer, a Records Secretary, a Correspondence Secretary and a Librarian — all wore a white tie and tails under their undergraduate gowns.

While the public debates were often noisy and lively as the speakers contended with a degree of heckling from the floor of the House, Ben's interest usually focused on the quality and style of the concluding remarks on topics of political or intellectual interest by the invited Chairmen. When these Chairmen were drawn from College staff his favourite speakers were David Greene and Owen Sheehy Skeffington. Of outsiders he remembered best Noel Hartnett, a Senior Counsel at the Irish Bar. All three have been dead for many years and because of their strong personalities are not necessarily remembered with universal affection. David Greene was probably the most likeable. He was the affable Professor of Irish who was a big man with a bushy golden beard stained by his habitual snuff-taking. He had a great booming voice often breaking — justifiably— into chuckles at the wit and insight of what he had to say. Owen Sheehy Skeffington was the physical opposite of Greene, pale, thin, apparently fragile and looking as if sheltering behind his spectacles. In debate, however, he was terrifyingly tough and had a style of argument that could cut and wound effortlessly. He was a University Senator and spoke out fearlessly as a liberal and atheist on issues which were often taboo in a conservative and largely Catholic country. In attacking the Fianna Fáil party and its famous leader Éamon de Valera his tongue often assumed tones of detestation, which seemed to some to be too strong to be taken seriously. Even to Ben as a Freshman, Noel Hartnett's debating style, really a cross between that of Greene and Skeffington, often generated expressions that were extreme enough to vitiate his credibility. Nevertheless, when he was good, he was very very good. Ben loved the weight of voice and apparent sincerity of argument that would capture his audiences, pushing them from time to time into corners of quiet self-doubt before a carefully constructed rallying cry drew them applauding to accept or reject the motion before the House as he had advocated.

The Hist's Private Business meeting was entirely in the hands of the undergraduate members and successive generations sought to bring their own touches to the Laws of the Society. These Laws were a remarkable set of procedural standing orders governing membership and debate, defining the duties and responsibilities of the Officers and Committee, and regulating how motions should be proposed and seconded, with the mechanics of amendment and voting. There were also measures designed to provide disciplinary motions and to assess performance. These ranged from fines to the annual Officers' Conduct Report prepared by a Sub-Committee chaired by the Senior Member of Committee. In Private Business ballot papers were distributed in which members could mark the contributions of members who had spoken on the public debate order paper. At the end of each year Officers and orators would be rated and awarded honours ranging from the 'Marked Thanks of the Society' to Honorary Membership. Gold and silver medals for debate were obviously particularly valued and there was also a Maiden Speaker's prize to encourage participation.

That the Hist's structure worked was a tribute to the Officers, most of whom would have given a lot of time to the Society over two to three years. Honor courses in Trinity were of four years — Junior Freshman, Senior Freshman, Junior Sophister, Senior Sophister — with medicine taking several more years. Ben saw that a number of the Officers were College Scholars or well known in their faculties as among the best and the more interesting students. Scholars wore distinctive gowns and had 'Sch.' after their names on the order paper. His knowledge of College characters came from the weekly publications *T.C.D. Miscellany* and *Trinity News* which often looked at the undergraduate population with the eyes of a gossip columnist.

On the one hand Ben wanted to be noticed and felt he could make his mark as a debater, on the other hand he felt that many of the views that he held could easily appear naive, and he certainly seemed to have little experience to match that brought to the ballot box by many maiden speakers. He thought of the small dark quixotic figure who had so dramatically launched his contribution to the debate 'That this House accepts the nationalization of the Suez Canal' by the electrifying opening, 'As I waded up the beach with my men under the smoke of Port Said . . .'

Of course the hall clapped and applauded. Here was a second year student who, because he had been in the Officer Training Corps of his public school, was a Commissioned Officer during his National Service and had led men ashore in the world's most recent classic water-borne invasion. When he met Peter Hinchcliffe subsequently he was surprised to find that he seemed to take his golf handicap much more seriously than his national service exploits or anything likely to be ahead of him in his College or professional career.

Ben took the plunge, making his maiden speech well down the order paper on the relatively non-controversial topic 'That Religion is for the Dreamer'. He began to look forward to Wednesday evenings. Instead of going home for tea, he would stay in College and go on Commons, that is to say the formal College dinner in the Dining Hall, where grace was said in Latin before and after meals and everyone wore gowns and the staff paraded from the adjoining Common Room to the High Table. The chat on Commons was often excellent and the long tables created opportunities to meet a lot of people, particularly students from other faculties living in rooms on the campus. After Commons he would sit through a debate and then in private business try his hand at raising 'Points of Order' and 'Points of Fact'. Like many Hist men before and since he would find this experience of formality and procedure invaluable in subsequent professional and organizational contexts. He learnt the importance of a well-written minute and saw how touches of wit could readily extract the sting from rivalries that might easily have developed into enmities.

STEVEN HARRIS — VICE-PRESIDENT FROM 1971

I arrived at College in October 1964 with my head full of romantic and no doubt erroneous notions of undergraduate life. The range of activities on offer to a Freshman was bewildering, from organ visiting (music not pathology) to jazz, from rowing to rock climbing, but I was drawn like a magnet to the Hist.

The Hist was always more than a debating society. It was a place where people from widely different backgrounds and divergent opinions met on common ground. Each man was accepted for himself and his opinions were listened to. There were Republicans and Loyalists; Catholics, Protestants, Atheists and Agnostics; Socialists and Conservatives; Politicians and Philosophers, Chemists and Classicists, Linguists and Lawyers, the hirsute, the smooth and the downright frivolous. All views could be expressed; if the views were passionately espoused and vigorously spoken, the manner of their expression was always such that those on either side of an argument could enjoy a drink together at the end of an evening. No consistency of viewpoint was expected; one could argue one thing one week, and its opposite the next. No one was there to advance their careers; it was all for the fun of it.

The Hist not only made connections between 'The Two Cultures' but was a bridge between students and their teachers, fostering the idea of the College as a community and not just a place where people came to teach and be taught. Honorary Members were often present, and not only at Honorary Members' debates, which gave us a sense that the Hist was bigger than ourselves, that we were only its present custodians with a duty both to the past and to the future.

This feeling of custodianship made me a doubter about the admission of women, at least at first. When a society is two hundred years old it can inhibit radical and irrevocable change. I also thought it was a decision to be taken by the Hist itself, not brought about by external pressure. In fact I was standing at the ballot box when visible, audible and tangible external pressure arrived in the shape of latter day suffragettes. My speech was soon lost in the commotion as the large doors from the Phil Conversation Room were burst open with noise and shouting from the women pressing their case for admission, from their supporters in the House and ripostes from indignant members. There was a bunch of Boat Club and Rugby Club heavies present; they tended to robust views and unsentimental attitudes and soon bundled out the unauthorised visitors and I carried on from where I left off. The distinguished guest that evening was Patrick Gordon-Walker, former UK Foreign Secretary; I was told he was impressed by my 'coolness under fire', but really, if you are in the middle of a speech and you are interrupted, there is not much you can do except wait until you can be heard again.

There used to be debates about every two years proposing the admission of women to the Hist, and later I came to the view that they should be admitted; perhaps I was less in awe of the burden of custodianship. Nevertheless the motions were defeated, largely by packing the house with backwoodsmen, people who used the Conversation Room but never or rarely attended the debates.

There was an important but little regarded section of the membership — the people who turned up to listen to the debates but never spoke. We, of the loquacious persuasion, value the sound of our own voices, but if there had been no one to listen we would have been rather pathetic. One faithful attender always came wearing his bicycle clips, presumably to make a quick getaway. I hope they got good entertainment, and there was certainly no discouragement to them from taking part. As a Freshman I was impressed by those magnificent Officers in tail coats and white bow ties, but I had nothing from anyone but encouragement to stand up and speak.

My maiden speech was on a motion to do with South Africa and apartheid. It was something I had views on but on which I knew no more than anyone else who could read newspapers. Looking back, I cannot imagine why I thought anyone might want to hear my views on the subject, but I soon realized that other speakers did not know much about what they were talking about. This phenomenon was codified by Gully Stanford as 'The Doctrine of Superior Ignorance'; put simply it means that once you see that no one knows much about a topic, you immediately become an expert in it. It is the creed of phoneys everywhere; it is a good skill to have, and it is useful to be able to spot it in others.

Of course there were speakers at debates who were knowledgeable, those who were passionate, those who were analytical and good at taking other people's arguments apart and those who were funny. I got a reputation for making funny speeches; the trouble was that when I tried to speak seriously people would either laugh in the wrong places or, finding nothing to laugh at, they thought my speech a failure. Making humorous speeches came about by accident; during my maiden speech I said something I thought was serious, paused for effect, and the house dissolved in laughter. I had no idea why people were laughing, and my bewildered innocence seemed to increase the jollity. From then on jollity took the upper hand; the joke had to be explained to me afterwards, but I didn't think it was funny. I had apparently unknowingly delivered a *double entendre* in dubious taste, and my skilful 'show' of innocence had successfully carried off the 'joke'.

After my maiden speech Jeremy Lucas came up to me to congratulate me on my speech, and said, 'You went to Harrow.' (Harrow is an English public school which had pretensions which I did not want to be associated with.) I confessed unwillingly that I had been there, and wondered how he knew. 'Well,' he said, 'You either went to Eton or Harrow and I went to Eton and you weren't there.' This was an uncomfortable truth; but I did not want to spend four years in Ireland as if Irish independence had never happened. The challenge for me was to experience being in Ireland rather than being in exile, without pretending to be something I was not. This was an entirely personal feeling, but being in the Hist helped me get to know Ireland and no one in the Hist ever suggested that there was anything reprehensible in being English, even though Ireland had struggled for so many years to be rid of England rule. There were a lot of Englishmen active in the Hist and they made, I think, a valuable contribution both to the Hist and to T.C.D. at large; two of the four Auditors in my years were English (Michael Cameron and Brian Williamson).

In my third year I was chosen to partner Brian Williamson, then Auditor, to represent the Hist in the *Irish Times* debating competition. The Hist had done very well in debating competitions in the two previous years, during which David McConnell and Cian Ó hÉigeartaigh had twice won the *Irish Times* trophy and once the *Observer* Mace as the best team in the British Isles. Brian and I had a hard act to follow, and came second in the *Irish Times* final. The topic for debate in the final was about the extent of involvement in the Common Market, and thirty years later the topic of the hour still concerns involvement in Europe. During my speech I was challenged by a question about reserve currencies and convertible currencies. I knew nothing about it. Brian Williamson is an economist and I saw his head go down; he knew how little I understood the question. However, I made a fluent and emphatic denial of the existence of Central Bank plans, which neither I nor the questioner could have known anything about, and Superior Ignorance carried the day.

Later Brian Williamson and I went to Glasgow to compete in the Scots-Irish Debate final. I remember nothing about the topic for debate, except that no one was interested in it. Brian was the best of the first round of speakers. The other contestants guessed that if I could make a half-way decent speech we would win, so they set out to spoil my efforts under a barrage of points of fact and order. I refused points of fact; I refused points of order until the Chairman pointed out that it was his prerogative. Each time I was interrupted I repeated the sentence I had last said, and such was the level of interruption that I said it several times. It seemed they could get on without me, so I turned my back, saw a piano nearby and went over to play it. I saw Brian's head go down once more. However, when I could get a word in edgeways, I repeated the same sentence again, and after that we were home. Brian's speech and my coolness under fire won the Scots-Irish debating trophy; I was grateful for the interruptions, because the speech I had prepared was not up to much anyway.

Despite the Hist's success in competitive debating it was just something we did for fun. It was not debating competitions nor the public debates, but the Private Business meetings which were the heart of the Hist, where ordinary members would harry the Officers, holding them to account, interpreting the Laws of the Society and generally trying to get them to trip up, and achieve the holy grail of midnight, and would then adjourn for refreshment and further discussion in the then TV Room at the top of the G.M.B., and after that in someone's rooms. The fact that women could not be in College after midnight, and could not have taken part in such late meetings was argued by some to be a bar to their admission.

Under the auditorship of Michael Cameron, playing the parliamentary game was sought to be extended to include 'Cabinet responsibility'. Brian Williamson, then Correspondence Secretary, wrote an article in *Trinity News* on matters concerning the Hist, without the permission of the Auditor and Committee. Michael Cameron wanted the Committee to censure Brian. Some people took it very seriously. There were two questions before the Committee, though it needed Occam's razor to distinguish between them. On the first question we went down the table and everyone had their twopenn'orth as to whether B. Williamson had been a naughty boy; by the time the Auditor came to me, at the bottom of the table, I had had enough, so I said that my view could be summed up in two words: 'Bull shit'. I rather hoped this would help abbreviate proceedings, but no. We went on to the second question, barely distinguishable from the first, and round we went again. By the time my turn came round the second time I was suffering serious discomfort in the gluteus maximus. All I could add was that it was not only bullshit, but horse piss as well. As I recall it, this helped move matters along. I hope I did my bit for irreverence and free speech.

At the end of my second year I stood for Auditor against Brian Williamson. William Young was another candidate. I don't think that either William or I were remotely plausible candidates, and I certainly did not want the job. However, everyone took it for granted that Brian would be elected, and I thought he should not be returned unopposed. The society took the right decision and elected Brian. In the following year everyone assumed I would be standing for the auditorship, the other likely candidate being Gully Stanford. I no more wanted to be Auditor then than in the previous year, but I had become, at least in some people's eyes, a plausible candidate. Because of the rule which forbids candidates for office to canvass for votes, expectations of my candidature were only increased by my denying such intentions. The best way to kill the speculation was for me to stand up in a private business meeting, announce my intention of standing, and ask for members' votes, thereby disqualifying myself from office. That is what I did.

Shortly after the Bicentenary celebrations, I got a letter from the Record Secretary telling me I had been elected a Vice-President of the Society. The Hist can never have elected a less distinguished Vice-President, but as the reported circumstances of my election were entirely in the spirit of the Hist, I was and am happy to accept the honour. The Auditor and Committee had proposed some no doubt well qualified person for election as Vice-President. The ordinary members, led by Shane Ross, wanted to oppose the Auditor and Committee, and cast around for a suitable candidate. I was not eligible for Honorary Membership, never having held office or received a gold medal, but I was eligible to be elected Vice-President, as there are no qualifications required for the office. I was not eligible for a medal in oratory because I had asked for one of my speeches to be unmarked (although the laws provided for it I had never seen anyone exercise the right) and I had not made enough marked speeches. Whether I would have got a medal anyway is open to speculation, but I wanted a speech unmarked. On this occasion the floor triumphed over the Auditor and Committee, and I am happy to have been chosen Vice-President by the votes of the irreverent.

DAVID FORD – AUDITOR 1968–69, GOLD MEDALLIST

Dramatic conflict was obviously in store for whoever was elected Auditor of the Hist for its 199th session in 1968–69. Student life around the western world was in turmoil, and Trinity was to join in, with a Maoist demonstration against the visit of the King and Queen of the Belgians that led to confrontations with police. In addition, the Civil Rights Movement was beginning in Northern Ireland, and Trinity was perhaps the only place where Northern Protestants and Catholics mixed with each other and also with students from the Republic and from England. And the Hist itself had its burning 'civil rights' issue: should women be admitted to the Society?

The admission of women to the Society had been debated for years and always defeated. My position was that they should certainly be admitted, but by constitutional means. This put me in between two extremes: the opponents of admission, and those who wanted to use unconstitutional means such as were being used by students around the world and by the Civil Rights Movement in Northern Ireland. All three positions were represented among those elected as my Officers and Committee members. As I sat through unruly Committee meetings I reflected on the impossibility of being expected to be a sort of Prime Minister but having no say about who my cabinet members were.

The climax of the campaign of interrupting meetings by supporters of the admission of women came when Conor Cruise O'Brien chaired a major Inter-University Debate, with participants from Irish, Scottish and English Universities. His daughter, Kate, had planned (with active support from within my Committee) a demonstration. She and some other women had come into the meeting in disguise. They jumped up, the meeting dissolved into chaos and her father supported her. Next day, on the front page of the *Irish Times*, there was a graphic picture of me facing Conor Cruise O'Brien as I attempted to restore order. My Censor, Joe Revington, was especially vocal in support of the interruption. I decided, with others, that drastic action was needed. I remember being especially grateful for the support of Senator Owen Sheehy Skeffington at the time — he was completely in favour of the admission of women but also passionately constitutional, and was very critical of the role of his cousin Conor Cruise O'Brien. What brought matters to a head was activating a rule that had never, so far as I could discover, been used before. It allowed the Committee to expel a member of the Society. The Committee voted by the narrowest of margins to expel the Censor. Then, predictably, I was impeached. Half my Committee also resigned. Shane Ross stayed!

The impeachment debate began around 8.00 p.m. Members were being dragged out of libraries and pubs by supporters of both sides. The intense debate went on till well after midnight. Then came the vote. The tellers announced: 131 votes in favour of impeachment, 132 against. Before a recount could be called I adjourned the meeting.

Then came the strangest part: after this extreme of antagonism and excitement, I was amazed at how peaceful things became. New Officers and Committee Members were elected. There was an orderly debate on the admission of women, and the whole admission process went through without more disruption. The first debate with women present was televised. And Marion O'Leary, who won the Maiden Speaker's Prize, came to the Honorary Members dinner, met the former Auditor Mike Cameron (who had written to me threatening to resign over the expulsion of the Censor) and now they are married.

IAN ASHE – AUDITOR 1969–70, GOLD MEDALLIST

When Hist 97 attracts America's Oliver North and France's Valery Giscard d'Estaing to events, it reminds me of Lord Hailsham's 1970 letter to the Hist observing that we had a 'good bag' of guests for the Bicentenary celebrations. Lord Hailsham, an Oxford Union President in 1929, recognized the primary obligation of a modern debating society — aim for the legendary personalities, within the society and without.

Whether it be Wolfe Tone, Winston Churchill, Andreas Papandreou or President Mary Robinson, debating societies depend on each personality as a beacon to attract the next speaker, hopefully a speaker who has also become a legend.

The essence of the Hist tradition lies in a formidable past and living membership. Who can ignore easily the names of Wolfe Tone, Bram Stoker, Robert Emmet, Thomas Davis, Edward Carson, Douglas Hyde, Diarmuid Coffey, Conor Cruise O'Brien, Frederick Boland, Thomas Moore, Mary Harney, Dick Spring, and Cian Ó hÉigeartaigh?

Diarmuid Coffey was a staff member of the Irish Volunteers in 1914 when it took cold courage and conviction to be a member. Patrick Pearse (never a member of the Hist nor a student of T.C.D.) in 1896 joined Douglas Hyde's Gaelic League and was heavily influenced by the separatist writings of Wolfe Tone and Thomas Davis. Pearse also enthused to his St Enda's students about Robert Emmet and the 'heroes of the last stand'. The links of the Hist with Irish independence are substantial and historical.

Added to these dominant and influential personalities in our membership came the controversy or fame of some guest speakers: Éamon de Valera, Winston Churchill, Eugene McCarthy, Andreas Papandreou, Alec Douglas-Home, Charles Haughey, Jack Lynch, Mary Robinson, Jan Masaryk, Patrick Mayhew, Oliver North, John Hume, Gerry Fitt, John Taylor, Lord Hailsham, Erskine Childers, and James Dillon.

For controversy, there was the epic moment when Rosaleen Mills in January 1969 became the first woman to address the Society, on the motion 'That this House reveres the memory of Mrs Pankhurst'. The Chair for that evening was Sheelagh Murnaghan, then Liberal M.P. in Stormont, and the Hist Debating Chamber was packed solid with men and women for the first time.

For drama, a highlight was the 1968 motion 'That Merger means Murder', when the dynamic Donogh O'Malley, Minister for Education, listened in silence to crowded student denunciation of his proposal to merge Trinity College and University College, Dublin.

The following vignettes encompass the alchemy of tradition, history and humour from the Bicentenary Week of 1970:

James Dillon exclaims aloud 'God Bless America' to silence his first heckler in the International Discussion.

Senator Eugene McCarthy, Andreas Papandreou, Michael Foot and Jack Lynch attend Commons together.

During the Bicentenary Address, Senator Edward Kennedy bids a heckler farewell with the words, 'There goes another great debater.'

Jack Lynch, Taoiseach, chairs the Hist International Discussion. Charles Haughey, Minister for Finance, opens the Hist Exhibition, *Art and Oratory*, at the National Gallery. Shortly after the Bicentenary Week both leaders conflict furiously in the continuum of Irish history.

Senator Mary Bourke (many years later to be elected President Robinson of Ireland) is the only woman to address the Hist at the celebrations, when she proposes the toast of the College Historical Society at the Bicentenary Dinner. This event was held in candlelight due to scarce electricity. Airs and songs are played on the College 1803 Broadwood Grand Piano.

Alec Reid, adjudicator at the Bicentenary Medal Debate for student debaters, invites his colleague judges to deliver the verdict from the balcony in the G.M.B. Unknown to him, the balcony could only bear the weight of two persons. The judges survived. Cambridge won.

Captain Yeoman Campbell, then eighty-one, was the oldest living member of the Hist at the 1970 celebrations. He deplored the students that do not fold the newspapers after use in the Conversation Room.

Tom Weldon, a former Garda Sergeant at Dáil Éireann, was a good friend of the Hist who had served the G.M.B. for eleven years. He was recalled from retirement to introduce Dr Frederick Boland at Senator Kennedy's Address. Tom provided his usual vigorous voice to the notice, 'Ladies and Gentlemen, your Chairman.'

In conclusion, these vignettes are what Lord Hailsham would describe as a 'good bag'. Personalities propel the Hist into the next century. Edmund Burke, our leading personality, commenced that road, which in 2000 will have travelled in four separate centuries of debate, a remarkable achievement by dedicated members and guest speakers, mandated to challenge the controversial issues of the day.

JAMES CONNOLLY – AUDITOR 1973–74, SILVER MEDALLIST

My involvement in the Hist was during the years immediately after the fervour of Bicentenary celebrations. Public meetings were well attended and the Society enjoyed unprecedented prestige both inside and outside the University. At that time continuous assessment and exam pressures were not comparable to those today and most students at some stage indulged themselves with attendance at, and involvement in, the College debates.

Changes were beginning to emerge; most university students in the early 1970s came from and lived in Dublin. Many 'politically aware' orators were devoting their energies to the now burgeoning S.R.C. rather than the Hist.

The 1974 Inaugural Meeting turned into a riot after a group of Internationalists and Marxist-Leninists locked themselves into the Exam Hall. They objected to 'free speech' being afforded to persons whom they identified as 'fascists' — such as the then Minister for Justice who was on the speaking platform for that evening's debate. Gardaí were called into College to dispel the protesters and restore order and to allow 'free speech' to be uttered in the Dining Hall before a greatly reduced audience. This was a long way from the 'ivory tower' image of the Hist of previous sessions.

By way of contrast, there was a lighthearted rivalry between the Hist and their rival Society, the Phil, whose meetings were more concerned with cultural than relevant issues. A cadre of Phil regulars master-minded a hoax at the expense of a Hist Intervarsity Debate. The debate was to be chaired by a supposedly notorious revolutionary of messianic reputation in Ghana, but exiled in London. The person who turned up, however, to take the Chair was in fact a Phil plant. The practical joke worked until near the end of the meeting when two robust officers of the Hist (having tumbled to the plot) were seen forcefully to remove the said personage from the Chair and throw him out of the meeting (another martyr for 'free speech').

Although primarily a debating society, the Hist provided through its billiard and study rooms and newspaper reading rooms a focal point where many College students relaxed in between lectures and tutorials. The survival and continuing prestige of the Hist is a tribute to all the hard work and loyalty of the Officers and Committee of successive generations. One of the continuing successes of the Hist from this time is the setting up in 1973 of the Edmund Burke Schools Debating Competition with a format very similar to university debating competitions. It would be remiss in any celebration of Edmund Burke not to recognize the value of the fostering by the Hist of this All-Ireland debating competition in ensuring a continuity of debating societies and standards for the future.

MICHAEL HANNA – AUDITOR 1975–76

To begin with, I should endeavour to put my year as Auditor in an historical context. Looking at it in reverse, I was succeeded as Auditor by my Treasurer, Mary Harney, who became the first female Auditor of the Society. Thus, I suppose the best I can do is identify myself as the last in a long distinguished and uninterrupted line of male Auditors. That is not much of a footnote for history. Still, history might be kind enough to regard me as the Hist equivalent of de Klerk[22].

One of the many advantages of active involvement in this Society at Officer level is the unending opportunities presented for meeting and getting to know persons ranging from the deeply fascinating to the utterly daft. Further, one takes one's first faltering steps towards the appreciation and application of one of life's essential skills, if not art forms — crisis management. What at the time might seem to be harrowing experiences take on a different and a more pleasant hue on recollection.

My first ordinary meeting as Auditor was the perennial law and order debate. A distinguished British Judge had agreed to address the Society, and the Correspondence Secretary at the time, David Alexander, went to the airport to meet him. I was deputed to meet the Chairman, then a distinguished member of the Bar, at the University Club. While waiting in the lobby of the club, I was approached by a person clearly speechless with drink. I could not understand a blessed word the man was saying. However, annoyance grew near to panic as, chiefly by gesture, this gentleman indicated the similarity of our ties. We were both wearing Hist ties and I was standing opposite our regrettably incoherent Chairman for the night. Remarkably, we got though the meeting — how I will never know. Indeed, a speech by a then (and since) eminent feminist/journalist stimulated a reaction of splenic conservatism peppered with unrepeatable

---

[22]   President of South Africa before Nelson Mandela.

expletives, sexual and otherwise, all uttered in an attempted 'piano' but issuing forth in a ribald 'fortissimo'. The night rounded off with a magnificent recovery by the Chairman, who delivered a splendid oration to the rapturous applause of those who stayed to see could he manage it and the unimaginable relief of your writer. The Chairman has long gone to a well-deserved rest in the ultimate Court of Appeal after a lifetime of unstinting and brilliant service to the law.

The law, too, featured when a special meeting of the Society was summoned as a mark of respect on the death of the late Mr Justice Gardner Budd, Vice-President and Honorary Member of the Society. A hushed and reverential assembly attended by the late Vice-President's son, Declan, now himself a Judge of the High Court, was called to order and the Record Secretary, George Birmingham, was asked to read the minutes of the last meeting. It was with growing horror that, too late, he and I remembered that the previous debate had been an Inter-Varsity affair with a ludicrous motion and suitably inane speeches. Alas, George had not stinted himself in his reporting of the events. Rather than treating the minutes as being read, he proceeded to deliver them in sepulchral and heart rending tones in an effort to lend them some dignity. This only made matters worse.

Fortunately, the meeting was carried off, and no one had to be carried out.

As in every year, various theme debates took place. The customary Arab-Israeli debate was its usual near-riotous success. The gay rights debate nearly exploded when I gently suggested to Noel Browne that he should draw his remarks to a close. I am grateful to the then Chairman, David Norris, for doing just about enough to ensure that I lived to pen these few words.

And, of course, inevitably the 'Crowd from the Students' Union' (or 'yips' as we used to call them) decided to get involved in the Society's business. The poor things! They could never understand our ways! I remember one such, an attractive girl by the name of Phil Connolly, making her maiden speech at the ballot box. Clearly having had enough, she proclaimed to the entire assembly, wide eyed with raging contempt, and to much applause, that the entire debate was a farce. Notwithstanding this outrageous affront to the Society and to the manner in which I was conducting the meeting, I followed tradition by writing to congratulate her on her maiden speech and to ask her to consider running for the Committee. As good fortune would have it, she showed it to me again in the recent past. Sixteen years of being married to me has not caused her to alter her view of that night!

GEORGE BIRMINGHAM – RECORD SECRETARY 1975–76, SILVER MEDALLIST

I joined the Hist on the first day of Freshers' Week. It was an obvious decision to make because the then Auditor, Declan Kiberd, had attended the same secondary school as I had and to some extent I had been something of a protégé of his, sharing an interest in debating and related activities. However, he must have been somewhat dubious about the merits of my arrival, when at the first Private Business of the session the dreaded Privileged Motion No. 1, seeking that the House do adjourn to consider his conduct was tabled by John Stephenson and I voted in favour, knowing nothing about the issues, but on the simple basis that it was late at night and the idea of an adjournment seemed like a good idea. I did not realize that the somewhat archaic language of Privileged Motion No. 1 concealed an impeachment motion. In fact my memory is that the Motion was carried, but it seemed in some fashion or another to have been declared null and void, and Declan served on with distinction.

The outstanding orator of the Hist, in the mid-70s, was David O'Sullivan, who subsequently came to prominence as a member of Peter Sutherland's cabinet. David was always forceful and often inspirational. I recall vividly a debate on the motion 'That an Independent, Secular, Palestinian State, in place of Israel, is the solution to the Middle East problem'. The debate was noteworthy in that not only had it attracted a sizeable student audience but also a very large degree of interest among the

Jewish community in Dublin, who attended in numbers and contributed to a highly-charged and emotional atmosphere. David's speech, while carefully balanced, was certainly not what the members of the friends of Israel had come to hear, but nonetheless, such was the force of his advocacy that it demanded their attention and was ultimately rewarded with a standing ovation.

A very different speaker, but often as effective, was Una Keating. She was a formidable force, particularly in the impromptu debate, when the motion before the house was a humorous one. Her heckles were feared by the pompous and the long-winded. I recall going with Una to attend an inter-society debate at the Cadet College in the Curragh. This debate coincided with a particularly tense time in recent Irish history, in that just days earlier, Seán Mac Stiofáin, then Chief of Staff of the I.R.A., had been convicted before the Special Criminal Court on a charge of membership and promptly resolved to engage in a hunger and thirst strike. At this stage, I do not remember what the motion was, but I do recall that, for whatever reason, one of the Cadet speakers found it necessary to observe that no one in Ireland was going hungry these days. It was an opening that Una could not resist and she did not. Given that Mac Stiofáin was actually on hunger strike in the Curragh Camp at the time, nobody was quite sure how to react and there was a degree of discomfort and shuffling of chairs on the part of the Senior Army Officers who were attending as observers. Una was not discommoded in the least.

For my own part I often found the politicking associated with the Hist and with the end of session elections, as absorbing as the debates themselves. It remains a source of some bemusement that a society, the constitution of which prohibited canvassing for elections, could absorb the attentions of so many politicos. The political skills formed in the Hist served a number of Hist debaters well in later years with a number of people going on either to seek and hold elective office or to gain prominence at national executive level or backroom adviser level in one or other of the political parties. I recall particularly the formidable campaign mounted for the Auditorship by Michael Hanna, and the following year by Mary Harney. These campaigns were directed by Gerry Murray, Librarian of the Society in the 1975–76 session, who was a truly formidable political operator. Gerry did not have to be told that the campaign did not begin on nomination night. His campaign on behalf of his favourite candidates began in Freshers' Week, as he made sure that potential voters were signed up as Hist members, and then continued throughout the year, as he made sure that his prospective voters attended the required number of meetings so as to qualify for the electoral register. Subsequently, I understand, his skills have been put at the service of the S.D.L.P. in his native Derry.

MARY HARNEY – AUDITOR 1976–77, SILVER MEDALLIST

I grew up in Newcastle, a farming community on the western fringes of County Dublin. Trips into town allowed me to form my first impressions of T.C.D., dominated by its impressive main façade. Here, the leading statesmen amongst its graduates, Henry Grattan and Edmund Burke, orate perpetually at each other across the narrowest part of College Green, while Oliver Goldsmith records it all rather cynically.

So it was not unnatural that, when I went to Trinity as a Fresher in 1972, I associated the place with politics, with debate, with literature and talk of every sort. Although my studies were in the so-called 'dismal science' of economics, my interests were political and, I suppose, disputatious. I was involved in the Hist almost from the beginning of my College career.

To the outsider, which was what I very much was, the feature of Trinity which strikes you immediately is its immense solidity in its historical setting. The Hist epitomized this for me, with its foundation by Edmund Burke in 1747 one year after the birth of his lapidary companion, Henry Grattan. Though its annals are replete with the props of Irish establishment over 250 years, the nationalist tradition is also well represented in its various guises by Emmet, Tone, Butt and more recent figures.

I was inherently involved in the Hist and its affairs throughout my

College career between 1973 and 1977. The variety of people, the eloquence and occasional passion of debate and, of course, the labyrinthine internal politics were very congenial to me. I was put on the Committee during my first year and remained there in various capacities until I became Auditor in 1977.

I was, as it happens, the Society's first woman Auditor in its history. I like to think of this as my first, but by no means last, exercise in mould-breaking. At the time (and still for all I know), it was customary for the Auditor of the Hist to be elected to membership of one of the clubs in St Stephen's Green. This perk was not accorded to me; with casuistry which would not disgrace a Jesuit, it was explained that the failure to elect me was not because I was a woman, but because I was not a man! That mould, too, has since been broken.

As you might expect, my term as Auditor, the guests I invited, and the whole tone of the Society, were of a political variety. I brought to debates my friend and mentor Jack Lynch, John Hume, and British Liberal Leader Jo Grimond, amongst others. I had, I think, no great difficulty in controlling the 'House', having watched my predecessors over the preceding three years. When I left the Hist, I felt it had equipped me well for a career in public life, on which I had already embarked.

Debate itself, has changed considerably over the past twenty years, mostly for the better. The level of sponsorship, the participation in transatlantic competitions and the funding available for foreign guests now greatly exceed anything available in the mid-seventies. But the atmosphere and spirit I see in my visits now are very reminiscent of the Society in my time and, no doubt, of the decades and centuries before.

PETER CHARLETON – AUDITOR 1977–78

The picture published in the *Irish Times* the next morning said it all. The Soviet Ambassador ascended the steps of the G.M.B. accompanied by Hist Officers while a flour bomb exploding about his head surreally transported the atmosphere of the annual British Inter-Varsities Debate into the realm of ideological strife and open warfare. Carl Jung has a theory about synchronicity. Similar things happen in similar but unconnected circumstances. It was always the case that something bizarre happened at this particular annual fixture. Maybe that was the reason why, in the final analysis, it was dropped. Could we take any more events like the Chairman from Africa who came from downstairs, but who managed to pass himself off with the liberal application of boot polish (an event I did not witness), the President of the 'other society' speechifying from the balcony and so outside of our jurisdiction, but within our earshot, and the Hitler-like interruptions of a since legendary Dublin figure twice physically ejected from the chamber, but still able to power his way back in with, dare I say, 'the strength of the mad' (something to which I can personally testify).

International events can influence the proceedings of obscure foreign debating societies. At this time, in 1977, China and the Soviet Union were having quite serious disputes as to the parameters of their borders. These disputes would not have arisen but for the clash of ideology. The Chinese had gone their own way, leaving behind the works of Lenin and adopting the beautiful, but perverted language of Mao Zedong as their sacred writ. I was soon to hear all about a notion with which, up to then, I was not even vaguely familiar.

A large black car carrying the Soviet Ambassador rolled up to the steps of the Graduates' Memorial Building. Assembled to meet him were the entire Committee and the representatives, two each, from five British university debating societies. A group of straggly students, numbering no more than about twenty, swiftly moved from their place of assembly at the corner of the building to the corner of his car. 'Down with the Soviet Social Imperialism', they chanted, prompting smiles and snorts of derision from our British friends. They swiftly retreated when eggs and flour bombs hit them in the face or bespattered their pristine tuxedos. His Excellency was swiftly ushered upstairs and the doors of the G.M.B. shut. A selected and carefully monitored audience was allowed into the chamber. The Ambassador took the chair.

Five minutes elapsed of quite turgid debate and then three further anorak-uniformed scruffies stood up and yelled, 'Down with Soviet Social Imperialism', aiming three eggs at the Soviet personage. One hit him full in the chest. The offenders were manfully ejected. The debate proceeded somewhat nervously on the motion 'That Men should be reared to be husbands and fathers'. This daft proposition, thought up by yours truly, was supposed to allow our British friends an opportunity to show off their sparkling wit as well as their oratorical powers. A prize of some bottles of good wine awaited the winning team. No one was either very witty or very erudite. It was one of those motions that fell flat on its face by being far too clever. The atmosphere of sterile debate was much improved by the yells coming from outside the building. The ideologues were having difficulties with their sloganising. One person would think of a suitable chant and the others would join in: 'Support the Chinese people's struggle for liberation'; 'Boycott Russian Imperialist products'. Inevitably it would return however to 'Smash/struggle against/down with Soviet Social Imperialism'.

At the end of the debate the Chairman, who had now vacated the chair, rose to speak. He had not seen the joke either, and proceeded to deliver a lengthy and somewhat leaden exegesis on how the Soviet system prepared men for fatherhood and the sociological imperatives of the creation of structures whereby New Men (in the 1920s Soviet meaning) could thrive.

At the adjournment we all engaged in polite chit-chat with the Ambassador and his secretary about 'how terrible it was that people could behave in this way'. With these sentiments His Excellency heartily agreed. I felt it my duty to go downstairs and commiserate with his chauffeur about the terrible reception which the Ambassador had received. The chauffeur could speak no English and I could speak no Russian. We were left grinning at one another and I retreated red-faced. The Ambassador was whisked away and our British guests retreated to their quarters.

That was the last British Inter-Varsities Debate held, at least during my time in College. I often wonder what the unfortunate English and Scots felt about the crazy country and the mad events it seemed to generate. Well, the worst sin is to be boring and at least we had been saved from what otherwise would have been a stultifying evening.

JOSEPH JACKSON – AUDITOR 1978–79, SILVER MEDALLIST

There is a wonderful continuity about the Hist; every year the Society is visited by the moth-eaten clothes of History dons — more often than not with the learned ones inside them. Ambassadors come and go and Inaugurals are held. At my Inaugural, Dublin's rotund Lord Mayor belched at an early stage in the proceedings and departed. After all one of the guests was Dr Garret Fitzgerald, whose contribution was bound to be thought provoking, and Dublin's first citizen was determined that the night should bring provocation of his pancreas and gastric juices but certainly not his cerebral faculties.

Nevertheless unusual things do happen and in my case it arose in the unlikely circumstance of an election to Honorary membership of an ex-Librarian. I read, with some amazement, that the candidate had been proposed twice before and had failed. An ex-Officer of the Hist failing to gain Honorary membership — it could happen to me! Thus motivated I made enquiry about his double rejection. Had he been caught in amorous embrace on the Committee Room table? No, hardly, or else he would have been an advisor to the Government within hours of his departure from College. Had he been caught with his hand in the till? Unlikely; first of all, the Hist 'till' is usually empty and, secondly, absconding with funds is a function reserved to Auditors and occasionally Treasurers.

The ex-Librarian's proposal for Honorary Membership came on at Private Business. Ten eligible electors cast their votes. Seven for the proposal and three against. Having found no good reason why this candidate had been twice rebuffed and not wishing to see an ex-Officer humiliated I was moved to make an Auditorial Ruling — that three quarters of ten was seven; ergo the ex-Librarian was an Honorary Member.

That was not the end of the saga. The following week Kenneth Ferguson proposed a motion that the minutes of the meeting at which the aforesaid Honorary Member had been elected should be expunged from the records of the Society. A large throng attended that night, mostly from the Science end of College, to judge from their ragged apparel. Ferguson rose to address the sans-culottes, his scholarly mane unaddressed by any grooming, save that wrought by being caught in the occasional downpour of rain.

'Not since the siege of Syracuse, when the brutal Roman besiegers cut down the noble Archimedes in his study has so much damage been done to the art of mathematics,' Ferguson declared. Science end gave unrestrained approval to this declamation and indicated this by waving their 'T' squares in the air.

A debate then ensued in which the late Archimedes was once more plunged into his apocryphal bath and forced to regurgitate his method of infinite sections. Dedekind's cut was reopened and Cantor's diagonal proof of the real number line continuum was rehearsed.

Despite the learned disputation and ignoring the Censor's threat to give them a whiff of grapeshot the mob voted to expunge the minutes. The week-long Honorary Member returned briefly to inform me, in rather huffy tones, that he had no intention of accepting an Honorary Membership which owed its origin to an Auditorial Ruling.

Lest upon the scaffold, you ruefully recall this histoire, absorb its moral now. That the power of Kings and Auditors is not infinite but the real number line is!

ALEXANDER OWENS – AUDITOR 1979–80

When I was asked by Declan Budd to write this piece I was also asked to provide a photograph of myself taken during my period of involvement in the Hist. Thankfully, I have retained no such embarrassing memento of the 'sartorial seventies'.[23]

Having got over the difficulty of the request for the photograph by the simple expedient of not providing one, the next challenge which I faced was the temptation to fill the piece with indiscreet revelations, settle a few old scores and do down my detractors! This is what everybody wants to read about. The Hist records for the most part provide details of attendances, meetings, votes, elections and so forth in a rather dry and formular fashion which conveys little about the atmosphere of the meetings or the personalities involved.

I suspect that most Auditors of the Hist have a detailed memory of how they got elected and how they went about the important business of trying to rid themselves of Officers and Committee members who got in their way. Other recollections are either pure invention or relate to things which happened to third parties or are very vague. Most of my memories fall into the 'pure invention' or 'very vague' categories.

Of the Opening Meeting of the 210th session I can remember but little. I remember nothing of the address that I delivered, not even its title. It was something about politics and was probably the most awful rubbish.[24] The first replying speaker was the late George Brown who complained in the nicest possible way that I had departed from the supplied script and that he had been got over to Ireland under false pretences to respond to points which I had not in fact made. The second reply was made by the late John M. Kelly, who was very gracious and complained, again in the nicest possible way, that he had heard all my 'new' and 'original' ideas many times

---

[23]   Editor's note: Thankfully, wives do keep photographs and cheerfully provide them.
[24]   Editor's note: The title given in the Annual Reports 1972–93 is 'Abuse of Power'.

before and that, in a sense, he too had been got to attend under false pretences. The final guest was a Fianna Fáil Senator who had been sent along in lieu of the late Brian Lenihan and who vanished without trace from the political scene shortly afterwards. I cannot remember his name but, at least, he had no complaints.

I remember very little of the other debates. There were some very good ones on Northern Ireland but most of them were unmemorable and I am afraid that some of them were very memorably awful. The largest meeting was the 1980 final of the *Observer* Mace Debating Competition. It must have been a success because, as far as I know, this was both the first and the last time that the final of this event was held in Ireland. As usual during this period the Hist had no team in the final, which was won by Charley Kennedy and Stephen Kerr of the Glasgow Union.

EOIN McCULLOUGH – AUDITOR 1982–83

When I was in the Hist, we spent a lot of time drinking. Indeed, on reflection, we probably regarded this as the primary purpose of our involvement in the Society. We tricked sponsors into providing plonk, we brewed beer, and on occasion we even bought it. In this regard, we perhaps did not differ very much from either predecessors or successors, but it might explain why I have considerable difficulty in remembering any individual episode that occurred at that time.

Thinking about the Hist through this haze, I suppose that we believed at the time that we were modernisers. We sought to increase membership, to obtain interesting guest speakers, and to become involved in non-debating activity. At least, we aspired to all this in the early part of the year. The great charm of the Hist is that it is sustained by its traditions, irrespective of the good intentions of the members or Committee. And so, each year ended with long sessions of private business, debates with no guests and minuscule attendances and, best of all, bitter and divisive elections. There were riots in Dublin on the day that Bobby Sands died, but we were upstairs in the workroom counting votes.

There were minor changes. In an early precursor of the boom in the native film industry, we rented out the Conversation Room to Michael Caine and Julie Walters to make *Educating Rita*. The Opening Meeting became the Inaugural Meeting again and was held later and later in the year. I spoke at one in late February, continuing a trend that had commenced some years before and that has continued since. That meeting was held in the Mansion House, College being affected by industrial action. As the Leader of the Labour Party was invited, and as he was unwilling to break a strike, we had to attend before the leaders of the F.W.U.I. in Parnell Square in order to obtain their permission for the meeting to proceed. They consented, subject to the inclusion in the order of events of a message of fraternal support. That may have been a change from previous practice at Opening Meetings. In a further daring and radical move involving films, we organized showings of the banned *Life of Brian* at enormous profit.

The central characteristic of my time in the Hist was that very little changed. We observed the same form of Private Business as had been observed from recorded time. The oldest jokes were always the most amusing. Members marked speeches for the purpose of awards at the end of the year, midnight was called, and Auditorial Rulings were given on important legal issues. It is, perhaps, not to the credit of those who became and stay involved, but I imagine that it is matters such as this that most people remember ten or twenty years later.

BRIAN MURRAY – AUDITOR 1984–85

The occasion not infrequently arises when conversation with those who were contemporaries of mine at the Hist (and I still seem to remain in touch with many) directs itself to our time in or around the Society. Most express fond and warm recollections, some manifest regret and others (for reasons all too obvious to those observing at the time) have a greatly impaired recollection of some, or all, of their four years.

If I were to apply one descriptive term to my own experiences, I think it would have to be 'instructive'. I do not recall precisely how, or why, I was attracted to the (then) foreboding ambience of the G.M.B., but by the end of my first year my interest in the internecine politics, history, and culture of College debating was overwhelming, and, by the end of my fourth year, obsessive.

In retrospect, I think that my experiences were defined by four particular features. The first was the intensity of the friendships and loyalties constructed in and around the Committee Room and the Debating Chamber. Inevitably, many of those wane with the passage of time, but some retain their vitality, not only in my own case, but also in those with whom I remain in touch.

The second was the prodigious consumption of alcohol which appeared to characterise the Society, at least in the mid 1980s. Most students drank a great deal at the time; but at the Hist, the combination of a common cause, generous sponsors, consequent opportunity and a general culture structured around the vortex of Dame Lane, the Buttery and the G.M.B. rooted the politics and debating at the Hist as firmly in the pub, as in the debating chamber. This, of course, distinguished us from our sanitised equivalents in U.C.D. and made us (or so we thought) infinitely more worldly-wise.

The third is a sense of brutality. The cocktail of youth, determination and ambition, which characterises all student politics, is a volatile one. Elections were unsavoury affairs, producing as many animosities, intense and impervious to the passage of time, as they did friendships and loyalties. Finally (and very much last), came the speaking. I was fortunate to participate in the Society when it boasted truly great speakers who could not only enliven Wednesday evening debates, but carry their weaker debating partners (me) to far flung competitions.

My wife was in College at the same time as I was. She has read a longer and far more amusing version of this note but constantly refrained, 'They can't print that!' Probably for the first time in my relationship with the College Historical Society, caution has got the better of me.

KERIDA NAIDOO – AUDITOR 1990–91

Although it will almost certainly go unremarked by historians, the Hist played a crucial role in the ending of the apartheid regime in South Africa and replacing it with a democratically elected government. This may be somewhat overstating our contribution; in fact it is an exaggeration so wild as to be an outrageous falsehood. It is true to say, however, that we anticipated the changes, which had already begun, with uncanny foresight. Or at least we heard about them.

It occurred to the Auditor and Committee of the 221st session that the increasingly likely release of Nelson Mandela from prison would soon deny student debating societies one of their most enduring topics and so we decided to have one more oratorical stab at the issue. To this end we invited the First Secretary from the South African Embassy in London to propose the motion to the effect that the boycott, both economic and cultural, then in place against South Africa in Europe and America should be lifted. Having initially encountered great difficulty in finding someone to share a platform with the First Secretary, we ultimately succeeded in persuading a Green Party T.D. to oppose him.

College was extremely anxious to avoid any sort of fracas and so security for the event was very tight, so much so that in order to ensure there would be some publicity attracting protesters present the Committee were forced to leak the fact of the First Secretary's attendance ourselves.

On the evening of the debate, therefore, there was a boisterous and gratifyingly large demonstration, consisting of student union members in addition to other groups including the socialist workers and anarcho-communist groups, determined that the debate should not proceed. They were unable to gain entry into the G.M.B. as College insisted the debate be limited to Society members and surprisingly few anarcho-communists had joined the Society during Freshers' Week; something to do with us being ivory tower establishmentarians who would be first up against the wall when the revolution came. Instead they assembled outside the building and jeered our dubious stance on apartheid while we riposted with taunts about their lamentable tailoring and poor grooming.

It then occurred to the Treasurer that this was an excellent opportunity to swell the Society's coffers and proceeded to sell membership to a number of the protesters. The result of his enterprise was that, when the debate started, there were half a dozen zealous protesters present in the chamber who loudly and very effectively obstructed the progress of the meeting.

It being impossible to conduct the meeting I directed the Censor to assemble a sub-Committee to remove the offending members. The resulting sub-Committee was almost certainly the largest ever, consisting as it did of almost the entire Committee and a fair number of able bodied ordinary members. Thankfully the protesters were a genial lot at heart and allowed themselves to be peacefully escorted from the chamber. I subsequently regretted their departure as the debate which followed was one of the dullest I ever attended.

BERNARD DUNLEAVY – AUDITOR 1991–92

My first memory of the Hist is of a time before I was actually a member, when I spoke in the final of the All-Ireland Schools Debating Competition in March 1989, which was hosted by the Society that year. I looked at the audience that evening in the Exam Hall with some wonder, having never spoken before a crowd of that size before. I determined to make an impression on them by delivering what I anticipated would be the winning speech. My plan, which had seemed perfect in theory, was fatally flawed in its execution in not allowing for the factor of other participants in the competition. So, history records me as the runner-up individual to John Smith, who was the schoolboy representative for Ulster that year.

The defeat I put behind me but the Hist had made an indelible impression and I determined that when I went to Trinity I would lose no time in joining the Society. I thought that my chance to make my mark had come when I delivered what I anticipated would be the winning speech in the Freshers' Debating Competition of Michaelmas Term 1989. I still maintain there was nothing wrong with the speech; nevertheless with a cruel inevitability I am recorded in the records of the Society as the runner-up individual to John Smith.

The most pleasant thing about banging your head against a brick wall is the enormous relief you get when you stop. So it was that myself and Smith ended the attrition and decided to speak together as a team for the Society, which we did with some success for the next four years.

It was my pleasure to represent the Society in debating chambers from Toronto to Glasgow but none of them compared to a hot and smoky G.M.B. on one of the nights when it was hazardously overcrowded as the Society prepared to debate the issue that had captured public imagination at that moment in time. I remember a near riot as anarchists attempted to prevent a representative of the South African Government speaking to a motion on apartheid. I recall also the vitriolic tone of what became for a few years at the end of the 1980s — the annual 'Abortion Debate'. And I remember the strange atmosphere the night the debate was adjourned as word filtered into the Chamber that fighting had begun in the Gulf War.

My best memories of the Hist are inevitably those of the University's Quatercentenary when the Society had the honour of opening the College's celebrations by hosting the 11th World Student Debating Championship. It was my privilege as Auditor that year to chair the final of the competition, and I have never been more proud of the Society than when regarding the audience that night, which included several thousand individuals from all around the world, who were acknowledging that evening the Hist's position as the most ancient and venerable institution of its kind.

All of the privileges afforded me as Auditor were the result for the most part of the hard work of an outstanding Committee. From that group I remember particularly my Treasurer, Brendan Fitzpatrick, whose tragically early death robbed the Society of one of its most devoted members.

My happiest memory of the Society, as is the way of all former Auditors, is of the night I was elected. A memory only slightly better than that of the night I relinquished that office and was able to pass the medal on to the 223rd Auditor of the Hist — John Smith!

MOTIONS DEBATED
1971–97

1971	27 January	That violence is necessary for an Irish Solution. Negative.
	28 April	That these islands should remain outside the E.E.C. Affirmative.
1972	23 February	That this House would support a Secular Constitution. Affirmative.
1973	24 January	That Social Work hinders progress. Negative.
	7 February	That we are well served by our mass media. Negative.
	4 April	That this House supports and welcomes the White Paper on Northern Ireland. Affirmative.
	14 November	That Profits are better than Prophets. Negative.
1974	23 October	That this House would be tough with the terrorists. Negative.

1975	26 February	That this House would oppose any compromise on the principle of immediate Majority Rule in South Africa and Rhodesia. Affirmative.
	12 November	That contraception will ruin Irish Society. Negative.
1976	10 November	That this House supports the Government's Anti-Terrorism legislation. Affirmative.
1977	26 January	That this House mourns the death of Irish Culture. Negative.
	16 November	That Gay Rights are Human Rights.
1978	18 January	That this House would legalise abortion.
	24 February	That this House supports an Independent Palestinian State.
	15 November	That Nuclear Power is a necessary evil. Negative.
1979	17 October	That Africa's best hope lies to the East and not to the West. Negative.
1980	9 January	That the Church has crucified Modern Ireland. Negative.
	27 February	That this House would legislate to curb the power of the Trade Unions. Negative.
1981	14 January	That this House would legalize divorce. Affirmative.
	15 April	That this House would dissolve the E.E.C. Negative.
1982	3 February	That Irish writers owe more to European influence than to Irish tradition. Negative.
	10 February	That our future prosperity lies in balanced budgets. Affirmative.

	31 March	That Seanad Éireann ought to be abolished. Negative.
	17 November	That the Abortion Referendum is a cosmetic exercise.
1983	19 October	That Socialism is an outmoded philosophy. Negative.
	2 November	That the New Ireland Forum will bring greater peace and stability to Ireland. Negative.
	9 November	That Property Tax is theft. Negative.
	30 November	That prostitution should be legalized. Affirmative.
	7 December	That censorship protects society. Negative.
1984	15 February	That Sinn Féin be proscribed. Negative.
	24 October	That our written Constitution has served us well. Tied vote.
1985	9 October	That this House would separate Church and State. Affirmative.
	30 October	That the Right to Strike is a danger to the Community. Negative.
1986	22 January	That Multinationals have served this country badly.
	5 March	That this House rejects the principle of Coalition.
	18 October	That scientific advance is logical regression.
	22 October	That No Surrender is No Solution. Affirmative.
	26 November	That the U.N. is an ineffectual organization. Affirmative.

1987	25 February	That this House would privatize its National Industries. Affirmative.
	11 November	That this House would decriminalize homosexuality.
1988	27 January	That Israel is the primary aggressor in the Middle East. Negative.
	17 February	That this House would repeal Section 31 of the Broadcasting Act. Affirmative.
	11 October	That the future of the Left is on the Right.
	9 November	That the time has come to talk to the Terrorists. Affirmative.
	30 November	That the share-owning democracy is a licence for greed. Affirmative.
1989	11 January	That Liberty rests on the rule of Law. Affirmative.
	18 January	That Feminism frustrates the Modern Woman. Affirmative. [Held on the anniversary of the admission of women to the Society.]
	1 March	That genetic engineering is good for Society.
	11 October	That this House would muzzle the Media. Negative.
	18 October	That the right to life is preferable to the right to choose. Negative.
	8 November	That this House would extradite terrorist suspects to Britain. Negative.
1990	28 February	That student radicalism has seen its day. Negative.

	4 April	That European Unity threatens Irish Culture. Affirmative.
	10 October	That this House would ordain women. Affirmative.
	17 October	That sanctions will not end Apartheid. Negative.
1991	23 January	That the British Occupation of North-Eastern Ireland makes the IRA campaign inevitable. Affirmative.
	23 October	That the Media's first duty is to the State. Affirmative.
1992	7 January	That Nationalism is a Hangover from History. Negative. [Final of the World Student Debating Championship]
	14 October	That this House would retain Articles 2 and 3 of the Constitution. Negative.
1993	27 January	That the death penalty is a necessity. Negative.
	13 October	That abortion is sometimes the lesser of two evils. Affirmative.
1994	19 January	That Human Rights should be the price for development aid. Affirmative.
	2 February	That this House favours a federal Europe. Affirmative.
	2 November	That the Free Market has failed the people of Ireland. Negative.
1995	7 April	That the safety of the Public outweighs the right to bail. Negative.
	4 October	That this House rejects the Catholic Church. Affirmative.

	11 October	That the private lives of public figures are of no concern to the body politic. Affirmative.
1996	7 February	That this House would check before it mates. Negative.
	9 October	That Decommissioning must precede all-party talks. Negative.
	20 November	That film diminishes the actor. Negative.
1997	11 February	That this House supports public funding for political parties. Negative.
	26 February	That Hong Kong will prosper under the Chinese. Negative.

REPORT
OF THE BICENTENARY
SUB-COMMITTEE

In keeping with the laws of the Society, the Bicentenary sub-Committee submitted its report to the Society at the Honorary Members' Debate held on Wednesday 24 April 1996. By then the sub-Committee felt confident of its ability to complete all its assigned tasks, including the publication of the present book. There may also have been a concern lest the Bicentenary sub-Committee, if it had not wound up, would be asked to organize in 1997 the simultaneous celebrations of the Bicentenary of the death of Burke, and the 250th anniversary of the founding of Burke's Club!

Mr Chairman, Mr Auditor, Ladies and Gentlemen of the College Historical Society, we, the surviving members of the sub-Committee, report as follows:

We record with regret the deaths, in the intervening period since the celebration of the Bicentenary of the Society in March 1970, of the Chairman of the sub-Committee, K. F. G. Purcell, a most active and hospitable Vice-President of the Society, the Honourable Mr Justice F. G. O. Budd, formerly Senator for T.C.D. and Judge of the Supreme Court, ex-Record Secretary, and also Dr F. H. Boland, then President of the Society and Chancellor of the University, ex-Correspondence Secretary, whose advice and assistance in respect of distinguished speakers from abroad was invaluable.

The sub-Committee was set up in 1968 during the Auditorship of W. A. C. Stanford and met both as a committee under the Chairmanship of K. F. G. Purcell and also in various sub-committees devoted to the organization of particular events during the celebratory week.

The programme of the week's events is annexed to this report.

The *Art and Oratory: College Historical Society Bicentenary Exhibition,* which was opened by Charles J. Haughey T.D., Minister for Finance, in the National Gallery of Ireland on Monday 2 March 1970, was the product of excellent co-operation between the Society and the Director Dr James White, and the staff, of the National Gallery. We are indebted to the Director for his helpful advice and assistance to Richard Marriott in the organization of this exhibition of portraits. The catalogue is a fitting memento of this Exhibition. A copy of the Catalogue is appended to this report.

On Tuesday 3 March 1970 Senator Edward Kennedy delivered the Bicentenary Address at a meeting in the Public Theatre over which Dr F. H. Boland presided. After a reception in the Provost's House, the Senator's address set the scene for a week of lively meetings. The contents of the debates and the discourse by Dr R. B. McDowell, Honorary Member and Vice-President, are recorded in the Anthology. Professor David McConnell still retains the pliers given to him as a security precaution by the Secretary to the Board in the preparations for Senator Kennedy's address!

On Wednesday 4 March 1970 An Taoiseach, Jack Lynch, took the Chair at an International Discussion in the Public Theatre in which Senator Eugene McCarthy, Professor Andreas Papandreou, James Dillon, Michael Foot M.P. and Dr Conor Cruise O'Brien spoke on the topic 'That the only Liberty . . . is a liberty connected with order' – Edmund Burke. Readers of the speeches will be intrigued by the reference by James Dillon to 'his friends the Maoists' and his invitation to them to consider George Orwell's *Animal Farm*. This is explicable in the context of security problems at that time for public meetings; a meeting in the R.D.S. shortly before March 1970, which was being attended by the Taoiseach and members of the Government, had been taken over by dissidents. Your Society reconciled the desire to hear, and allow to be heard, every point of view with the need for an orderly and fair forum; the leader of those very dissidents, who had taken control of the microphone at the R.D.S., and who had chaired a recent debate of the Society, was invited and was seated beside a large member of the rugby team, proficient in the first official language dear to his heart and well able to explain the need for adherence to the arranged procedures of the meeting. A group of vociferous Maoists chanted loud and long outside the doors of the Public Theatre. One vivid memory is of the sight of Ross Hinds standing with arms folded surveying the scene in the Public Theatre with his back to the doors, outside which the noise of protesters surged and swelled. This interruption was used dramatically by James Dillon to enhance his powerful speech in favour of freedom of speech.

Later that memorable night in the Guest rooms in No. 40 occupied by Michael Foot, and through the courtesy of that good friend of the Society, a less formal exchange of ideas took place. It is now difficult to convey how bright a light on the American political stage the meteoric ascent of Senator Eugene McCarthy had thrown, but the Officers and members of the sub-Committee, who poured a libation that night in the company of Eugene McCarthy, Andreas Papandreou, Jack Lynch and Conor Cruise O'Brien, will have a clearly etched memory of the scene in No. 40 with the incandescence of the Senator from Minnesota and with the pithy and sage comments from Andreas Papandreou biding his time in the background. If you love liberty, read his warning about the influential oligarchies which subvert power in a representative democracy.

On Thursday 5 March 1970 Professor R. B. McDowell delivered a public address 'Personalities in the Hist' to a packed house in the G.M.B. This sparklingly witty review was an excellent aperitif before the Bicentenary Dinner in the Dining Hall. Your Honorary Secretary had visited Dr McDowell in the Rubrics earlier that day to remind him of the time of the meeting and of the dinner; it is with regret that I have to confess that the whereabouts of the notes, which I assisted him to locate that afternoon, and on which the Address was based, is unknown; so be wary if you are throwing out old envelopes in the Committee Room. Incidentally, the Editor of this Address in the Anthology maintains that there is a clear, lucid and topical theme of thought consistently maintained in the speech, despite seeming deviations and diversions.

The dinner was well organized by Gardner Budd and Ross Hinds. The musical accompaniment included renderings of works by composers who were members of the Society. A copy of the menu is appended.

On Friday 6 March 1970 The Hon. Mr Justice T. C. Kingsmill Moore, Vice-President, took the Chair for the Irish Debate 'That Emmet's Epitaph be Now Written'. Michael O'Kennedy T.D., John Hume M.P., Gerry Fitt M.P., Michael O'Leary T.D., Erskine Childers T.D., Minister for Health, and Vincent Browne, Editor of *Magill*, addressed the meeting.

On Saturday 7 March 1970 the Dance in the Dining Hall, ably organized by Robert Kirkpatrick, rounded off the week of celebrations.

Copies of five letters of congratulations received by the Auditor are appended as typical of expressions of appreciation at the success of the Bicentenary. These include the letters from Dr A. J. McConnell, then Provost, and from Senator Mary Bourke.

Press and television coverage was extensive. Senator Edward Kennedy's acceptance of the invitation extended by Dr F. H. Boland on behalf of the Society ensured international interest. The brilliance and world-wide reputation of the speakers ensured a huge audience for both debates. Members of the Society travelled from far and near to attend the Celebrations. Publicity was co-ordinated by David J. McConnell.

The meticulous efficiency of Alan J. Craig as Honorary Treasurer ensured a careful account was kept of every penny of income and expenditure. The Bicentenary sub-Committee left no financial deficit, rather a credit of good reputation and excellent publicity for the Society and the College.

Security had posed problems at a time of turbulent unrest and demonstrations. Your sub-Committee co-operated with the College and State authorities to ensure the safety of our distinguished guests; but the brunt of the arranging for orderly access to, and uninterrupted proceedings at, the meetings rested with the sub-Committee who took unobtrusive steps to deter unwelcome disorder. The Maoist heckler, who had hidden in the organ in the Public Theatre, interrupted Senator Edward Kennedy, and was assisted to leave the Gallery swiftly.

The sub-Committee came into being in 1968 at the initiative of the then Auditor, William A. C. Stanford, after late night discussions in the Rubrics with the Convenor/Honorary Secretary. The planning and arrangements progressed under the Auditorship of David F. Ford, often at meetings in the home of the Chairman, K. F. G. Purcell, whose genial hospitality restored any feathers ruffled by the Secretary's remarks about tasks not carried out. The work of staging the actual celebrations fell on Ian T. Ashe, the Auditor in 1970, and he and his Committee discharged their duty admirably in co-operation with the Bicentenary sub-Committee.

The proposed Anthology was one task not completed. It is your Sub-

Committee's hope that the material will have matured in the meantime — what is a mere twenty-five years in the life of this Society? The Anthology is annexed to this Report.

We the surviving members of your sub-Committee for the Bicentenary, request your approval of this Report on our endeavours on behalf of your Society.

We remain:

William A. C. Stanford	Auditor 1968
David F. Ford	Auditor 1969
Ian T. Ashe	Auditor 1970
Richard R. Marriott	Exhibition
Robert W. Kirkpatrick	Dance
D. Ross Hinds	Dinner
David J. McConnell	Press Officer
Alan J. Craig	Treasurer
Declan N. O. Budd	Convenor and Secretary

24 April 1996

APPENDICES

The following Appendices are attached [to the original report]:

1. Programme of the week's events
2. Catalogue of the Exhibition
3. Dinner Menu
4. Letters of congratulation
5. Anthology of the College Historical Society [This volume, published as *The Hist and Edmund Burke's Club*]

INDEX

as otherwise it is almost impossible to condemn bad actions without
also condemning him from whom they proceed — Mr Mohun for
the bill. Mr Hamilton against it. there being an equality of
voices Mr Pres. gave it against the bill. The assembly dismiss

Mr Burke President.
Mr Mohun.
Mr Dennis Sec. Mr Hamilton

Tuesday the
May the 12
1747.

Mr Buck fined for absence. sends an Epistle to the Pr
who orders it to be preserved, and likewise recorded in
proceedings of the assembly, that he may more fully
himself. Mr Pres. harangues from the chair, says he rep
the dignity of the assembly, and wou'd act with the u
rigour, and wou'd was there no law do it thro' his ben
and regard to the society, that he wou'd act absolu
free within the laws.

Pres: Speech

Mr Hamilton reads his paper on pride, Mr Pres: re
while the assembly criticize upon it. Mr Hamilton
the thanks of the assembly.

Hamilton

Mr Mohun order'd to declaim in praise of poetry

Declamation
on Poetry.
P.F. 14.
On pride and
Servility

Thesis propos'd, whether an absolute pride or servile comp
in a Pres: be most commendable —— Mr Dennis a
favour of the former, urges that pride is the token
that it springs from vanity the ruling passion
it will necessarry to preserve order and even so
Mr Hamilton argues in favour of Humility says
and by that preserves the laws, whereas Pride tho
from vanity was vicious as it was an excess.
Mr Dennis urges that if vanity was laudable its
wd be so great a fault as the opposite vice, that
in a Pres: rather incurs contempt than esteem,
the laws were destroy'd, but that Pride preserves
(as it is in the Pres: breast) and the society itself.
Mr Pres: recapitulates the whole determines i
be the least faulty of Extremes but recommends the

On Poetry

Mr Mohun declaims in favour of poetry. Pra